D1605640

The Elements of System Design

The Elements of System Design

Amer A. Hassan
John E. Hershey
Jim Schroeder
Guy R. L. Sohie
R. K. Rao Yarlagadda

ACADEMIC PRESS, INC.
Harcourt Brace & Company

Boston San Diego New York
London Sydney Tokyo Toronto

This book is printed on acid-free paper. ∞

ACADEMIC PRESS, INC.
525 B. Street, Suite 1900, San Diego, CA 92101-4495

United Kingdom Edition published by
ACADEMIC PRESS LIMITED
24–28 Oval Road, London NW1 7DX

Library of Congress Cataloging-in-Publication Data

The Elements of system design/Amer A. Hassan ... [*et al.*].
p. cm.
Includes bibliographical references and index.
ISBN 0-12-343060-7 (alk. paper)
1. System design. I. Hassan, Amer A.
QA76.9.S88E43 1994
620′.001′171—dc20 93-38585
CIP

Printed in the United States of America
93 94 95 96 EB 9 8 7 6 5 4 3 2 1

Contents

Contributors

Amer A. Hassan, General Electric Research and Development Center, Schenectady, New York

John E. Hershey, General Electric Research and Development Center, Schenectady, New York

Jim Schroeder, Department of Engineering, University of Denver, Denver, Colorado

Guy R. L. Sohie, General Electric Research and Development Center, Schenectady, New York

R. K. Rao Yarlagadda, Oklahoma State University, Stillwater, Oklahoma

To Adnan and Khalid, my bridge to education
To Beirut, I miss you—*Amer A. Hassan*

To the memory of my uncle, Ship's Master Christian Dahlgard,
whose wisdom I am only beginning to understand—*John E. Hershey*

To Sarah, Sunny, and Tae for their patience and understanding
throughout this project—*Jim Schroeder*

To my wife and children—*Guy R. L. Sohie*

To my students, it has been a pleasure—*R. K. Rao Yarlagadda*

Foreword

The world continues to change at a frenetic pace. Engineering has been affected as well as almost all the scientific disciplines. The world market is considering technology more and more as a commodity. This is keenly felt by large-scale system designers. With emphasis on cost and development time becoming ever more acute, it is evident that long-term research and the quest for optimal solutions will be deemphasized in favor of getting something done with "off-the-shelf" componentry. The luxury of developing specific expensive modules will simply not obtain as an option for many system designers.

The good news is that a lot of off-the-shelf technology is already available. The bad news is that we are not educating engineers to this new reality. Engineering curricula must become more relevant to the practicing engineer's role.

System engineering is essentially the study of multidimensional trade-offs. The individual who guides the development of a system must be sensitive to these trade-offs, be able to direct their performance, and evaluate the work so directed. This is not an easy task as the lead system's engineer will be involved in many other factors, such as cost, logistics, and personnel management.

The five authors have been colleagues and friends for many years. We have individually and collectively worked on many system problems over our professional lifetimes. It is our belief that almost any large system will involve four main disciplines:

- Signal processing,
- Control,
- Communications,
- Computation.

We believe that most system designers are formally exposed to each of these disciplines at some time in their education but never as parts of a larger whole. The purpose of this book is to bring these four disciplines into contact with one another and allow a single course to cover them all as a review or as a fresh look at the possibilities of interplay and trade-off so essential and characteristic of good large-scale system design.

The book's chapters can be read as "stand-alone" segments and may be useful to mathematicians and computer scientists as well as engineers.

Amer A. Hassan
John E. Hershey
James E. Schroeder
Guy R. L. Sohie
Rao R. K. Yarlagadda

Chapter 1

Introduction to Signal Analysis

Chapter's Purpose

This chapter deals with the analysis of periodic and aperiodic signals using Fourier analysis. These are extended to the study of discrete signals and their analysis using discrete and fast Fourier transforms. Filtering and approximation of filter functions are discussed. A brief introduction to the short-time Fourier analysis along with analog and digital filter synthesis has been presented. Most of the material presented in this chapter takes the systems approach. The chapter is concluded using a thumbnail sketch of pattern recognition and illustrates an example of using a simple speech signal. In general, the material presented in this chapter is basic and can be found in most communication theory and signal processing texts. A list of references can be found at the end of the chapter.

Signals

A signal is a pattern used to convey a message; for example, Morse code, smoke signals, a set of flags, traffic lights, or speech signal. Here, we will consider a signal to be the variation of a quantity, such as voltage, current, pressure, or temperature, with respect to a variable such as time. The two variables we will be interested in are the time t and the signal identified by $x(t)$. If the variable t can take any real value from $-\infty < t < \infty$, such as $t = 2.345612\ldots$, then t is called a *continuous variable*. Note that ... simply means that the number of digits could be infinite. On the other hand, if the variable t can take only discrete values, then t is called a *discrete variable*; for example, variable t can take any integer value between 1 and 10.

Textbooks rarely begin with physical examples, such as speech, because they are hard to study. Therefore, simple examples are usually considered first, such as a step function, identified here as $u(t)$ and given by

$$u(t) = \begin{cases} 0, & t < 0 \\ 1, & t > 0 \end{cases} \tag{1.1}$$

Note the ambiguity at $t = 0$, as it is not defined at this value. One could define at $t = 0$ explicitly as 0 or 1 or 0.5, the average value. The pulse function is defined by

$$\Pi\left(\frac{t-(a+b)/2}{(b-a)}\right)=\begin{cases}0, & t<a\\ 1, & a<t<b\\ 0, & t>\mathrm{b}\end{cases} \tag{1.2}$$

Note again the ambiguity at $t = a$ and $t = b$. The pulse is centered at $t = (a + b)/2$ and the width is $(b - a)$. Another function of interest is the exponential function, defined as

$$x(t)=\begin{cases}\mathrm{e}^{-t}, & t>0\\ 0, & t<0\end{cases} \tag{1.3}$$

Clearly, one can build more complex functions by using these simple functions. For example, the ramp function, $x(t) = 0$, $t < 0$ and $x(t) = t$, $t > 0$, can be obtained by integrating the unit step function, the parabolic function, $x(t) = 0$, $t < 0$ and $x(t) = t^2/2$, $t > 0$, by integrating the ramp function, and so forth. Also the ramp function can be obtained by taking the derivative of the parabolic function. Taking the derivatives of discontinuous functions such as unit step functions do create problems. To handle some of these problems, we define the impulse function, also called the *dirac delta function*, by

$$\delta(t)=\begin{cases}0, & t\neq 0\\ \infty, & t=0\end{cases} \tag{1.4a}$$

with

$$\int_{-\infty}^{\infty}\delta(t)\,\mathrm{d}t=1 \tag{1.4b}$$

The impulse can be approximated. For example,

$$\delta(t)=\lim_{\varepsilon\to 0}\frac{1}{\varepsilon}\left[\Pi\left(\frac{t}{\varepsilon}\right)\right]$$

Obviously other functions can be used to approximate delta functions. An interesting application involves the delta function in an integral:

$$\int_{-\infty}^{\infty}x(t)\delta(t-t_0)\,\mathrm{d}t=x(t_0) \tag{1.5}$$

where $x(t)$ is any test function that is continuous at $t = t_0$. The delta function can be related to the unit step function and

$$\int_{-\infty}^{t}\delta(\alpha)\,\mathrm{d}\alpha=\begin{cases}1, & t>0\\ 0, & t<0\end{cases} \tag{1.6}$$

For $t = 0$, it is generally not given and can be defined as (1/2). Also, the derivative of a unit step function is a delta function. Noting that the derivative of the unit step function does not exist at $t = 0$, one might wonder how to relate the preceding. This can be visualized by using approximations.

A function $x(t - t_0)$ is obtained from $x(t)$ by delaying the function by t_0 seconds. When $t_0 < 0$, the function is, of course, advanced by t_0 seconds. It can be shown that

$$\delta(at + b) = \frac{1}{|a|}\delta\left(t + \frac{b}{a}\right), \qquad a \neq 0 \tag{1.7}$$

Also, if $x(t)$ is continuous at $t = t_0$, then

$$x(t)\delta(t - t_0) = x(t_0)\delta(t - t_0) \tag{1.8}$$

Earlier we pointed out that a delta function is a derivative of a unit step function. We can extend this through a limiting process, so that the derivative of a delta function is a doublet and the argument can be extended to higher orders.

Periodic and Aperiodic Functions

A signal is periodic if and only if

$$x(t) = x(t + T), \qquad -\infty < t < \infty \tag{1.9}$$

for some T. The smallest such number is called the *fundamental period.* If (1.9) is not true, then the function $x(t)$ is called an *aperiodic function.* Examples of periodic functions include trignometric functions like sine and cosine functions. The function

$$x(t) = A_0 \cos(2\pi f_0 t + \theta_0) \tag{1.10}$$

is a periodic function with period

$$T = (1/f_0) \tag{1.11}$$

where A_0, f_0, and θ_0 are assumed to be constants.

The next question that comes to mind is, Where do you come across periodic functions? Note that *periodic* means "forever." In many situations, we assume the function is periodic on a short-time basis. That is, the function repeats only for a short time. Consider the example of a speech waveform shown in Figure 1.1 corresponding to the part *sho* in *show*, which is obtained by first converting the acoustic signal into an electrical signal. The recorder is turned on, then the word is spoken. The portion identified

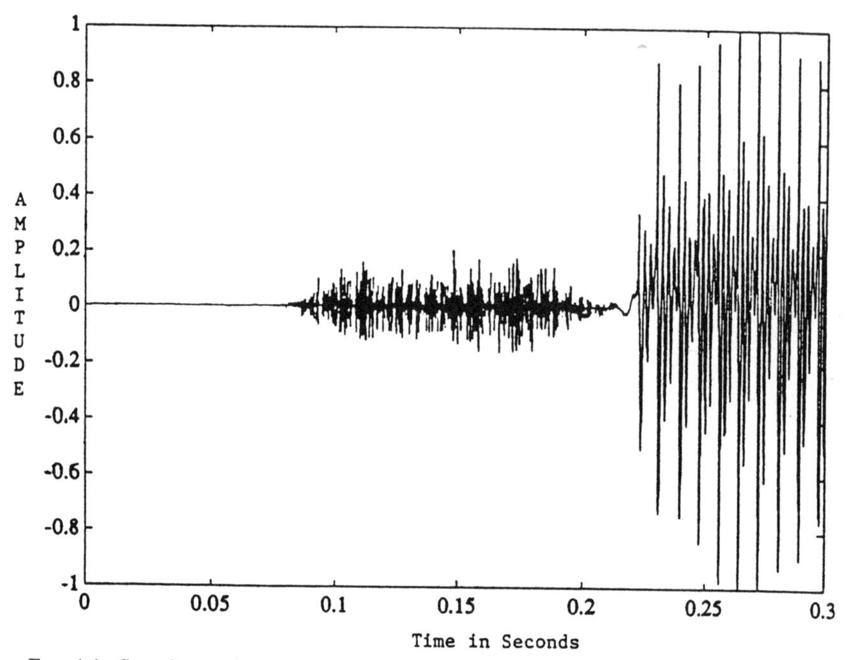

FIG. 1.1. Speech waveform illustrating the parts silence, and *sho* in the word *show* (speech waveforms courtesy of Dr. Scott King).

by silence is the time prior to speech. There is still a signal with small amplitude, which is identified as noise. This may have come from background or from the recorder itself. The second portion represents *sh* and the third portion represents *o* in *show*. It can be seen from the figure that the vowel sound appears like it is repeating itself, albeit for a short time. So, we can define such signals as periodic on a short-time basis. Any function given for a short interval can be used to define a function that is periodic by repeating the given function. The waveform corresponding to the phoneme *sh* is not periodic.

Consider an example from machine vision in a robotics problem. A robot has a picture of the head of a hexagonal bolt and a square bolt as shown in Figure 1.2. Here we have a two-dimensional signal (a picture). We can measure the distances from the x and y axes, respectively, and identify the variations by $x_a(t)$ (or $x_b(t)$) and $y_a(t)$ (or $y_b(t)$), corresponding to the square bolt and the hexagonal bolt, respectively. Two signals can be constructed from these: namely,

$$\begin{aligned} z_a(t) &= x_a(t) + \mathrm{j}y_a(t) \\ z_b(t) &= x_b(t) + \mathrm{j}y_b(t) \end{aligned} \tag{1.12}$$

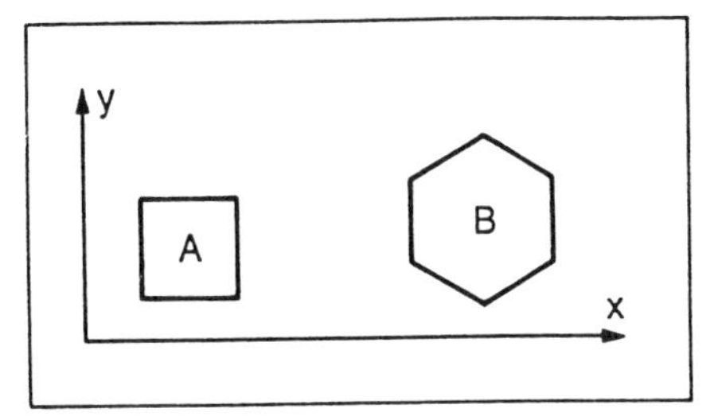

FIG. 1.2. Example of a machine vision problem, square and hexagonal bolts.

where $z_a(t)$ and $z_b(t)$ are now complex functions. The variable t is the time as we go around the circumference of the heads of the bolts. Clearly, $z_a(t)$ and $z_b(t)$ are periodic functions. If we know one period of a periodic signal, we have all the information about that signal.

Now, in the robotics problem, we want to distinguish between the two bolts. One variable we can use is the period. If z_a and z_b have periods T_a and T_b, respectively, then we can use a threshold $T_h = (T_a + T_b)/2$. If the measured period is larger than T_h, it is the hexagonal bolt. Otherwise, it is the square bolt. If both have the same circumference, we may need more "features" to distinguish one from the other. Clearly, recognition is a major problem in any area of science, and invariably signal analysis is the first step in these recognition problems. What other variables can we use? Well, if we look at the speech example, we can see that the consonant sound appears to have more oscillations than the vowel sound. On the other hand, the vowel sound has a larger amplitude than the consonant. So, features based on amplitudes and the number of zero crossings can be used as a measure [1]. Well, we have a third item in the speech waveform in Figure 1.1, the silence portion, where the speaker did not utter. This is simply the background noise. How do we separate that from the speech signal. Its amplitudes are fairly small and a feature can be based on these amplitudes. What happens if we want to recognize different phonemes? There ar 42 (or 44) different phonemes used in the speech analysis for the English language. This leads to the Fourier analysis, which is discussed later. But first a brief discussion of classification of signals [2].

Energy and Power Signals

For an arbitrary signal $x(t)$, the energy contained in this signal is given by

$$E = \lim_{T \to \infty} \int_{-T/2}^{T/2} |x(t)|^2 \, dt = \int_{-\infty}^{\infty} |x(t)|^2 \, dt \tag{1.13}$$

If we assume $x(t)$ to be the voltage source across a 1 ohm, resistor, then E gives the total energy delivered by the source. This is some times called the normalized energy or simply the energy in the signal. Noting that power is the time average value of the energy, we can define the normalized power of a signal over time T by

$$P = \lim_{T \to \infty} \frac{1}{T} \int_{-T/2}^{T/2} |x(t)|^2 \, dt \tag{1.14}$$

For periodic signals with period T, this reduces to

$$P = \frac{1}{T} \int_{-T/2}^{T/2} |x(t)|^2 \, dt = \frac{1}{T} \int_{T} |x(t)|^2 \, dt \tag{1.15}$$

Note that the last equality points out that the period could be any one period.

A signal $x(t)$ is classified as an energy signal if and only if $0 < E < \infty$ and therefore $P = 0$. A signal $x(t)$ is classified as a power signal if and only if $0 < P < \infty$ and therefore $E \to \infty$. Clearly, the periodic signal is a power signal. Randomly varying signals are classified as power signals. Time limited signals, such as a pulse, are energy signals. If a signal does not satisfy any of these properties, it is neither.

Fourier Series

A real periodic signal $x(t)$ with period T can be represented by

$$x_p(t) = \frac{a_0}{2} + \sum_{n=1}^{\infty} \left(a_n \cos \frac{2\pi}{T} nt + b_n \sin \frac{2\pi}{T} nt \right) \tag{1.16}$$

The coefficients a_n and b_n can be solved by noting that

$$\begin{aligned} &\int_T \cos \frac{2\pi}{T} mt \sin \frac{2\pi}{T} nt \, dt = 0 \qquad \text{for all } m \text{ and } n \\ &\int_T \cos \frac{2\pi}{T} mt \cos \frac{2\pi}{T} nt \, dt = \begin{cases} 0, & m \neq n \\ T/2, & m = n \end{cases} \\ &\int_T \sin \frac{2\pi}{T} mt \sin \frac{2\pi}{T} nt \, dt = \begin{cases} 0, & m \neq n \\ T/2, & m = n \end{cases} \end{aligned} \tag{1.17}$$

and

$$\begin{aligned} a_n &= \frac{2}{T} \int_T x(t) \cos \frac{2\pi}{T} nt \, dt \\ b_n &= \frac{2}{T} \int_T x(t) \sin \frac{2\pi}{T} nt \, dt \end{aligned} \tag{1.18}$$

The expression in (1.16) is usually referred to as the *real Fourier series* or simply the *Fourier series*. The expression in (1.16) used a set of basis functions [3]; namely,

$$\left\{1, \quad \cos 2\pi \frac{n}{T} t, \quad \sin 2\pi \frac{n}{T} t, \quad n = 1, 2, \ldots\right\}$$

The functions are independent and orthogonal, as shown in (1.17).

The complex Fourier series can be expressed using the orthogonal basis functions:

$$\{e^{jn(2\pi/T)t}, \quad n = \ldots, \quad -1, 0, 1, \ldots\}$$

and

$$x_p(t) = \sum_{n=-\infty}^{\infty} X_n \, e^{jn(2\pi/T)t} \tag{1.19a}$$

where

$$X_n = \frac{1}{T} \int_T x(t) \, e^{-jn(2\pi/T)t} \, dt \tag{1.19b}$$

where again $x(t)$ is assumed to be a periodic signal with period T.

In signal processing, we have many applications where the discontinuities are common. The next question one might ask is, How many terms should be kept in the Fourier series representation? (Certainly not infinite number of terms.) This leads to the question of convergence and uniqueness. By looking at few examples, one can see that the sum containing more and more terms tend to approximate a function better and better. If the given periodic function $x(t)$ has discontinuities and Fourier series are used to approximate $x(t)$, then there will be a considerable amount of error near the discontinuity, no matter how many terms are used in the sum. This effect is called the *Gibb's phenomenon*. The Fourier series expansion is unique if a set of conditions called *Dirichlet conditions* is satisfied. These are (1) The periodic function $x(t)$ is absolutely integrable over a period; (2) it has a finite number of maxima and minima; or (3) $x(t)$ has a finite number of discontinuities. If these conditions are satisfied, then the Fourier series converge to $x(t)$ pointwise for every value of t where $x(t)$ is continuous and piecewise differentiable or to the midpoint of the discontinuity at each discontinuity.

Also, if $x(t)$ is square integrable over one period, then the mean squared error between $x(t)$ and the Fourier series expansion of this function, $x_p(t)$, will approach 0 as the number of terms approaches infinity. That is, $\int_T |x(t) - x_p(t)|^2 \, dt = 0$. In this sense, the function $x(t)$ is expressed in terms of equality in $x(t) = x_p(t)$. The power in the periodic signal $x_p(t)$ is given by

$$P = \sum_{n=-\infty}^{\infty} |X_n|^2 \tag{1.20}$$

which is usually referred to as *Parseval's theorem*.

In signal processing, we have many applications where the discontinuities are common, and convergence to the midpoint at the discontinuity is an important point to remember. Higher frequency terms, i.e., the terms corresponding to large values of n, are important as the signal becomes closer to a waveform having a discontinuity. For example, approximating a rectangular pulse waveform, which has a discontinuity, the values a_n and b_n decrease only linearly, whereas approximating a triangular wave, which has a discontinuity only in the waveforms derivative, the a_n and b_n decrease quadratically.

Many important properties of the Fourier series are useful. First, the Fourier series coefficients uniquely describe the periodic function $x(t) = x_p(t)$. For simplicity, we will use $x_p(t)$ for a periodic function in the following. To identify the Fourier series relationship, it is generally written

$$x_p(t) \Leftrightarrow X_n \tag{1.21}$$

Computing the coefficients can be cumbersome. In many test signals, such as a pulse, triangular, and other waveforms, the coefficients can be derived by using some simple relationships. The X_0 term can be computed by simply computing the area under the function over one period and normalized with respect to the period. Many of the functions we are interested in can be considered a sum of simpler functions with the same period T, and superposition principle can be used. That is,

$$\sum_i x_{pi}(t) \Leftrightarrow \sum_i X_{ni} \tag{1.22}$$

Second,

$$\frac{\mathrm{d}^r}{\mathrm{d}t^r} x_{pi}(t) \Leftrightarrow (\mathrm{j}n2\pi f_0)^r X_{ni} \qquad (n \neq 0) \tag{1.23}$$

This important relation is useful in computing the Fourier coefficients for a piecewise linear function, where $f_0 = (1/T)$. Consider the periodic function $x(t)$ with period T shown in Figure 1.3. This type of a waveform will be useful in designing digital filters, where the function will be given in terms of frequency, f, rather than time. The Fourier series coefficients can be obtained by considering one period of $y(t) = (\mathrm{d}/\mathrm{d}t)x(t)$. The Fourier series coefficients corresponding to $y(t)$ are given by

$$Y_n = \frac{1}{T}\int_T y(t)\,\mathrm{e}^{-\mathrm{j}(2\pi/T)nt}\,\mathrm{d}t$$

$$= \frac{1}{T}\int_T (A\delta(t - T_1)\,\mathrm{e}^{(-\mathrm{j}2\pi/T)nt} - A\delta(t - T_2)\,\mathrm{e}^{(-\mathrm{j}2\pi/T)nt})\,\mathrm{d}t \tag{1.24}$$

$$= \frac{1}{T}A(\mathrm{e}^{(-\mathrm{j}2\pi/T)nT_1} - \mathrm{e}^{(-\mathrm{j}2\pi/T)nT_2}) \tag{1.25}$$

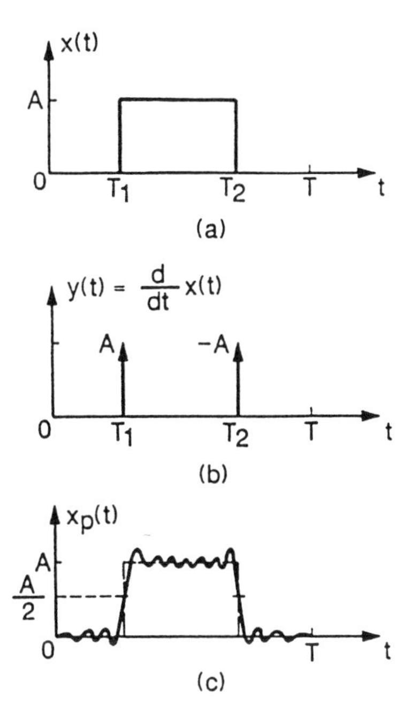

FIG. 1.3. (a) An example of a periodic function, $x(t)$; (b) derivative of the periodic function, $y(t)$; (c) expansion of $x(t)$ (via) Fourier series, $x_p(t)$ (only one period is shown).

and

$$Y_n = \left(jn\frac{2\pi}{T}\right)X_n, \qquad n \neq 0,$$

where $f_0 = 1/T$ is used. X_0 needs to be determined separately and is equal to $[A(T_2 - T_1)/T]$. The Fourier series expansion is

$$x_p(t) = \sum_{n=-\infty}^{\infty} X_n \, e^{(-jn2\pi/T)t} \tag{1.26}$$

One period of the resultant Fourier series expansion is plotted in Figure 1.3c. Note the overshoots and the undershoots before and after the discontinuity corresponding to the discontinuity. There is a lower bound of 9% overshoot (and undershoot also) even when infinite number of terms are considered. Recall the phenomenon of overshoots and undershoots before and after the discontinuity referred earlier as the Gibb's phenomenon.

Functions similar to the derivative of the periodic function, such as the integral of the periodic function, can be used in deriving Fourier series coefficients.

Fourier Transform

If the signal is not periodic, i.e., it is aperiodic, the Fourier transform is used. The forward transform is given by

$$X(f) = F[x(t)] = \int_{-\infty}^{\infty} x(t)\,\mathrm{e}^{-\mathrm{j}2\pi ft}\,\mathrm{d}t \tag{1.27a}$$

and the inverse transform is given by

$$x(t) = \int_{-\infty}^{\infty} X(f)\,\mathrm{e}^{\mathrm{j}2\pi ft}\,\mathrm{d}f \tag{1.27b}$$

One can use the symbol to identify the Fourier transform pair by

$$x(t) \leftrightarrow X(f) \tag{1.27c}$$

Instead of the frequency variable f, $\omega = 2\pi f$, the radian frequency is sometimes used. If so,

$$X(\omega) = \int_{-\infty}^{\infty} x(t)\,\mathrm{e}^{-\mathrm{j}\omega t}\,\mathrm{d}t \quad \text{and} \quad x(t) = \frac{1}{2\pi}\int_{-\infty}^{\infty} X(\omega)\,\mathrm{e}^{\mathrm{j}\omega t}\,\mathrm{d}\omega \tag{1.28}$$

Instead of $X(\omega)$, some texts use $X(\mathrm{j}\omega)$ indicating that the variable is $\mathrm{j}\omega$. Note the difference between the two terms $\mathrm{e}^{-\mathrm{j}\omega t}$ in the forward transform and $\mathrm{e}^{\mathrm{j}\omega t}$ in the inverse transform. The transform and its inverse in (1.27) can be derived using the Fourier series results earlier with

$$X(f) = \lim_{T\to\infty} [TX_n].$$

The existence and uniqueness aspects can be discussed in a similar manner.

Laplace Transform

In circuits and in control theory, Laplace transforms are widely used. Most engineers tend to use these more than the Fourier transforms. For the Fourier transform of a function to exist, it must be absolutely integrable. This can be alleviated by introducing a convergency factor $\mathrm{e}^{-\sigma t}$, where σ is a real number such that $\int_{-\infty}^{\infty} |x(t)\,\mathrm{e}^{-\sigma t}| < \infty$. Consider the Fourier transform of $x(t)\,\mathrm{e}^{-\sigma t}$. That is,

$$F[x(t)\,\mathrm{e}^{-\sigma t}] = X_I(f) = \int_{-\infty}^{\infty} (x(t)\,\mathrm{e}^{-\sigma t})\,\mathrm{e}^{-\mathrm{j}2\pi ft}\,\mathrm{d}t \tag{1.29}$$

and the inverse transform

$$x(t)\,\mathrm{e}^{-\sigma t} = \int_{-\infty}^{\infty} X_I(f)\,\mathrm{e}^{\mathrm{j}2\pi ft}\,\mathrm{d}f$$

or

$$x(t) = \int_{-\infty}^{\infty} X_I(f)\, e^{\sigma t}\, e^{j2\pi ft}\, df \tag{1.30}$$

Note that $\sigma + j2\pi f$ appears in both the integrals in (1.29) and (1.30). Introducing a new variable $s = \sigma + j2\pi f$, we have the bilateral Laplace transform

$$X_b(s) = \int_{-\infty}^{\infty} x(t)\, e^{-st}\, dt = \int_{-\infty}^{0} x(t)\, e^{-st}\, dt + \int_{0}^{\infty} x(t)\, e^{-st}\, dt \tag{1.31a}$$

and the inverse

$$x(t) = \frac{1}{2\pi j} \int_{\sigma - j\infty}^{\sigma + j\infty} X_b(s)\, e^{st}\, ds \tag{1.31b}$$

Equations in (1.31) are generally referred to as a *bilateral Laplace transform pair* (note the subscript b) or sometimes called the *complex-Fourier transform pair*. To have $X_b(s)$, we must find a convergence factor $\sigma = \text{Re}(s) = \alpha$ for the first integral and $\sigma = \text{Re}(s) = \beta$ for the second integral and $\alpha < \text{Re}(s) < \beta$ in (1.31a).

The Laplace transform used most is the one-sided or the unilateral transform, defined by

$$X_I(s) = \int_{0^-}^{\infty} x(t)\, e^{-st}\, dt \tag{1.32}$$

where the lower limit is 0^- rather then 0^+, which allows for handling any discontinuity at $t = 0$. The inverse Laplace transform is given by

$$x(t) = \frac{1}{2\pi j} \int_{\sigma_1 - j\infty}^{\sigma_1 + j\infty} X_I(s)\, e^{+st}\, ds \tag{1.33}$$

where $\sigma_1 > \sigma_c$; σ_c is the abscissa of convergence.

The Fourier and the Laplace transform tables are available, and it is only natural to consider obtaining one from the other. If $x(t) = 0$ for $t < 0$ and

$$\int_0^{\infty} |x(t)|\, dt < \infty, \qquad \text{then} \quad F[x(t)] = X_I(s)|_{s = j2\pi f}$$

Clearly, if $x(t) = e^{-at} u(t)$, $a > 0$, then

$$\int_0^{\infty} |e^{-at}|\, dt < \infty \tag{1.34}$$

and

$$F[e^{-at} u(t)] = \frac{1}{a + j\omega} = \left.\frac{1}{s + a}\right|_{s = j2\pi f} \tag{1.35}$$

On the other hand, if $a = 0$, then (1.34) is not true and therefore (1.35) is not true. Note that when $a = 0$, the function has a pole on the imaginary axis, specifically at the origin. For special cases where simple poles exist on the imaginary axis, a simple method can be used to find the Fourier transforms from the Laplace transforms.

Consider the case of a function that has the Laplace transform, and the region of convergence is the entire right half-plane. Let the Laplace transform be $X_I(s)$ with simple poles on the imaginary axis and the other poles on the left half-plane. Clearly, the region of convergence cannot include the imaginary axis because of the poles on the imaginary axis. Fourier transforms exist for these cases in the limit. These will involve delta functions. Let the Laplace transform of the function be

$$X_I(s) = X_0(s) + \sum_n \frac{a_n}{s - \mathrm{j}\omega_n}, \qquad \omega_n = 2\pi f_n \tag{1.36}$$

Where $X_0(s)$ represents the portion that does not include the poles on the imaginary axis, and the second term obviously represents simple poles on the imaginary axis. The corresponding Fourier transform is given by

$$X(f) = X_I(s)|_{s=\mathrm{j}2\pi f} + \sum_n \frac{a_n}{2}\delta(f - f_n) \tag{1.37}$$

For the special case of a unit step function, the Laplace transform is

$$\int_0^\infty u(t)\,\mathrm{e}^{-st}\,\mathrm{d}t = \frac{1}{s} \tag{1.38}$$

and the corresponding Fourier transform is

$$F[u(t)] = \frac{1}{s}\bigg|_{s=\mathrm{j}2\pi f} + \frac{1}{2}\delta(f) = \frac{1}{\mathrm{j}2\pi f} + \frac{1}{2}\delta(f) \tag{1.39}$$

From these we can see that the Fourier and the Laplace transforms can be related in some cases. However, these transforms are distinct, and neither one is a generalization of the other.

Important Fourier Transform Theorems

The theorems presented here can be found in any of the basic texts on signal analysis or communication theory. The proofs of most of these follow from the definition of the transform [2].

Let $X_i(f)$ be the Fourier transform of $x_i(t)$, written as

$$x_i(t) \leftrightarrow X_i(f), \qquad i = 1, 2, \ldots, N \tag{1.40}$$

then the superposition theorem states that

$$\sum_{i=1}^{N} a_i x_i(t) \leftrightarrow \sum_{i=1}^{N} a_i X_i(f) \tag{1.41}$$

where the terms a_i are constants. For the following, we assume $x(t) \leftrightarrow X(f)$. The scale-change theorem states that

$$x(at) \leftrightarrow \frac{1}{|a|} X\left(\frac{f}{a}\right) \tag{1.42}$$

where a is a constant. The time delay theorem states that

$$x(t - t_0) \leftrightarrow X(f)\,\mathrm{e}^{-\mathrm{j}2\pi f t_0}. \tag{1.43}$$

The duality theorem states that

$$X(t) \leftrightarrow x(-f) \tag{1.44}$$

indicating that, if a table of Fourier transforms is available, then we can double the table by using the preceding. The frequency shifting and modulation theorems state that

$$x(t)\,\mathrm{e}^{\mathrm{j}2\pi f_0 t} \leftrightarrow X(f - f_0) \tag{1.45a}$$

and

$$x(t) \cos 2\pi f_0 t \leftrightarrow \tfrac{1}{2}X(f - f_0) + \tfrac{1}{2}X(f + f_0) \tag{1.45b}$$

The differentiation and integration theorems state that

$$\frac{\mathrm{d}^k x(t)}{\mathrm{d}t^k} \leftrightarrow (\mathrm{j}2\pi f)^k X(f) \tag{1.46}$$

$$\int_{-\infty}^{t} x(\alpha)\,\mathrm{d}\alpha \leftrightarrow \frac{X(f)}{\mathrm{j}2\pi f} + \frac{1}{2} X(0)\delta(f) \tag{1.47}$$

The two widely used operations are the convolution, which is useful in system analysis, and the correlation, which is useful in comparing signals. The convolution operation is generally defined between two signals $x_1(t)$ and $x_2(t)$:

$$x_1(t) * x_2(t) = \int_{-\infty}^{\infty} x_1(\tau) x_2(t - \tau)\,\mathrm{d}\tau = \int_{-\infty}^{\infty} x_2(u) x_1(t - u)\,\mathrm{d}u \tag{1.48}$$

The convolution theorem states that

$$x_1(t) * x_2(t) \leftrightarrow X_1(f) X_2(f) \tag{1.49a}$$

Correspondingly, the multiplication theorem states that

$$x_1(t) x_2(t) \leftrightarrow X_1(f) * X_2(f) \tag{1.49b}$$

where

$$X_1(f) * X_2(f) = \int_{-\infty}^{\infty} X_1(u)X_2(f-u)\,du$$

These two theorems state that the convolution in time (frequency) corresponds to the multiplication in frequency (time).

The autocorrelation of an energy signal $x(t)$ is given by

$$\phi(\tau) = x(\tau) * x(-\tau) = \int_{-\infty}^{\infty} x(u)x(\tau + u)\,du \tag{1.50a}$$

and its transform

$$\Phi(f) = X(f)X^*(f) = |X(f)|^2 \tag{1.50b}$$

which is called the *energy spectral density*. In considering the periodic signals with period T, the autocorrelation is defined by

$$r(\tau) = \frac{1}{T}\int_T x_p(t)x_p(t+\tau)\,dt \tag{1.50c}$$

and the power spectral density is $R(f) = F[r(\tau)]$.

The autocorrelation function is a function of τ (not time t), where τ is the time shift between $x(t)$ and $x(t + \tau)$. A simple application may involve in finding the delay of a signal. Assuming that there is no corruption in the received signal, the cross correlation of the transmitted signal $x(t)$ and the received signal $y(t) = x(t - a)$ will give us the information. That is, if the crosscorrelation is defined by

$$c(\tau) = \int_{-\infty}^{\infty} x(u)y(u+\tau)\,dt \tag{1.50d}$$

then $c(\tau)$ is maximum when $a = \tau$, giving the desired delay.

A Few Important Transform Examples

Some important functions are basic to many signal processing functions. These include impulses, pulse functions, sinusoids, and others. The transforms of these can be computed by using the basic definition. Some of these follow for future references.

$$F[\delta(t - t_0)] = e^{-j2\pi f t_0} \tag{1.51a}$$

$$F\left[\Pi\left(\frac{t-t_0}{\tau}\right)\right] = (\tau)\,\mathrm{sinc}(f\tau)\,e^{-j2\pi f t_0} \tag{1.51b}$$

$$F[\cos 2\pi f_i t] = \frac{1}{2}\delta(f - f_i) + \frac{1}{2}\delta(f + f_i) \tag{1.51c}$$

$$F[e^{-\alpha t}u(t)] = \frac{1}{\alpha + j2\pi f}, \qquad \alpha > 0 \tag{1.51d}$$

Note the sinc function in (1.51b) is defined by $\mathrm{sinc}(f\tau) = (\sin \pi f\tau)/\pi f\tau$. Interestingly, $\mathrm{sinc}(f\tau) = 0$ for $f\tau = \pm 1, \pm 2, \ldots$, and is equal to 1 for $f\tau = 0$. It is bounded by 1 and, for larger values of $f\tau$, is inversely proportional to $(f\tau)$.

Magnitude and Phase Spectra

When $x(t)$ is real, which is true in most of our applications, the transform $X(f)$ has some nice properties. Noting that the Fourier transform is generally complex, we can obviously express a complex function $X(f)$ in its polar form,

$$X(f) = |X(f)|\, e^{j\theta(f)} \tag{1.52a}$$

or in its rectangular form,

$$X(f) = \mathrm{Re}[X(f)] + j\,\mathrm{Im}[X(f)] \tag{1.52b}$$

The amplitude $|X(f)|$ is generally transformed into base 20 log scale, i.e., $20 \log|X(f)|$, for easier plotting and is measured in decibels. For example, if $X(f) = \alpha/\alpha + j2\pi f$, $\alpha > 0$, the amplitude and phase spectra are respectively given by

$$\begin{aligned} A(f) &= 20 \log|X(f)| = 10 \log\left[\frac{1}{1 + |(2\pi f/\alpha)^2|}\right], \\ \theta(f) &= -\tan^{-1}\left(\frac{2\pi(f)}{\alpha}\right) \end{aligned} \tag{1.52c}$$

respectively. These are plotted in Figure 1.4. The units (dBs) originated as a measure of attentuation in a standard telephone cable, where 1 dB is equal to the attenuation of 1 mile of standard telephone cable. It is also the smallest audio power level that could be discerned by a human ear.

The value $|X(f_i)|$ gives the amplitude of the function at $f = f_i$. For example, at $f = \alpha/2\pi$ in (1.52c), $|X(\alpha/2\pi)| = 1/\sqrt{2}$ and in dB, it is -3 dB. It is some times referred to as a 3 dB frequency.

The magnitude spectrum of the delta function is 1 indicating that the delta function has all frequencies. The delta function $\delta(t - t_0)$ is obviously a delayed function, and the delay can be seen from the phase. First, $F[\delta(t - t_0)] = e^{-j2\pi f t_0}$, indicating the phase function is given by $\theta(f) = -2\pi f t_0$. Second, the delay is t_0 seconds. The group delay or simply

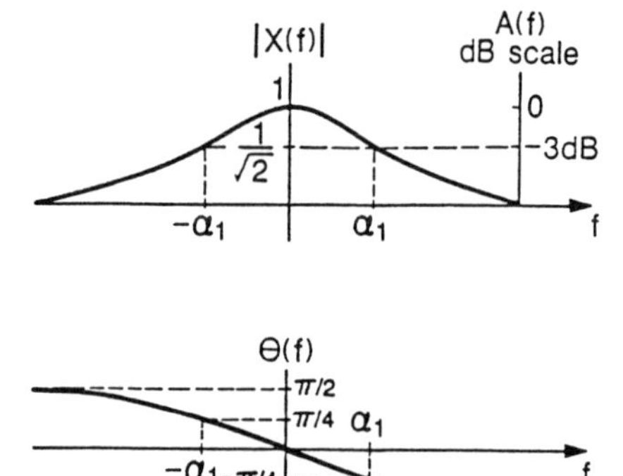

FIG. 1.4. Plots of amplitude and phase spectra ($\alpha_1 = \alpha/2\pi$).

the delay is defined by

$$T_G(f) = -\frac{1}{2\pi}\frac{\mathrm{d}}{\mathrm{d}f}\theta(f) \tag{1.53}$$

The transform of a cosine function, i.e., $F[\cos 2\pi f_i t]$, has two delta functions at $f = f_i$ and $-f_i$ indicating the frequency locations. See (1.51c). The delays are important. For example, if a function contains several frequencies and if different frequencies are delayed differently, clearly the resulting sum will not be a good (may not be any good at all) approximation of the original function. Human ears are rather insensitive to slight delays. However, a computer dealing with pulses is very senstitive to phase errors.

Another interesting result is the Rayleigh's energy theorem, which states that for an energy signal, $x(t)$,

$$E = \int_{-\infty}^{\infty} |x(t)|^2 \, \mathrm{d}t = \int_{-\infty}^{\infty} |X(f)|^2 \, \mathrm{d}f \tag{1.54}$$

Recall the Parseval's theorem in the periodic case. Note its similarity to this theorem.

Time-Frequency Widths

The delta function $\delta(t)$ is nonzero only at one point, whereas its spectrum is a constant for all frequencies. That is, its frequency, or spectral, width is ∞. Next, we are interested in the uncertainty principle of Fourier analysis, which points out that the product of the spectral width and the time duration of a signal cannot be less than a minimum value of $(1/4\pi)$.

First, let the transform of the real energy signal $x(t)$ to be $X(f)$. The energy content of the signal is

$$E = \int_{-\infty}^{\infty} |x(t)|^2 \, \mathrm{d}t < \infty$$

and the center of gravity of the function, $x^2(t)$, $\bar{t}$, is given by

$$\bar{t} = \frac{1}{E} \int_{-\infty}^{\infty} t x^2(t) \, \mathrm{d}t \tag{1.55a}$$

and let the dispersion of the signal around $\bar{t}$ be defined by

$$(\Delta t)^2 = \frac{1}{E} \int_{-\infty}^{\infty} (t - \bar{t})^2 x^2(t) \, \mathrm{d}t < \infty \tag{1.55b}$$

Note that (1.55a) and (1.55b) appears very similar to the analysis of statistical signals, where we study the mean and the variance. In a similar manner, we can define these for the transform $X(f)$. These are

$$E = \int_{-\infty}^{\infty} |X(f)|^2 \, \mathrm{d}f \tag{1.55c}$$

$$\bar{f} = \frac{1}{E} \int_{-\infty}^{\infty} f |X(f)|^2 \, \mathrm{d}f = 0 \tag{1.55d}$$

$$(\Delta f)^2 = \frac{1}{E} \int_{-\infty}^{\infty} (f - \bar{f})^2 |X(f)|^2 \, \mathrm{d}f = \frac{1}{E} \int_{-\infty}^{\infty} f^2 |X(f)|^2 \, \mathrm{d}f \tag{1.55e}$$

Note that (1.55c) follows from the Raleigh's energy theorem discussed earlier; (1.55d) follows from the fact that the integrand is an odd function and $\bar{f} = 0$; (1.55e) then follows. The spectral bandwidth of the signal Δf is a measure of the frequency width of the signal. Earlier, we have defined the 3 dB bandwidth, as the frequency width of the signal for which $20 \log |X(f)|$ satisfies

$$-3 \text{ dB} \le 20 \log |X(f)| \le 0 \quad \text{for} \quad f_1 \le f \le f_2$$

where $|X(f)|$ assumed to be normalized. That is, $|X(f)|_{\max} = 1$. We can generalize this to α dB bandwidth by saying that

$$-\alpha \text{ dB} \le 20 \log |X(f)| \le 0 \quad \text{for} \quad f_1 \le f \le f_2$$

One could wonder, why do we consider α dB bandwidths when a general definition is available? The reason for this is that the frequency bandwidth or spectral bandwidth can be infinity. For example, the transform of the pulse function $\Pi(t)$ is $\operatorname{sinc}(f)$ and

$$(\Delta f)^2 = \frac{1}{E}\int_{-\infty}^{\infty} f^2 \operatorname{sinc}^2(f)\, \mathrm{d}f \to \infty$$

where E, the energy in the pulse is 1. The finiteness of $\int_{-\infty}^{\infty} f^2|X(f)|^2\, \mathrm{d}f$ also means that

$$\lim_{f\to\infty} f^2|X(f)|^2 = 0$$

To avoid some of these problems, α dB widths are usually defined. For the case of the rectangular pulse, the spectral width of the pulse

$$\Pi\left(\frac{t - ((t_1 + t_2)/2)}{t_2 - t_1}\right)$$

is defined by $1/(t_2 - t_1)$, i.e., the inverse of the time width. Clearly, most of the energy is contained in the main lobe of $X(f)$, i.e., between

$$-\frac{1}{(t_2 - t_1)} < f < \frac{1}{(t_2 - t_2)}.$$

Interestingly, the product of spectral width and time width is given by

$$\left[\frac{1}{(t_2 - t_1)}\right](t_2 - t_1) = 1,$$

where we have used only the frequency width corresponding to positive frequencies. Note that there are no negative frequencies in reality. They are used for mathematical convenience. As a rule of thumb, we can state that time-bandwidth product is a constant. This product will be used later in evaluating windows.

Gaussian functions are widely used in probability theory and are useful here. The Fourier transform of a Gaussian function is also a Gaussian function. That is, for

$$x(t) = \mathrm{e}^{-at^2} \tag{1.56a}$$

we have

$$F[\mathrm{e}^{-at^2}] = \sqrt{\frac{\pi}{a}}\,\mathrm{e}^{-(2\pi f)^2/4a} \tag{1.56b}$$

Clearly, $\bar{t} = 0$, since $tx^2(t)$ is an odd function. Also, using tables, we can see that

$$(\Delta t)^2 = \frac{1}{4a}$$

$$(\Delta f)^2 = \frac{a}{4\pi^2}$$

Interestingly, the time-bandwidth product

$$(\Delta t)(\Delta f) = \frac{1}{4\pi} \tag{1.57a}$$

is a constant. However, in general, it can be shown that the time-bandwidth product is lower bounded. That is,

$$\frac{1}{4\pi} \leq (\Delta t)(\Delta f) \tag{1.57b}$$

This can be used to select a bandwidth measure, when the time width is limited, whereas the frequency width is unlimited.

Digital Representation of Analog Signals

Most signals, such as speech and many others, are analog signals. That is, they are functions of the continuous variable t. Images, on the other hand, are two-dimensional signals. Digitizing a one-dimensional signal, say $x(t)$, generally involves a three step process:

1. A sampler samples the signal at periodic intervals $t = nT_s$, where T_s corresponds to the sampling interval.
2. A quantizer maps the exact sampled values of $x(t)$ into one of L quantization levels.
3. The encoder assigns a unique code word to each of the L quantization levels.

There are obviously other ways of representing a signal. For example, the speech signal can be decomposed into 42 (or 44) English phonemes, which is clearly an application-dependent case. Here we will be interested in the general digitization process that is application independent. Multidimensional cases, such as images, can be dealt with by considering each dimension at a time.

In the first step, we are interested in obtaining the sampled values $x(nT_s)$ from the signal. How close we select the sampled values is a function of the frequency content of the signal. The classical Nyquist low-pass sampling theorem states that a signal can be reconstructed from the samples, if the sampling rate, $f_s = (1/T_s)$, which is the inverse of the time between samples. Explicitly, if $x(nT_s)$ corresponds to the sample values of the signal, then $x(t)$ can be obtained by using the interpolation formula [2]:

$$x(t) = \sum_{n=-\infty}^{\infty} x(nT_s) \operatorname{sinc}(f_s t - n) \tag{1.58}$$

where the sinc function was defined before.

The expression in (1.58) is a generalized Fourier series expansion of $x(t)$ using the orthogonal function set

$$\{\text{sinc}(f_s t - n),\ n = 0, \pm 1, \ldots\} \tag{1.59}$$

The orthogonal condition, of course, is

$$\int_{-\infty}^{\infty} \text{sinc}(f_s t - n)\,\text{sinc}(f_s t - m)\,dt = \begin{cases} k_n, & n = m \\ 0, & n \neq m \end{cases} \tag{1.60}$$

where $k_n = (1/f_s)$. The expression in (1.58), as mentioned earlier, is really an interpolation formula in the sense that knowing $x(nT_s)$, the sum interpolates between the sample points nT_s and $(n + 1)T_s$. At the sample point, say, $t = kT_s$, (1.58) reduces to $x(kT_s)$.

As pointed out earlier, the Nyquist sampling theorem states that a signal can be reconstructed from its samples if the sampling rate is at least twice the highest frequency in the signal. The sampling theorem does not tell you where to sample. As an example, say, $x(t) = \sin 2\pi t$. The highest frequency is 1 Hz. If the sampling rate is 2 Hz, i.e., two samples per second, then sampling $x(t)$ at $t = 0, \pm 1/2, \pm 1, \ldots$, gives the output exactly 0. On the other hand, sampling at $t = \pm 1/4, \pm 3/4, \ldots$, gives $x(k/2 + 1/4) = \pm 1$ for $k = 0, \pm 1, \pm 2, \ldots$. To avoid some of these problems, the sampling rate is taken higher than the Nyquist rate. Normally, 2.1 to 10 times the highest frequency in the input signal is used as the sampling frequency. For speech, the highest frequency is generally assumed to be around 3.5 kHz. The sampling rate is generally taken as 8 kHz or 10 kHz. For music, such as for compact discs, approximate frequency range is few Hertz to 20 kHz. The sampling rate is usually assumed to be 41 kHz. For seismic signals, the frequency is very low, few Hertz to about few hundred Hertz. Some common seismic sampling rates are 500 Hz and 1000 Hz. In summary, the sampling rate is application dependent. The preceding is for low-pass signals. If the signal is a bandpass signal, then different approaches are used to determine the sampling frequencies. See [2] for bandpass sampling theorem.

To find the spectrum of the sampled signal, the instantaneous sampled waveform is assumed to be

$$x_s(t) = \sum_{n=-\infty}^{\infty} x(nT_s)\delta(t - nT_s) \tag{1.61}$$

where T_s is the sampling interval. The transform

$$\begin{aligned} F[x_s(t)] &= F\left[x(t) \sum_{n=-\infty}^{\infty} \delta(t - nT_s) \right] \\ &= X(f) * f_s \sum_{n=-\infty}^{\infty} \delta(f - nf_s) = f_s \sum_{n=-\infty}^{\infty} X(f - nf_s) \end{aligned} \tag{1.62}$$

where we have used the facts that multiplication in the time domain corresponds to the convolution in the frequency domain, and

$$F\left[\sum_{n=-\infty}^{\infty} \delta(t - nT_s)\right] = f_s \sum_{n=-\infty}^{\infty} \delta(f - nf_s) \tag{1.63}$$

The last item is interesting, as the time domain function and the transform have the same general form. Another such interesting result is the Fourier transform of a Gaussian function (see (1.56)), which is also a Gaussian function.

Before we consider the second step in the sampling process, we should point out that if a signal is sampled below the Nyquist rate, then aliasing errors will result. This is due to the fact that adjacent spectral bands overlap (see (1.62)). Most of the signals we deal with are not frequency limited. So, before sampling, a bandlimiting filter is generally used. Filters will be considered a bit later.

In the second step of the sampling process, the sampled values, $x(nT_s)$, having infinite precision, need to be quantized so that the quantized value has only a finite precision. Clearly, in any realistic computer, the data need to have a finite precision. The quantizer maps the exact sampled values, $x(nT_s)$, into say L quantization levels. An example of such a quantizer is shown in Figure 1.5. In the example, eight quantization levels are assumed corresponding to a 3 bit representation, which corresponds to the third step. A unique code word is used to represent each level. For example, all the values between 1/2 and 3/2 are mapped to one and a binary representation may be 100 corresponding to level 4. Clearly, the coarser the quantization is, the greater is the error (diference between the original signal and the quantized signal). Greater error obviously means the discrete signal is noisier. Discretization noise of course is the difference between the signal, say, $x(t)$, and the quantized signal $x_q(t)$, i.e., the output of the quantizer. Let the signal power be S and the noise power be N, then the ratio of course is the signal-to-noise (S/N) ratio. It is generally measured in

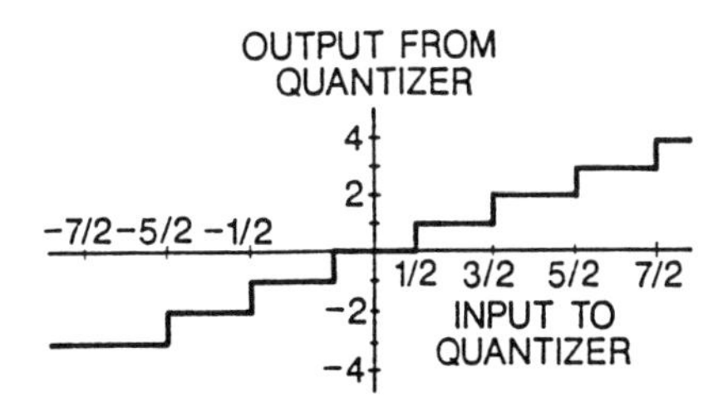

FIG. 1.5. Quantizer.

terms of a log scale, specifically in terms of dB and is 10 log (S/N) decibels. A rule of thumb, based on signal-to-noise ratios, is 1 bit for every 6 dB of signal-to-noise ratio. For speech 8 bits per sample and for compact discs 16 bits per sample are used. Obviously, for speech, fewer bits per sample can be used if only intelligibility and not fidelity is needed. For a sampling rate of 8 kHz with 8 bits per sample, it follows that 64 kbps is the data rate. For compact discs, the approximate rate is 1.3 Mbps, where two channels are assumed corresponding to stereo. This does not even include coding for error protection. For a video signal, the maximum frequency is assumed to be 5 MHz. With 8 bits/sample corresponding to a sampling rate of 11 MHz, the bit rate is 88 Mbps. Facsimile machines scan the page line by line and the data bits are based on the intensity of the light reflected by points. An 8.5 by 11 inches page sampled 200 points per inch gives $200 \times 200 \times 8.5 \times 11 \cong 3.74$ Mbits per page. Since the delay time for transmission of a page is not critical, data rate is critical only for the amount of time used. Using a modem (modulator-demodulator) with a 9.6 kbs takes approximately 6.5 minutes. Various data compression algorithms are available that can be used to reduce the data rate. For example, a white page corresponds to all zeros. Run length coding [4] is an effective way, which uses the runs of bits to reduce the number of bits for transmission.

Data Analysis

In data analysis, we are interested in processing signals that are represented by a sequence of numbers, say,

$$x = \{x(n)\}, \qquad -\infty < n < \infty \tag{1.64}$$

where $x(n)$ is the nth number in the sequence. Special cases include the unit-sample sequence, $\delta(n)$, defined by

$$\delta(n) = \begin{cases} 0, & n \neq 0 \\ 1, & n = 0 \end{cases} \tag{1.65}$$

which can be used to represent arbitrary sequences. Sequences, say, x and y, can be manipulated by the following rules:

1. The product of sequences, $x \cdot y = \{x(n)y(n)\}$.
2. The sum of two sequences, $x + y = \{x(n) + y(n)\}$.
3. The multiplication of a sequence by a constant a, $a \cdot x = \{ax(n)\}$. A sequence y is a delayed (usually termed *shifted* in digital terminology) version of x if $y(n) = x(n - n_0)$, where n_0 is an integer.

A simple example of a shifted sequence is

$$\delta(n - n_0) = \begin{cases} 0, & n \neq n_0 \\ 1, & n = n_0 \end{cases} \tag{1.66}$$

Interestingly, with the preceding simple rules, an arbitrary sequence $x(n)$ can be written as [5]

$$x(n) = \sum_{k=-\infty}^{\infty} x(k)\delta(n - k) \tag{1.67}$$

Transformations

In our study here, we will be interested in unique transformations that map one signal $x(t)$ ($x(n)$ for digital) into another sequence, say, $y(t)$ ($y(n)$ for digital). This transformation is symbolically written as

$$y(t) = T[x(t)] \tag{1.68}$$

for the continuous case and, for the discrete case,

$$y(n) = T[x(n)] \tag{1.69}$$

Before proceeding further, we should point out that the continuous case is represented in terms of a continuous variable t, whereas in the discrete case an arbitrary integer variable n (sometimes k) is used. The basic concepts are very similar, and we can use the continuous case for discussion. Three classes of systems are of interest to us, and they can be defined by putting constraints on T, the transformation. These are linearity, time invariance, and causality.

Given the responses $y_1(t)$ and $y_2(t)$ corresponding to the respective inputs $x_1(t)$ and $x_2(t)$, then a system is linear if and only if

$$T[a_1x_1(t) + a_2x_2(t)] = a_1y_1(t) + a_2y_2(t) \tag{1.70}$$

where a_1 and a_2 are some constants. Let $y(t)$ be the response to the input $x(t)$. A system is time invariant if $y(t - t_0)$ is the response to the input $x(t - t_0)$. That is, if the input is delayed, then the output of the time invariant system is correspondingly delayed. In the digital case, the system is usually referred to as shift invariant rather than time invariant.

Finally, a causal system is a system for which the output for anytime t_0 depends on the inputs for $t \leq t_0$ only. That is, the response does not depend on the future inputs.

Based on these concepts, we can characterize a linear system. First, we will consider analog systems. If the response to a delta function is $h(t)$, then the response to an input $x(t)$ is given by the convolution integral (see (1.48))

$$y(t) = h(t) * x(t) = \int_{-\infty}^{\infty} x(u)h(t-u)\,du \tag{1.71}$$

For a derivation of this concept, see any text on signal analysis (for example, [2]). Clearly, when $x(t) = \delta(t)$, $X(f) = 1$, and

$$Y(f) = H(f) \tag{1.72}$$

which is generally called the *transfer function* and $h(t)$ is the impulse response.

The discretized version can be derived by approximating the convolution integral. Noting that the integral of a function is simply the area under the function, we can use, say, the rectangular integration rule and at $t = kT_s$, we have

$$y(kT_s) = \sum_{n=-\infty}^{\infty} x(nT_s)h((k-n)T_s)T_s \tag{1.73}$$

where we have used the fact that the area of the rectangle strip is width times the height of the strip. Noting that T_s is a constant, we generally drop it and write

$$y(k) = \sum_{n=-\infty}^{\infty} x(n)h(k-n) = \sum_{n=-\infty}^{\infty} h(n)x(k-n) \tag{1.74}$$

Clearly, (1.74) could be derived for the discrete case, and for such a case, $h(n)$ is called the *unit sample response*. It should be noted that if (1.74) were used to determine the convolution integral, it would have to be multiplied by T_s.

For most digital signals and systems,

$$x(n) = 0 \text{ for } n < 0 \text{ and for } n \geq L$$
$$h(n) = 0 \text{ for } n < 0 \text{ and for } n \geq N$$

That is,

$$\begin{aligned} y(k) &= \sum_{n=0}^{L-1} x(n)h(k-n) \\ &= \sum_{n=0}^{N-1} h(n)x(k-n) \end{aligned} \tag{1.75}$$

Clearly, $y(k) = 0$ for $k < 0$ and for $k > N + L - 2$. The preceding can be written in a matrix form. For simplicity, let

$$h_n \equiv h(n) \tag{1.76a}$$

$$\begin{bmatrix} y(0) \\ y(1) \\ y(2) \\ \cdot \\ \cdot \\ \cdot \\ y(N-1) \\ y(N) \\ \cdot \\ \cdot \\ \cdot \\ y(N+L-2) \end{bmatrix} = \begin{bmatrix} h_0 & 0 & 0 & \cdots & 0 \\ h_1 & h_0 & 0 & \cdots & 0 \\ h_2 & h_1 & h_0 & \cdots & 0 \\ \cdot & \cdot & \cdot & \cdots & \cdot \\ \cdot & \cdot & \cdot & \cdots & \cdot \\ \cdot & \cdot & \cdot & \cdots & \cdot \\ h_{N-1} & h_{N-2} & h_{N-3} & \cdots & \cdot \\ 0 & h_{N-1} & h_{N-2} & \cdots & \cdot \\ \cdot & \cdot & \cdot & \cdots & h_0 \\ \cdot & \cdot & \cdot & \cdots & \cdot \\ \cdot & \cdot & \cdot & \cdots & h_{N-2} \\ 0 & 0 & 0 & \cdots & h_{N-1} \end{bmatrix} \begin{bmatrix} x(0) \\ x(1) \\ \cdot \\ \cdot \\ \cdot \\ x(L-1) \end{bmatrix} \tag{1.76b}$$

In symbolic form, this can be written as

$$\mathbf{y} = H\mathbf{x} \tag{1.76c}$$

where $\mathbf{x}$ and $\mathbf{y}$ are vectors of dimensions L and $N + L - 1$, respectively, and H is an $(N + L - 1)$ by L matrix.

Earlier when we discussed the convolution integral, we pointed out that the convolution in the time domain corresponds to the multiplication in the frequency domain (see (1.49)). Similar results can be obtained in the digital domain also. This is done by noting the coefficient matrix structure in (1.76b). The columns are shifted versions of each other. These types of matrices can be discussed in terms of discrete Fourier transform matrices and circulant matrices. These will be discussed next.

The Discrete Fourier Transform

Earlier we briefly discussed the continuous Fourier transform and its inverse transform. The computation involves integrals and clearly the analytical computation is possible only in a very few cases. In many cases, such as speech processing, the signal is available as a waveform rather than a function. This leads to digital processing and digital Fourier transform is obviously the next step. First, the signal needs to be sampled using the sampling theorem and the integral needs to be approximated using an approximation, such as the rectangular approximation. The Fourier transform

$$X(f) = \left[\int_{-\infty}^{\infty} x(t)\,\mathrm{e}^{-\mathrm{j}2\pi ft}\,\mathrm{d}t \right]$$

can be approximated by

$$X(f) \cong \sum_{k=-\infty}^{\infty} T_s x(kT_s)\,\mathrm{e}^{-\mathrm{j}2\pi fkT_s} \tag{1.77}$$

where T_s is the sampling interval, selected according to the Nyquist sampling theorem discussed earlier. Most signals are assumed to be nonzero only for a finite interval. Assuming $x(t) = 0$ for $t < 0$ and $t \geq NT_s$, where N is some integer, Eq. (1.77) can be written as

$$X(f) = T_s \sum_{k=0}^{N-1} x(kT_s)\,\mathrm{e}^{-\mathrm{j}2\pi fkT_s} \tag{1.78}$$

which is periodic with period $(1/T_s)$. Sampling $X(f)$ at intervals of $(1/NT_s)$, we have

$$X\left(n\frac{1}{NT_s}\right) = T_s \sum_{k=0}^{N-1} x(kT_s)\,\mathrm{e}^{-\mathrm{j}(2\pi/N)kn}, \qquad n = 0, 1, \ldots, N-1.$$

Since T_s and $(1/NT_s)$ are constants, they are usually omitted. The discrete Fourier transform is defined by

$$X(n) = \sum_{k=0}^{N-1} x(k)\,\mathrm{e}^{-\mathrm{j}(2\pi/N)nk}, \qquad n = 0, 1, \ldots, N-1 \tag{1.79}$$

and are usually referred to as *discrete Fourier transform* (DFT) *coefficients*.

Using analysis similar to the preceding, we can approximate the inverse Fourier transform also. Or, better yet, we can find the inverse transform directly from (1.79). To do this, $X(n)$ can be written in a matrix form

$$\begin{bmatrix} X(0) \\ X(1) \\ \vdots \\ X(N-1) \end{bmatrix} = \begin{bmatrix} 1 & 1 & \cdots & 1 \\ 1 & \mathrm{e}^{-\mathrm{j}(2\pi/N)} & \cdots & \mathrm{e}^{-\mathrm{j}(2\pi/N)(N-1)} \\ \vdots & \vdots & \vdots & \vdots \\ 1 & \mathrm{e}^{-\mathrm{j}(2\pi/N)(N-1)} & \cdots & \mathrm{e}^{-\mathrm{j}(2\pi/N)(N-1)^2} \end{bmatrix} \begin{bmatrix} x(0) \\ x(1) \\ \vdots \\ x(N-1) \end{bmatrix} \tag{1.80a}$$

or in compact form

$$\mathbf{X} = A_{\mathrm{DFT}}\mathbf{x} \tag{1.80b}$$

where A_{DFT} is usually referred as DFT matrix and is an $N \times N$ matrix with a typical entry, say (n, k) entry,

$$A_{\mathrm{DFT}}(n, k) = \mathrm{e}^{-\mathrm{j}(2\pi/N)(k-1)(n-1)}. \quad (1.81\mathrm{a})$$

$$= W^{(k-1)(n-1)}, \qquad 1 \le n \le N,\ 1 \le k \le N \quad (1.81\mathrm{b})$$

where we have used for simplicity

$$W = \mathrm{e}^{-\mathrm{j}(2\pi/N)} \quad (1.81\mathrm{c})$$

Interestingly, $((1/\sqrt{N})A_{\mathrm{DFT}})$ is a symmetric unitary matrix. That is, $A_{\mathrm{DFT}} = A_{\mathrm{DFT}}^{T}$ and

$$\frac{1}{N} A_{\mathrm{DFT}} A_{\mathrm{DFT}}^{*} = I \quad (1.82)$$

an identity matrix. From this, it follows that

$$\mathbf{x} = \frac{1}{N} A_{\mathrm{DFT}}^{*} \mathbf{X} \quad (1.83)$$

which is not too surprising since the forward and the inverse continuous Fourier transforms are very similar except for the sign in $\mathrm{e}^{\pm \mathrm{j}2\pi f t}$ ($-$ for the forward transform and $+$ for the inverse transform). If an algorithm can be developed for the forward transform, the inverse transform is a simple modification, which involves conjugation (W to W^*) and the scale factor $(1/N)$.

Equations (1.80) and (1.83) point out that they are linear transformations and they convert one set of data from one domain to another (time to frequency and frequency to time). Clearly, to implement (1.80) (or (1.83)) requires N^2 complex multiplications and additions. Obviously, the number of computations gets larger as N gets larger. Various fast algorithms are available to implement the discrete Fourier transform. One of the algorithms considered classic is usually referred to as the *Cooley–Tukey algorithm*. This is also referred to as a *fast Fourier transform* (FFT) and is applicable when N, the number of points, is a power of 2 [5]. An outline of this follows.

The principle behind this algorithm is to express an N-point DFT by two $(N/2)$ points DFTs. This can be seen from [5–7]:

$$\begin{aligned} X(n) &= \sum_{k=0}^{N-1} x(k)\,\mathrm{e}^{-\mathrm{j}(2\pi/N)nk} \\ &= \sum_{k=0}^{(N/2)-1} x(2k)\,\mathrm{e}^{-\mathrm{j}(2\pi/(N/2))nk} + \sum_{k=0}^{(N/2)-1} x(2k+1)\,\mathrm{e}^{-\mathrm{j}(2\pi/N)(2k+1)n} \\ &= A(n) + B(n)\,\mathrm{e}^{-\mathrm{j}(2\pi/N)n}, \qquad n = 0, 1, \ldots, N-1 \end{aligned} \quad (1.84)$$

with

$$A(n) = \sum_{k=0}^{(N/2)-1} x(2k)\, e^{-j(2\pi/(N/2))nk}, \qquad B(n) = \sum_{k=0}^{(N/2)-1} x(2k+1)\, e^{-j(2\pi/(N/2))nk} \tag{1.85}$$

Note that $A(n)$ and $B(n)$ are DFTs of even and odd samples, respectively. Since an N-point DFT is reduced to two $(N/2)$-point DFTs, the number of operations is reduced by approximately half. Successive application of this algorithm allows for the reduction of the number of computations from N^2 to compute (1.80) to $N(\log_2 N)$ by this algorithm for N, a power of 2. Obviously, the power of this algorithm really shows as N gets larger.

In the following, the FFT algorithms are presented for an N point, $(N = 2^\nu)$, case [7]. For simplicity, we will use the symbol W in (1.81c). Clearly,

$$W^{nk} = e^{-j(2\pi/N)(nk)} \tag{1.86}$$

Expressing n and k in terms of binary representations, we have

$$n = n_{\nu-1}2^{\nu-1} + n_{\nu-2}2^{\nu-2} + \cdots + n_0 = \sum_{i=0}^{\nu-1} n_i 2^i \tag{1.87a}$$

$$k = k_{\nu-1}2^{\nu-1} + k_{\nu-2}2^{\nu-2} + \cdots + k_0 = \sum_{i=0}^{\nu-1} k_i 2^i \tag{1.87b}$$

where n_i and k_i, $i = 0, 1, \ldots, \nu - 1$, can take on values 0 and 1 only. The binary equivalence can be written as

$$(n)_2 = n_{\nu-1}n_{\nu-2}\ldots n_0 \tag{1.88a}$$

$$(k)_2 = k_{\nu-1}k_{\nu-2}\ldots k_0 \tag{1.88b}$$

Noting that $W^N = 1$, we can write

$$W^{nk} = W^{nk(\mathrm{mod}(N))} \tag{1.89}$$

The product nk can be written as

$$nk = k_{\nu-1}2^{\nu-1}\left(\sum_{i=0}^{\nu-1} n_i 2^i\right) + \cdots + k_0\left(\sum_{i=0}^{\nu-1} n_i 2^i\right) \tag{1.90a}$$

Noting that $2^\nu = N$, we can simplify the expression

$$nk\,\mathrm{mod}(N) = k_{\nu-1}2^{\nu-1}n_0 + k_{\nu-2}2^{\nu-2}\left(\sum_{i=0}^{1} n_i 2^i\right) + \cdots + k_0\left(\sum_{i=0}^{\nu-1} n_i 2^i\right) \tag{1.90b}$$

Since W is an exponential function, it follows that

$$W^{nk\,\mathrm{mod}(N)} = W^{k_{\nu-1}2^{\nu-1}n_0} W^{k_{\nu-2}2^{\nu-2}(\sum_{i=0}^{1} n_i 2^i)} \cdots W^{k_0(\sum_{i=0}^{\nu-1} n_i 2^i)} \quad (1.91)$$

Let $x(k)$ be a typical entry in $\mathbf{x}$ (i.e., the $(k+1)$th entry) and let $X(n)$ be a typical entry in $\mathbf{X}$ (i.e., the $(n+1)$th entry in $\mathbf{X}$). For future use, let us use a subscript on $\mathbf{x}$ and define

$$\mathbf{x}_0 \equiv \mathbf{x} \quad (1.92)$$

and

$$\begin{aligned} X(n) &= X(n_{\nu-1}n_{\nu-2}\ldots n_0) \\ &= \sum_{k_0=0}^{1}\sum_{k_1=0}^{1}\cdots\sum_{k_{\nu-1}=0}^{1} x_0(k_{\nu-1}k_{\nu-2}\ldots k_0)W^{nk} \end{aligned} \quad (1.93)$$

Using (1.89) and (1.91), we have

$$\begin{aligned} X(n) = \sum_{k_0=0}^{1} W^{k_0(\sum_{i=0}^{\nu-1} n_i 2^i)} &\left[\sum_{k_1=0}^{1} W^{2k_1 \sum_{i=0}^{\nu-2} n_i 2^i} \right. \\ &\times \left. \left[\cdots \left[\sum_{k_{\nu-1}=0}^{1} W^{k_{\nu-1}n_0 2^{\nu-1}} x_0(k_{\nu-1}k_{\nu-2}\ldots k_0) \right] \cdots \right] \right] \end{aligned}$$

Now, let us identify

$$\begin{aligned} x_1(n_0k_{\nu-2}\ldots k_0) &= \sum_{k_{\nu-1}=0}^{1} x_0(k_{\nu-1}k_{\nu-2}\ldots k_0)W^{k_{\nu-1}n_0 2^{\nu-1}} \\ x_2(n_0n_1k_{\nu-3}\ldots k_0) &= \sum_{k_{\nu-2}=0}^{1} x_1(n_0k_{\nu-2}\ldots k_0)W^{k_{\nu-2}2^{\nu-2}(\sum_{i=0}^{1} n_i 2^i)} \\ &\vdots \\ x_l(n_0n_1\ldots n_{l-1}k_{\nu-l-1}\ldots k_0) &= \sum_{k_{\nu-l}=0}^{1} x_{l-1}(n_0n_1\ldots n_{l-2}k_{\nu-l}\ldots k_0) \\ &\quad \times W^{k_{\nu-l}2^{\nu-l}(\sum_{i=0}^{l-1} n_i 2^i)} \\ &\vdots \\ x_\nu(n_0n_1\ldots n_{\nu-1}) &= \sum_{k_0=1}^{1} x_{\nu-1}(n_0n_1\ldots n_{\nu-2}k_0)W^{k_0(\sum_{i=0}^{\nu-1} n_i 2^i)} \end{aligned} \quad (1.94)$$

with

$$X(n_{\nu-1}n_{\nu-2}\ldots n_0) \equiv x_\nu(n_0n_1\ldots n_{\nu-1}) \quad (1.95)$$

Note the arguments of x_l and x_{l-1}:

Argument of x_{l-1}: $n_0n_1\ldots n_{l-2}k_{\nu-l}k_{\nu-l-1}\ldots k_0$

Argument of x_l: $n_0n_1\ldots n_{l-2}n_{l-1}k_{\nu-l-1}\ldots k_0$

From this, we can see that the arguments are the same except $k_{\nu-l}$ in the x_{l-1} argument and n_{l-1} in the x_l argument. Noting that n_{l-1} (and $k_{\nu-l}$) are either 1 or 0, we can write

$$x_l(n_0 n_1 \ldots n_{l-2}\, 0\, k_{\nu-l-1} \ldots k_0) = x_{l-1}(n_0 n_1 \ldots n_{l-2}\, 0\, k_{\nu-l-1} \ldots k_0) + W^p x_{l-1}(n_0 n_1 \ldots n_{l-2}\, 1\, k_{\nu-l-1} \ldots k_0) \tag{1.96}$$

where

$$p = 2^{\nu-l}\left(\sum_{i=0}^{l-2} n_i 2^i\right) \tag{1.97}$$

Note $n_{l-1} = 0$ in determining the value of p in (1.97). Similarly,

$$x_l(n_0 n_1 \ldots n_{l-2}\, 1\, k_{\nu-l-1} \ldots k_0) = x_{l-1}(n_0 n_1 \ldots n_{l-2}\, 0\, k_{\nu-l-1} \ldots k_0) + W^{p_1} x_{l-1}(n_0 n_1 \ldots n_{l-2}\, 1\, k_{\nu-l-1} \ldots k_0) \tag{1.98}$$

where

$$p_1 = 2^{\nu-l}\left(\sum_{i=0}^{l-2} n_i 2^i\right) + 2^{\nu-1} = p + 2^{\nu-1} \tag{1.99}$$

and where $n_{l-1} = 1$ was used. Interestingly, for any arbitrary n, $0 \le n \le N-1$, N, a power of 2, we can write

$$\begin{bmatrix} x_l(n_0 n_1 \ldots n_{l-2}\; 0\; k_{\nu-l-1} \ldots k_0) \\ x_l(n_0 n_1 \ldots n_{l-2}\; 1\; k_{\nu-l-1} \ldots k_0) \end{bmatrix} = \begin{bmatrix} 1 & W^p \\ 1 & W^{p_1} \end{bmatrix} \begin{bmatrix} x_{l-1}(n_0 n_1 \ldots n_{l-2}\; 0\; k_{\nu-l-1} \ldots k_0) \\ x_{l-1}(n_0 n_1 \ldots n_{l-2}\; 1\; k_{\nu-l-1} \ldots k_0) \end{bmatrix} \tag{1.100}$$

indicating the relationship between x_l and x_{l-1}, and l varies from 1 to ν, and the argument of $x(a)$, a, satisfies $0 \le a < 2^\nu - 1$. The arguments are expressed in binary form in (1.100). Interestingly,

$$W^{p_1} = W^p W^{2^{\nu-1}} = -W^p \tag{1.101}$$

Example

Consider the case $N = 4 = 2^\nu = 2^2$. The data set is given by $x(k)$, $k = 0, 1, 2, 3$. By definition, we write $x_0(k) \equiv x(k)$. In matrix form, we have

$$\begin{bmatrix} X(0) \\ X(1) \\ X(2) \\ X(3) \end{bmatrix} = \begin{bmatrix} 1 & 1 & 1 & 1 \\ 1 & W^1 & W^2 & W^3 \\ 1 & W^2 & W^4 & W^6 \\ 1 & W^3 & W^6 & W^9 \end{bmatrix} \begin{bmatrix} x_0(0) \\ x_0(1) \\ x_0(2) \\ x_0(3) \end{bmatrix} \tag{1.102}$$

The data vector $\mathbf{x}_0$, the successive vectors $\mathbf{x}_l$, $l = 1, 2$, and the transform vectors can be written in terms of the binary arguments. These are

$$\begin{bmatrix} x_0(00) \\ x_0(01) \\ x_0(10) \\ x_0(11) \end{bmatrix}, \quad \begin{bmatrix} x_1(00) \\ x_1(01) \\ x_1(10) \\ x_1(11) \end{bmatrix}, \quad \begin{bmatrix} x_2(00) \\ x_2(01) \\ x_2(10) \\ x_2(11) \end{bmatrix}, \quad \begin{bmatrix} X(00) \\ X(01) \\ X(10) \\ X(11) \end{bmatrix}$$

Now, using (1.100), we have successively

$$\begin{bmatrix} x_1(00) \\ x_1(01) \\ x_1(10) \\ x_1(11) \end{bmatrix} = \begin{bmatrix} 1 & 0 & W^0 & 0 \\ 0 & 1 & 0 & W^0 \\ 1 & 0 & W^2 & 0 \\ 0 & 1 & 0 & W^2 \end{bmatrix} \begin{bmatrix} x_0(00) \\ x_0(01) \\ x_0(10) \\ x_0(11) \end{bmatrix} \tag{1.103}$$

$$l = 1, \qquad \nu = 2, \qquad \nu - l = 2 - 1 = 1$$

and

$$\begin{bmatrix} x_2(00) \\ x_2(01) \\ x_2(10) \\ x_2(11) \end{bmatrix} = \begin{bmatrix} 1 & W^0 & 0 & 0 \\ 1 & W^2 & 0 & 0 \\ 0 & 0 & 1 & W^1 \\ 0 & 0 & 1 & W^3 \end{bmatrix} \begin{bmatrix} x_1(00) \\ x_1(01) \\ x_1(10) \\ x_1(11) \end{bmatrix} \tag{1.104}$$

$$l = 2, \qquad \nu = 2, \qquad \nu - l = (2 - 2) = 0$$

and, finally

$$\begin{bmatrix} X(0) \\ X(1) \\ X(2) \\ X(3) \end{bmatrix} = \begin{bmatrix} x_2(00) \\ x_2(10) \\ x_2(01) \\ x_2(11) \end{bmatrix} \tag{1.105}$$

where the argument of $X(n_1 n_0)$ is bit reversed from the argument of $x_2(n_0 n_1)$.

A few illustrations are in order. First, the (3, 4) entry in the coefficient matrix in (1.104) is given by (see 1.97)) W^1, where the power $p = 1$ is obtained from

$$p = 2^{2-2}\left(\sum_{i=0}^{0} n_i 2^i\right) = 1(1 \times 2^0) = 1$$

and in the (4×4) entry

$$p_1 = p + 2^{\nu-1} = 1 + 2 = 3$$

The manipulations identified earlier (Equations (1.104)–(1.106)) are usually shown by a flow graph. For example, the equation

$$x_1(10) = x_0(00) + W^2 x_0(10)$$

is represented as shown in Figure 1.6, where W^2 below the line indicates the multiplier and no number indicates that the power of W is 0; therefore the multiplier is 1. Note that $W^2 = -1$ for a 4-point DFT. The flow graph for Eqs. (1.103)–(1.105) is shown in Figure 1.7.

In matrix form, the fourth-order DFT matrix can be written as

$$A_{\mathrm{DFT}} = \begin{bmatrix} 1 & 1 & 1 & 1 \\ 1 & W & W^2 & W^3 \\ 1 & W^2 & W^4 & W^6 \\ 1 & W^3 & W^6 & W^9 \end{bmatrix}$$

$$= \begin{bmatrix} 1 & 0 & 0 & 0 \\ 0 & 0 & 1 & 0 \\ 0 & 1 & 0 & 0 \\ 0 & 0 & 0 & 1 \end{bmatrix} \begin{bmatrix} 1 & 1 & 0 & 0 \\ 1 & -1 & 0 & 0 \\ 0 & 0 & 1 & W^1 \\ 0 & 0 & 1 & -W^1 \end{bmatrix} \begin{bmatrix} 1 & 0 & 1 & 0 \\ 0 & 1 & 0 & 1 \\ 1 & 0 & -1 & 0 \\ 0 & 1 & 0 & -1 \end{bmatrix} \qquad (1.106)$$

where the entries in the matrices can be read from the flow graph, where W^3 is written as $-W^1$. Since $A_{\mathrm{DFT}}^T = A_{\mathrm{DFT}}$, we can also write the preceding as

$$A_{\mathrm{DFT}} = \begin{bmatrix} 1 & 0 & 1 & 0 \\ 0 & 1 & 0 & 1 \\ 1 & 0 & -1 & 0 \\ 0 & 1 & 0 & -1 \end{bmatrix} \begin{bmatrix} 1 & 1 & 0 & 0 \\ 1 & -1 & 0 & 0 \\ 0 & 0 & 1 & 1 \\ 0 & 0 & W^1 & -W^1 \end{bmatrix} \begin{bmatrix} 1 & 0 & 0 & 0 \\ 0 & 0 & 1 & 0 \\ 0 & 1 & 0 & 0 \\ 0 & 0 & 0 & 1 \end{bmatrix} \qquad (1.07)$$

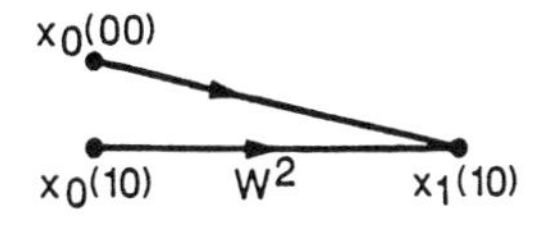

FIG. 1.6. Example of flow graph notation.

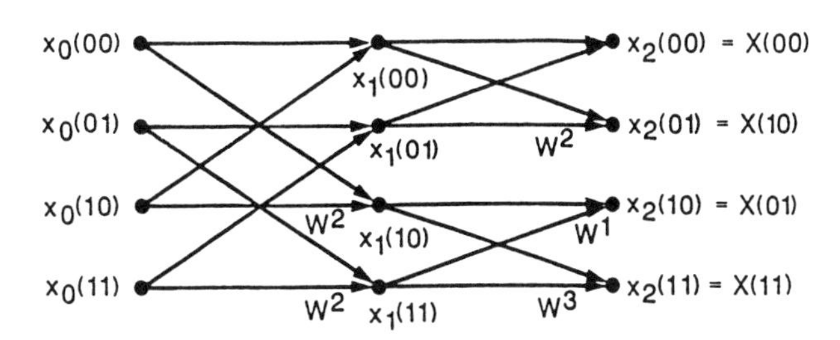

FIG. 1.7. FFT flow graph for Eqs. (1.104)–(1.106), $N = 4$; output data are in shuffled order.

and the corresponding flow graph is shown in Figure 1.8. From this we can see that, if we know one flow graph, we can draw the other one by inspection from the first. The derivation obviously follows in a very similar way.

It should be pointed out that the in-between values in computing the DFTs by using the different algorithms are obviously not the same. Also, for an N point DFT, with $N = 2^\nu$, we use ν stage plus reordering the data (or the transforms). Note, for example, in the first case, see (1.105) and Figure 1.7. We have used

$$x_2(0, 0) = X(0, 0), \quad x_2(0, 1) = X(1, 0), \quad x_2(1, 0) = X(0, 1), \quad \text{and} \quad x_2(1, 1) = X(1, 1).$$

Note the addresses associated with $x_2(a, b)$ and $X(b, a)$: the bits are simply reversed. In the second case, see Figure 1.8, $x(0, 0) = x_0(0, 0)$,

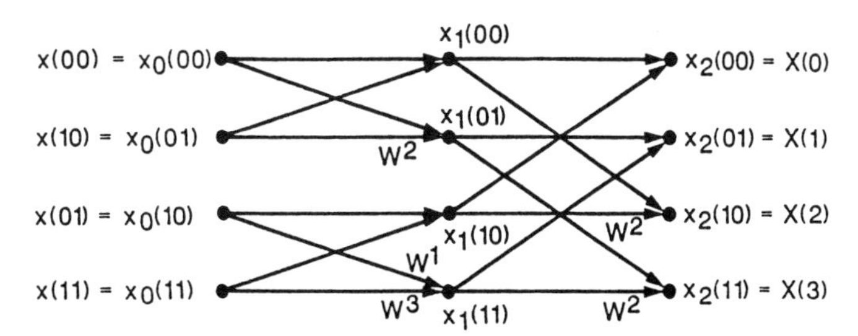

FIG. 1.8. FFT flow graph using (1.107), $N = 4$; data are in shuffled order.

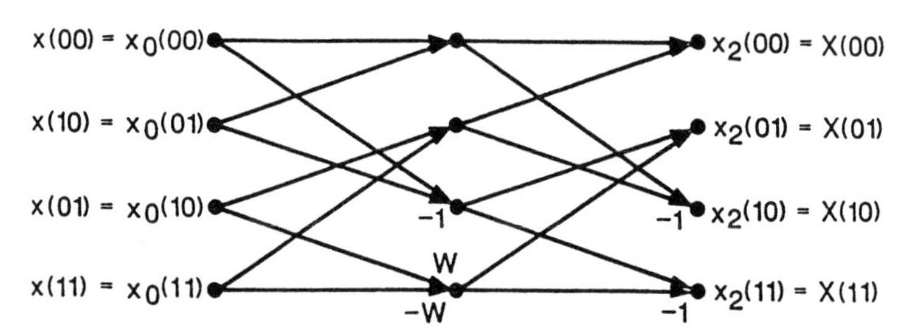

FIG. 1.9. FFT flow graph using (1.108).

$x(1, 0) = x_0(0, 1)$, $x(0, 1) = x_0(1, 0)$, and $x(1, 1) = x_0(1, 1)$, where the addresses in the arguments of $x_0(a, b)$ are bit reversed from the arguments of $x(b, a)$. An interesting aspect is that the structure is different from stage to stage. However, at each stage, two inputs are used to get two outputs at a time.

Another variation of the algorithm, is to make the structures the same. For the previous case, we have

$$A_{\mathrm{DFT}} = \begin{bmatrix} 1 & 1 & 0 & 0 \\ 0 & 0 & 1 & 1 \\ 1 & -1 & 0 & 0 \\ 0 & 0 & 1 & -1 \end{bmatrix} \begin{bmatrix} 1 & 1 & 0 & 0 \\ 0 & 0 & 1 & 1 \\ 1 & -1 & 0 & 0 \\ 0 & 0 & W^1 & -W^1 \end{bmatrix} \begin{bmatrix} 1 & 0 & 0 & 0 \\ 0 & 0 & 1 & 0 \\ 0 & 1 & 0 & 0 \\ 0 & 0 & 0 & 1 \end{bmatrix} \qquad (1.08)$$

where (1.108) is obtained from (1.107) by permuting the second (third) column to the third (to second) column in the first matrix and permuting the second and third rows in the second matrix. Note that bit reversal ordering is still there, and the multipliers are different. The flow graph is shown in Figure 1.9. Other variations can be discussed, of course.

Circulant Matrices

An $N \times N$ matrix C is called a *circulant matrix* if it can be written in the form [4]

$$C = \begin{bmatrix} c_0 & c_1 & \cdots & c_{N-1} \\ c_{N-1} & c_0 & \cdots & c_{N-2} \\ \vdots & \vdots & & \vdots \\ c_1 & c_2 & \cdots & c_0 \end{bmatrix} \qquad (1.109)$$

A fourth order example is

$$C = \begin{bmatrix} c_0 & c_1 & c_2 & c_3 \\ c_3 & c_0 & c_1 & c_2 \\ c_2 & c_3 & c_0 & c_1 \\ c_1 & c_2 & c_3 & c_0 \end{bmatrix} \tag{1.110}$$

Some of the interesting aspects of circulant matrices are

1. There are only N distinct elements in the Nth order circulant matrix.
2. If we know the first column or the first row, we can write the entire matrix.
3. Most important, it can be expressed as

$$C = \frac{1}{N} A_{\text{DFT}} D A_{\text{DFT}}^{*} = \frac{1}{N} A_{\text{DFT}}^{*} \Lambda A_{\text{DFT}} \tag{1.111}$$

where A_{DFT} is the discrete Fourier transform (DFT) matrix discussed earlier and the diagonal matrices $D = \text{dia}(d_{11}, d_{22}, \ldots, d_{NN})$ and $\Lambda = \text{dia}(\lambda_{11}, \lambda_{22}, \ldots, \lambda_{NN})$ can be explicitly written as

$$\begin{bmatrix} d_{11} \\ d_{22} \\ \vdots \\ d_{NN} \end{bmatrix} = A_{\text{DFT}} \begin{bmatrix} c_0 \\ c_1 \\ \vdots \\ c_{N-1} \end{bmatrix}, \quad \begin{bmatrix} \lambda_{11} \\ \lambda_{22} \\ \vdots \\ \lambda_{NN} \end{bmatrix} = A_{\text{DFT}} \begin{bmatrix} c_0 \\ c_{N-1} \\ \vdots \\ c_1 \end{bmatrix} \tag{1.112}$$

It is interesting to point out that discrete convolution can be formulated in terms of a circulant matrix and eigenvalue–eigenvector decomposition. This can be seen as an extension to the analog convolution that can be computed via Fourier transforms, discussed earlier (see (1.49)). That is, the convolution of $x_1(t)$ and $x_2(t)$ can be computed by first computing $X_1(f)$ and $X_2(f)$, then computing the product $X_1(f)X_2(f)$, and finally computing the inverse transform of the product.

Discrete Convolution via DFT

The first step in this approach is to expand the coefficient matrix H in (1.76), which is an $(N + L - 1) \times L$ matrix, to a square circulant matrix.

As an example, let $L = 2$ and $N = 3$. For this,

$$H = \begin{bmatrix} h_0 & 0 \\ h_1 & h_0 \\ h_2 & h_1 \\ 0 & h_2 \end{bmatrix}, \quad \mathbf{y} = \begin{bmatrix} y_0 \\ y_1 \\ y_2 \\ y_3 \end{bmatrix}, \quad \mathbf{x} = \begin{bmatrix} x_0 \\ x_1 \end{bmatrix}, \quad \mathbf{y} = H\mathbf{x} \tag{1.113}$$

The circulant matrix corresponding to H is given by

$$H_c = \begin{bmatrix} h_0 & 0 & h_2 & h_1 \\ h_1 & h_0 & 0 & h_2 \\ h_2 & h_1 & h_0 & 0 \\ 0 & h_2 & h_1 & h_0 \end{bmatrix} \tag{1.114}$$

and

$$\begin{bmatrix} y_0 \\ y_1 \\ y_2 \\ y_3 \end{bmatrix} = H_c \begin{bmatrix} x_0 \\ x_1 \\ 0 \\ 0 \end{bmatrix} = H_c \mathbf{x}_a \tag{1.115}$$

Note that (1.115) reduces to (1.113), where $\mathbf{x}_a$ in (1.115) is a padded vector obtained from $\mathbf{x}$. Since H_c can be decomposed using DFT matrices (see (1.111)), we can write

$$\mathbf{y} = \frac{1}{N} A^*_{\mathrm{DFT}} \Lambda A_{\mathrm{DFT}} \mathbf{x}_a \tag{1.116}$$

Now,

$$(A_{\mathrm{DFT}} \mathbf{y}) = \Lambda (A_{\mathrm{DFT}} \mathbf{x}_a) \tag{1.117}$$

where (Λ) and $(A_{\mathrm{DFT}} \mathbf{x}_a)$ correspond to filter and data DFT coefficients. Taking IDFT (inverse DFT of $(\Lambda A_{\mathrm{DFT}} \mathbf{x}_a)$) will give $\mathbf{y}$, the result of convolution.

In summary, to compute the convolution, $h(n) * x(n)$, where $x(n)$, $0 \leq n \leq L - 1$, corresponds to the data, and $h(n)$, $0 \leq n \leq N - 1$ corresponds to a filter, we go through the following steps.

1. Pad, i.e., add $(N - 1)$ zeros to the data:

$$\mathbf{x}_a = (x_0, x_1, \ldots, x_{L-1}, 0 \ldots 0)^T$$

2. Pad $(L - 1)$ zeros to the h vector to form

$$\mathbf{h}_a = (h_0, h_1, \ldots, h_{N-1}, 0 \ldots 0)^T$$

3. Find the discrete Fourier transforms of the two vectors to obtain $\mathbf{X}_a$ and $\mathbf{H}_a$; multiply the coefficients:

$$\mathbf{Y}_a(k) = H_a(k)\mathbf{X}_a(k)$$

4. Take the inverse discrete Fourier transform of $\mathbf{Y}_a(k)$ resulting in the data corresponding to the convolution. The data corresponding to the convolution can be extracted from the final step.

Since the fast Fourier transform (FFT) is one of the most efficient algorithms and is optimal when the number of points is a power of 2, more zeros can be added to $\mathbf{x}_a$ and $\mathbf{h}_a$ so that the number of entries in $\mathbf{x}_a$ and $\mathbf{h}_a$ is a power of 2 and FFT algorithms can be used.

Discrete Correlation

The discrete correlation of the two signals x_n, $0 \le n \le L - 1$, h_n, $0 \le n \le N - 1$ is defined by

$$y_n = \sum_{m=0}^{N-1} h_m x_{n+m} \tag{1.118}$$

The corresponding matrix representation is given by

$$\begin{bmatrix} y_{-(N-1)} \\ y_{-(N-2)} \\ \cdot \\ \cdot \\ y_0 \\ y_1 \\ \cdot \\ \cdot \\ \cdot \\ y_{(L-1)} \end{bmatrix} = \begin{bmatrix} h_{N-1} & 0 & \cdots & 0 \\ h_{N-2} & h_{N-1} & \cdots & 0 \\ \cdot & \cdot & \cdots & ; \\ \cdot & \cdot & \cdots & ; \\ \cdot & \cdot & \cdots & h_{N-1} \\ \cdot & \cdot & \cdots & h_{N-2} \\ h_0 & h_1 & \cdots & \cdot \\ 0 & h_0 & \cdots & \cdot \\ \cdot & \cdot & \cdots & \cdot \\ 0 & 0 & \cdots & h_0 \end{bmatrix} \begin{bmatrix} x_0 \\ x_1 \\ \cdot \\ \cdot \\ \cdot \\ x_{L-1} \end{bmatrix} = H\mathbf{x} \tag{1.119}$$

Note the structure of the coefficient matrix has the same general form as in the case of the convolution, except that the entries are reversed. That is, the first column in the matrix H starts with h_{N-1} (rather than h_0), then $h_{N-2}, \ldots, h_0$, and then a set of zeros. Since the coefficient matrix has the same general form as the convolution matrix (see (1.76b)), we can construct a circulant matrix and use DFT as before.

Deconvolution

In an earlier section, convolution of two signals was discussed, where one signal could be considered as the impulse response of a system and the other as the input. In the continuous case, the response can be represented by the convolution integral

$$y(t) = \int_{-\infty}^{\infty} h(u)x(t-u)\,\mathrm{d}u \tag{1.120a}$$

where $h(t)$ is the impulse response of the system and $x(t)$ is the input and the transform

$$Y(f) = H(f)X(f) \tag{1.120b}$$

An example is the signal measured by a nonideal instrument where $x(t)$ is the desired signal and $y(t)$ is what we have obtained. If $H(f) = 1$, then $x(t) = y(t)$. Obviously, we do not have infinite band width instruments. In addition, the measured signal is not always perfect. That is, the received signal is generally corrupted by noise, usually additive. In other words, the received signal is

$$r(t) = y(t) + n(t) \leftrightarrow R(f) = Y(f) + N(f) \tag{1.121}$$

where $n(t)$ is the additive noise term. Other noises such as multiplicative and convolutive noises are possible. However, additive noise is the most common one. This type of noise can be handled easier than the others. In the absence of noise of course, you could solve the problem by first computing $X(f) = Y(f)/H(f)$, and taking the inverse transform. This implies $H(f)$ is not zero for all values of f, which is obviously not always true. What we would like to do is apply the so-called optimal filter, say, $\Phi(f)$, such that the deconvolved signal, say $\hat{x}(t)$, is as close as possible to the original signal $x(t)$. The phrase *as close as possible* needs to be clarified further. One avenue is to minimize the error in the least squares sense. That is, we would like to minimize

$$E = \int_{-\infty}^{\infty} |x(t) - \hat{x}(t)|^2\,\mathrm{d}t \tag{1.122a}$$

Using the Rayleigh's energy theorem, we have

$$\int_{-\infty}^{\infty} |x(t) - \hat{x}(t)|^2\,\mathrm{d}t = \int_{-\infty}^{\infty} |X(f) - \hat{X}(f)|^2\,\mathrm{d}f \tag{1.122b}$$

where $X(f) = F[x(t)]$ and $\hat{X}(f) = F[\hat{x}(t)]$. Let

$$\hat{X}(f) = \left[\frac{[Y(f) + N(f)]}{R(f)}\Phi(f)\right]$$

Using this, we have

$$E = \int_{-\infty}^{\infty} \frac{1}{|R(f)|^2} [|Y(f)|^2|1 - \Phi(f)|^2 + |N(f)|^2|\Phi(f)|^2] \, df$$

where we assumed that the signal $y(t)$ and the noise are uncorrelated; therefore the integral of their product integrated over the entire frequency resulted in a zero term. Taking the derivative with respect to $\Phi(f)$ and equating to zero results in

$$\Phi(f) = \frac{|Y(f)|^2}{|Y(f)|^2 + |N(f)|^2} \tag{1.123}$$

which is the classical Wiener filter (function) [3]. But, the signal $y(t)$ and the noise $n(t)$ are not available separately. Generally, the signal is bandlimited with a hump, whereas the noise is broadband. The noise spectrum can be extrapolated from the tail(s) (outside the hump of the signal spectrum). The signal frequency band is assumed to be generally known. The sum of the squares of the spectra $|Y(f)|^2 + |N(f)|^2$ is approximately equal to $|R(f)|^2$, the measured spectra. Even the crude extrapolations give generally good results. Various other spectral estimation methods might be useful in specific applications [5]. The preceding analysis can obviously be extended to the digital domain.

In the digital domain, time domain deconvolution is a popular method. This can be stated in terms of matrices. Given the system of equations,

$$\mathbf{y} = H\mathbf{x} \tag{1.124}$$

where H is the convolution matrix discussed earlier. The received vector $\mathbf{r}$ is the output vector $\mathbf{y}$ corrupted by additive noise. That is,

$$\mathbf{r} = \mathbf{y} + \mathbf{n} = H\mathbf{x} + \mathbf{n} \tag{1.125}$$

where $\mathbf{n}$ is the noise vector.

Let r_i and y_i be the ith entries of the $(N + L - 1) = M$ dimensional vectors $\mathbf{r}$ and $\mathbf{y}$, respectively. Also, let E be the error defined by

$$E = \sum_{i=0}^{M-1} |r_i - y_i|^p = \|\mathbf{r} - H\mathbf{x}\|_p \tag{1.126}$$

where $1 \leq p \leq \infty$ is of interest. For $0 < p < 1$, we do not have a proper linear normed space, and therefore it is not of much interest. For $1 \leq p \leq \infty$, the Lp norm estimate $\mathbf{x}$ is obtained by minimizing

$$\sum_{i=0}^{M-1} |r_i - (H\mathbf{x})_i|^p, \qquad 1 \leq p < \infty \tag{1.127a}$$

$$\max_i |r_i - (H\mathbf{x})_i| \qquad \text{for } p = \infty \tag{1.127b}$$

The three values of p that are of most interest are $p = 1$, the least absolute value deviation; $p = 2$, the least squares deviation; and $p = \infty$, the Tchebysheff (or minimax) approach. The L_p, $p = 1, 2$, and ∞ estimators are maximum likelihood estimators that are asymptotically unbiased and considered the best estimators when the errors are from Laplacian, Gaussian, and uniform distributions, respectively.

For $1 < p < 2$, the errors are assumed to come from a mixture of Gaussian and Laplacian or some p-normed distribution [27]. The L_p solutions that are of interest to us are for $1 \leq p \leq 2$, and these can be obtained by iterative algorithms [8]. The iteratively reweighted least squares algorithm for solving (1.124) is

$$\mathbf{x} = (H^T W(k) H)^{-1} H^T W(k) \mathbf{r} \tag{1.128a}$$

where $W(k)$ is a diagonal matrix with its diagonal entries defined by

$$W_{ii}(k) = \begin{cases} |\mathbf{r} - H\mathbf{x}|_i^{p-2}, & (\mathbf{r} - H\mathbf{x})_i > \varepsilon \\ \varepsilon^{p-2}, & (\mathbf{r} - H\mathbf{x})_i \leq \varepsilon \end{cases} \tag{1.128b}$$

where ε is some small positive number. When $p = 2$, the solution is

$$\mathbf{x} = (H^T H)^{-1} H^T \mathbf{r} \tag{1.129}$$

which is the L_2 solution and $(H^T H)^{-1} H^T$ is sometimes referred to as the *pseudo inverse* of H. For some of the computational problems associated with L_p solutions, see [10]. L_1 solutions are particularly useful when there are isolated errors and the L_1 solutions are not always unique. It is interesting to point out that the system of equations in (1.124) is overdetermined. The solution in (1.129) implies that $(H^T H)$ is nonsingular. If this is not so, then a method usually referred to as *diagonal loading* is used, where $(H^T H)$ is replaced by $(H^T H + \sigma I)$ and σ is a small positive number and I is an identity matrix. A result similar to the one in (1.129) for the underdetermined case, i.e., when there are more unknowns than equations, can be obtained by using the least squares solution. If $\mathbf{y} = B\mathbf{x}$, where the dimension of $\mathbf{x}$ is larger than $\mathbf{y}$, then the least squares solution is given by $\mathbf{x} = B^T (BB^T)^{-1} \mathbf{y}$, where again note the inverse.

The selection of p in (1.126) for a particular problem is not always easy except in ideal situations, as pointed out earlier. A rule of thumb for selecting p is used by Money [9], based upon the kurtosis (k). *Kurtosis* is defined as the fourth moment normalized by the square of the variance. The value of p given by

$$p = \left(\frac{9}{k^2} + 1 \right), \qquad 1 \leq p \leq \infty \tag{1.130}$$

is useful. The three popular values for p [9] follow:

$$\begin{aligned} k > 3.8 \quad &\text{use} \quad L_1 \\ 2.2 < k < 3.8 \quad &\text{use} \quad L_2 \\ k < 2.2 \quad &\text{use} \quad L_\infty \end{aligned} \tag{1.131}$$

For the three distributions mentioned earlier, the kurtosis k can be computed and these are $k = 1.8$ (Uniform), 3 (Gaussian), and 6 (Laplacian).

Power Spectral Density

Earlier we have studied the autocorrelation function. The *power spectral density*, PSD (or simply spectral density), of a function $x(t)$ is defined as the Fourier transform of the autocorrelation of $x(t)$. In the digital domain, of course, the PSD is defined as the discrete Fourier transform of the autocorrelation sequence. Different terminology is used to define power and one of these is

$$p = \sum_{n=0}^{N-1} |x(nT)|^2 \tag{1.132}$$

which is the total power in the signal, whereas

$$\int_0^T |x(t)|^2 \, \mathrm{d}t \cong T \sum_{n=0}^{N-1} |x(nT)|^2 \tag{1.133}$$

is the time-integral squared amplitude.

There are various methods used to estimate the PSD. The direct method, which is sometimes referred to as the *periodogram approach*, is to find the PSD estimate directly from the data. The indirect method first estimates the autocorrelation and then takes the Fourier transform to compute the PSD [14, 15].

For a given function $x(t)$, let $x_k = x(kT)$ be the samples of the function $x(t)$. Let the discrete Fourier transform coefficients be given by

$$X_n = \sum_{k=0}^{N-1} x_k \, \mathrm{e}^{-\mathrm{j}(2\pi/N)nk}, \qquad n = 0, 1, \ldots, N-1 \tag{1.134}$$

then the periodogram estimate of the power spectrum is defined at $(N/2 + 1)$ frequencies [14]

$$f_n = \frac{n}{NT}, \qquad n = 0, 1, \ldots, \frac{N}{2} \tag{1.135}$$

with

$$p(0) = p(f_0) = \frac{1}{N^2}|X_0|^2$$

$$p(f_n) = \frac{1}{N^2}[|X_n|^2 + |X_{N-n}|^2], \qquad n = 1, 2, \ldots, N/2 - 1 \quad (1.136)$$

$$p(f_{N/2}) = \frac{1}{N^2}|X_{N/2}|^2$$

where f_n is defined only for positive frequencies. Some texts omit the scale factors.

These power spectral density values are only estimates. The question is, How good are these estimates? We can ask some educated questions. That is, how good are these estimates on the average? First, there is leakage. Recall from the window analysis discussed earlier, a rectangular window has a spectrum that is a sinc function. Also, a windowed sinusoid at a frequency $f = f_0$ results in a spectrum corresponding to two sinc functions located at $f = \pm f_0$. The sinc function has a main lobe and sidelobes. The spectrum of a sinusoid has to have two delta functions. See, for example, (1.51c). Therefore, there is a leakage into the sidelobes. Some of the window functions reduce the effect of the sidelobes at the expense of reducing the spectral resolution. Most signals we consider have more than one frequency. Except for some test signals, most signals have a continuous spectrum indicating the difficulty associated with leakage. In beam-forming type applications, one looks at the problem of identifying frequency locations. Obviously frequency separation is an interesting test case the algorithms use. For example, if a signal, containing two frequencies that are close is transmitted, then, from the received signal corrupted by noise, can we still separate the two frequencies? The tendency of course is that the two main lobes will become one main lobe. Different algorithms, such as L_p and others, have been used for such applications [10]. The resolution by some of the classical methods, as a rule of thumb, is the reciprocal of the data duration. Another problem to consider is the aliasing problem due to sampling.

The estimate of the frequency locations is critical in communication theory problems. Statistically, the expected value of the frequency locations is a function of many things, mainly the frequency locations and how far apart they are, the window function, and the type of estimator used under different noise conditions. The second measure is the variance of the periodogram estimates. As the number of data points increase, that is, using a longer time width or by using a faster sampling rate, the periodogram estimates do not become more accurate unfortunately. The variance of the periodogram estimate at a frequency, say $f = f_n$ is equal to the square of the expected value at that frequency. Various techniques are available to reduce the variance of the estimates, see [5]

Parametric Model Approaches to Spectral Estimation

In conventional signal analysis, approximation methods in filtering are very common. Some of these will be discussed later. Polynomial curve fitting is another approach in modeling signals. The basic idea in parametric model approaches is to represent the signal $x(n)$ by its past p-samples, and if an input is present, then the signal is written in terms of the linear difference equation:

$$x(n) = -\sum_{k=1}^{p} a_k x(n-k) + \sum_{k=0}^{q} b_k r(n-k) \tag{1.137}$$

where $x(n)$ is the output sequence and $r(n)$ is the input sequence. The equation in (1.137) can also be written as

$$x(n) = \sum_{k=0}^{\infty} h(k) r(n-k) \tag{1.138}$$

Note the upper limit on the summation. Define the z-transform functions (see [5])

$$\begin{aligned} X(z) &= \sum_{n=-\infty}^{\infty} x(n) z^{-n} \\ H(z) &= \sum_{n=0}^{\infty} h(n) z^{-n} \\ R(z) &= \sum_{n=-\infty}^{\infty} r(n) z^{-n} \end{aligned} \tag{1.139}$$

We assumed $h(n) = 0$ for $n < 0$, i.e., a causal filter in (1.139). The Fourier transforms of $x(n)$, $h(n)$, and $r(n)$ are defined by

$$\begin{aligned} X(e^{j\omega T}) &= \sum_{n=-\infty}^{\infty} x(n)\, e^{-j\omega nT}, \qquad H(e^{j\omega T}) = \sum_{n=0}^{\infty} h(n)\, e^{-j\omega nT} \\ R(e^{j\omega T}) &= \sum_{n=-\infty}^{\infty} r(n)\, e^{-j\omega nT}, \qquad \omega = 2\pi f \end{aligned} \tag{1.140a}$$

Clearly, these can be obtained from (1.139) by using $z = e^{j\omega T}$. The factor T is generally omitted or incorporated with ω and written as

$$X(e^{j\Omega}) = \sum_{n=-\infty}^{\infty} x(n)\, e^{-jn\Omega}, \qquad H(e^{j\Omega}) = \sum_{n=0}^{\infty} h(n)\, e^{-jn\Omega} \tag{1.140b}$$

and

$$R(e^{j\Omega}) = \sum_{n=-\infty}^{\infty} r(n)\, e^{-jn\Omega}$$

where

$$\Omega = \omega T \tag{1.140c}$$

Clearly, the Fourier transform functions in the Ω domain are periodic with period 2π, and in the ω domain, they are periodic with period $(2\pi/T)$.

The functions in (1.139) are related by

$$H(z) = \frac{X(z)}{R(z)} = \frac{1 + \sum_{k=1}^{q} b_k z^{-k}}{1 + \sum_{k=1}^{p} a_k z^{-k}} = \frac{N(z)}{D(z)} \tag{1.141a}$$

and

$$H(z) = 1 + \sum_{k=0}^{\infty} h_k z^{-k} \tag{1.141b}$$

In the preceding, we assumed $b_0 = 1$, $h_0 = 1$, and $h_k \equiv h(k)$ for simplicity. If b_0 and h_0 are not equal to 1, then a constant needs to be introduced, usually in the form of a gain constant.

The polynomials $N(z) = 1 + \sum_{k=1}^{q} b_k z^{-k}$ and $D(z) = 1 + \sum_{k=1}^{p} a_k z^{-k}$ are assumed to have the zeros all inside the unit circle to guarantee that $H(z)$ is a stable function and a minimum phase function. These functions are useful in designing filters. Special cases of the general model just given are useful [5, 15]. These are (1) the autoregressive moving average filter (ARMA) of order (p, q); (2) moving average filter (MA) of order q; and (3) the autoregressive filter (AR). These are explicitly written.

$$\text{ARMA:} \quad H_{\text{ARMA}}(z) = \frac{1 + \sum_{k=1}^{q} b_k z^{-k}}{1 + \sum_{k=1}^{p} a_k z^{-k}} = \frac{N(z)}{D(z)} \tag{1.142a}$$

$$\text{MA:} \quad H_{\text{MA}}(z) = 1 + \sum_{k=1}^{q} b_k z^{-k} = A(z) \tag{1.142b}$$

$$\text{AR:} \quad H_{\text{AR}}(z) = \frac{1}{1 + \sum_{k=1}^{p} c_k z^{-k}} = \frac{1}{C(z)} \tag{1.142c}$$

The identification of AR, MA, and ARMA models by different polynomials are given so that they can be related at a later time.

The filter response is given by substituting $z = e^{j\omega T}$, $\omega = 2\pi f$, and is for the ARMA model

$$H(e^{j\omega T}) = \frac{1 + \sum_{k=1}^{q} b_k\, e^{-j2\pi f k T}}{1 + \sum_{k=1}^{p} a_k\, e^{-j2\pi f k T}} \tag{1.143a}$$

where the subscript ARMA is omitted for simplicity. In many texts, this expression is identified sometimes as $H(e^{j\omega})$, or $H(e^{j2\pi f})$, or $H(e^{j\Omega})$, or simply $H(f)$. We will use here $H(e^{j\omega})$. $H(e^{j\omega})$ is a continuous function of the frequency f. The filter designs are based upon selecting the parameters for the situation at hand, and the details are discussed at a later time.

Before discussing the concepts associated with relating the various models, two comments are appropriate. First, considering the moving average filter, we have

$$H_{MA}(e^{j\omega}) = 1 + \sum_{k=1}^{q} b_k e^{-j\omega kT} \tag{1.143b}$$

which can be related to the classical Fourier series. Second, the ARMA filters are designed by some transformations using a mapping between the unit circle of the z-plane and the imaginary axis of the s-plane. More on this later. The autoregressive approach and the moving average approaches are obviously special cases of ARMA approaches. However, each is considered separately and the techniques use the special forms.

The autoregressive (AR) model is widely used in the spectral estimation. Consider the special case in (1.137)

$$x(n) = -\sum_{k=1}^{p} a_k x(n-k) + r(n). \tag{1.144}$$

We can interpret this in two different ways. First, a direct interpretation is the response of a discrete data system with $r(n)$ being the input. The second interpretation is predicting the next sample from the last p samples. The difference between $x(n)$, the present sample, and the linear combination of the past samples, $(-\sum_{k=1}^{p} a_k x(n-k))$, is the error. That is, $r(n)$ can be considered an error sequence. The principle of course is to select a_k such that the error is minimum, i.e., $\sum_n x^2(n) \gg \sum_n r^2(n)$. In many texts, instead of the minus sign in $-\sum_{k=1}^{p} a_k x(n-k)$, a plus sign is used. The coefficients $(-a_k)$ (or simply a_k) are called *predictive coefficients*. Linear prediction is a very popular area in speech, seismic, and other signal processing areas. In these cases the signals are generally smooth and oscillatory. Recall the discussion earlier on voiced and unvoiced speech signals. Linear prediction extrapolates with reasonable accuracy through many cycles of the signal. Clearly, the accuracy generally depends upon the order of the prediction p, and it depends on the number of poles required to approximate a signal. The polynomial extrapolation is another method signal analysts use at times. Unfortunately, polynomial extrapolation becomes inaccurate after a cycle or so.

All three models—AR, MA, and ARMA—are used in different applications. However, all are related, at least in the limit [15]. The MA model originated from the Fourier series and ARMA approaches from transfer function analysis. Although the AR model is a special case of the ARMA model, it is sometimes used as a first step for the other two models [15].

The AR model discussed earlier is given in (1.142c), written in the general term

$$H_{\mathrm{AR}}(z) = \left[1\bigg/\left(1 + \sum_{k=1}^{p} c_k z^{-k}\right)\right] = [1/C(z)] \tag{1.145}$$

With $p \to \infty$ the relation to the ARMA model can be derived

$$\begin{gathered}\frac{N(z)}{D(z)} = \frac{1}{C(z)} \quad \text{or} \quad C(z)N(z) = D(z) \\ \left(1 + \sum_{k=1}^{\infty} c_k z^{-k}\right)\left(1 + \sum_{k=1}^{q} b_k z^{-k}\right) = \left(1 + \sum_{k=1}^{p} d_k z^{-k}\right)\end{gathered} \tag{1.146}$$

Consider an example with $p = q = 2$ in (1.146). With this, the preceeding can be expressed as

$$\begin{aligned}&(1 + c_1 z^{-1} + c_2 z^{-2} + c_3 z^{-3} + \cdots)(1 + b_1 z^{-1} + b_2 z^{-2}) \\ &\qquad = (1 + d_1 z^{-1} + d_2 z^{-2}) \\ &1 + (c_1 + b_1)z^{-1} + (b_2 + c_2 + b_1 c_1)z^{-2} + (c_3 + b_1 c_2 + b_2 c_1)z^{-3} + \cdots \\ &\qquad = 1 + d_1 z^{-1} + d_2 z^{-2}\end{aligned}$$

Equating the coefficients, we have

$$\begin{aligned}1 &= 1 \\ c_1 + b_1 &= d_1 \\ b_2 + c_2 + b_1 c_1 &= d_2 \\ c_3 + b_1 c_2 + b_2 c_1 &= 0, \ldots\end{aligned}$$

Solving for c_k and ($c_0 = 1$) by definition, we have

$$\begin{aligned}c_0 &= 1 \\ c_1 &= d_1 - b_1 c_0 \\ c_2 &= d_2 - b_2 c_0 - b_1 c_1 \\ c_3 &= -(b_1 c_2 + b_2 c_1), \ldots\end{aligned}$$

We can generalize this and write

$$c_n = \begin{cases} 0, & n < 0 \\ 1, & n = 0 \\ d_n - \sum_{k=1}^{q} b_k c_{n-k}, & 1 \le n \le p \\ -\sum_{k=1}^{q} b_k c_{n-k}, & n > p \end{cases} \tag{1.147a}$$

Note the initial conditions, $c_{-1}, c_{-2}, \ldots, c_{-q} = 0$. Recall that ARMA($p$, q) model indicates that the highest power coefficient in the numerator is p, and in the denominator, it is q.

On the other hand, we can relate an AR(∞) model to an ARMA (p, q) model. How could that be? Note the AR model is assumed to have an infinite number of terms. We can solve the problem in two steps. First, solve for the MA part of the ARMA model. From the last step, we have

$$c_n = -\sum_{k=1}^{q} b_k c_{n-k}, \qquad n > p \tag{1.147b}$$

That, is

$$\begin{bmatrix} c_{p+1} \\ c_{p+2} \\ \vdots \\ c_{p+q} \end{bmatrix} = -\begin{bmatrix} c_p & c_{p-1} & \cdots & c_{p-q+1} \\ c_{p+1} & c_p & \cdots & c_{p-q+2} \\ \vdots & & & \\ c_{p+q-1} & c_{p+q-2} & \cdots & c_p \end{bmatrix} \begin{bmatrix} b_1 \\ b_2 \\ \vdots \\ b_q \end{bmatrix} \tag{1.148}$$

where the coefficient matrix has the Toeplitz structure. Fast algorithms are available for solving such systems of equations [15]. The AR part of the ARMA model can be obtained from the relation (see (1.146))

$$D(z) = N(z) \cdot C(z)$$

and the time functions can be derived from the discrete convolution. Namely,

$$d_n = c_n * b_n \quad \text{or} \quad d_n = c_n + \sum_{k=1}^{q} b_k c_{n-k} \tag{1.149}$$

for $1 \le n \le p$. The values of h_k in (1.141b) can be related to those of a_k and b_k in (1.141a) (see [15]).

Windowing

Measurement of a signal can obviously be limited to a finite time. That is, we will be looking at a signal through a window. The simplest of all windows is the Fourier or rectangular or the box car window and is defined by

$$w_F(t) = \begin{cases} 1, & |t| \le \dfrac{T}{2} \\ 0, & |t| > \dfrac{T}{2} \end{cases} \tag{1.150}$$

If $x(t)$ is the signal under consideration, then $(x(t)w_F(t))$ is the windowed signal. That is, the windowed signal is the same as $x(t)$ for $|t| \le T/2$ and 0 elsewhere. For example, if $x(t)$ is a sinusoid, say, $x(t) = \cos 2\pi f_1 t$, then the windowed signal $x_w(t) = (x(t)w_F(t))$ is given by

$$w_w(t) = \begin{cases} \cos 2\pi f_1 t, & |t| \le \dfrac{T}{2} \\ 0, & |t| > \dfrac{T}{2} \end{cases} \tag{1.151a}$$

Its Fourier transform is given by

$$X_w(f) = \frac{T_0}{2} \frac{\sin(T/2)2\pi(f - f_1)}{2\pi(f - f_1)(T/2)} + \frac{T_0}{2} \frac{\sin(T/2)2\pi(f + f_1)}{2\pi(f + f_1)(T/2)} \tag{1.151b}$$

which is a sum of two sinc functions. Recall that Fourier transform of a cosine function is a sum of two delta functions. See (1.51c). Interestingly, it can be seen that as $T \to \infty$, the two sinc functions become two delta functions. That is, the larger the window is, the more sharp is the spectrum. The bandwidth for arbitrary signals is sometimes arbitrarily defined. See the discussion earlier on time–frequency widths and (1.57). For example, the frequency width is infinity for a rectangular window. Recall that a signal cannot be both time limited and frequency limited. So, as a rule of thumb, take the bandwidth of the window functions as a multiple of the first zero crossing of the window spectrum. In the case of a rectangular window with a window of T secs, $w_F(t) = \Pi(t/T)$, where the $\Pi(\cdot)$ function was defined in (1.2) (At $|t| = T/2$, it is assumed as 1), the magnitude of the transform is given by (see (1.51b))

$$|W_F(f)| = \left| \frac{\sin(2\pi f(T/2))}{(2\pi f(T/2)} \right| \tag{1.152}$$

indicating that the first zero crossing is at $f = 1/T$. For this case, the time-bandwidth product is $\Delta t \cdot \Delta f = 1$, as pointed out before. A word of caution, some books use the entire main lobe width (i.e., both positive and negative frequencies, rather than only positive frequencies, introducing a factor of 2 difference) in their frequency width.

The rectangular window is the simplest of all. However, it has problems. Various measures are used to evaluate windows. These include the main lobe width, the time–bandwidth product, and heights of the sidelobes compared to the height of the main lobe. The object is to make the main lobe as narrow as possible and the sidelobes fall off as fast as possible. For the rectangular window, the spectrum falls off rather slowly. So, for comparison purposes, the first sidelobe height is compared with the main lobe height. Let $W_F(f_1)$ be the maximum corresponding to the sidelobes, then for the rectangular window

$$20 \log \left| \frac{W_F(f_1)}{W_F(0)} \right| \cong -13.4 \text{ dB}$$

In digital signal processing, the window weights can be defined:

$$w(n), \qquad n = 0, 1, \ldots, N-1 \tag{1.153a}$$

For a rectangular window, $w_n = 1$, for $n = 0, 1, \ldots, N-1$. The corresponding transform is given by ($\Omega = \omega T$ is used in the following; see (1.140c))

$$W(\mathrm{e}^{\mathrm{j}\Omega}) = \sum_{n=0}^{N-1} \mathrm{e}^{-\mathrm{j}\Omega k} = [(1 - \mathrm{e}^{-\mathrm{j}\Omega N})/(1 - \mathrm{e}^{-\mathrm{j}\Omega})] = \mathrm{e}^{-\mathrm{j}\Omega((N-1)/2)} \frac{\sin(N\Omega/2)}{\sin(\Omega/2)} \tag{1.153b}$$

and

$$|W(\mathrm{e}^{\mathrm{j}\Omega})| = |\sin(\Omega N/2)/\sin(\Omega/2)| \tag{1.153c}$$

Note the difference in the expression for the continuous case in (1.152) and the preceding, especially the denominator. The parameters can be given in either the continuous or digital domain. The results are very close. Another parameter of interest is how fast the amplitude is going down, sometimes identified by the asymptotic sidelobe decay rate. For the rectangular window, this is -6 dB/octave. Recall that sampling introduces aliasing. These need to take into consideration. The 3 dB bandwidth (sometimes referred to as *half-power bandwidth*), in the digital case, is usually given in terms of a normalized value with respect to a discrete frequency bin of $(1/(NT))$ Hz. It is (0.89) bins [15] for a rectangular window.

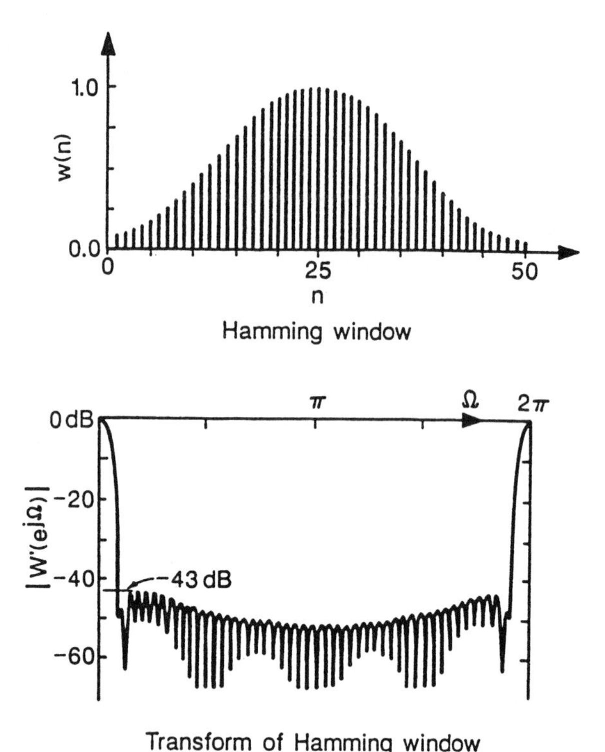

FIG. 1.10. Hamming window and its magnitude transform, where the transform is shown for one period:

$$|w'(e^{j\Omega})| = \left|\sum_{n=0}^{N-1} w(n)\, e^{-j\Omega n}\right|$$

Other windows are popular. These include Hamming, Kaiser, Gaussian, Dolph–Tchebychev and many others. A widely used window is the Hamming window, sometimes called a *raised cosine window*, given by

$$w(n) = 0.54 + 0.46 \cos\left[2\pi\left(n - \left(\frac{N-1}{2}\right)\right)\Big/ N - 1\right],$$

$$N \text{ is odd}, \qquad n = 0, 1, \ldots, N-1 \qquad (1.154)$$

where we assumed N to be odd. Clearly, a similar expression can be given for even cases. The magnitude spectrum for the Hamming window is shown in Figure 1.10, where one period in the Ω domain is shown. The highest sidelobe level is -43 dB with an asymptotic sidelobe decay rate of -6 dB/octave. The 3 dB bandwidth is approximately 1.3 bins.

The truncated Gaussian window function is for N-odd

$$w(n) = e^{-(1/2)(2\alpha f(n))^2} \qquad \text{with,} \quad f(n) = \frac{n - ((N-1)/2)}{(N-1)} \tag{1.155}$$

The highest sidelobe level is -42 dB with a sidelobe decay rate of -6 dB/octave with a 3 dB normalized band width of 1.33 bins. α in (1.55) in a parameter and a common value for α is 2.5. Recall that the Gaussian function is in principle the minimum uncertainty window. Note the equality in (1.56).

Another important window is the Kaiser window, which has the interesting property that the window and the transform are narrow in a certain sense [17]. The prolate spheroidal functions have this nice property. The weights are given by

$$w(n) = \begin{cases} \dfrac{I_0[\alpha\sqrt{1-(n/N)^2}]}{I_0(\alpha)}, & |n| \le N \\ 0, & |n| > N \end{cases} \tag{1.156a}$$

where I_0 is the zeroth-order Bessel function of the first kind and can be evaluated by

$$I_0(\alpha) = 1 + \sum_{n=1}^{\infty} \left(\frac{(\alpha/2)^n}{n!} \right)^2 \tag{1.156b}$$

Noting the factorials in the denominator, very few terms are needed to approximate this function. The transform of the Kaiser window has some very nice properties. The digital transform of the window is not available in closed form. For the continuous case, see [17]. The parameter α can be used to reduce the highest sidelobe level. For example for $\alpha \cong 4$, the sidelobe level is approximately -45 dB, whereas for $\alpha \cong 10$, the sidelobe level is approximately -100 dB. Reducing the sidelobe levels increases the window width.

The last window we will consider here is the Dolph–Tschebyscheff (or simply Tschebyscheff) window, which has the interesting property that all the peaks of the sidelobes are at a constant level. The window is first defined in the frequency domain by [15]

$$W(e^{j\omega T}) = \frac{\cos[(N-1)\cos^{-1}\{\alpha \cos(\pi f T)\}]}{\cos h[(N-1)\cosh^{-1}(\alpha)]} \tag{1.157}$$

where $\alpha = \cos h[\cosh^{-1}(10^{(\beta/20)})/(N-1)]$ and β is the ratio of main lobe to sidelobe level in dB. The time domain function is obtained by taking the inverse transform of this function.

Poissons Sum Formula

If $w(t)$ is any arbitrary function with $W(f)$ its Fourier transform, then the Poisson sum formula is given by [3]

$$\sum_{m=-\infty}^{\infty} w(t + mT) = \frac{1}{T} \sum_{m=-\infty}^{\infty} W\left(\frac{m}{T}\right) e^{j2\pi(m/T)t} \tag{1.158}$$

Its digital equivalent is given as follows. Let $w(n)$ be any sequence with its z-transform

$$W(z) = \sum_{n=-\infty}^{\infty} w(n)z^{-n}$$

then the digital Poisson formula is given by [5]

$$\sum_{m=-\infty}^{\infty} w(n + mR) = \frac{1}{R} \sum_{p=0}^{R-1} W(e^{j(2\pi/R)p})\, e^{j(2\pi/R)pn} \tag{1.159}$$

Interestingly, the digital formula is different in the sense that the righthand side of the equation has a finite number of terms, instead of infinite number of terms, and is over the z transforms of $w(n)$ evaluated on the unit circle at R equally spaced points.

Interestingly,

$$\left(\frac{R}{W(e^{j0})} \sum_{m=-\infty}^{\infty} w(n + mR)\right) \cong 1 \tag{1.160}$$

indicating that the sum adds up to approximately 1 and is exact if the window is band limited. For details, see [16]. The error, i.e., the difference between the two sides in (1.160), is given by

$$\begin{aligned} e_R(n) &= \frac{R}{W(e^{j0})} \sum_{m=-\infty}^{\infty} w(n + mR) - 1 \\ &= \sum_{p=1}^{R-1} \left[\frac{W(e^{j\omega'_p})}{W(e^{j0})}\right] e^{jn\omega'_p} \end{aligned} \tag{1.161}$$

with $\omega'_p = (2\pi p/R)$ indicating that the error can be computed from the samples of the window sequence. See [11] for various bounds for the error. In that paper, the rectangular, Tchebysheff, Hamming, and Kaiser windows were compared using the same time–bandwidth products. Based on this analysis, Kaiser window has the smallest rms error and is also flexible. It was recommended for short-time Fourier synthesis and system identification. Note that (1.160) is an interesting result in the sense that we can process one windowed signal separately from the other windowed ones.

Linear Prediction

Recall that we have represented the response of a system or a predicted signal from its past samples and the inputs (see (1.137)). With $x(n) = s_n$, $r_n = r(n)$, we have

$$s_n = -\sum_{k=1}^{p} a_k s_{n-k} + G \sum_{l=0}^{q} b_l r_{n-l} \tag{1.162}$$

with $b_0 = 1$, where a_k, b_l, and G are the parameters of the system. The gain G is explicitly identified here. Earlier it was taken as 1. Solving for $S(z) = Z[s_n]$, we have

$$S(z) = \frac{G \sum_{l=0}^{q} b_l z^{-l}}{1 + \sum_{k=1}^{p} a_k z^{-k}} R(z) \tag{1.163}$$

Many times G is taken inside and $G \cdot b_l$ is rewritten. Recall also that we talked explicitly about three cases; namely, ARMA, AR, and MA models. Consider the all-pole model

$$s_n = -\sum_{k=1}^{p} a_k s_{n-k} + G r_n \tag{1.164}$$

where r_n can be considered an input for an all-pole model system. In the case of linear prediction, we can assume $Gr(n) = e(n)$ and it represents the error between the signal s_n and its predicted value.

Assuming that the signal is deterministic for the following analysis, the total squared error is

$$E = \sum_n e_n^2 = \sum_n \left(s_n + \sum_{k=1}^{p} a_k s_{n-k} \right)^2$$

which can be minimized by setting

$$\frac{\partial E}{\partial a_k} = 0, \qquad 1 \le k \le p$$

This gives

$$\sum_{k=1}^{p} a_k \sum_n s_{n-k} s_{n-i} = -\sum_n s_n s_{n-i}, \qquad 1 \le i \le p \tag{1.165}$$

Defining

$$R_i = \sum_{n=-\infty}^{\infty} s_n s_{n+i} \tag{1.166}$$

as the autocorrelation coefficients of the signal, with lag i, we can write (1.165) in the form

$$\sum_{k=1}^{p} a_k R_{i-k} = -R_i, \qquad 1 \le i \le p \tag{1.167a}$$

Note that $R_{-i} = R_i$ and $R_{i-k} = R_{|i-k|}$. Explicitly, (1.167a) can be written in the form

$$\begin{bmatrix} R_0 & R_1 & \dots & R_{p-1} \\ R_1 & R_0 & \dots & R_{p-2} \\ \vdots & & & \\ R_{p-1} & R_{p-2} & \dots & R_0 \end{bmatrix} \begin{bmatrix} a_1 \\ a_2 \\ \vdots \\ a_p \end{bmatrix} = - \begin{bmatrix} R_1 \\ R_2 \\ \vdots \\ R_p \end{bmatrix} \tag{1.167b}$$

where the coefficient matrix $\Phi = (\phi_{ij})$ with $\phi_{ij} = R_{|i-j|}$. Clearly, the coefficient matrix is a symmetric Toeplitz matrix. In practice, the signal s_n is known only over a finite interval. Without loosing any generality, we can therefore consider a windowed signal defined by

$$s'_n = \begin{cases} s_n w_n, & 0 \le n \le N-1 \\ 0, & \text{otherwise} \end{cases}$$

where w_n represents the samples of a window function of length N. Earlier, we introduced a speech example and pointed out the change in the spectral character of the signal. Speech is considered as a nonstationary signal. It is considered stationary on a short-time basis. Such a signal can be windowed, and the spectral aspects of the windowed signal can be computed on a short-time basis. The autocorrelation coefficients are given by

$$R_i = \sum_{n=0}^{N-1-i} s'_n s'_{n+i} \tag{1.168}$$

Note the tapering. That is, for $i = 0$ all the entries s'_n are included in computing R_0, where as fewer and fewer values of s'_i are used in computing R_i, $i \neq 0$. The set of equations in (1.167a) is usually referred to as a set of normal equations, and they are used in prediction. Clearly, knowing the values of a_k in (1.164) will allow computing the future values from the past values. Another application where the normal equations are used is in deconvolution.

Recall that the discrete convolution, in the presence of noise, can be expressed in the form $\mathbf{r} = H\mathbf{x} + \mathbf{n}$, where $\mathbf{r}$ is the received vector, H has a special form (see (1.125)), and $\mathbf{n}$ is the noise vector. It was pointed out that the L_2 solution of this overdetermined system of equations is given by $\mathbf{x} = (H^T H)^{-1} H^T \mathbf{r}$. This can be derived by using the matrix concepts. Noting that and premultiplying $\mathbf{r}$ by H^T, we have

$$H^T \mathbf{r} = (H^T H)\mathbf{x} + (H^T \mathbf{n}) \cong (H^T H)\mathbf{x} \tag{1.169}$$

Assuming the inverse of (H^TH) exists, we can solve for $\mathbf{x}$, and the L_2 solution is given by

$$\mathbf{x} = (H^TH)^{-1}H^T\mathbf{r} \tag{1.170a}$$

which is what we had before. Keep in mind that $\mathbf{x}$ in (1.170a) may not satisfy $\mathbf{r} = H\mathbf{x}$ exactly, as $\mathbf{r}$ includes the noise vector. It is an L_2 estimate.

The matrix (H^TH) is a symmetric Toeplitz matrix, and the entries are given by

$$(H^TH)_{ki} = \sum_{j=0}^{N-1-|k-i|} h_j h_{j+|k-i|} \tag{1.170b}$$

Clearly, they have the same general form as the entries in (1.168). Similarly, $H^T\mathbf{r}$ can be expressed as

$$\mathbf{d} = H^T\mathbf{r} \tag{1.170c}$$

where

$$d_i = \sum_{j=0}^{N-1} h_j r_{j+i}, \qquad 0 \le i \le N + L - 2 \tag{1.170d}$$

The system of equations in (1.169) are very useful in signal processing, which we can see from the correlation and the deconvolution points of view. Clearly, the system of equations in (1.169), $H^T\mathbf{r} = (H^TH)\mathbf{x}$, is a set of normal equations.

Solutions of Normal Equations

In this section we will be interested in obtaining solutions for normal equations. To consider both the correlation and deconvolution cases, we will write the normal equations in the general form as follows for simplicity.

$$\begin{bmatrix} R_0 & R_1 & \cdots & R_{p-1} \\ R_1 & R_0 & \cdots & R_{p-2} \\ \vdots & & & \\ R_{p-1} & R_{p-2} & \cdots & R_0 \end{bmatrix} \begin{bmatrix} \hat{a}_1 \\ \hat{a}_2 \\ \vdots \\ \hat{a}_p \end{bmatrix} = \begin{bmatrix} d_1 \\ d_2 \\ \vdots \\ d_p \end{bmatrix} \tag{1.171}$$

The unknowns are assumed to be values of $\hat{a}_i$ without losing any generality.

Note the difference in the righthand side of the equations in (1.167b) and (1.171). They are different. The unknowns are a_i in the first case and $\hat{a}_i$ in the second case. Fast algorithms use the solution of (1.167b) to obtain the solution in (1.171) [19, 29]. Four basic methods deal with these systems:

1. Durbin's method
2. Levinson's method
3. Trench's method
4. Iterative methods.

We will discuss the first two methods and an iterative technique. Before we do this, let us consider some important properties of Toeplitz matrices.

First, a matrix E with ones along the cross diagonal and zeros everywhere else, called an *exchange matrix*, is

$$E = \begin{bmatrix} & & & & 1 \\ & & & \cdot^{\cdot^{\cdot}} & \\ & & 1 & & \\ & 1 & & & \\ 1 & & & & \end{bmatrix}$$

A real matrix A is said to be *persymmetric* if

$$EA^TE = A \tag{1.172}$$

where A^T corresponds to the transpose of A.

A symmetric Toeplitz is persymmetric. For future discussion, we define a kth-order Toeplitz matrix as

$$A_T(k) = \begin{bmatrix} R_0 & R_1 & \cdots & R_{k-1} \\ R_1 & R_0 & \cdots & R_{k-2} \\ \vdots & \vdots & & \\ R_{k-1} & R_{k-2} & \cdots & R_0 \end{bmatrix} \tag{1.173a}$$

where the subscript T is used to denote a Toeplitz matrix. Also, let

$$\mathbf{t}(k) = -\begin{bmatrix} R_1 \\ R_2 \\ \vdots \\ R_k \end{bmatrix} \tag{1.173b}$$

With these, it follows that

$$A_T(k+1) = \begin{bmatrix} A_T(k) & -E\mathbf{t}(k) \\ -\mathbf{t}^T(k)E & R_0 \end{bmatrix}$$

These allow for fast implementations to solve the normal equations.

Durbin's Method

This method computes the solution for the system of equations given in (1.167b) recursively. Define

$$A_T(k)\mathbf{a}(k) = \mathbf{t}(k) \tag{1.174}$$

$$\begin{bmatrix} A_T(k) & -E\mathbf{t}(k) \\ -\mathbf{t}^T(k)E & R_0 \end{bmatrix} \begin{bmatrix} \mathbf{a}_1(k+1) \\ a_2(k+1) \end{bmatrix} = \begin{bmatrix} \mathbf{t}(k) \\ -R_{k+1} \end{bmatrix} \tag{1.175a}$$

or

$$A_T(k+1)\mathbf{a}(k+1) = \mathbf{t}(k+1) \tag{1.175b}$$

Durbin's method computes $\mathbf{a}(k+1)$ from $\mathbf{a}(k)$ and the solution of the system of equations in (1.167b) is given by $\mathbf{a} = \mathbf{a}(p)$.

Premultiplying (1.175a) by $[\mathbf{a}^T(k)E \quad 1]$, we have

$$[\mathbf{a}^T(k)E \quad 1] \begin{bmatrix} A_T(k) & -E\mathbf{t}(k) \\ -\mathbf{t}^T(k)E & R_0 \end{bmatrix} \begin{bmatrix} \mathbf{a}_1(k+1) \\ a_2(k+1) \end{bmatrix} = [\mathbf{a}^T(k)E \quad 1] \begin{bmatrix} \mathbf{t}(k) \\ -R_{k+1} \end{bmatrix}$$

or

$$(\mathbf{a}^T(k)EA_T(k) - \mathbf{t}^T(k)E)\mathbf{a}_1(k+1) + (R_0 - \mathbf{a}^T(k)\mathbf{t}(k))a_2(k+1)$$

$$= (-R_{k+1} + \mathbf{a}^T(k)E\mathbf{t}(k)) \tag{1.176}$$

The coefficient of $\mathbf{a}_1(k+1)$ is $(\mathbf{a}^T(k)A_T(k) - \mathbf{t}^T(k))E = 0$, which follows from (1.174). Therefore

$$a_2(k+1) = \frac{R_{k+1} - \mathbf{a}^T(k)E\mathbf{t}(k)}{-R_0 + \mathbf{a}^T(k)\mathbf{t}(k)} \equiv C_{k+1} \tag{1.177}$$

Using this in the first equation in (1.175a), we have

$$A_T(k)\mathbf{a}_1(k+1) - E\mathbf{t}(k)C_{k+1} = \mathbf{t}_k$$

and using (1.174), it follows that

$$\mathbf{a}_1(k+1) = \mathbf{a}(k) + C_{k+1}E\mathbf{a}(k) \tag{1.178}$$

Equations (1.177) and (1.178) provide a recursive solution and can be expressed in a matrix form as

$$\mathbf{a}(k+1) = \begin{bmatrix} \mathbf{a}_1(k+1) \\ a_2(k+1) \end{bmatrix} = \begin{bmatrix} \mathbf{a}(k) \\ 0 \end{bmatrix} + C_{k+1}\begin{bmatrix} E\mathbf{a}(k) \\ 1 \end{bmatrix} \tag{1.179a}$$

with the final solution

$$\mathbf{a} = \mathbf{a}(p) \tag{1.179b}$$

Levinson's Algorithm

Levinson's algorithm computes the solution of (1.171) in two steps. First step is Durbin's algorithm. The solution again is recursive. Defining

$$A_T(k)\hat{\mathbf{a}}(k) = \mathbf{d}(k) \tag{1.180a}$$

$$\begin{bmatrix} A_T(k) & -E\mathbf{t}(k) \\ -\mathbf{t}^T(k)E & R_0 \end{bmatrix}\begin{bmatrix} \hat{\mathbf{a}}_1(k+1) \\ \hat{a}_2(k+1) \end{bmatrix} = \begin{bmatrix} \mathbf{d}(k) \\ d_{k+1} \end{bmatrix} \tag{1.180b}$$

or

$$A_T(k+1)\hat{\mathbf{a}}(k+1) = \mathbf{d}(k+1) \tag{1.180c}$$

Premultiplying (1.180b) by $[\mathbf{a}^T(k)E \quad 1]$, we have

$$[\mathbf{a}^T(k)E \quad 1]\begin{bmatrix} A_T(k) & -E\mathbf{t}(k) \\ -\mathbf{t}^T(k)E & R_0 \end{bmatrix}\begin{bmatrix} \hat{\mathbf{a}}_1(k+1) \\ \hat{a}_2(k+1) \end{bmatrix} = [\mathbf{a}^T(k)E \quad 1]\begin{bmatrix} \mathbf{d}(k) \\ d_{k+1} \end{bmatrix}$$

Noting (1.174) and solving for $\hat{a}_2(k+1)$, we have

$$\hat{a}_2(k+1) = \frac{d_{k+1} + \mathbf{a}^T(k)E\mathbf{d}(k)}{R_0 - \mathbf{a}^T(k)\mathbf{t}(k)} \equiv W_{k+1} \tag{1.181a}$$

and

$$\hat{\mathbf{a}}_1(k+1) = \hat{\mathbf{a}}(k) + W_{k+1}E\mathbf{a}(k) \tag{1.181b}$$

which is obviously a recursive solution.

Another interesting algorithm is by Trench [19], which is not discussed here. Many of these algorithms are computationally efficient, and they require computations on the order of p^2, as opposed to the methods by Gauss and Cholesky, which require the computations on the order of p^3, where p is the number of unknowns in the system. These are compared with iterative methods in the next section. The main criticism of the above methods lies in the practical instability in computing (1.177).

Iterative Techniques

If an approximate solution of (1.171) is desired, then iterative techniques, such as conjugate gradient methods, play an important role [20]. This is especially true if there is a need for solving a new set of normal equations of like order for successive signals, such as the case in seismic signal processing. Noting that for successive traces, the solution of (1.171) may not vary drastically. One can use the previously known solution as the initial solution for the next set. The initial solution may be solved by, say the Levinson's algorithm. In the following section, we will discuss the conjugate gradient method and its implementation using the fast Fourier transform algorithms.

In symbolic form, let Eq. (1.171) be written as

$$A_T\hat{\mathbf{a}} = \mathbf{d} \tag{1.182}$$

where $\hat{\mathbf{a}}$ and $\mathbf{d}$ are p-dimensional vectors, and A_T is a symmetric positive definite Toeplitz matrix.

Conjugate Gradient Method

The solution of (1.182) can be obtained using the following procedure, in p steps.

1. Assume an arbitrary solution for $\hat{\mathbf{a}}$, $\hat{\mathbf{a}}_0$
2. Compute $\mathbf{b}_0 = \mathbf{r}_0 = \mathbf{d} - A_T\hat{\mathbf{a}}_0$
3. Find successively at the kth step:

$$\begin{aligned} C_k &= \|r_k\|^2(\mathbf{b}_k^T A_T \mathbf{b}_k)^{-1} \\ \hat{\mathbf{a}}_{k+1} &= \hat{\mathbf{a}}_k + C_k\mathbf{b}_k \\ \mathbf{r}_{k+1} &= \mathbf{r}_k - C_k A_T \mathbf{b}_k \\ d_k &= \|r_{k+1}\|^2\|r_k\|^{-2} \\ \mathbf{b}_{k+1} &= \mathbf{r}_{k+1} + d_k\mathbf{b}_k \end{aligned}$$

The solution of (1.182) is given by

$$\hat{\mathbf{a}} = \sum_{k=0}^{p-1} (\mathbf{b}_k^T\mathbf{d})(\mathbf{b}_k^T A_T \mathbf{b}_k)^{-1}\mathbf{b}_k \tag{1.183}$$

The number of computations required by the preceding is rather large when compared to the other methods discussed earlier. Most of these are for the computation of

$$\mathbf{Q}_k \equiv A_T\mathbf{b}_k \tag{1.184}$$

This number can be reduced significantly by using a fast Fourier transform algorithm and the structure of the Toeplitz matrix.

Use of FFT in Computing (1.184)

Construct a symmetric circulant from A_T in the form

$$A_{\text{cirs}} = \begin{bmatrix} R_0 & R_1 & \cdots & R_{p-1} & R_p & \cdots & R_{N-1} \\ R_1 & R_0 & \cdots & R_{p-2} & R_{p-1} & \cdots & R_{N-2} \\ \vdots & \vdots & \vdots & \vdots & & \vdots & \vdots \\ R_{p-1} & R_{p-2} & \cdots & R_0 & R_1 & \cdots & \cdot \\ R_p & R_{p-1} & \cdots & R_1 & R_0 & \cdots & \cdot \\ \vdots & \vdots & \vdots & \vdots & \vdots & \vdots & \vdots \\ R_{N-1} & R_{N-2} & \cdots & \cdot & \cdot & \cdots & R_0 \end{bmatrix} \tag{1.185a}$$

where

$$R_{N-j} = R_j \qquad j = 1, 2, \ldots, p - 1$$

$$R_j = 0 \qquad p \le j \le N - p$$

From these, we can see that

$$N = 2(p - 1) + 1 + \beta \tag{1.185b}$$

with β being the smallest integer such that

$$-1 \le \beta \le \frac{N}{2} - 3 \tag{1.185c}$$

and N being a power of 2. Equations (1.185a–c) apply for $p > 2$. For $p = 1$, $N = 1$ and for $p = 2$, $N = 2$.

Example

$$A_T = \begin{bmatrix} R_0 & R_1 & R_2 \\ R_1 & R_0 & R_1 \\ R_2 & R_1 & R_0 \end{bmatrix}$$

$$A_{\text{cirs}} = \begin{bmatrix} R_0 & R_1 & R_2 & R_1 \\ R_1 & R_0 & R_1 & R_2 \\ R_2 & R_1 & R_0 & R_1 \\ R_1 & R_2 & R_1 & R_0 \end{bmatrix}$$

With the equations in (1.185), (1.184) can be computed using

$$\left[\frac{\mathbf{Q}_k}{\mathbf{Q}_k'}\right] = \frac{1}{N} A_{\mathrm{DFT}}^* \left\{ \Lambda \left\{ A_{\mathrm{DFT}} \left[\frac{\mathbf{b}_k}{0}\right] \right\} \right\} \tag{1.186}$$

See (1.111) for the decomposition of A_{cirs}.

The vector $\mathbf{Q}_k'$ need not be computed. It is clear that FFT can be used to compute (1.186) and save computational time, especially when the size of the system of normal equations is large (p in (1.171)).

Even with (1.186), the number of computations is significantly higher when compared to the methods discussed earlier. Levinson's alorithm calls for $2.5p^2$ operations, while the algorithm of trench calls for $2p^2$ operations to solve a set of Toeplitz normal equation in p unknowns. In general, iterative techniques depend upon the number of iterations required to solve the equations. If the number of iterations to compute $\hat{\mathbf{a}}$ can be reduced, then the preceding method appears to have potential. Also, if an approximate solution is known, then the solution can be obtained in fewer iterations than the number p used in (1.183). See [20] for more details.

Ideal Analog Filter Functions

An ideal filter has the property that if a signal is the input to this system, it allows some frequencies to go though with little attenuation and the others are blocked or greatly attenuated. There are four basic types of filters: low-pass, high-pass, band-pass, and band-elimination filters. To explain this further, see the block diagram representation in Figure 1.11, where $x(t)$ is the input, $y(t)$ is the output, and $h(t)$ is the impulse response of the system. The impulse response of course is the response of the system when $x(t) = \delta(t)$, the delta function. The Fourier transform of $h(t)$, $H(f)$, is the filter transfer function. Since we are interested in blocking, say, a frequency band, filters are generally defined in terms of the magnitude function $|H(f)|$. When the phase or the delay is important, then the phase characteristic, $H(f)$, is important.

The transfer characteristic of an ideal low-pass filter is shown in Figure 1.12, where the subscript Lp is used on H to denote the low-pass case.

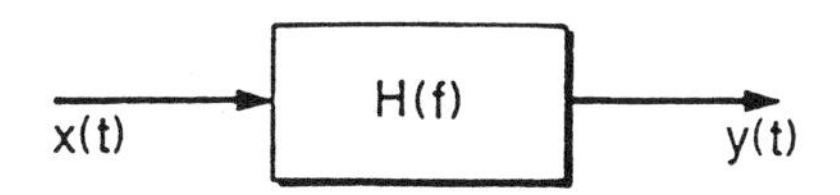

FIG. 1.11. Block diagram representation of a filter.

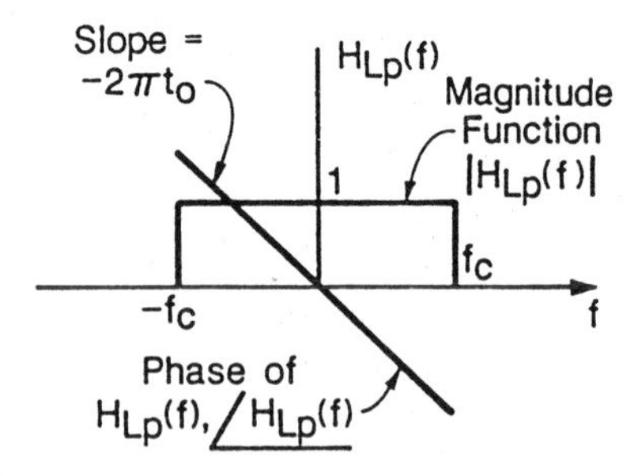

FIG. 1.12. Ideal low-pass characteristic in terms of magnitude and phase.

The system function $H_{\mathrm{Lp}}(f)$ is given by

$$H_{\mathrm{Lp}}(f) = \Pi\left(\frac{f}{2f_c}\right) e^{-2\pi f t_0} \tag{1.187}$$

where f_c is referred to as the *cutoff frequency*. The output $y(t)$ can be computed from the inverse transform of $H_{\mathrm{Lp}}(f)X(f)$. The impulse response of the ideal low-pass filter; that is,

$$y(t) = h(t)$$

is given by

$$h(t) = 2f_c \operatorname{sinc}[2f_c(t - t_0)] \tag{1.188}$$

The impulse response is the response to the input, an impulse, applied at $t = 0$. The response is not zero for $t < 0$ indicating that there is output before the input is applied. This implies that the ideal low-pass characteristic is physically unrealizable. The width of the main pulse (lobe) is $(1/f_c)$ and the height of the pulse is $2f_c$ and is centered at $t = t_0$. Thus, the pulse width–amplitude product is constant. If the delay time is defined as the difference between the time of impulse excitation and the time at which the main lobe of the impulse response is maximum, then t_0 is the time delay. The response is distorted as the filter can transmit only a limited range of frequencies. Note that as $f_c \to \infty$, the peak of $h(t)$ approaches infinity and the width approaches 0. Now a brief discussion on other types of filter functions. As in the low-pass case, the filter functions, such as high-pass, band-pass, and band-elimination filters, are specified in terms of magnitude functions. The actual transfer functions are usually derived by using frequency transformations from the low-pass functions. The ideal magnitude transfer functions are shown in Figure 1.13, where the subscripts Hp, Bp, and Be are used to denote the high-pass, band-pass and band-elimination filter functions, respectively.

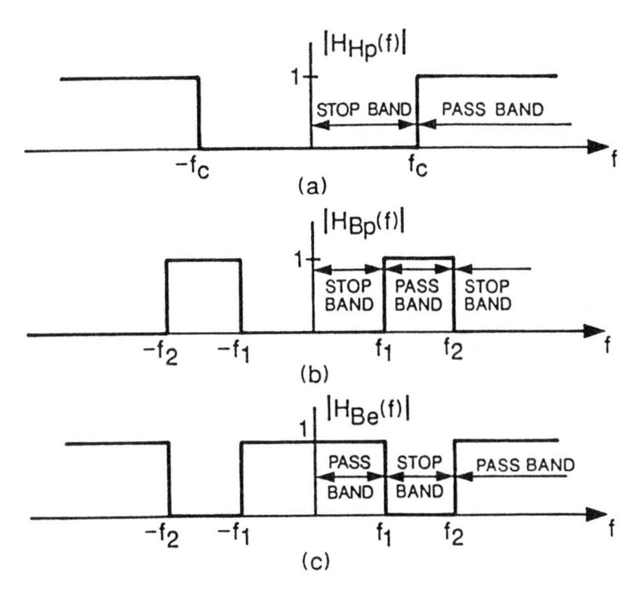

FIG. 1.13. Ideal magnitude filter functions: (a) high-pass function, (b) band-pass function, (c) band-elimination function.

As pointed out earlier, the low-pass ideal filter function is not physically realizable. The same goes with the other ideal functions. We can make a general statement that brickwall type functions are physically unrealizable, which leads to the part of approximating the ideal functions by physically realizable functions as close as possible. A set of specifications is given (see Figures 1.14a–d) for each of the four filter types mentioned. Since the amplitude function $|H(f)|$ is even, the specifications (see for example, [21]) are given for $f \geq 0$. In most cases, the amplitudes are specified in terms of dB (decibels), i.e., $20 \log_{10} |H(f)|$. Subscripts on H are identified to denote different filter type functions.

Low-Pass Filter Specifications

The pass and stop band specifications are given by

$$\left.\begin{array}{lll} \text{Pass band:} & 0 \leq |f| \leq f_c, & \dfrac{1}{1+\varepsilon^2} \leq |H_{\mathrm{Lp}}(f)|^2 \leq 1 \\[2ex] \text{Stop band:} & |f| \geq f_r, & |H_{\mathrm{Lp}}(f)|^2 \leq \dfrac{1}{A^2} \end{array}\right\} f_c < f_r \qquad (1.189)$$

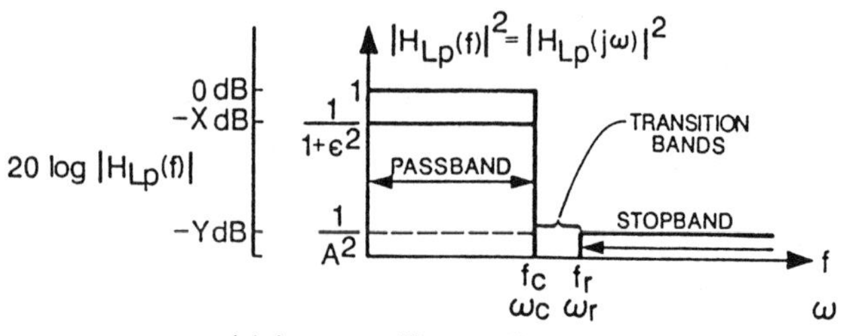

(a) Low-pass filter specifications (Non ideal)

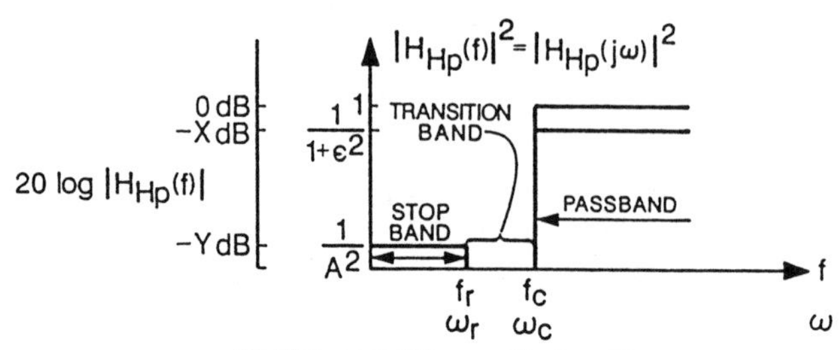

(b) High-pass filter specifications (Non ideal)

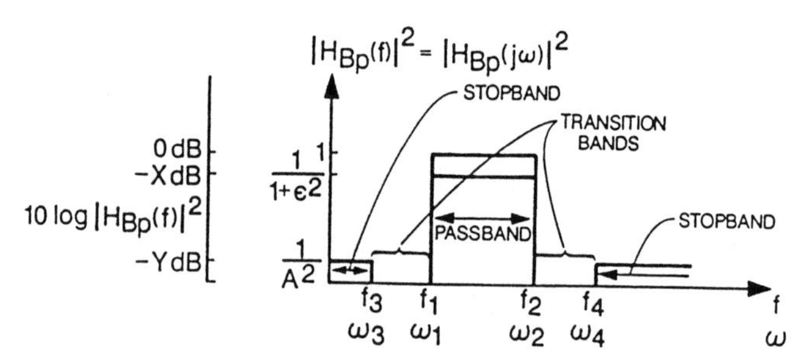

(c) Band-pass filter specifications (Non ideal)

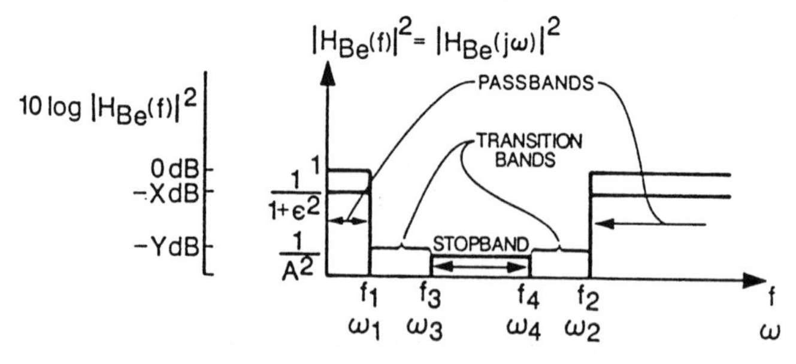

(d) Band-elimination filter specifications (Non ideal)

FIG. 1.14. Nonideal filter specification.

High-Pass Filter Specifications

$$\left.\begin{array}{lll}\text{Pass band:} & f_c \le |f| \le \infty, & \dfrac{1}{1+\varepsilon^2} \le |H_{\mathrm{Hp}}(f)|^2 \le 1 \\ \text{Stop band:} & 0 \le |f| \le f_r, & |H_{\mathrm{Hp}}(f)|^2 \le \dfrac{1}{A^2}\end{array}\right\} f_r < f_c \quad (1.190)$$

Band-Pass Filter Specifications

$$\left.\begin{array}{l}\text{Pass band: } f_1 \le |f| \le f_2, \quad \dfrac{1}{1+\varepsilon^2} \le |H_{\mathrm{Bp}}(f)|^2 \le 1 \\ \text{Stop band: } 0 \le |f| \le f_3, \quad f_4 \le |f| \le \infty, \quad |H_{\mathrm{Bp}}(f)| \le \dfrac{1}{A^2}\end{array}\right\} f_3 < f_1 < f_2 < f_4 \quad (1.191)$$

Band-Elimination Filter Specifications

$$\left.\begin{array}{l}\text{Pass band:} \\ 0 \le |f| \le f_1, \quad f_2 \le |f| < \infty, \quad \dfrac{1}{1+\varepsilon^2} \le |H_{\mathrm{Be}}(f)|^2 \le 1 \\ \text{Stop band:} \\ f_3 \le |f| \le f_4, \quad |H_{\mathrm{Be}}(f)|^2 \le \dfrac{1}{A^2}\end{array}\right\} f_1 < f_3 < f_4 < f_2 \quad (1.192)$$

All the four cases are shown in Figure 1.14, where the power levels are shown in dB scales. In addition to f_i, values of ω_i are shown, where $\omega_i = 2\pi f_i$, for later use. Note that $H(j\omega)$ with appropriate subscripts is used also on the figures.

There are four popular approximation techniques in analog filter theory [12, 21]:

1. Butterworth approximation
2. Tschebyscheff I and II approximations
3. Elliptic filter approximation
4. Bessel filter approximation

In the communication theory literature, the frequency f is generally used, whereas in circuits, filters, and others, ω is generally used. Instead of writing the function $H(f)$, filter designers use $H(j\omega)$.

Butterworth Approximation

The magnitude characteristic of the low-pass Butterworth approximation (BA) is given by

$$|H_{\mathrm{BA}}(j\omega)|^2 = \frac{1}{1 + \varepsilon^2(\omega/\omega_c)^{2n}} \tag{1.193}$$

where we have used ω rather than the frequency $f = (\omega/2\pi)$. In the pass and stop bands, this function satisfies

$$0 \le |\omega| \le \omega_c \qquad 1 \ge |H_{\mathrm{BA}}(j\omega)|^2 \ge [1/(1 + \varepsilon^2)]$$

$$|\omega| \ge \omega_r \qquad |H_{\mathrm{BA}}(j\omega)|^2 \le \frac{1}{A^2} \tag{1.194}$$

The magnitude plots are shown in Figure 1.15 for $n = 1$ and 2. Clearly, ε controls the pass-band constraints and A controls the attenuation in the stop band, which determines the order of the filter. In this case, $n = 2$ satisfies the specifications. The transfer function, $H_{\mathrm{BA}}(s)$, where s is the conventional Laplace transform variable, can be obtained by equating

$$H_{\mathrm{BA}}(s)H_{\mathrm{BA}}(-s) = 1/[1 + \varepsilon^2(-s^2/\omega_c^2)^n]|_{s=j\omega} = |H_{\mathrm{BA}}(j\omega)|^2 \tag{1.195}$$

The transfer function

$$H_{\mathrm{BA}}(s) = \frac{a_o}{D(s)} = \prod_{k=1}^{n} \frac{a_o}{(s - s_k)}, \qquad a_o = \prod_{k=1}^{n} (-s_k) \tag{1.196}$$

where the poles of the function, i.e., the roots of $D(s)$, are given by [21]

$$s_{2\nu+1} = \left(\frac{\omega_c}{\varepsilon^{(1/n)}}\right) e^{j(2\nu+1+n)(\pi/2n)}, \qquad \nu = 0, 1, 2, \ldots, n-1 \tag{1.197}$$

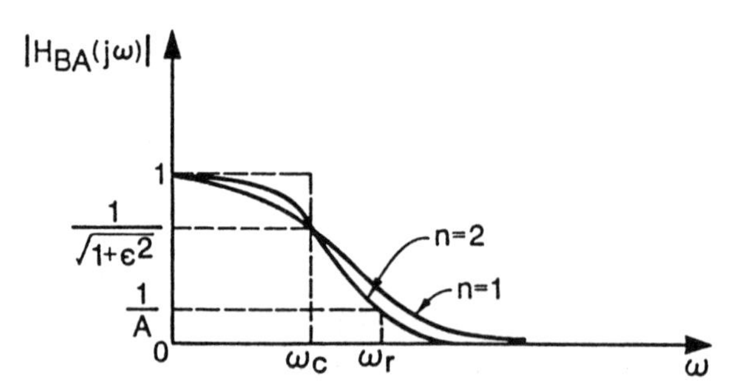

FIG. 1.15. Butterworth approximation to the low-pass filter.

The design formula for determining n, the order of the filter, is [12]

$$n = \frac{\ln\sqrt{A^2 - 1} - \ln(\varepsilon)}{\ln(\omega_r/\omega_c)} \cong \frac{\ln(A/\varepsilon)}{(f_r/f_c) - 1} \tag{1.198}$$

where we have used $(\omega_i = 2\pi f_i)$ and an approximation. Butterworth approximation is sometimes referred to as a *maximally flat approximation* because the characteristic is monotonic for all ω and $(2n - 1)$ derivatives are 0 at $\omega = 0$.

Tschebyscheff I Approximation

The magnitude characteristic of a Tschebyscheff I filter is

$$|H_{T_1}(j\omega)|^2 = \frac{1}{1 + \varepsilon^2 C_n^2(\omega/\omega_c)} \tag{1.199}$$

where

$$C_n(x) = \begin{cases} \cos(n \cos^{-1} x), & |x| \leq 1 \\ \cosh(n \cosh^{-1} x), & |x| > 1 \end{cases} \tag{1.200}$$

which can be determined from the polynomial form by relating $C_n(x)$ to a recursive relation,

$$C_{n+1}(x) = 2xC_n(x) - C_n(x) \tag{1.201}$$

with $C_o(x) = 1$ and $C_1(x) = x$.

It can be shown that these polynomials exhibit equal ripple characteristics for $0 \leq |x| \leq 1$, and for large x, we can approximate them by $C_n(x) \cong 2^{n-1}x^n$. From these properties we can see that $|H_{T_1}(j\omega)|^2$ has a low-pass characteristics. Figure 1.16 illustrates the characteristic for $n = 2$ and $n = 3$. Note that $C_n^2(0) = 0$ for n odd and $C_n^2(0) = 1$ for n even and the value of $H_{T_1}(j\omega)$ is 1 when n is odd and $\sqrt{[1/(1 + \varepsilon^2)]}$ when n is even at

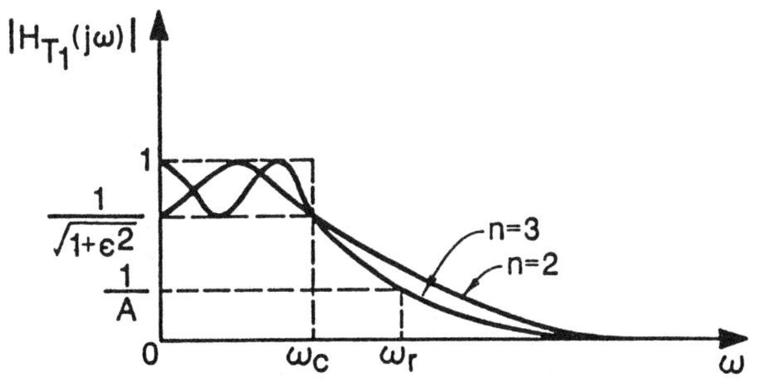

FIG. 1.16. Tschebyscheff I approximation to the low-pass filter.

$\omega = 0$. As in the Butterworth case, the transfer function can be computed as

$$H_{T_1}(s) = \frac{a_1}{\prod_{k=1}^{n}(s/\omega_c - s_k)} \qquad a_1 = \begin{cases} \prod_{k=1}^{n}(-s_k), & n \text{ odd} \\ \prod_{k=1}^{n}(-s_k)\dfrac{1}{\sqrt{1+\varepsilon^2}}, & n \text{ even} \end{cases} \tag{1.202}$$

and [21]

$$s_k = -\sinh\left(\frac{1}{n}\sinh^{-1}\frac{1}{\varepsilon}\right)\sin\frac{(2k+1)}{2n}\pi + j\cosh\left(\frac{1}{n}\sinh^{-1}\frac{1}{\varepsilon}\right)\cos\frac{2k+1}{2n}\pi$$

$$k = 0, 1, 2, \ldots, n-1$$

where ω_c, as before, is the cutoff frequency. The design equation for determining the order of the filter n is

$$n = \frac{\cosh^{-1}(\sqrt{A^2 - 1}/\varepsilon)}{\cosh^{-1}(\omega_r/\omega_c)} \cong \frac{\ln(2A/\varepsilon)}{[2(\omega_r - \omega_c)/\omega_c]^{1/2}} \tag{1.203}$$

and ε is computed as in the Butterworth case. Tschebyscheff I magnitude characteristic has an equal ripple characteristic in the pass band and monotonic characteristic in the stop band. The inverse Tschebyscheff (or Tschebyscheff II) has equal ripple in the stop band and maximally flat property near $\omega = 0$ in the pass band, which is discussed next.

Tschebyscheff II Approximation

The magnitude characteristic of this approximation is

$$|H_{T_2}(j\omega)|^2 = \frac{1}{1 + \varepsilon^2\left[\dfrac{C_n(\omega_r/\omega_c)}{C_n(\omega_r/\omega)}\right]^2} \tag{1.204}$$

where $C_n(x)$ is defined as before. The ε value and the design equation, i.e., the value of n, is the same as in type I case. The transfer function can be computed in a manner similar to the Tschebyscheff I. Note that the transfer function in the earlier case is an all-pole function, whereas in the Tschebyscheff II, the transfer function has zeros on the imaginary axis and can be determined from the Tschebyscheff polynomials. Figure 1.17 illustrates the magnitude characteristic for $n = 2$ and 3. Note the value of $\lim_{\omega \to \infty} |H_{T_2}(j\omega)|$ for n even and n odd.

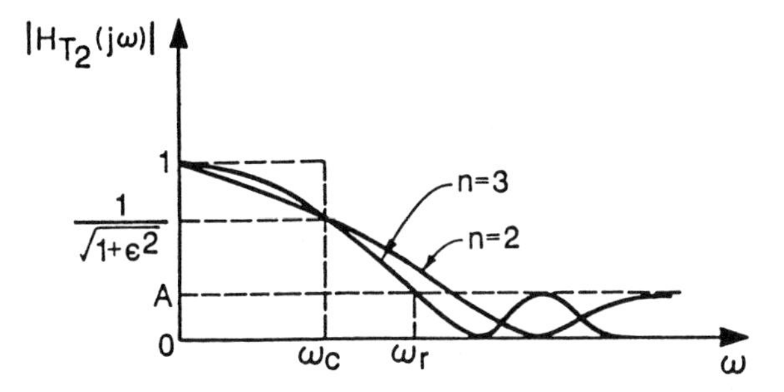

FIG. 1.17. Tschebyscheff II approximation to the low-pass filter.

Elliptic Filter Approximation

In the last two approximations, the magnitude characteristics have ripples in the pass band (Tschebyscheff I) and in the stop band (Tschebyscheff II), respectively. A filter function that has equal ripple characteristics both in the pass and stop bands is a very useful function. It can be written as [21]

$$R_n(\omega) = \frac{\omega(\omega_1^2 - \omega^2)(\omega_2^2 - \omega^2)\ldots(\omega_l^2 - \omega^2)}{(1 - \omega_1^2\omega^2)(1 - \omega_2^2\omega^2)\ldots(1 - \omega_l^2\omega^2)}, \quad n \text{ odd}$$
$$= \frac{(\omega_1^2 - \omega^2)(\omega_2^2 - \omega^2)\ldots(\omega_l^2 - \omega^2)}{(1 - \omega_1^2\omega^2)(1 - \omega_2^2\omega^2)\ldots(1 - \omega_l^2\omega^2)}, \quad n \text{ even} \tag{1.205}$$

where the integer n determines the complexity of the function. For n even, $n = 2l$ and for n odd, $n = 2l + 1$. Interestingly, $R_n(1/\omega) = 1/[R_n(\omega)]$. The magnitude function

$$|H_E(j\omega)|^2 = \frac{1}{1 + \varepsilon^2 R_n^2(\omega)}$$

where $R_n(\omega)$ has zeros in the range $0 \le \omega < 1$ and poles in the complimentary range $1 < \omega \le \infty (0 < \omega_1 < \omega_2 \cdots < \omega_l < 1)$. Clearly, for a given n, an infinite number of R_n exist. The function R_n becomes unique when n, the order of the function, and ω_r, the start of the stop band, are specified [21]. Frequency normalizations and transformations will be discussed later.

The actual values of ω_i can be determined by considering the elliptic integral of the first kind defined by

$$K(k) = \int_0^{\pi/2} \frac{d\phi}{(1 - k^2 \sin^2 \phi)^{1/2}} \tag{1.206}$$

and

$$R_n(\omega) = \begin{cases} sn\left[n\dfrac{K(k_1)}{K(k)}sn^{-1}\left(\dfrac{\omega}{\omega_c}; k\right); k_1\right], & n \text{ odd} \\ sn\left[K(k_1) + n\dfrac{K(k_1)}{K(k)}sn^{-1}\left(\dfrac{\omega}{\omega_c}; k\right); k_1\right], & n \text{ even} \end{cases} \tag{1.207}$$

where $x = sn(y;\ k)$ is the elliptic sine function and $sn^{-1}(x;\ k) = y$ is the inverse elliptic function. There are good references [12], as well as tables [22], to determine $K(k)$ and $sn(\cdot;\ \cdot)$.

The value of k is determined by

$$k = \omega_c/\omega_r \tag{1.208a}$$

where, as before, ω_c and ω_r are the edges of the transition band of the low-pass filter. The constant k_1 is determined from the allowable ripple in the pass band, and

$$k_1 = \frac{\varepsilon}{\sqrt{A^2 - 1}} \tag{1.208b}$$

where ε and A were defined as before. The order of the filter, n, is given by the design equation [12]

$$n = \frac{K(\sqrt{1 - k_1^2})K(k)}{K(k_1)K(\sqrt{1 - k^2})} \tag{1.209a}$$

which can be approximated by

$$n \cong \frac{2}{\pi^2}\ln\left(\frac{4A}{\varepsilon}\right)\ln\left(\frac{8\omega_c}{\omega_r - \omega_c}\right) \tag{1.209b}$$

The location of the poles and zeros of the transfer function can be obtained in a two-step process [12]. First, for n odd, the zeros and poles are, respectively, given in the u–v domain for $l = 0, \pm 1, \ldots, \pm(n - 1)/2$:

$$\begin{aligned} &\text{Zeros:} \quad u_l + jv_l = -K(\sqrt{1 - k^2}) + j\frac{2l}{n}K(k) \\ &\text{Poles:} \quad \overline{u_l} + j\overline{v_l} = -u_0 + j\frac{2l}{n}K(k) \end{aligned} \tag{1.210a}$$

and for n even, the zeros and poles are, respectively, given by for $l = -n/2$, $-n/2 + 1, \ldots, n/2 - 1$:

$$\text{Zeros:} \quad u_l + jv_l = -K(\sqrt{1 - k^2}) + j\frac{2l + 1}{n}K(k)$$

$$\text{Poles:} \quad \overline{u_l} + j\overline{v_l} = -u_0 + j\frac{2l + 1}{n}K(k) \tag{1.210b}$$

$$u_0 = -j\frac{K(k)}{nK(k_1)}sn^{-1}\left(\frac{j}{\varepsilon}; k_1\right)$$

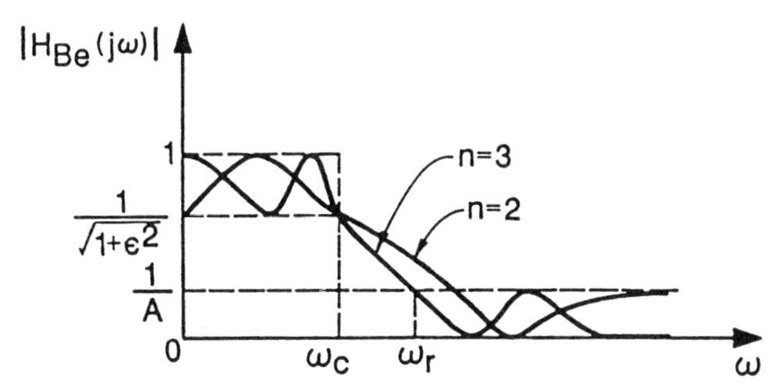

FIG. 1.18. Elliptic approximation to the low-pass filter function.

The actual locations of the poles and zeros of the transfer function are determined by substituting (1.210) in

$$s = j\omega_c sn(-j(u + jv);\ k)$$

where k is as defined in (1.208a).

Figure 1.18 illustrates the low-pass magnitude characteristics for $n = 2$ and $n = 3$. Note again the characteristic at $\omega = 0$ and as $\omega \to \infty$.

Comparing the Butterworth, Tschebyscheff, and elliptic filters for a given set of specifications, the order of the filter, i.e., n, satisfy the following:

$$n_B \geq n_T \geq n_E$$

where the subscripts are identified explicitly for B for Butterworth, T for Tschebyscheff, and E for elliptic. The elliptic filter approximation of degree n is the best obtainable using a ratio of nth-degree polynomials. Clearly, when the transition band is narrow, i.e., (ω_c/ω_r) is near 1, elliptic filter approximation gives the best results as far as the magnitude characteristic is concerned. As a rule of thumb, the sharper the slope in the transition band, of the magnitude of the transfer function, say, $|G(j\omega)|$, the more nonlinear the phase, $\phi(\omega) = \arg(G(j\omega)) = \tan^{-1}[\mathrm{Im}(G(j\omega)/\mathrm{Re}\, G(j\omega)]$ is, where $\mathrm{Re}(\cdot)$ corresponds to the real part and $\mathrm{Im}(\cdot)$ corresponds to the imaginary part. Since the group delay is defined by

$$T_G = -\frac{d}{d\omega}\phi(\omega) \tag{1.211}$$

the group delay is generally a nonlinear function of frequency. Delay correction may be required if a constant delay is desired in the frequency range of interest.

Noting that if

$$G_d(j\omega) = \frac{\prod_{i=1}^{n}(a_i - jb_i\omega)}{\prod_{i=1}^{n}(a_i + jb_i\omega)} \tag{1.212}$$

where $a_i > 0$ and $b_i > 0$ (for stability reasons), it follows that $|G_d(j\omega)| = 1$, a constant, and the phase spectrum is given by

$$\phi_d(\omega) = -\sum_{i=1}^{n} 2\tan^{-1}\left(\frac{b_i}{a_i}\omega\right) \tag{1.213a}$$

The group delay is given by

$$-\frac{d}{d\omega}\phi_d(\omega) = \sum_{i=1}^{n}\left[\frac{2(b_i/a_i)}{1 + [(b_i/a_i)\omega)]^2}\right] \tag{1.213b}$$

Generally, the delay (or the phase) is adjusted, i.e., a_i and b_i in (1.212) are adjusted such that the total function $[G_f(j\omega)G_d(j\omega)]$ has the desired magnitude and delay (or the phase) characteristics, where $G_f(j\omega)$ is the filter function. Bessel functions are usually used in determining $G_d(j\omega)$. For a detailed discussion, see [21].

Frequency Transformations

In the last section, we considered the generation of low-pass functions. It was pointed out that $\omega = 2\pi f$ is commonly used rather than f. Various tables are available corresponding to different types of approximations. The tables generally give in terms of s domain polynomials ($s = j\omega$), corresponding to a cutoff frequency of $\omega_c = 1$. Such a transfer function is usually referred to as a *prototype normalized function*, $H_{\mathrm{Lpn}}(s)$. If the cutoff frequency is ω_c, then the corresponding low-pass function is given by

$$H_{\mathrm{Lp}}(s) = H_{\mathrm{Lpn}}(s/\omega_c) \tag{1.214a}$$

where we have used the transformation $s \to (s/\omega_c)$. The high-pass function can be obtained from $H_{\mathrm{Lpn}}(s)$ by using the transformation $s \to (\omega_c/s)$. That is, low(high) frequencies become high(low) frequencies, and

$$H_{\mathrm{Hp}}(s) = H_{\mathrm{Lpn}}(\omega_c/s) \tag{1.214b}$$

Similarly, the band-pass function can be obtained from $H_{\mathrm{Lpn}}(s)$ by using the transformation $s \to (s^2 + \omega_0^2)/Bs$, where $B = (\omega_2 - \omega_1)$, and, $\omega_0^2 = \omega_1\omega_2$. The ω_1 and ω_2 were referred to earlier as the edge frequencies of the band-pass filter. The corresponding band-pass function is given by

$$H_{\mathrm{Bp}}(s) = H_{\mathrm{Lpn}}\left(\frac{s^2 + \omega_0^2}{Bs}\right) \tag{1.214c}$$

Finally, the band-elimination function can be obtained from $H_{\mathrm{Lpn}}(s)$ by using the transformation $s \to Bs/(s^2 + \omega_0^2)$ and the corresponding

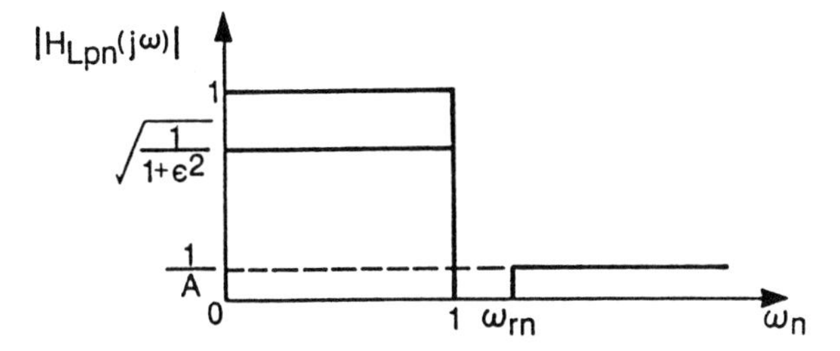

FIG. 1.19. Normalised low-pass filter specifications.

band-elimination function is given by

$$H_{\mathrm{Be}}(s) = H_{\mathrm{Lpn}}\left(\frac{Bs}{s^2 + \omega_0^2}\right) \tag{1.214d}$$

where $B = (\omega_2 - \omega_1)$ and $\omega_0^2 = \omega_1\omega_2$ (see Figure 1.14d).

Clearly the preceding discussion centers around the point of finding the low-pass, high-pass, band-pass, and band-elimination functions from a normalized low-pass function. The next question we want to answer is, If the specifications are given for low-pass, high-pass, band-pass, and band-elimination filters, how do we transform these specifications into normalized low-pass specifications (see Figure 1.19)? This is discussed next.

The low-pass filter specifications are easy to transform to a normalized low-pass case since the amplitudes remain the same and the frequencies are normalized, i.e., $\omega_{c_n} = 1$, and

$$\omega_{r_n} = \frac{\omega_r}{\omega_c} \tag{1.215a}$$

Also, $|H_{\mathrm{Lp}}(j\omega_c)| = |H_{\mathrm{Lpn}}(j1)|$ and $|H_{\mathrm{Lp}}(j\omega_r)| = |H_{\mathrm{Lpn}}(j\omega_{r_n})|$. See Figures 1.14a and 1.19. The high-pass filter specifications can be transformed to a normalized low-pass filter specifications by

$$\omega_{c_n} = 1 \quad \text{and} \quad \omega_{r_n} = (\omega_c/\omega_r) \tag{1.215b}$$

Also, $|H_{\mathrm{Hp}}(j\omega_c)| = |H_{\mathrm{Lpn}}(j1)|$ and $|H_{\mathrm{Hp}}(j\omega_{\mathrm{r}})| = H_{\mathrm{Lpn}}(j\omega_{r_n})|$. See Figures 1.14b and 1.19. The band-pass filter specifications can be transformed to a normalized low-pass filter specifications by

$$\omega_{c_n} = 1 \quad \text{and} \quad \omega_{r_n} = \min\{|\alpha_1|, |\beta_1)\}, \tag{1.215c}$$

where

$$\alpha_1 = [(-\omega_3^2 + \omega_1\omega_2)/\omega_3(\omega_2 - \omega_1)]$$

$$\beta_1 = [(\omega_4^2 - \omega_1\omega_2)/\omega_4(\omega_2 - \omega_1)]$$

The reason for the possibility of $|\alpha_1|$ and $|\beta_1|$ are the two sides of the band-pass spectrum and the minimum value between $|\alpha|$ and $|\beta|$ allows for finding the tighter specification. See Figures 1.14c and 1.19.

Finally, the band-elimination filter specifications can be transformed to a normalized low-pass filter specifications by

$$\omega_{c_n} = 1 \quad \text{and} \quad \omega_{r_n} = \min\{|\alpha_2|, |\beta_2|\} \tag{1.215d}$$

where

$$\alpha_2 = [\omega_3(\omega_2 - \omega_1)/(-\omega_3^2 + \omega_1\omega_2)]$$

$$\beta_2 = [\omega_4(\omega_2 - \omega_1)/(-\omega_4^2 + \omega_1\omega_2)]$$

where again the reason for finding the minimum is to find the tighter specifications. See Figures 1.14d and 1.19.

Digital Filter Functions

In digital filters, the input and the output variables are sequences of numbers. The input could be a sequence of numbers obtained by sampling an analog signal, such as speech, or they could be just numbers, such as stock prices, on a day-to-day basis. We can consider both the cases by starting with an arbitrary signal $x(kT)$, $k = 0, 1, \ldots$. Note that T is used rather than T_s for ease in the following. In a digital signal, we can assume $T = 1$. The sequence of numbers $x(kT)$ are processed so that the output sequence of numbers are $y(kT)$. Both sequences must have a finite number of digits so that they can reside in a register of a digital computer. For the analysis here, none of these restrictions is considered. See [18] for a discussion on finite register effects. Assuming the system under consideration is a linear, shift invariant system, the output, i.e. the response, can be expressed by

$$y(nT) = \sum_{k=0}^{n} h(nT - kT)x(kT) \tag{1.216}$$

where $h(nT)$ characterizes the behavior of the discrete linear system. We can identify $h(nT) = y(nT)$ when $x(0) = 1$ and $x(nT) = 0$, $n \neq 0$ and $h(nT)$ is the unit sample response. Instead of Laplace transforms, we can use the z-transforms and (see Eq. (1.139))

$$H'(z) = \sum_{k=0}^{\infty} h(kT)z^{-k} \tag{1.217a}$$

and the output z-transform

$$Y(z) = H'(z)X(z). \tag{1.217b}$$

In the following, we are interested in the design of filters, i.e., determine $H'(z)$ for a given set of specifications of a filter. Various techniques are available to achieve this goal [6].

Impulse Invariance Method

In this method, a digital filter is designed such that the digital impulse response is equal to the sampled impulse response of a given continuous filter. First, consider a simple transfer function in the s-domain

$$H(s) = \frac{A_i}{s + s_i} \tag{1.218a}$$

The corresponding impulse response is

$$h(t) = A_i \mathrm{e}^{-s_i t} u(t)$$

where $u(t)$ is the usual unit step function. Clearly,

$$h(kT) = A_i \mathrm{e}^{-s_i kT}, \qquad k \geq 0$$

The corresponding z-transform of this is given by

$$H'(z) = A_i \sum_{k=0}^{\infty} \mathrm{e}^{-s_i kT} z^{-k} = \frac{A_i}{1 - \mathrm{e}^{-s_i T} z^{-1}} \tag{1.218b}$$

where we assumed that $|\mathrm{e}^{-s_i T} z^{-1}| < 1$. Note the prime superscript on $H'(z)$ is introduced to differentiate from $H(\cdot)$. We can generalize this and consider the multiple pole case. That is, if

$$H(s) = \frac{A_i}{(s + s_i)^m} \tag{1.218c}$$

then the corresponding z-domain function is

$$H'(z) = \left[\frac{(-1)^{m-1}}{(m-1)!} \frac{\partial^{m-1}}{\partial a^{m-1}} \left(\frac{A_i}{1 - \mathrm{e}^{-aT} z^{-1}} \right) \right]_{|a = s_i} \tag{1.218d}$$

Almost all the filter transfer functions considered are simple pole cases. Complex pole cases can be handled by using these results and combining the terms corresponding to the complex and its conjugate:

$$\frac{s + a}{(s + a)^2 + b^2} \Rightarrow \frac{1 - \mathrm{e}^{-aT}(\cos bT) z^{-1}}{1 - 2\,\mathrm{e}^{-aT} \cos bT z^{-1} + \mathrm{e}^{-2aT} z^{-2}} \tag{1.219a}$$

$$\frac{b}{(s + a)^2 + b^2} \Rightarrow \frac{\mathrm{e}^{-aT} \sin(bT) z^{-1}}{1 - 2\,\mathrm{e}^{-aT} \cos bT z^{-1} + \mathrm{e}^{-2aT} z^{-2}} \tag{1.219b}$$

Clearly, if the s-domain transfer function is given by $H(s) = \sum_{i=1}^{N} H_i(s)$, where $H_i(s)$ are one of the functions given previously, see (1.218c) or (1.219a) or (1.219b), then the corresponding z-domain function $H'(z) = \sum_{i=1}^{N} H_i'(z)$. H_i' can be obtained from the preceding.

One of the main problems with the impulse invariance method is in frequency folding (see the discussion on sampling theory). One way to avoid such a problem is to use a transformation that will map the entire complex s-plane into the horizontal strip in a plane bounded by the lines $s = -j(\omega_s/2)$ and $s = +(j\omega_s/2)$. However, a digital filter represented by $H'(z)$ must be periodic in ω with period ω_s. Therefore, this transformation must also map the entire complex s-plane identically in each of the other strips bounded by $s = j(n - \frac{1}{2})\omega_s$ and $s = j(n + \frac{1}{2})\omega_s$, where n is an integer. A simple transformation that has this property is the bilinear transformation.

Bilinear Transformation Method

Consider

$$s = j\omega_A = \tan\frac{s_1 T}{2} = \frac{1 - e^{-j\omega_D T}}{1 + e^{j\omega_D T}} = \frac{1 - z^{-1}}{1 + z^{-1}} = \frac{z - 1}{z + 1} \qquad (1.220a)$$

where we have used explicitly ω_A to represent the analog frequency, ω_D to represent the digital frequency ($s_1 = j\omega_D$). The analog frequency ω_A is given by

$$\omega_A = \tan\frac{\omega_D T}{2} \qquad (1.220b)$$

The transformation is nonlinear and sometimes referred to as *frequency warping*. The functions $H(j\omega_A)$ and $H'(e^{j\omega_D T})$ take on the same values for $\omega_A = \tan(\omega_D T/2)$. The transformation has some interesting properties. Equation (1.220a) can be rewritten as

$$z = \frac{1 + s}{1 - s} \qquad (1.221)$$

and, for $s = \alpha + j\beta$, we have

$$|z| = \sqrt{\frac{(1 + \alpha)^2 + \beta^2}{(1 - \alpha)^2 + \beta^2}} \qquad (1.222a)$$

which implies that

$$\alpha \begin{matrix} < \\ = \\ > \end{matrix} 0 \Leftrightarrow |z| \begin{matrix} < \\ = \\ > \end{matrix} 1 \qquad (1.222b)$$

This makes it very nice for designing digital filters from the s-domain functions. If $H(s)$ is a stable analog filter, i.e., all the poles are on the left side of the s-plane, then the corresponding digital filter obtained by the bilinear transformation (Eq. 1.220a) is also a stable filter. That is, the poles of the digital filter function are located inside the unit circle of the z-plane. The following steps can be used for the design.

1. Identify the critical frequencies and the ranges of the frequencies corresponding to the filter. Note the digital filter response is periodic with period ω_s and we will be concerned in the frequency range 0 to $(\omega_s/2)$. See Figure 1.20 for an example in the low-pass case, where (0 to ω_{Dc}) is the passband, (ω_{Dc} to ω_{Dr}) is the transition band, and (ω_{Dr} to $\omega_s/2$) is the stop band. That is, (0 to $\omega_s/2$) is the entire frequency range we are interested in. The other cases, such as high pass, bandpass and band elimination, can be similarly defined. Note that $H'(e^{j\omega_D T})$ is periodic with period ω_s. T is the sampling interval.
2. Compute the analog frequencies using $\omega_{Ai} = \tan(\omega_{Di} T/2)$. Transform the digital filter specifications to analog filter specifications. For example, see Figure 1.20b for the low-pass case.
3. Find $H(s)$, the s-domain transfer function, for the appropriate analog filter specifications. This generally involves a couple of steps: (a) finding the prototype (normalized) analog low-pass function and

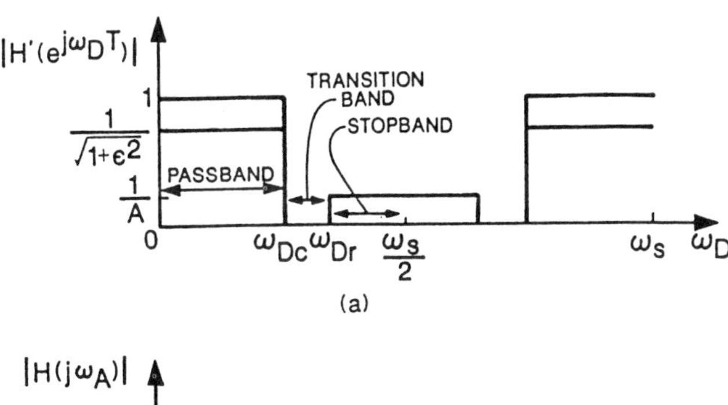

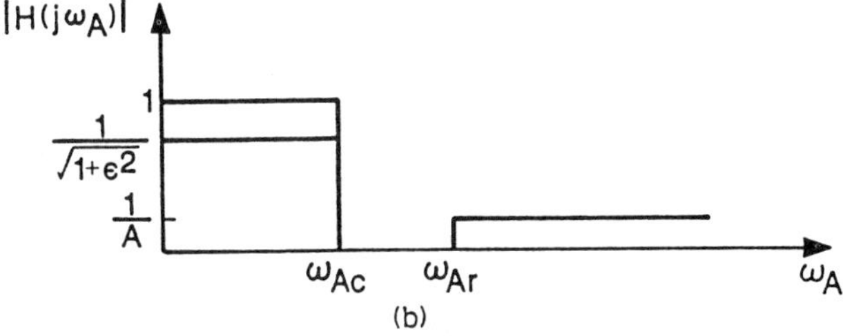

FIG. 1.20. Specifications of (a) a digital low-pass filter and (b) analog filter specifications corresponding to it, $\omega_{Ai} = \tan(\omega_{Di} T/2)$.

(b) finding the transfer function corresponding to the appropriate analog filter specifications by using the appropriate frequency transformations discussed earlier.

4. Replace s by $[(z - 1)/z + 1]$ and simplify. This results in a rational function in z, $H'(z)$, which is physically realizable and stable.

The actual digital filter implementation may involve different approaches. In the following, we will consider a simple approach using cascade method of realization. The model

$$Y(z) = H'(z)X(z) \tag{1.223}$$

where $X(z)$ is the input transform, $Y(z)$ is the output transform, and $H'(z)$ is the z-domain transfer function of the filter. In the cascade realization, $H'(z)$ is factored into k second-order functions (one of them is a first-order function if the degree of $H'(z)$ is odd). Clearly, if $H'(z)$ is an nth-order function, then $n = 2k$ (or $2k - 1$). Now,

$$H'(z) = H_1'(z)H_2'(z) \ldots H_k'(z)$$

and the realization is shown in Figure 1.21a, where $X_1(z) = X(z)$,

$$H_j'(z) = \frac{b_{0j} + b_{1j}z^{-1} + b_{2j}z^{-2}}{1 + a_{1j}z^{-1} + a_{2j}z^{-2}}, \qquad X_{j+1}(z) = H_j'(z)X_j(z) \tag{1.224}$$

Of course, if there is a first-order function, then we can assume $b_{2j} = a_{2j} = 0$. A simple implementation of (1.224) is shown in Figure 1.21b,

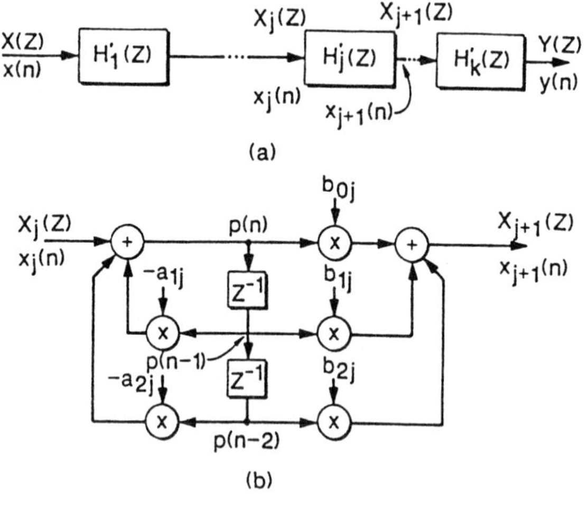

FIG. 1.21. (a) Cascade realization. (b) Realization of one section.

where a_{ij}, b_{ij} are multiplier constants, $\times$ represent multipliers, $+$ represent summers, the arrows indicate the directions of the signals, and (z^{-1}) block represents the delay. The intermediate variables are $p(n)$, $p(n-1)$, and $p(n-2)$ in Figure 1.21b, where

$$\begin{aligned} p(n) &= x_j(n) - a_{1j}p(n-1) - a_{2j}p(n-2) \\ x_{j+1}(n) &= b_{0j}p(n) + b_{1j}p(n-1) + b_{2j}p(n-2) \end{aligned} \tag{1.225}$$

Using z-transforms, i.e., $z[p(n)] = P(z)$, $z[p(n-k)] = z^{-k}P(z)$ and $z[x_{j+l}(n)] = X_{j+l}(z)$, we have

$$P(z) = \frac{X_j(z)}{1 + a_{1j}z^{-1} + a_{2j}z^{-2}}$$

and

$$X_{j+1}(z) = \frac{b_{0j} + b_{1j}z^{-1} + b_{2j}z^{-2}}{1 + a_{1j}z^{-1} + a_{2j}z^{-2}} X_j(z) \tag{1.226}$$

giving the desired result. Structures other than cascade structures can be used to realize a given transfer function. Parallel structures and companion form structures have also been used [6].

The filter structures discussed earlier are usually referred to as *infinite impulse response* (IIR) filters. The name evolves from the fact that the unit sample response is of infinite duration. For example, if

$$Y(z) = \frac{b_0 + b_1 z^{-1} + b_2 z^{-2}}{1 + a_1 z^{-1} + a_2 z^{-2}} X(z) \tag{1.227a}$$

then

$$(1 + a_1 z^{-1} + a_2 z^{-2})Y(z) = (b_0 + b_1 z^{-1} + b_2 z^{-2})X(z)$$

and taking the inverse transform, we have

$$y(n) = -(a_1 y(n-1) + a_2 y(n-2)) + b_0 x(n) + b_1 x(n-1) + b_2 x(n-2) \tag{1.227b}$$

Say for example, $a_1 \neq a_2 \neq 0$ and $x(0) = 1$ (unit sample), and $x(n) = 0$, $n \neq 0$, then the response could last for an infinite duration. Note that the denominator of the transfer function is a polynomial with a nonzero set of coefficients, which results in a feedback structure. There are special cases wherein the denominator polynomial is a factor of the numerator polynomial and the response will be of finite duration. Some digital band-pass filters are designed that way (see [6]). Next, we will consider the finite impulse response (FIR) filters.

Finite Impulse Response Filters

A system characterized by

$$Y(z) = \left(\sum_{k=0}^{N-1} h_k z^{-k}\right) X(z) \tag{1.228a}$$

results in the difference equation

$$y(n) = \sum_{k=0}^{N-1} h_k x(n-k) \tag{1.228b}$$

Clearly, if the input is $x(0) = 1$ and $x(n) = 0$, $n \neq 0$, then the unit sample response is

$$y(n) = h_n, \qquad 0 \leq n \leq N-1$$

which obviously lasts for N samples and the sample values are h_n. The filter function $H'(z) = \sum_{k=0}^{N-1} h_k z^{-k}$ is a finite impulse response filter function, and $H'(e^{j\omega T})$ is the frequency response of the filter and the amplitude, and the phase responses can be computed from this function. For a causal FIR filter, the impulse response begins at $n = 0$ and ends at, say, $N - 1$; $h(n)$ must satisfy the following [28]

$$h(n) = h(N-1-n), \qquad 0 \leq n \leq N-1 \tag{1.229a}$$

in order that the sequence has a linear phase. This can be seen from

$$\begin{aligned} H'(e^{j\omega T}) &= \sum_{n=0}^{N-1} h_n e^{-j\omega nT} \\ &= \sum_{n=0}^{(N/2)-1} h_n e^{-j\omega nT} + \sum_{n=0}^{(N/2)-1} h_{N-1-n} e^{-j\omega(N-1-n)T} \end{aligned}$$

where N is assumed even. Using (1.229a), we have

$$H'(e^{j\omega T}) = (e^{-j\omega((N-1)/2)T})\left\{\sum_{n=0}^{(N/2)-1} 2h_n \cos\left[\omega\left(n - \left(\frac{N-1}{2}\right)\right)T\right]\right\} \tag{1.229b}$$

where the first term is the complex term and the second term is real. In the case of N odd, $H'(e^{j\omega T})$ can be written in the form

$$\begin{aligned} H'(e^{j\omega T}) = (e^{-j\omega((N-1)/2)T})\Bigg\{ & h\left(\frac{N-1}{2}\right) \\ & + \sum_{n=0}^{(N-3)/2} 2h_n \cos\left[\omega\left(n - \left(\frac{N-1}{2}\right)\right)T\right]\Bigg\} \end{aligned} \tag{1.229c}$$

where again the first term is complex and the second term is real. Clearly, the phase is linear and a delay in the output is given by $((N - 1)/2)$ samples, which is an integer number of samples in the case of N odd, and in the case of N even, the delay in the output is $((N - 1)/2)$ samples, which is obviously not an integer. If the linear phase is necessary, i.e., the group delay is constant, then the FIR filters are ideal. There are several approaches of FIR filter design. A simple approach of course is to use Fourier series expansion of $H'(e^{j\omega T})$, where $H'(e^{j\omega T})$ is the desired function, such as a low-pass function. Identify the specifications. Noting that filter specifications in the digital domain are periodic, expand the filter specifications in terms of Fourier series. The problem, of course, is if the filter specifications are ideal, i.e., the function is a brickwall type function, then there will be ripples before and after the discontinuity. Recall the Gibb's phenomenon. To reduce the ripples, we can do few things. We can increase the transition band, shape the transition band response, and at the same time control the ripple size in the passband and satisfy the attenuation requirements in the stop bands. The approach we are going to follow is by using windows [28].

Recall the rectangular window, which is a pulse in the analog case and a sampled version of the pulse in the digital case. Other windows, such as a Hamming window, were defined earlier. Let the rectangular window be defined by

$$w_F(n) = \begin{cases} 1, & N_1 \leq n \leq N_2 \\ 0, & \text{otherwise} \end{cases} \tag{1.230}$$

Also, let $h_d(n)$ be the impulse response of the infinite impulse response digital filter. The impulse response of the finite impulse response filter can be expressed by

$$h(n) = h_d(n)w(n) \tag{1.231a}$$

where $w(n)$ is some window function, such as a rectangular window or a Hamming window, and $h_d(n)$ is the impulse response of the desired IIR filter. That is, $h_d(n)$ is the inverse Fourier transform of $H_d(e^{j\omega T})$. Note that n is used, rather than nT (i.e., T is suppressed). Noting that multiplication in the time domain corresponds to the convolution in the frequency domain, the Fourier transform of $h(n)$ is given by

$$H'(e^{j\omega T}) = H_d'(e^{j\omega T}) * W'(e^{j\omega T}) \tag{1.231b}$$

Noting that $H'(e^{j\omega T})$ is periodic with period $(2\pi/T)$, it can be written in terms of the normalized form, $H'(e^{j\Omega})$, which is periodic with period 2π. Now

$$H'(e^{j\Omega}) = H_d'(e^{j\Omega}) * W'(e^{j\Omega}) \tag{1.231c}$$

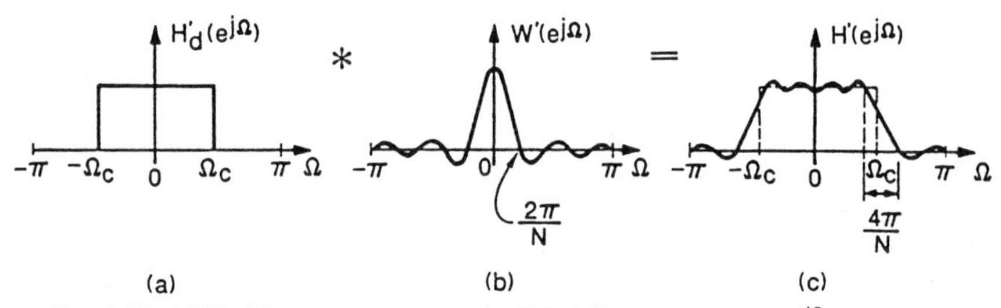

FIG. 1.22. (a) Ideal frequency response of a digital filter (low-pass) $H_d'(e^{j\Omega})$; (b) rectangular window function response, $W'(e^{j\Omega})$; (c) result of convolution, $H_d'(e^{j\Omega}) * W'(e^{j\Omega}) = H'(e^{j\Omega})$.

where $W'(e^{j\Omega})$ is the Fourier transform of the window function. Consider Figure 1.22, where $H_d'(e^{j\Omega})$ is the ideal low-pass filter function (Figure 1.22a). $W'(e^{j\Omega})$ is the Fourier transform of the rectangular window (Figure 1.22b). $H'(e^{j\Omega})$ is the result of the convolution (Figure 22c). From our earlier discussion, the main lobe width is $(2\pi/N)$ for the rectangular window. The first sidelobe level is -13.3 dB (-43 dB) for a rectangular (Hamming) window. For a Kaiser window, this is a variable and can be adjusted. The transform's main lobe width of a window is $k'(2\pi/N)$, where k' depends on the window. If the transition width of the filter is given by $(\Omega_2 - \Omega_1)$, where Ω_i are the edges of the transition band (see Figure (1.20a) in the low-pass case, where the transition band width is $(\Omega_{Dr} - \Omega_{Dc})$), then

$$\Omega_2 - \Omega_1 \geq k' \frac{2\pi}{N} \tag{1.232}$$

where $k' = 2$ (rectangular window), 4 (Hamming window), and k' is variable for a Kaiser window. This equation determines the value of N. To determine an integer number of samples of delay, select an integer N larger than the value determined by (1.232) that gives the desired number of samples for the delay.

The following step-by-step procedure can be used for the design [28].

1. Select a window type that satisfies the stop-band requirements. Minimum stopband attenuations for a rectangular window in -21 dB and, for a Hamming window, it is -53 dB. It is variable for a Kaiser window [5].
2. Select the number of points in the window to satisfy the transition width. This obviously varies with the type of the window. The number of points N, an integer, must satisfy

$$N \geq \frac{2\pi}{(\text{transition width})} \cdot k' \tag{1.233}$$

where k' is window dependent (4 for a Hamming window). The Hamming window is very popular.

3. The size of the window also depends upon the desired phase delay and the delay is given by $(N - 1)/2$ points.
4. The parameters can be adjusted in an iterative fashion to satisfy the filter design requirements. That is, find $H'(e^{j\Omega})$ from $h(n)$ and see if it satisfies the design requirements. If not, adjust the parameters and iterate.

Various other techniques are also available, see [5].

Short-Time Analysis

The concept of short-time Fourier analysis and synthesis is fundamental to describing any quasi-stationary (slowly time-varying) signal. If the signal properties change relatively slowly with time, a variety of short-time processing methods can be used to extract certain properties of the signal. Specifically, we mean that short segments of the signal can be isolated and processed as if they were short segments from a signal with fixed properties. Speech processing is an area where short-time analysis is used.

Most of the short-time processing techniques can be represented mathematically in the form [1]

$$Q_n = \sum_{m=-\infty}^{\infty} T[x(m)]w(n - m) \tag{1.234}$$

where $x(m)$ is the signal and $w(m)$ is the window sequence. The signal (possibly after linear filtering) is subjected to a transformation, $T[\cdot]$, which may be either linear or nonlinear. This sequence is multiplied by a window sequence positioned at n and the product terms are added.

As an example, consider the short-time energy of a signal. The energy in a discrete signal $x(m)$ is defined as

$$E = \sum_{m=-\infty}^{\infty} x^2(m) \tag{1.235}$$

which gives us very little information about the time-dependent properties of the signal. Using (1.234), a simple definition of short-time energy is

$$E_n = \sum_{m=n-N+1}^{n} x^2(m) \tag{1.236}$$

where we have used $T[x(m)] = x^2(m)$ and the window is the rectangular window. Note the subscript on E.

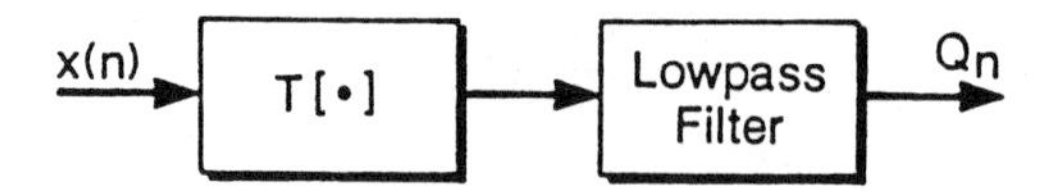

FIG. 1.23. Block diagram representation of Eq. (1.234).

Equation (1.234) can be represented by a block diagram representation, as shown in Figure 1.23. This follows from the fact that (1.234) is in the form of a discrete convolution of the window, $w(n)$, with the sequence, $T[x(n)]$. The low-pass aspects can be seen by looking at the transform of the window function. For example, see $W'(e^{j\Omega})$, the transform of the rectangular window function in Figure 1.22b.

Another function that is of interest is the autocorrelation function on a short-time basis. This function is

$$R_n(k) = \sum_{m=-\infty}^{\infty} x(m)w(n-m)x(m+k)w[n-(k+m)] \quad (1.237a)$$

which can be expressed in the form (note: $R_n(k) = R_n(-k)$)

$$R_n(k) = \sum_{m=-\infty}^{\infty} x(m)x(m-k)h_k(n-m) \quad (1.237b)$$

with

$$h_k(n) = w(n)w(n+k) \quad (1.237c)$$

Short-Time Fourier Transform

We would like to consider a function that reflects the time-varying properties of the signal on a short-time basis. Let $x(n)$ be a signal to be defined for all n, and let $X_n(e^{j\Omega})$ be the short-time Fourier transform of $x(n)$ evaluated at time n and frequency Ω (say Ω_k). Let this be defined as [1]

$$X_n(e^{j\Omega}) = \sum_{m=-\infty}^{\infty} x(m)w(n-m)\,e^{-j\Omega m} \quad (1.238a)$$

$$X_n(e^{j\Omega_k}) = \sum_{m=-\infty}^{\infty} x(m)w(n-m)\,e^{-j\Omega_k m} \quad (1.238b)$$

To use the time-dependent transform, the sequence must be absolutely summable. The window function, $w(n)$, is assumed to be of finite duration and the windowed sequence is absolutely summable for signals in real world. Also, note that the window selectively determines the portion of $x(n)$ being analyzed.

One can interpret (1.238) in two different ways. The first one is that of a filter bank analysis in which $X_n(e^{j\Omega})[X_n(e^{j\Omega_k})]$ is considered a function of n for a fixed $\Omega(\Omega_k)$. With this, (1.238b) can be written as a convolution:

$$X_n(e^{j\Omega_k}) = [x(n)\, e^{-j\Omega_k n}] * w(n)$$

where $w(n)$ is a window function and it has a low-pass filter characteristics. The modulation of x_n by $e^{-j\Omega_k n}$ corresponds to the shifting of frequency spectrum of $x(n)$ at frequency Ω_k to 0. The second interpretation of (1.238a) is as the normal Fourier transform of the sequence $[w(n - m)x(m)]$.

For a given value of n, $X_n(e^{j\Omega})$ has the same properties as the normal Fourier transform. The input sequence $x(n)$ can be recovered exactly from the time-varying Fourier transform $X_n(e^{j\Omega})$ by noting that it is the normal Fourier transform of the sequence $[w(n - m)x(m)]$. Therefore,

$$w(n - m)x(m) = \frac{1}{2\pi} \int_{-\pi}^{\pi} X_n(e^{j\Omega})\, e^{j\Omega m}\, d\Omega \qquad (1.239a)$$

If $w(0) \neq 0$, then

$$x(n) = \frac{1}{2\pi w(0)} \int_{-\pi}^{\pi} X_n(e^{j\Omega})\, e^{j\Omega n}\, d\Omega \qquad (1.239b)$$

This points out the fact that $x(n)$ can be recovered exactly from $X_n(e^{j\Omega})$ if $X_n(e^{j\Omega})$ is known for all values of Ω over one period and if $w(0) \neq 0$.

Basic Concepts of Pattern Recognition Methods

In an early part of this chapter, we considered a speech example and pointed out three simple cases; namely, no signal (or simply noise), a voiced part of a speech signal, and an unvoiced part of a speech signal. In the second example, we looked at an example of an image, wherein there are two bolts, a hexagonal bolt and a square bolt. The problem is how to distinguish one from the other. The concept, the theory and applications, of pattern recognition, is a vast area. In almost all the applications, processing the signal is a first step. The area is rather wide and we will consider only some rudimentary concepts [25] and use these concepts to illustrate the proposed.

One of the simplest problems is determining the existence or nonexistence of the signal. First, it may appear simple, but it is a difficult problem if noise is present. Second, if a signal is present before or after the silence, how do we determine the onset of the signal or silence? Third, how do we determine the starts and stops of different parts of the signal, such as phonemes? Fourth, how do we identify a phoneme, a word, a sentence, etc.?

With a simple knowledge of Fourier transforms, one would think, take the transform and see what frequencies we have at hand. Obviously, it is not that simple. Why? Remember the spectrum changes from phoneme to phoneme. That is, the signal is nonstationary. Nonstationary signal analysis is a vast area. It is beyond the scope here.

Consider two signals $x_1(t)$, $0 \leq t \leq T_1$ and $x_2(t)$, $0 \leq t \leq T_2$, and the sum $y(t) = x_1(t) + x_2(t - T_1)$ has the transform

$$Y(f) = X_1(f) + e^{-j2\pi f T_1} X_2(f)$$

where $X_i(f)$ are the transforms of $x_i(t)$. Note the delay, T_1, in $x_2(t - T_1)$. From this it is clear that the transform gives a mixture of the transforms of the two signals. Obviously, taking the Fourier transform of a word, a sentence, etc. does not tell you much. The problem is that we are dealing with nonstationary signals. Fortunately, speech is a stationary signal on a short-time basis. The spectral character of a speech signal stays the same within 10 to 20 milli seconds. So, we can consider that and investigate the recognition aspects. There are many aspects one may have to consider, such as what portion of speech we are considering. It is difficult to segment a speech signal into phonemes. In the following, we will look at the speech signal shown in Figure 1.1 and again in Figure 1.24a for ease corresponding to the portion of the word *sho* in the sentence "show the rich lady out" for a male voice. The signal is sampled at 8000 samples per second, and Figure 1.24a shows 2400 samples, i.e., for 0.3 secs. The signal, shown in the analog form for ease, is then windowed with a rectangular window of width 160 sample points (20 msec) every 20 points. Let the sample values be given by

$$x_n(k) = x[n(c) + k], \qquad 0 \leq k \leq 159, \quad 0 \leq n \leq 119 \tag{1.240}$$

In other words, we have extracted 160 sample points at a time by using a rectangular window, shifted the window by $c(=20)$ data points. It follows that there is an overlap of 140 points between successive windows. The process is continued until the data is exhausted. Clearly there is no overlap in the beginning and end of the data (end effects). The windowed data $x_n(k)$ can be processed to obtain the desired information. Note the window used is a rectangular window and other windows can be appropriately used of course.

In Figure 1.24b, the root mean square (RMS) values are plotted. The RMS values are computed every 20 samples; that is,

$$y_{\text{RMS}}(n) = \sqrt{(1/160) \sum_{k=1}^{160} x_n^2(k)}, \qquad 0 \leq n \leq 119 \tag{1.241}$$

From the plot, we can see that there are three major regions: a low-level RMS region, corresponding to silence region (lowest energy region); a middle-level RMS region, corresponding to the nonvowel sound *sh*; and finally the highest level RMS region, corresponding to the vowel region from (*ow*). The plot allows for identifying and segmenting these regions. The exact identification of the phoneme onsets and the ends may not always be possible.

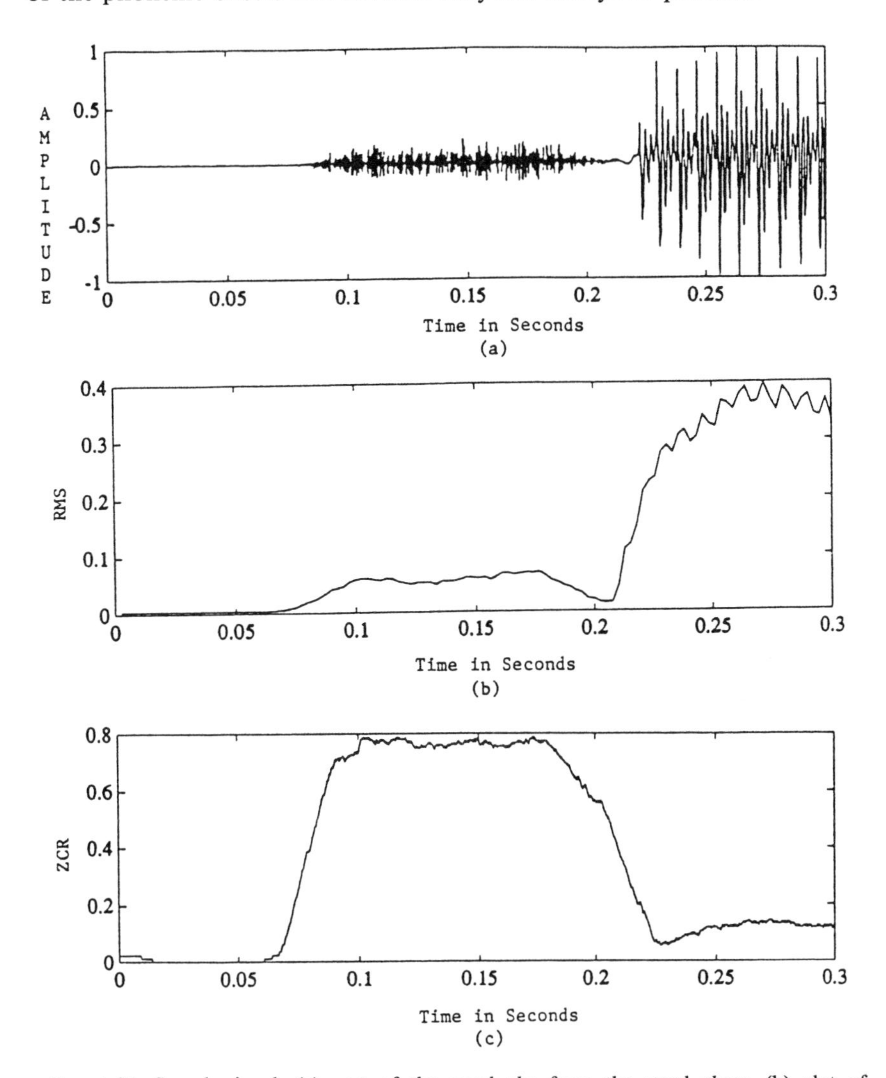

FIG. 1.24. Speech signal: (a) part of the word *sho* from the word *show*, (b) plot of RMS values using Eq. (1.241), (c) plot ZCR using Eq. (1.242) (waveforms courtesy of Dr. Scott King).

In Figure 1.24c, the zero crossing rate (ZCR), defined by

$$p_{ZCR}(n) = \frac{1}{2N} \sum_{k=1}^{N} |\text{sgn}\, x_n(k+1) - \text{sgn}\, x_n(k)| \tag{1.242}$$

is plotted, where the window length is taken as 160, as before, corresponding to a rectangular window. The ZCR is calculated with $c = 1$ in (1.240). The ZCR is a measure of the frequency content of the signal. As before, from the plot, we can see three regions, again corresponding to the silence, unvoiced, and voiced regions. The silence region is hard to predict, as it depends on the noise level and its frequency content. In our example, the noise is essentially negligible. Comparitively, the unvoiced part, i.e., the middle portion in the plot corresponding to *sh* has a higher frequency content than the voiced part *o*. Based on these two simple measures, the speech signal can be adaptively segmented on a short-time basis:

Low frequency and high energy:	voiced portion
High frequency and low energy:	unvoiced portion
Very low energy:	silence

For a more detailed discussion, see Rabiner and Schafer [1].

Now we have segmented the speech, how can we recognize the phonemes? For that matter, what are some simple pattern recognition techniques? An important step in this process is to find a set of discriminatory properties or features of the signal that will allow for classifying it into its class. For the example earlier, we used short-time energy and short-time zero crossing rates as features. Recognition of digits, one, two, three, etc., based on their acoustical waveforms is a simple pattern recognition problem. This would involve identification of the types of the phonemes, vowels, semivowels, dipthongs, etc. based on important features of the segment of the signal. Identifying features for pattern classification is a major problem. A brief introduction to this topic follows.

There are basically three types of features: physical, structural, and mathematical. The first two features are routinely used by humans, as they can be detected by the human sensory organs, such as the eye or ear, and the sensation of touch. Image processing is an area where these are used. Color is used as a physical feature, and structural features are used, such as buildings, roads, specific objects. Here we will be interested in the extraction of mathematical features that allow classification. Mathematical features are more general, and they can be easily implemented on a digital computer.

The first thing that comes to a signal analyst's mind when analyzing a signal is the Fourier analysis. That is, can the Fourier transform, or perhaps another transform, be used to come up with some mathematical features? So, let us look at the three segments we have considered earlier. Figure 1.25 gives the magnitude spectral plots obtained by using the following steps. Three segments are selected from silence and from *ow*, and *sh* from the word *show* illustrated in Figure 1.24a. The segments are windowed with 160 sample Hamming windows (20 msec), starting at 0.015 sec (for silence), at 0.1512 sec (for *sh*), and at 0.25 sec (for *ow*). The windowed signals are parametrized using the linear predictive analysis (LPC) discussed earlier.

Recall that in the LPC approach, the windowed signal, say $x(n)$, $0 \leq n < 160$, is parametrized in the form

$$x(n) = \sum_{k=1}^{p} a_k x(n-k) + \varepsilon(n) \tag{1.243a}$$

where $\varepsilon(n)$ is assumed to be the error signal, and the transfer function is assumed to be of the form

$$H'(z) = \frac{\sigma}{1 - \sum_{k=1}^{p} a_k z^{-k}} \tag{1.243b}$$

where σ is the gain constant of the model. The constant p corresponds to the order of the prediction. For each of the three cases, a tenth-order LPC model, i.e., $p = 10$, is used. The LPC spectrum can be obtained by substituting $z = e^{j\omega T}$. Figure 1.25 gives the LPC magnitude spectra, $20 \log |H'(e^{j\omega T})|$, for the three segments mentioned previously.

The noise-imbedded silence portion has a variable spectra with no special character. The vocal tract, which is an acoustical tube, has natural frequencies that are a function of its shape. These natural frequencies are usually called *formants*, and they provide important information about the spectrum and the resulting speech. The peaks of the spectrum correspond to formants. Notice the low-frequency character of the voiced portion and the three main peaks (see Fig. 1.25c). Clearly, these frequencies can be used in a pattern recognition model to distinguish this vowel from other vowels. Average formant frequencies for English vowels by adult speakers were given by, for example, Peterson and Barney [23]. Vowels are generally distinguished by the first three formants.

A very important parameter for speech and speaker recognition is the fundamental frequency or pitch. Voiced speech involves the vibration of the vocal chords, and pitch is referred to the fundamental frequency of the vibration. Pitch estimation is an important problem. One approach is find the period of the voiced region using the autocorrelation function on a short-time basis. Pitch periods could vary from 2 to 20 msec. A typical range is about 4 to 12 msec. The pitch period can also be estimated by

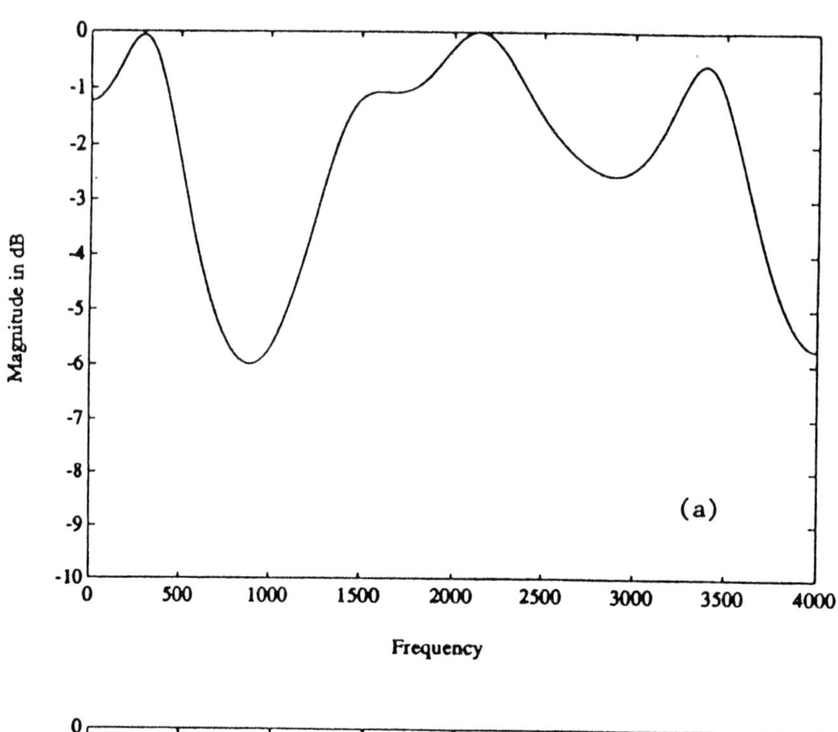
Magnitude in dB
0
-1
-2
-3
-4
-5
-6
-7
-8
-9
-10
0
500
1000
1500
2000
2500
3000
3500
4000
Frequency
(a)

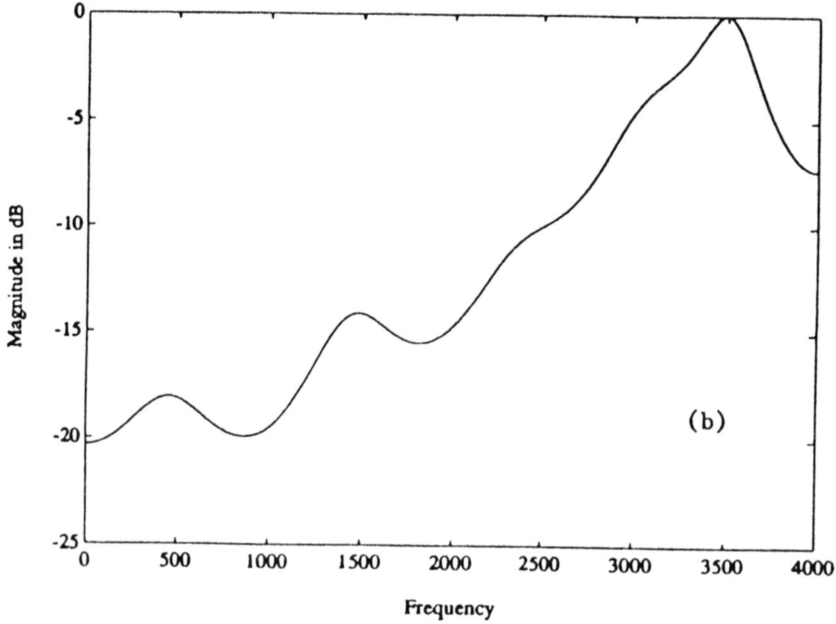
Magnitude in dB
0
-5
-10
-15
-20
-25
0
500
1000
1500
2000
2500
3000
3500
4000
Frequency
(b)

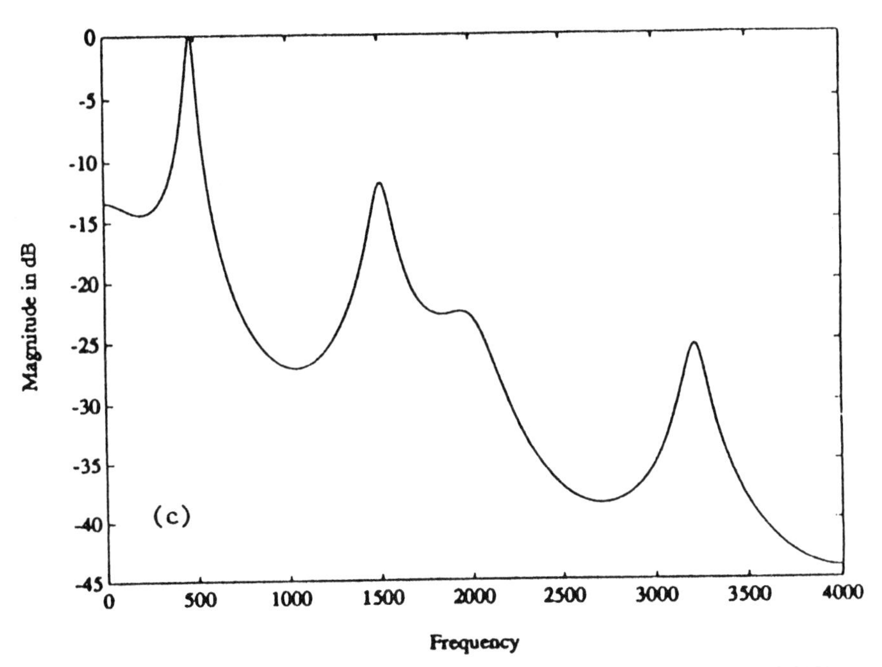

FIG. 1.25. LPC spectrums of (a) a portion of silence segment, data started at 0.0151 sec; (b) a portion of unvoiced segment *sh*, data started at 0.15125 sec; (c) a portion of voiced segment *ow*, data started at 0.25 sec. For the signal, see Figure 1.24a. All segments are Hamming windowed with 160 samples and the LPC model is a tenth-order model (waveforms courtesy of Dr. Scott King).

locating the fundamental spectral peak. Unfortunately, this is unreliable in situations where the speech signal is bandpass filtered, as in the case of a telephone signal. Clearly, pitch and the formant frequencies can be used in the speech and the speaker recognition model.

Finally, the unvoiced (*sh*) spectra is shown in Figure 1.25b. Compared to the voiced counterpart, the main spectral peaks are fewer and the main peak is at a much higher frequency than in the voiced case. The number of coefficients in the LPC model for an unvoiced case can be much lower than the voiced case. The order p corresponds to the number of poles required to represent adequately a given segment of the signal. Clearly, p in the unvoiced case is lower than in the voiced case.

Pattern classfication is an important problem in many areas. Speech recognition and speaker recognition are no exceptions. One of the important methods used in pattern recognition is the minimum distance pattern classification [25]. The reason for this is its simplicity. It is discussed briefly next.

Without loosing any generally, let $\mathbf{v}_k$ be an n-dimensional vector containing some of the important aspects of the ith signal, such as some important features like frequency locations, for example, formant frequencies for a speech signal, and others. The patterns of each class generally cluster around a representative pattern of that class, usually called a *prototype pattern*. If there are N patterns, then there are N prototype patterns, say $\mathbf{z}_1, \mathbf{z}_2, \ldots, \mathbf{z}_N$, where $\mathbf{z}_j$ represents n-dimensional vectors. The problem is, given an n-dimensional vector, say $\mathbf{v}_k$, to classify this vector as one of the N patterns.

As mentioned earlier, a simple measure is distance. The distance between two vectors, say $\mathbf{v}_k$ and $\mathbf{z}_i$, is given by

$$D(\mathbf{v}_k - \mathbf{z}_i) = \sqrt{\sum_{j=1}^{n} (v_{kj} - z_{ij})^2} \tag{1.244}$$

where v_{kj} and z_{ij} are the jth components of the vectors $\mathbf{v}_k$ and $\mathbf{z}_i$, respectively. Clearly, (1.244) is an L_2 measure, and such a measure can be used to classify a particular vector to a class. It is easy to visualize for $n = 2$. Figure 1.26 illustrates two classes of patterns with $\mathbf{z}_1$ and $\mathbf{z}_2$ as prototype pattern vectors. A simple boundary is chosen that separates the two patterns. For this simple case, if the received vector $\mathbf{v}_k$ is to the right (left) of the decision boundary, then the vector $\mathbf{v}_k$ belongs to class 2(1). This obviously can be extended to N classes. That is, the vector $\mathbf{v}_k$ belongs to class i, if $D(\mathbf{v}_k, \mathbf{z}_i)$ is the smallest number. In case of ties, i.e., $D(\mathbf{v}_k, \mathbf{z}_i) = D(\mathbf{v}_k, \mathbf{z}_l)$, for some i and l, then no decision can be made.

Finally, the LPC model is a good model for speech coding. These models can be used effectively to reduce the data rates. To compare data rates,

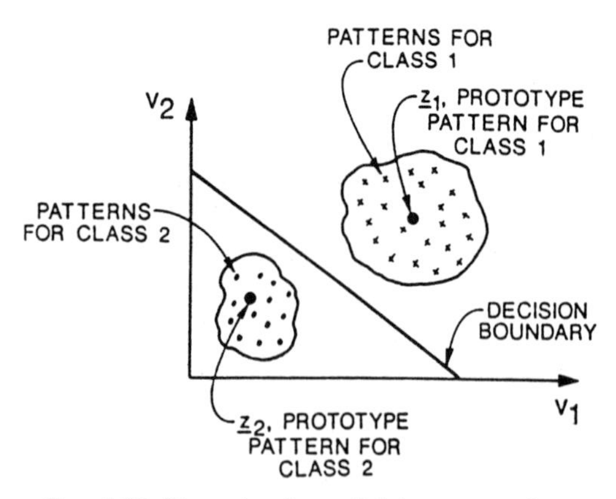

FIG. 1.26. Example of two disjoint pattern classes:

$$\mathbf{v}_k = \begin{bmatrix} v_{k1} \\ v_{k2} \end{bmatrix}, \quad \mathbf{z}_1 = \begin{bmatrix} z_{11} \\ z_{12} \end{bmatrix}, \quad z_2 = \begin{bmatrix} z_{21} \\ z_{22} \end{bmatrix}.$$

a conventional standard, usually referred to as the *toll-quality speech* corresponds to sampling speech at 8 KHz sampling rate with 8 bits per sample, which gives an effective rate of 64 kbps. This is obviously very high. So, a simple way to code speech is to use a set of bits to represent the LPC parameters, usually in the form of reflection coefficients (RCS) or line spectrum pairs (LSPS), decide whether voiced or unvoiced, and if voiced, give the pitch period information for a segment of windowed speech. Using this approach, there are several coding methods in the literature that use a few hundred bits to a few thousand bits. The popular ones include 2.4, 4.8, and 9.6 kbps; and there are others that use even few hundred bits or less. The very low bit rate coders generally lack the speaker identity in the speech, and they tend to be machinelike (monotonic). For information, for example, see [24].

This chapter presented some of the basic concepts associated with analog and digital signals, using continuous and discrete Fourier transforms. Concepts associated with analog and digital filtering and simple pattern recognition ideas are also included. The contents include a very small portion of the material available on the general topic of signal analysis. References are given if the reader is interested in further detail.

Problems

Consider the design of a system that determines the quality of a watermelon by using a nondestructive test. The proposed system uses several concepts discussed in this chapter. The following gives a few ideas of how one could design such a system. In pattern recognition, the tests could be either subjective or objective. Objective measures are easy to implement. Each of the problems that follow is useful in the proposed design in some sense, and of course, they are useful in other areas also.

The proposed test is based upon the impulse response of the watermelon. The input could be a tap or a light knock on the melon by a small hammer approximating an impulse. Assume the response $h(t)$ can be modeled in the form

$$h(t) = [A_1 \cos \omega_1 t + A_2 \cos \omega_2 t] \prod \left[\frac{t - (\tau/2)}{\tau} \right]$$

where A_1 and A_2 constants, $f_i = \omega_i / 2\pi$, $i = 1, 2$ are the two frequencies, and $\Pi(t)$ is the pulse function defined in (1.2). Assume $f_2 = 2(f_1)$.

1. Compute the Fourier transform of $h(t)$, $H(f)$.
2. Compute the energy spectral density of the signal, i.e., $G(f) = |H(f)|^2$, sketch the function $G(f)$, and see the effect of windowing the signal by increasing τ. What is the effect of changing the rectangular

window to, say, the Hamming window? Obviously, if f_1 and f_2 are close, it is possible that the energy spectral density may have only a single peak. Experiment with by varying τ or $(f_2 - f_1)$ to see the effect.

3. Sample the signal using rates of 0.75, 1, 1.5 times the Nyquist rate. Identify the problems related to under sampling. Using an N-point DFT and IDFT, sketch the functions to see the effects of sampling. Obviously, this problem will be easier if a PC or a main frame is used. If available, use $N = 64$, and $f_1 = 1$ kHz. If not available, assume $f_1 = 0.5$ Hz and $N = 8$. Sketch the functions after taking the IDFT.
4. Interpolation is an important part of signal analysis. A simple approach is by using DFT.

   (a) Compute $h(n)$ and its DFT, $H(k)$, $k = 0, 1, \ldots, N - 1$.
   (b) In the middle of the DFT sequence add $(l - 1)N$ zeros, and let this sequence be $H_I(k)$.
   (c) Take the IDFT of $H_I(k)$. The sequence will have (lN) samples. The time interval between the resultant samples is (T/l).

   Obviously, the larger is the value of l, the more samples we have and the more detail in the resultant signal. It is important to note that if the sampling frequency is not high enough, then the sampled signal will loose detail and interpolation will not restore the information. Why? Illustrate this using the results in Problem 3. What are some of the problems if l is not an integer (and $[(l - 1)N]$ obviously has to be an integer).
5. Decimation is opposite to the interpolation discussed in Problem 4. Starting with part b in Problem 4, you can go backward and obtain N samples from lN samples by deleting $(l - 1)N$ DFT samples and taking IDFT. In Problem 4, we purposely added zeros. In a decimation problem, they may have been obtained from a signal. By equating $(l - 1)N$ samples to zero in the middle of the spectrum, we are essentially using the low-pass filter operation. Can we use this procedure for other filter operations? If so, how?
6. Using the samples from $h(t)$, say, $t = 0, 1, \ldots, N - 1$, compute the LPC spectrum. Use, $N = 64$, if a PC is available. If not, use $N = 8$. Compare the peaks from the given signal. What happens if you add noise to $h(t)$? What should be p, the order of the prediction? Assume a white noise source if a PC is available. Add a colored noise that has a peak in the middle of the two peaks, and see the effect as the other two peaks (assume additive noise) by varying the amplitude of the spectrum in the middle.

7. Find the Butterworth, Tchebysheff I and II, and elliptic filter functions corresponding to the following low-pass specifications. Assume $(\omega_r/\omega_c) = 1.5$ and allow for $\varepsilon = 1$ in the pass-band and stop-band attenuation to $A = 20$.
8. Consider the same specifications as in Problem 7 for a digital filter problem. Use a sampling rate of $(4\omega_r/2\pi)$. Give the z-domain function.
9. For the specifications given in Problem 8, derive a finite impulse response filter using a Hamming window.
10. Consider the statement on the watermelon problem. Based on a large number of samples, the following information can be used to identify a tasty watermelon. The average values for A_1 and A_2 are 2 and 1, respectively. It has been determined that the actual values are not as important as the ratio of the value (A_2/A_1), and assume the important frequencies are normalized to 1 and 2 Hz. That is, $f_{1,\text{norm}} = (f_1/1\ \text{kHZ})$ and $f_{2,\text{norm}} = (f_2/2\ \text{kHz})$. The individual frequencies are considered important. Classify the following information to see whether the three cases will identify the good from the bad by using the least squared error:

$$E = \sqrt{\left(\frac{A_2}{A_1} - 0.5\right)^2 + (f_{1,\text{norm}} - 1)^2 + (f_{2,\text{norm}} - 2)^2}$$

You can assume the melon is good if $E \leq 0.1$.

A_2/A_1	$f_{1,\text{norm}}$	$f_{2,\text{norm}}$
0.55	1.2	1.8
0.4	0.8	2.2
0.5	1.1	2.1

References

[1] Rabiner, L., and R. W. Schafer. (1978). *Digital Processing of Speech Signals*. Prentice-Hall, Englewood Cliffs, NJ.
[2] Ziemer, R., and W. Tranter. (1990). *Principles of Communications: Systems, Modulation, and Noise*, 3rd ed. Houghton Mifflin Company, Boston.
[3] Papoulis A. (1962). *Signal Analysis*. McGraw-Hill, New York.
{4[Hershey, J., and R. Yarlagadda. (1986). *Data Tansportation and Protection*. Plenum, New York.
[5] Oppenheim, A. V., and R. W. Schafer. (1975). *Digital Signal Processing*. Prentice-Hall, Englewood Cliffs, NJ.
[6] Gold, B., and C. Rader. (1969). *Digital Processing of Signals*. McGraw-Hill, New York.
[7] Brigham, E. O. (1974). *The Fast Fourier Tansform*. Prentice-Hall, Englewood Cliffs, NJ.
[8] Byrd, R. H., and D. A. Payne. (1979). "Convergence of the Iteratively Reweighted Least Squares Algorithms for Robust Regression," Johns Hopkins University, Baltimore, Tech. Rept. #313.

[9] Money, A. H. (1982). "The Linear Regression Model: Lp Normed Estimation and the Choice of *p*," *Commun. Statist. Simmulation Computation* **11**, 89–109.
[10] Schroeder, J., and R. Yarlagadda. (1991). "Lp Normed Minimization with Application to Linear Predictive Modeling for Sinusoidal Frequency Estimation," *Signal Processing* **24**, 1–24.
[11] Yarlagadda, R., and J. Allen. (1982). "Aliasing Errors in Short-Time Analysis," *Signal Processing* **4**, 79–84.
[12] Storer, J. E. (1957). *Passive Network Synthesis*. McGraw-Hill, New York.
[13] Giordano, A. A., and F. M. Hsu. (1985). *Least Squares Estimation with Applications to Digital Signal Processing*. John Wiley and Sons, New York.
[14] Press, W. H., B. P. Flannery, S. A. Teukolsky, and W. T. Vetterling. (1989). *Numerical Recipes*. Cambridge University Press, Cambridge.
[15] Marple, S. L., Jr. (1987). *Digital Spectral Analysis with Applications*. Prentice-Hall, Englewood Cliffs, NJ.
[16] Allen, J. B. (1977). "Short-Time Spectral Analysis, Synthesis, and Modification by Discrete Fourier Transform," *IEEE Trans. ASSP* **ASSP-25**, 235–238.
[17] Kaiser, J. F. (1966). "Digital Filters,". In *System Analysis by Digital Computer* (F. F. Kuo and J. F. Kaiser, eds.). Wiley and Sons, New York.
[18] DeFatta, D. J., J. G. Lucas, and W. S. Hodgkiss. (1988). *Digital Signal Processing: A System Design Approach*. John Wiley and Sons, New York.
[19] Trench, W. F. (1969). "An Algorithm for the Inversion of Finite Toeplitz Matrices," *J. SIAM* **12**, 515–522.
[20] Yarlagadda, R., and B. N. Suresh Babu. (1980). "On the Application of FFT to the Solution of a System of Normal Equations," *IEEE Trans. on Circuits and Systems* **CAS-27**, 151–154.
[21] Weinberg, L. (1962). *Network Analysis and Synthesis*. McGraw-Hill, New York.
[22] *Handbook of Mathematical Functions with Formulas, Graphs, and Mathematical Tables* (M. Abromowitz and I. A. Stegun, eds.). (1970). U.S. Dept. of Commerce, National Bureau of Standards, Applied Mechanics Series-55.
[23] Peterson, L. C., and H. Barney. (1952). "Control Methods Used in a Study of Vowels," *J. Acoust. Soc. Am.* **24**, 175–184.
[24] O'Shaughnessy, D. (1987). "Speech Communications, Human and Machine," Addison-Wesley, Reading, MA.
[25] Tou, J. T., and R. C. Gonzalez. (1974). *Pattern Recognition Principles*, Addison-Wesley, Reading, MA.
[26] Parson, T. (1986). *Voice and Speech Processing*. McGraw-Hill, New York.
[27] Pham, T. T., and R. J. P. diFigueiredo. (1989). "Maximum Likelihood Estimation of a Class of Non-Gaussian Densities with Application to Lp Deconvolution," *IEEE Trans. ASSP* **37**, 73–82.
[28] Ludeman, L. C. (1986). *Fundamentals of Digital Signal Processing*. Harper & Row, New York.

Chapter 2

An Overview of Linear Systems and Discrete-Time Kalman Filtering

The focus of this chapter is on the description of a discrete-time linear system both in the time domain and the z-domain, with applications to systems with feedback and discrete-time Kalman filtering. We will develop three fundamental methods for describing a discrete linear system: linear difference equations, discrete impulse function, and discrete state variable representation. All three methods have counterparts within continuous time linear system theory; most classical results from conventional continuous time linear systems carry over to the analysis and design of discrete-time linear systems in a natural manner.

Analogous to the role Laplace transformations play in simplifying the analysis and design of continuous time systems, z-transform methods offer a powerful tool for the designer of discrete-time systems. Although developed by mathematicians over 200 years ago, the z-transform has been applied by engineers in the analysis of discrete-time problems by transforming a discrete sequence into a function of the complex variable z. Thus, similar to Laplace transformation methods, we may invoke the concept of transfer functions or use the z-transform to recast the set of difference equations, which relate the output of a linear system to the system input, into an equivalent algebraic expression.

With time domain and z-domain theory well in hand, two system design problems will be briefly reviewed: the minimum energy control problem, and the quadratic index controller design. Finally, the important field of discrete-time Kalman filtering will be developed.

Discrete Linear Systems—Time Domain

Measurable physical quantities, human-made or naturally occurring, present within our environment may be continuous in nature or intrinsically discrete. Examples of continuous variables (frequently a function of time) abound: atmospheric temperature, speech and music, voltage and currents used to control electronic devices such as clocks and radios, and aircraft sensor data used by modern flight control computers to fly a prescribed air navigational route. Other quantities, such as a sequence of closing stock market quotes recorded over a three-month period, are inherently discrete in nature. Most systems in our modern society, regardless of whether the system processes continuous quantities or discrete quantities, probably contain a digital processing element. Thus, it is desirable to consider techniques for discrete system analysis. Once the province of complex, costly, military-oriented systems, discrete-time system concepts have penetrated the commercial consumer marketplace. Compact disc players, for example, contain digital filters to alter musical characteristics for some desired purpose.

Fortunately, most concepts from continuous-time linear system theory possess a discrete-time counterpart. This enables the practicing engineer, perhaps schooled solely in continuous-time concepts, to rapidly learn the jargon and principles of discrete-time linear system analysis. Linear differential equations used to relate system input and output quantities are replaced by linear difference equations. System impulse response characterization, fundamental to continuous-time linear system analysis, carries over to discrete-time systems directly. State variable representation, a powerful tool exploited by system engineers to land a person on the moon, is particularly well-suited for complex discrete-time system analysis and design. Likewise, the familiar concepts of controllability and observability from control theory are conveniently defined for discrete-time systems. Finally, linear difference equations with time-varying coefficients may be accommodated with relative ease.

Linear Difference Equations

Difference equations serve as discrete-time counterparts of differential equations, long considered a powerful technique that relates the input and output variables of continuous time systems. The differential equation description of continuous systems is so fundamental to modern engineering analysis that the subject is introduced during the freshman year of study; indeed, study of this historic and fascinating branch of mathematics continues unabated throughout the undergraduate and graduate curricula.

For a linear time-invarient system, a difference equation may be expressed

$$\sum_{k=0}^{N} a_k y(n-k) = \sum_{k=0}^{M} b_k x(n-k), \qquad n \geq 0 \tag{2.1}$$

where a_k and b_k are known scalar constants; $x(n)$ and $y(n)$ are the system input and output, respectively. In general, of course, the constants may be complex, but for most applications, a_k and b_k will be real. The input-output description given by equation (2.1) is quite general and thus may be invoked to describe a wide variety of discrete-time linear systems. Examples where a difference input–output description is particularly useful include numerous physical dynamic systems, such as a satellite platform that requires extensive orbital analysis plus the plethora of discrete-time control system algorithms required for stabilization. Another common application of difference equations, pervasive in the world of modern digital signal processing, involves modeling some desired filtering algorithm to analyze or modify a data set or perhaps an electrical signal carrying information, such as speech or music, in a controlled fashion.

An advantage of the difference equation representation given by (2.1) is that the system output, $y(n)$, may be computed recursively if required or desired, as is common in real-time applications. This procedure, analogous to solving differential equations on an analog computer, may be accomplished in a straightforward manner by solving (2.1) for $y(n)$. Thus,

$$y(n) = \frac{1}{a_0}\left[\sum_{k=0}^{M} b_k x(n-k) - \sum_{k=1}^{N} a_k y(n-k)\right], \qquad n \geq 0 \tag{2.2}$$

with $y(-k)$, $k = 1, 2, \ldots, N$ representing the initial conditions for the difference equations, and $x(n-k)$, $n \geq 0$, $k = 0, 1, \ldots, M$ is a known input function or sequence of discrete numbers. Clearly, for computer-based processing, either real-time or off-line, Eq. (2.2) maps directly into a "for" loop. Additionally, a hardware implementation of (2.2) is convenient. Both ideas may be illustrated via a simple first-order example.

Consider the difference equation with $M = N = 1$, $a_0 = b_0 = 1$, and $a_1 = -0.5$.

$$y(n) = x(n) + 0.5y(n-1) \tag{2.3}$$

Let the initial condition $y(-1) = 0$, and $x(n) = u(n)$, $n \geq 0$, where $u(n)$ is the discrete step function. The recursion $y(n)$ defined by (2.3), $n \geq 0$, may be programmed directly on a computer as shown in Table 2.1 over $n = 0, 1, \ldots, 19$, and $y(n)$ is plotted in Figure 2.1. A digital hardware implementation utilizing an adder, gain, and delay Δ of Eq. (2.3) for

TABLE 2.1

COMPUTER PROGRAM IMPLEMENTATION OF EQUATION (2.3)

```
y(0) = x(0)
for n = 1:19
    y(n) = x(n) + 0.5 * y(n - 1)
end
```

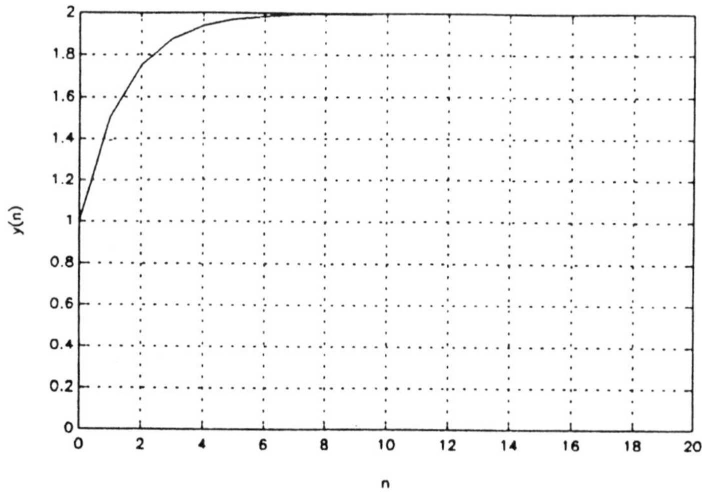

FIG. 2.1. $y(n)$, $n = 0, 1, \ldots, 19$, from Eq. (2.3) implemented by computer code in Table 2.1.

arbitrary $x(n)$ is given in Figure 2.2. A network such as shown in Figure 2.2 is not unique; many different network topologies implement Eq. (2.3) or more generally Eq. (2.1) and (2.2), each with differing pros and cons. This field falls properly into digital filtering and numerous excellent textbooks provide detailed discussion [1–11].

A disadvantage of solving difference equations in the preceding manner, natural though the technique may be for on-line or off-line processing, is that an analytical solution, if indeed one exists, is usually not readily apparent. When solving textbook problems, a recognizable geometric series may obtain, but such is not often the case for real-world problems. Thus, for system analysis and design purposes, it is highly desirable to find analytical solutions to a set of difference equations. Perhaps the most common time-domain technique for solving difference equations to obtain an expression for arbitrary n is by determining the homogeneous and particular solutions for Eq. (2.1), then appealing to the principle of superposition by writing the

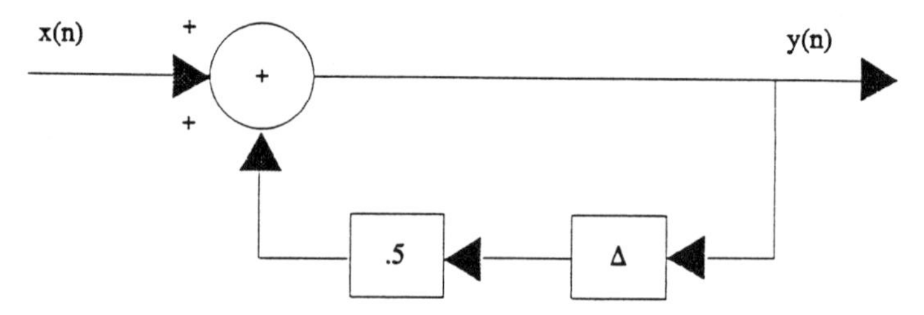

FIG. 2.2. Digital hardware implementation for Eq. (2.3).

complete solution as the sum of the two components. Since z-transform methods are very powerful, familiar to most practicing engineers, and ultimately serve our purposes better, we refer the interested reader to the numerous textbooks available for time-domain solution of difference equations [1–11].

Impulse Response Representation

A second convenient method of relating system input and output variables is through the system impulse response, $h(n)$ depicted graphically in Figure 2.3. By definition, $h(n)$ is simply the output of a system when the input is a unit impulse function, $x(n) = \delta(n)$, with zero initial conditions. For the discrete-time convolution formulas

$$y(n) = \sum_{k=-\infty}^{\infty} x(k)h(n-k) \tag{2.4}$$

or

$$y(n) = \sum_{k=-\infty}^{\infty} x(n-k)h(k) \tag{2.5}$$

that relate the system output, $y(n)$, to the system input, $x(n)$, through the impulse response, $h(n)$, we have assumed a linear shift-invariant system. It is easy to justify Eq. (2.4) or Eq. (2.5) by noting that $x(n)$ may be expressed

$$x(n) = \sum_{k=-\infty}^{\infty} x(k)\delta(n-k) \tag{2.6}$$

assuming shift invariance, and observing that an input $\delta(n-k)$ produces an output $h(n-k)$; then by assuming linearity, the output, $y(n)$, corresponds to the weighted sum in Eq. (2.6), as given in Eq. (2.4). Equation (2.5) follows directly from (2.4). If the system is not shift invariant, $h(n)$ is not a function of $(n-k)$, but rather of (n, k); in this case, the simple discrete convolution formula given by Eq. (2.4) may not be used, but could be replaced by

$$y(n) = \sum_{k=-\infty}^{\infty} x(k)h(n, k) \tag{2.7}$$

and computations carried out. As simplified mathematical expressions are unlikely to obtain from Eq. (2.7), it may be easier to solve (2.2) recursively.

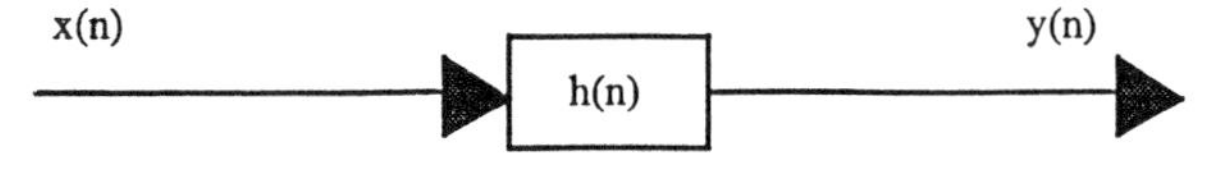

FIG. 2.3. Discrete-time system with input $x(n)$, impulse response $h(n)$, and output $y(n)$.

Matters deteriorate quickly if additionally the system is nonlinear; except for a few textbook problems, generally speaking, one must resort to a brute force solution to the difference equations relating system input and output. The same comments apply as well if the system contains time-varying coefficients. For the most part, we restrict the discussion, for reasons of mathematical simplification and widespread real-world application, to linear, shift-invariant, constant coefficient systems.

If system impulse response $h(n)$ is unknown, a frequent occurence, several methods are available for computing (more likely estimating!) $h(n)$. One may simply use $x(n) = \delta(n)$ in Eq. (2.2) and solve the resulting series. For the example defined by Eq. (2.3), this procedure produces the impulse response

$$h(n) = (0.5)^n, \qquad n \geq 0 \tag{2.8}$$

which from Eq. (2.4) or (2.5) results in

$$y(n) = 2 - (0.5)^n, \qquad n \geq 0 \tag{2.9}$$

Equation (2.9) is exactly the function already graphed in Figure 2.1. An analytical solution, such as given by (2.9), is naturally convenient for system analysis or if $y(n)$ for specific values of n is desired. Other methods may be used to find $h(n)$ from Eq. (2.2), but will not be discussed since z-transform techniques are easier to use and will be reviewed later in this chapter. In real-world situations, the task of estimating $h(n)$ may be formidable; fortunately copious literature exists to aid the engineer in this endeavor (termed *system identification*) [12, 13]. A simple example will be presented in the section on z-transforms to illustrate the basic concept of estimating $h(n)$ from measured time series data. The design of sophisticated discrete-time control systems, for example, is commonly preceded by a system identification step to estimate $h(n)$.

State-Variable Representation

The linear difference equation (with possibly time-varying coefficients) may be generalized by the state-variable approach. A major advantage of using state variables for linear system analysis and design is that this approach reveals the hidden workings of complex network topologies. By contrast, analysis and design based upon only linear difference equations (Eq. 2.1) or equivalently a convolution relationship (Eq. 2.4) relate just the output variable to the input variable; the internal structure of the linear system is not apparent and not unique. A second advantage is that the state variable method admits a unified representation of single input–single output systems and multiple input–multiple output systems. Linear systems

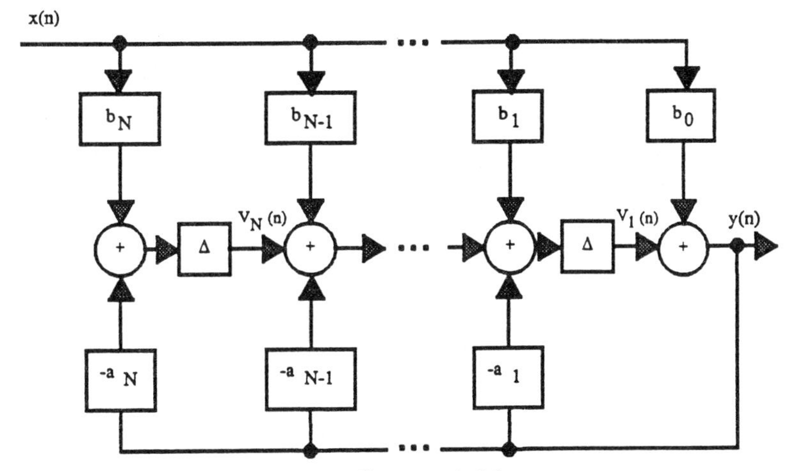

FIG. 2.4. First canonical form.

with time-varying coefficients are accommodated via the state-variable approach with relative ease. Finally, state-variable equations map onto current computer structures.

The concept of state variables, although a fairly simple idea when one becomes adjusted to the notation, is best introduced by a single input–single output example, followed by the general case. The first canonical form for implementation of Eq. (2.2) is shown in Figure 2.4. The state vector $\mathbf{v}(n)$, is given by the N-dimensional vector

$$\mathbf{v}(n) = [v_1(n)v_2(n) \dots v_N(n)]' \tag{2.10}$$

The state-variable equations for the single input–single output time-invariant linear system shown in Figure 2.4 are

$$\mathbf{v}(n+1) = A\mathbf{v}(n) + \mathbf{b}x(n) \tag{2.11a}$$

$$y(n) = \mathbf{c}\mathbf{v}(n) + dx(n) \tag{2.11b}$$

where matrix A is $N \times N$, b is an $N \times 1$ column vector, $\mathbf{c}$ is a $1 \times N$ row vector, and d is a scalar. Matrix A, vector $\mathbf{b}$, vector $\mathbf{c}$, and scalar d are defined respectively by

$$A = \begin{bmatrix} -a_1 & 1 & 0 & \dots & 0 \\ -a_2 & 0 & 1 & \dots & 0 \\ \vdots & & & & \\ -a_N & 0 & 0 & \dots & 0 \end{bmatrix} \tag{2.12a}$$

$$\mathbf{b} = \begin{bmatrix} b_1 - a_1 b_0 \\ b_2 - a_2 b_0 \\ \vdots \\ b_N - a_N b_0 \end{bmatrix} \tag{2.12b}$$

$$\mathbf{c} = [1 \quad 0 \quad 0 \quad \ldots \quad 0] \tag{2.12c}$$

$$d = b_0 \tag{2.12d}$$

As a specific example, from Figure 2.4, let $a_0 = b_0 = 1$, $b_1 = y_2$, $b_2 = -1$, and $a_1 = a_2 = -\frac{1}{4}$. For this case $v(n) = [v_1(n)v_2(n)]'$, and the state equation representation is

$$\mathbf{v}(n + 1) = A\mathbf{v}(n) + \mathbf{b}x(n) \tag{2.13a}$$

$$y(n) = \mathbf{cv}(n) + dx(n) \tag{2.13b}$$

where

$$A = \begin{bmatrix} \frac{1}{4} & 1 \\ \frac{1}{4} & 0 \end{bmatrix} \tag{2.13c}$$

$$\mathbf{b} = \begin{bmatrix} \frac{3}{4} \\ \frac{-3}{4} \end{bmatrix} \tag{2.13d}$$

$$\mathbf{c} = [1 \quad 0] \tag{2.13e}$$

$$d = 1 \tag{2.13f}$$

The second canonical form is given next. For this standard form, the state equations are

$$\hat{\mathbf{v}}(n + 1) = \hat{A}\hat{\mathbf{v}}(n) + \hat{\mathbf{b}}\mathbf{x}(n) \tag{2.14a}$$

$$\mathbf{y}(n) = \hat{\mathbf{c}}\hat{\mathbf{v}}(n) + \hat{\mathbf{d}}\mathbf{x}(n) \tag{2.14b}$$

with

$$\hat{A} = \begin{bmatrix} 0 & 1 & 0 & \ldots & 0 \\ 0 & 0 & 1 & \ldots & 0 \\ \vdots & & & & \vdots \\ 0 & 0 & & \ldots & 1 \\ -a_N & -a_{N-1} & & \ldots & -a_1 \end{bmatrix} \tag{2.15a}$$

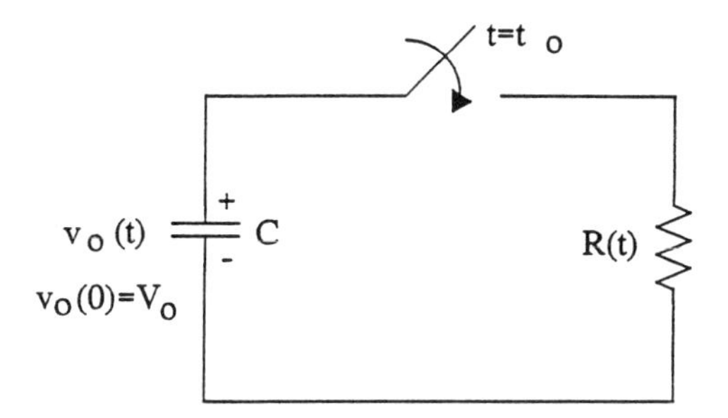

FIG. 2.5. Time-varying R-C circuit example.

$$\hat{\mathbf{b}} = \begin{bmatrix} 0 \\ 0 \\ \vdots \\ 1 \end{bmatrix} \tag{2.15b}$$

$$\hat{\mathbf{c}} = [a_N b_0 - b_N \quad \ldots \quad a_2 b_0 - b_2 \quad a_1 b_0 - b_1] \tag{2.15c}$$

$$\hat{d} = b_0 \tag{2.15d}$$

With the two state descriptions defined by Eqs. (2.13) and (2.14), it can be shown that a nonsingular matrix P exists such that

$$\mathbf{v}(n) = P\hat{\mathbf{v}}(n) \tag{2.16}$$

Additionally, with transformation matrix P, it may be shown that

$$\hat{A} = PAP^{-1}, \qquad \hat{\mathbf{b}} = P^{-1}\mathbf{b}, \qquad \hat{\mathbf{c}} = \mathbf{c}P, \qquad \text{and} \qquad \hat{d} = d \tag{2.17}$$

Clearly, in addition to relating the first and second canonical forms, numerous transformations from one network implementation to another may be defined simply by choosing P to be any nonsingular $N \times N$ matrix. The transformation $\hat{A} = PAP^{-1}$ is termed a *similarity transformation* and occurs frequently in matrix theory.

A state equation defined by Eq. (2.13), for $n \geq 0$ and initial condition $\mathbf{v}(0) = \mathbf{v}_0$ may be solved by the iteration

$$\mathbf{v}(n) = A^n\mathbf{v}(0) + \sum_{j=0}^{n-1} A^{n-j-1}\mathbf{b}x(j) \tag{2.18}$$

The quantity A^n is termed the *state transition matrix*, denoted

$$\Phi(n) = A^n \tag{2.19}$$

The Cayley–Hamilton theorem states that any matrix A, arbitrary size $N \times N$, satisfies its own characteristic equation:

$$\det(A - \lambda I) = 0 \tag{2.20}$$

which may be used to find an analytical expression for A^n if it is not desired or practical to solve the state equations via iteration. We omitted an example for this procedure however, since z-transform methods greatly simplify the task of computing $\Phi(n) = A^n$ and will be demonstrated in a later section.

The impulse response of the system described for state-variable equations may be devised by setting $\mathbf{v}(0) = 0$ and $x(n) = \delta(n)$. Following this procedure, we find that

$$h(n) = \mathbf{c}A^{n-1}\mathbf{b} + \mathrm{d}\delta(n) \tag{2.21}$$

The next step is to generalize the state-variable representation developed for a single input–single output system to a multiple input–multiple output system. Such a generalized system will be the most useful for linear system analysis and design. We consider both purely digital systems and hybrid systems; we use a normalized sampling period of $T = 1$ sec. We restrict our attention to linear systems, but consider difference equations with time-varying coefficients as well as the constant coefficient case.

A continuous-time system may be represented by a set of first-order differential equations in state equation format. In an analogous manner, a purely discrete system, in state-variable form, is represented by a set of first-order difference equations. Since many physical problems consist of both continuous-time and discrete-time elements, we also will blend both analog and discrete state-variable equations into a hybrid set of differential and difference equations.

In vector matrix form, we may express a linear, time-varying system in state variable form as

$$\dot{\mathbf{x}}(t) = A(t)\mathbf{x}(t) + B(t)\mathbf{u}(t) \tag{2.22}$$

$$\mathbf{y}(t) = C(t)\mathbf{x}(t) + D(t)\mathbf{u}(t), \tag{2.23}$$

where $A(t)$ is an $n \times n$ square matrix, $B(t)$ is $n \times p$, $C(t)$ is $q \times n$, and $D(t)$ is $q \times p$. The vector $\mathbf{x}(t)$ is an $n \times 1$ column matrix, termed the *state vector*,

$$\mathbf{x}(t) = [x_1(t) \quad x_2(t) \quad \ldots \quad x_n(t)]' \tag{2.24}$$

The system input vector,

$$\mathbf{u}(t) = [u_1(t) \quad u_2(t) \quad \ldots \quad u_p(t)]' \tag{2.25}$$

is a $p \times 1$ column vector, and the output vector, $y(t)$ is defined as

$$\mathbf{y}(t) = [y_1(t) \quad y_2(t) \quad \ldots \quad y_q(t)]' \tag{2.26}$$

which is a $q \times 1$ column vector. For a linear, time-invariant system, the coefficient matrix elements are constant and consequently Eqs. (2.22) and (2.23) may be written

$$\dot{\mathbf{x}}(t) = A\mathbf{x}(t) + B\mathbf{u}(t) \tag{2.27}$$

$$\mathbf{y}(t) = Cx(t)D\mathbf{u}(t) \tag{2.28}$$

which is the case for many systems arising in engineering applications. Although we will generally restrict our attention to systems possessing constant coefficients, which admit transform methods such as the z-transform and the Laplace transform, it is worthwhile to remember that a state-variable problem formulation is reasonably amenable to solution for systems with time-varying coefficients. For a time-varying system, the state transition matrix, $\phi(t, t_0)$, is an $n \times n$ matrix that satisfies the state equations

$$\dot{\mathbf{x}} = A(t)\mathbf{x}(t) \tag{2.29}$$

that is,

$$\dot{\phi}(t, t_0) = A(t)\phi(t, t_0) \tag{2.30}$$

with the initial condition $\phi(t_0, t_0) = I$, where I is the $n \times n$ identity matrix, and t_0 is some arbitrary starting time. It may be shown that an analytic solution for the state transition matrix is

$$\phi(t, t_0) = \exp\left[\int_{t_0}^{t} A(\tau)\,\mathrm{d}\tau\right] \tag{2.31}$$

If Eq. (2.31) is not easily expressed in closed form, the exponential function may be expanded in the conventional manner, and the resulting infinite series truncated to a finite number of terms so that a desired numerical accuracy is obtained. Although not obvious, $\phi(t, t_0)$ cannot be singular, a comforting fact indeed.

For the time-invariant case, Eq. (2.31) via straightforward integration reduces to

$$\phi(t - t_0) = \exp[A(t - t_0)] \tag{2.32}$$

without loss of generality, we let $t_0 = 0$ and write

$$\phi(t) = \exp[At] \tag{2.33}$$

a convenient and compact form of the state transition matrix for a linear system with constant coefficients. The transition matrix may also be expressed as the infinite series (truncated for computer implementation)

$$\phi(t) = \sum_{k=0}^{\infty} \frac{A^k t^k}{k!} \tag{2.34}$$

for cases where Eq. (2.33) does not possess a convenient closed form solution, not uncommon when analyzing real-world systems. As for time-varying cases, in analogous fashion, we have that $\phi(0) = I$, where I is an $n \times n$ identity matrix, $\phi(t)$ is nonsingular (A assumed finite), and $\phi^{-1}(t) = \phi(-t)$, a handy identity.

With a state transition matrix determined, that satisfies the homogeneous state equation (2.29), and combining the solution of the nonhomogeneous time-varying state equations, we may write the total solution for the system state vector $\mathbf{x}(t)$ as

$$\mathbf{x}(t) = \phi(t, t_0)\mathbf{x}(t_0) + \int_{t_0}^{t} \phi(t, \tau)B(\tau)\mathbf{u}(\tau)\, d\tau \tag{2.35}$$

at any time t and t_0. For the time-invariant (constant coefficient) case, Eq. (2.35) simplifies to

$$\mathbf{x}(t) = \phi(t - t_0)\mathbf{x}(t_0) + \int_{t_0}^{t} \phi(t - \tau)B(\tau)\mathbf{u}(\tau)\, d\tau \tag{2.36}$$

Note that Eqs. (2.35) and (2.36) are composed of two easily recognized parts: a term dependent only upon the initial state and the state transition matrix, and a convolution integral consisting of the state transition matrix and the input. The two parts are termed, respectively, in a variety of manner: homogeneous solution and nonhomogeneous solution (i.e., particular integral), force-free response and forced response, and perhaps less frequently, the zero-input response and the zero-state response.

Time-Varying State Equation Example

Since it is not uncommon for a linear system to contain elements with time-varying characteristics, it is worthwhile to consider a simple example of this case. For simplicity, we consider a first-order system, which obviously does not require the generality of a state variable representation, since we wish to emphasize the time-varying aspects of the solution.

Consider the R-C circuit in Figure 2.5 with a known time-varying resistor, $R(t) = R_0 - (2/C)t$, constant capacitance C, with initial voltage $V_C(0) = V_0$. We wish to find $V_C(t)$, over the time interval $t_0 \le t \le R_0C/2$, with $R_0C/2$ chosen for physical realizability. The switch closes at $t = t_0$.

The differential equation for $V_C(t)$ in the circuit is

$$R(t)C\frac{\mathrm{d}V_C}{\mathrm{d}t} + V_C(t) = 0, \qquad V_C(0) = V_0 \tag{2.37}$$

A set of state equations may be written

$$\dot{x} = \frac{-1}{R(t)C}x(t) + (0)u(t) \tag{2.38}$$

$$y(t) = (1)x(t) + (0)u(t), \tag{2.39}$$

where, from Eqs. (2.27) and (2.28), we have that $A = [-1/R(t)C]$, $B = [0]$, $C = [1]$, and $D = [0]$. With $A(\tau)$ as given, the state-transition matrix, actually a scalar function in this example, becomes

$$\phi(t, t_0) = \sqrt{\frac{R_0C - 2t}{R_0C - 2t_0}} \tag{2.40}$$

Note that $\phi(t, t_0) = 1$, which does not prove Eq. (2.40) correct, but is a quick and easy check that does catch many algebraic errors. With $\phi(t, t_0)$ as defined in Eq. (2.40), and $x(0) = V_0$, from Eq. (2.35), we may write the solution as

$$x(t) = V_0 \cdot \sqrt{\frac{R_0C - 2t}{R_0C - 2t_0}} \tag{2.41}$$

valid for

$$t_0 \le t \le \frac{R_0C}{2}, \qquad 0 \le t_0 \le \frac{R_0C}{2} \tag{2.42}$$

The solution as given by Eq. (2.41) appears strange (i.e., no decaying exponentials are present) simply because we are generally unaccustomed to solving even simple R-C first-order circuit example problems with time-varying coefficients. Although Laplace transform and z-transform methods are not generally applicable as an aid in time-varying coefficient problems, the state-variable method produced a solution in a simple and straightforward manner. Extension of this technique for higher order systems is relatively easy and will be illustrated by example for the constant coefficient case.

As a final note, we compute the power, $P(t)$, dissipated in $R(t)$ directly and find that

$$P(t) = \frac{V_0^2}{R_0 - 2t_0/C}, \qquad t_0 \le t \le \frac{R_0C}{2} \tag{2.43}$$

A surprising result is that the power dissipated in $R(t)$ is constant! Note that for $t = R_0C/2$, $V_C(t) = 0$, and the current through $R(t) \to \infty$!

Constant-Coefficient State-Variable Example

In this example, we introduce a method for diagonalizing the system state matrix, as previously discussed and summarized in Eq. (2.17), termed *modal decomposition*, in addition to solving state-variable equations by conventional techniques. For this example, with state equations defined by (2.27) and (2.28), let

$$A = \begin{bmatrix} 0 & 1 \\ 8 & -2 \end{bmatrix}, \quad B = \begin{bmatrix} 1 \\ 1 \end{bmatrix}, \quad C = [1 \quad 0], \quad D = [0 \quad 0], \quad \mathbf{x}(0) = \begin{bmatrix} 0 \\ 0 \end{bmatrix},$$

$$\text{and} \quad \mathbf{u}(t) = \begin{bmatrix} u_1(t) \\ u_2(t) \end{bmatrix} \tag{2.44}$$

Equation (2.34) may be used to approximate the state transition matrix, but for this example, transform methods (illustrated later) lead to an analytic solution. The state transition matrix is easily shown to be given by

$$\phi(t) = \frac{1}{6}\begin{bmatrix} 2\,e^{-4t} + 4\,e^{2t} & -e^{-4t} + e^{2t} \\ -8\,e^{-4t} + 8\,e^{2t} & 4\,e^{-4t} + 2\,e^{2t} \end{bmatrix} \tag{2.45}$$

Given the state transition matrix defined by Eq. (2.45), with $t_0 = 0$, and zero initial conditions, we may use Eq. (2.36) to compute the solution:

$$\mathbf{x}(t) = \frac{1}{6}\begin{bmatrix} \dfrac{-9}{4} - \dfrac{1}{4}e^{-4t} + \dfrac{5}{2}e^{2t} \\ -6 + e^{-4t} + 5\,e^{2t} \end{bmatrix} \tag{2.46}$$

Setting $t = 0$ in Eq. (2.46) leads to $\mathbf{x}(0) = (0 \ \ 0)'$, which serves as a partial check on the solution. Note that $\mathbf{x}(t)$ is seen to represent an unstable system in this example, but the resulting instability is of no concern (mathematically!) for state-variable-based system analysis.

Although the preceding solution method is straightforward and easily implemented on an analog or digital computer, modal decomposition provides another and simpler method of solution. Additionally, modal decomposition decouples the system by diagonalizing the A matrix and shows clearly the relative importance of each system mode (here each mode is defined by an exponential term) to the final solution. Finally, the new set of state variable equations produced by modal decomposition represent a canonical form.

Modal decomposition is accomplished via the similarity transformation

$$\Lambda = P^{-1}AP \tag{2.47}$$

where A is the $n \times n$ system matrix, and P is an $n \times n$ matrix whose columns are any set of eigenvectors formed from the distinct eigenvalues of A. If A contains repeated eigenvalues, a slightly modified solution method is required, and the Jordan canonical form is obtained. A new set of state variables may be written in canonical form (decoupled since Λ is diagonal) as

$$\dot{\mathbf{z}}(t) = \Lambda \mathbf{z}(t) + \Gamma \mathbf{u}(t) \tag{2.48}$$

with

$$\Gamma = P^{-1}B \tag{2.49}$$

and

$$\mathbf{x}(t) = P\mathbf{z}(t) \tag{2.50}$$

where $\mathbf{x}(t)$ are the state variables of the original system. Since Λ is diagonal, the solution of Eq. (2.48) for $\mathbf{z}(t)$ is trivial, and although a new state transition matrix could be defined, it is not required or particularly useful.

For this simple 2×2 example, the eigenvalues of A, computed from $\det(A - I\Lambda) = 0$, with I a 2×2 identity matrix, are $\lambda_1 = -4$ and $\lambda_2 = 2$. The ith eigenvector, e_i, may be computed from λ_i conveniently from $(A - I\lambda_i)e_i = 0$. Alternatively, we might wish to compute the adjoint $(A - I\lambda_i)$, in which case it is known that the columns of the adjoint matrix are eigenvectors of A. Regardless of solution method, from A we form the eigenvectors

$$\mathbf{e}_1 = \begin{pmatrix} 1 \\ -4 \end{pmatrix}, \qquad \mathbf{e}_2 = \begin{pmatrix} 1 \\ 2 \end{pmatrix} \tag{2.51}$$

and thus matrix P becomes

$$P = \begin{pmatrix} 1 & 1 \\ -4 & 2 \end{pmatrix} \tag{2.52}$$

with

$$P^{-1} = \frac{1}{6}\begin{pmatrix} 2 & -1 \\ 4 & 1 \end{pmatrix} \tag{2.53}$$

From Eq. (2.47), we compute the decoupled system state matrix Λ as

$$\Lambda = \begin{pmatrix} -4 & 0 \\ 0 & 2 \end{pmatrix} \tag{2.54}$$

and from Eq. (2.49), we find

$$\Gamma = \frac{1}{6}\begin{pmatrix} 1 \\ 5 \end{pmatrix} \tag{2.55}$$

Expanding Eq. (2.48), we have the set of decoupled state equations

$$\begin{aligned} \dot{z}_1(t) &= -4z_1(t) + \tfrac{1}{6}u(t) \\ \dot{z}_2(t) &= 2z_2(t) + \tfrac{5}{6}u(t) \end{aligned} \tag{2.56}$$

which are easily solved, resulting in

$$\begin{aligned} z_1(t) &= (\tfrac{1}{24} - \tfrac{1}{24}\,\mathrm{e}^{-4t})u(t) \\ z_2(t) &= (-\tfrac{5}{12} + \tfrac{5}{12}\,\mathrm{e}^{2t})u(t) \end{aligned} \tag{2.57}$$

that define the two system modes for this 2×2 example. Finally, from Eq. (2.50), we see the interaction of system modes defined by Eq. (2.57) by expressing

$$\begin{aligned} x_1(t) &= z_1(t) + z_2(t) \\ x_2(t) &= -4z_1(t) + 2z_2(t) \end{aligned} \tag{2.58}$$

which, if $z_1(t)$ and $z_2(t)$ are replaced by Eq. (2.57), is of course the same solution previously computed via the state transition matrix technique and summarized by Eq. (2.46). In this example, one could have guessed the modes correctly from the form of Eq. (2.46), set up two equations in two unknowns, and solved for Λ and Γ. In general, however, model decomposition is not so easily guessed, and an organized solution procedure as just summarized is necessary. Note that one could arbitrarily pick some nonsingular matrix P and develop a new set of state variable equations whenever desired, perhaps to search for system implementations via hardware that exhibits improved numerical accuracy. Picking P as prescribed here for model decomposition, however, guarantees that the new state equations are decoupled. Decoupled state equations are solvable in an easy manner and clearly show the relative importance of individual system modes upon final system dynamics. To illustrate this concept graphically, the system modes $z_1(t)$ and $z_2(t)$ are plotted in Figure 2.6, with the original state variables $x_1(t)$ and $x_2(t)$ plotted in Figure 2.7.

The preceding two examples have demonstrated that a state-variable approach to system analysis is unified, compact, powerful, and admits analysis of time-varying linear systems in a systematic manner. So far we have restricted our attention to continuous-time systems for completeness (many real-world systems naturally consist of both continuous-time and discrete-time elements, but the extension of state-variable concepts to purely discrete systems is easily accomplished). Discrete- state equations may arise by sampling a continuous system for computer simulation or because the data and processing systems are inherently discrete. As was the

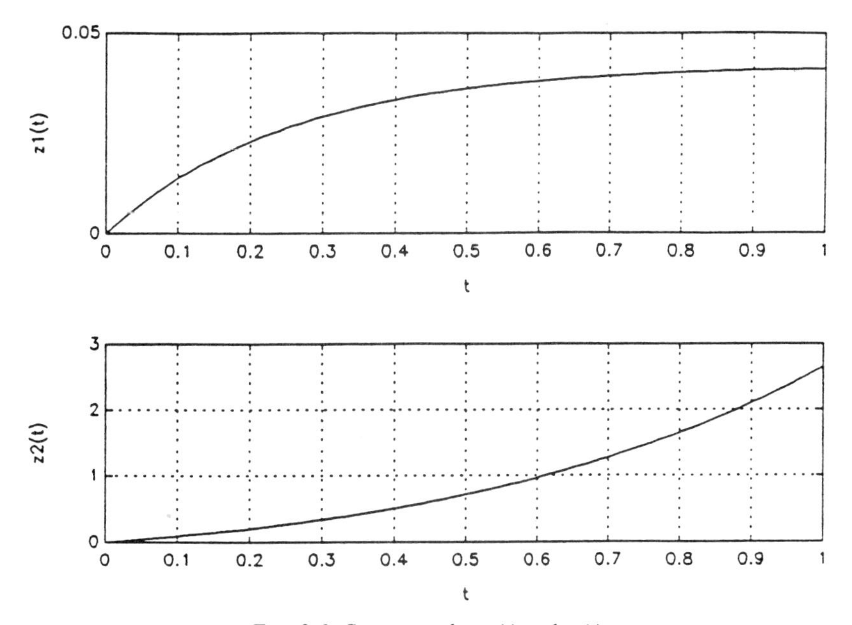

FIG. 2.6. System modes $z_2(t)$ and $z_2(t)$.

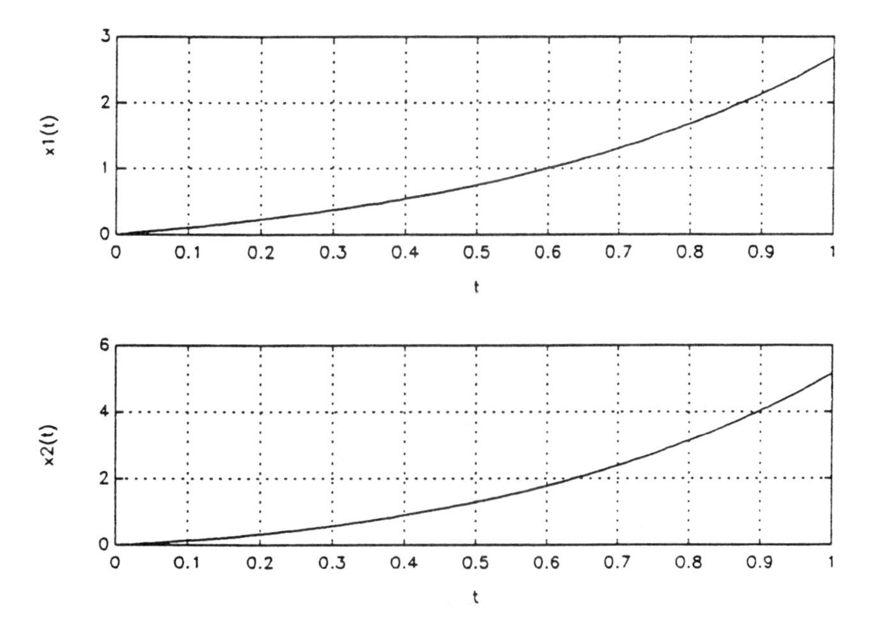

FIG. 2.7. System state variables $x_1(t)$ and $x_2(t)$.

case for continuous-time systems, both constant-coefficient linear systems and time-varying coefficient linear systems may be accommodated with relative ease.

Discrete state equations for a general linear system with time-varying coefficients may be written

$$\mathbf{x}(k+1) = A(k)\mathbf{x}(k) + B(k)\mathbf{u}(k) \tag{2.59}$$

$$\mathbf{y}(k) = C(k)\mathbf{x}(k) + D(k)\mathbf{u}(k) \tag{2.60}$$

With the time-varying discrete-time transition matrix defined by

$$\phi(k, n) = A(k-1)A(k-2)A(k-3)\ldots A(n+1)A(n) \tag{2.61}$$

the solution to Eq. (2.59) is given by

$$\mathbf{x}(k) = \phi(k, 0)\mathbf{x}(0) + \sum_{n=1}^{k} \phi(k, n)B(n-1)\mathbf{u}(n-1) \tag{2.62}$$

when evaluating Eq. (2.63), note that when $n = k$, $\phi(k, n) = In$, and when $n = k - 1, \phi(k, n) = A(k-1)$; for $0 \leq n \leq k-2, \phi(k, n)$ is defined by Eq. (2.61) in an obvious manner. Unfortunately, for the time-varying coefficient case, computation of the transition matrix defined by Eq. (2.61) may not be simple if an analytical expression is sought for $\phi(k, n)$. High-speed computers, however, are easily programmed to compute $\phi(k, n)$ by brute force.

For systems with constant coefficients the state equations reduce to

$$\mathbf{x}(k+1) = A\mathbf{x}(k) + \mathbf{B}\mathbf{u}(k) \tag{2.63}$$

$$\mathbf{y}(k) = C\mathbf{x}(k) + \mathbf{D}\mathbf{u}(k) \tag{2.64}$$

The solution to Eq. (2.63) may be expressed

$$\mathbf{x}(k) = A^{k}x(0) + \sum_{n=1}^{k} A^{k-n}B(n-1)\mathbf{u}(n-1) \tag{2.65}$$

which is the same as Eq. (2.62), since the discrete transition matrix with A constant is given by

$$\phi(k, n) = A^{k-n} \tag{2.66}$$

Thus, Eq. (2.62) may be used to represent a solution for $\mathbf{x}(k)$ for both the time-varying coefficient case and the constant-coefficient case with $\phi(k, n)$ defined appropriately. Actually, the discrete transition matrix, $\phi(k, n)$, may be defined in general by Eq. (2.61) and noting that, for A constant, $\phi(k, n)$ simplifies to Eq. (2.66). The advantage of expressing the discrete transition matrix defined by Eq. (2.66) is that several different methods may be used to obtain an analytical expression, which is convenient for system analysis and design.

One property of the discrete transition matrix $\phi(k, n)$ is notable. If the inverse exists, then we have

$$\phi^{-1}(k, n) = \phi(n, k) \tag{2.67}$$

but unlike the continuous-time case, $\phi^{-1}(k, n)$ is *not* required to exist for validity of the state-variable solution defined in Eq. (2.65) or (2.62). In other words, A may be singular.

As with continuous-time systems, model decomposition techniques may be applied to discrete-time state equations to simplify solution or provide additional insight into system dynamics. For the state-variable transformation

$$\mathbf{x}(k) = P\mathbf{z}(k) \tag{2.68}$$

where again, P is defined by

$$P = [\mathbf{e}_1 \quad \mathbf{e}_2 \quad \dots \quad \mathbf{e}_n], \tag{2.69}$$

with $\mathbf{e}_i$, the ith eigenvector, corresponding to the ith eigenvalue of A. If A possesses distinct eigenvalues, then the similarity transformation

$$\Lambda = P^{-1}AP \tag{2.70}$$

may be used to write a set of decoupled state equations

$$\mathbf{x}(k + 1) = \Lambda\mathbf{z}(k) + \Gamma\mathbf{u}(k) \tag{2.71}$$

$$\mathbf{y}(k) = C(k)P\mathbf{z}(k) + D(k)\mathbf{u}(k), \tag{2.72}$$

where

$$\Gamma = P^{-1}B \tag{2.73}$$

If A contains repeated eigenvalues, then Eq. (2.71) is still quite useful, as the new state variables, $\mathbf{z}(t)$, are as nearly decoupled as possible. When the eigenvalues of A are distinct, then of course Λ is diagonal and the solution to Eq. (2.71) is

$$\mathbf{z}(k) = \Lambda^k\mathbf{z}(0) + \sum_{n=1}^{k} \Lambda^{k-n}P^{-1}B(n - 1)\mathbf{u}(n - 1) \tag{2.74}$$

Substituting $\mathbf{x}(k) = P\mathbf{z}(k)$ and $\mathbf{z}(0) = P^{-1}\mathbf{x}(0)$ results in

$$\mathbf{x}(k) = P\Lambda^kP^{-1}\mathbf{x}(0) + \sum_{n=1}^{k} P\Lambda^{k-n}P^{-1}B(n - 1)\mathbf{u}(n - 1) \tag{2.75}$$

which by comparison to Eq. (2.65) shows that

$$A^k = P\Lambda^kP^{-1} \tag{2.76}$$

which is a convenient method for computing the discrete transition matrix, $\phi(k, n)$.

Discrete-Time State-Variable Example

Consider the discrete-time state-variable equations (2.63) and (2.64) with

$$A = \begin{bmatrix} \frac{1}{2} & \frac{1}{4} \\ \frac{1}{4} & \frac{1}{2} \end{bmatrix}, \quad B = \begin{bmatrix} 1 & 0 \\ 0 & 1 \end{bmatrix}, \quad C = [1 \quad 1], \quad \text{and} \quad D = [0 \quad 0] \tag{2.77}$$

Our goal is to find $\mathbf{x}(k)$ and $\mathbf{y}(k)$ via model decomposition. From $\det(A - I\lambda) = \lambda^2 - \lambda + \frac{3}{16} = 0$, we find $\lambda_1 = \frac{3}{4}$ and $\lambda_2 = \frac{1}{4}$. From $(A - I\lambda_i)\mathbf{e}_i = 0$ we form two eigenvectors $\mathbf{e}_1 = (1 \quad 1)'$ and $\mathbf{e}_2 = (1 \quad -1)'$, which gives the transformation matrix

$$P = \begin{bmatrix} 1 & 1 \\ 1 & -1 \end{bmatrix} \tag{2.78}$$

with

$$P^{-1} = \begin{bmatrix} \frac{1}{2} & \frac{1}{2} \\ \frac{1}{2} & -\frac{1}{2} \end{bmatrix} \tag{2.79}$$

Now, from Eq. (2.70), we compute

$$\Lambda = \begin{bmatrix} \frac{3}{4} & 0 \\ 0 & \frac{1}{4} \end{bmatrix} \tag{2.80}$$

and from Eq. (2.73)

$$\Gamma = \begin{bmatrix} \frac{1}{2} & \frac{1}{2} \\ \frac{1}{2} & -\frac{1}{2} \end{bmatrix} \tag{2.81}$$

The decoupled state equations become

$$\mathbf{z}(k+1) = \begin{bmatrix} \frac{3}{4} & 0 \\ 0 & \frac{1}{4} \end{bmatrix} \mathbf{z}(k) + \begin{bmatrix} \frac{1}{2} & \frac{1}{2} \\ \frac{1}{2} & -\frac{1}{2} \end{bmatrix} \mathbf{u}(k) \tag{2.82}$$

$$\mathbf{y}(k) = [2 \quad 0]\mathbf{z}(k) \tag{2.83}$$

with the discrete transition matrix

$$\Lambda^k = \begin{bmatrix} (\frac{3}{4})^k & 0 \\ 0 & (\frac{1}{4})^k \end{bmatrix} \tag{2.84}$$

From Eq. (2.76), we then compute

$$A^k = \begin{bmatrix} \frac{1}{2}(\frac{3}{4})^k + \frac{1}{2}(\frac{1}{4})^k & \frac{1}{2}(\frac{3}{4})^k - \frac{1}{2}(\frac{1}{4})^k \\ \frac{1}{2}(\frac{3}{4})^k - \frac{1}{2}(\frac{1}{4})^k & \frac{1}{2}(\frac{3}{4})^k + \frac{1}{2}(\frac{1}{4})^k \end{bmatrix} \tag{2.85}$$

and finally, via Eq. (2.75), the solution for state variables, $\mathbf{x}(k)$, is expressed

$$\mathbf{x}(k) = A^k \mathbf{x}(0) + \sum_{n=1}^{k} A^{k-n} \mathbf{u}(n-1) \tag{2.86}$$

$$\mathbf{y}(k) = [1 \quad 1]\mathbf{x}(k) \tag{2.87}$$

Since $\mathbf{x}(k) = P\mathbf{z}(k)$, we may also write $\mathbf{x}(k)$ as a sum of system modes

$$\mathbf{x}(k) = \mathbf{e}_1 z_1(k) + \mathbf{e}_2 z_2(k) \tag{2.88}$$

where, from Eq. (2.74),

$$\mathbf{z}(k) = \begin{bmatrix} (\frac{3}{4})^k & 0 \\ 0 & (\frac{1}{4})^k \end{bmatrix} \mathbf{z}(0) + \sum_{n=1}^{k} \begin{bmatrix} (\frac{3}{4})^{k-n} & 0 \\ 0 & (\frac{1}{4})^{k-n} \end{bmatrix} \begin{bmatrix} \frac{1}{2} & \frac{1}{2} \\ \frac{1}{2} & -\frac{1}{2} \end{bmatrix} \mathbf{u}(n-1) \tag{2.89}$$

For an interesting numerical example, set $\mathbf{u} = (0 \quad 0)'$, $\mathbf{x}(0) = (1 \quad 1)'$, in which the state natural response becomes

$$\mathbf{x}(k) = \begin{bmatrix} (\frac{3}{4})^k \\ (\frac{3}{4})^k \end{bmatrix} \tag{2.90}$$

and the exponential term, $(\frac{1}{4})^k$, has been suppressed. The reason for this phenomena can be easily seen by expressing the natural response in decoupled form with $\mathbf{z}(0) = P^{-1}\mathbf{x}(0) = (1 \quad 0)'$, as

$$\mathbf{z}(k) = \Lambda^k \mathbf{z}(0) = \begin{bmatrix} (\frac{3}{4})^k \\ 0 \end{bmatrix} \tag{2.91}$$

from which it can be seen that the system mode associated with $\lambda = \frac{1}{4}$, $\lambda = \frac{1}{4}$, possesses zero contribution. From Eq. (2.88) we could have them written

$$\mathbf{x}(k) = \begin{bmatrix} 1 \\ 1 \end{bmatrix} \left(\frac{3}{4}\right)^k \tag{2.92}$$

which is, of course, exactly the same result given by Eq. (2.90). In general, however, for the arbitrary initial condition, $\mathbf{x}(0)$, both system modes will be excited.

A slightly more general case results, for example, if we let $\mathbf{x}(0) = (2 \quad 1)'$, $\mathbf{u} = (0 \quad 0)'$. Now $\mathbf{z}(0) = P^{-1}\mathbf{x}(0) = (\frac{3}{2} \quad \frac{1}{2})'$, and the decoupled natural response is given by

$$\mathbf{z}(k) = \begin{bmatrix} \frac{3}{2}(\frac{3}{4})^k \\ \frac{1}{2}(\frac{1}{4})^k \end{bmatrix} \tag{2.93}$$

and the discrete state-variable solution, from Eq. (2.88), is

$$\mathbf{x}(k) = \begin{bmatrix} 1 \\ 1 \end{bmatrix} \cdot \frac{3}{2} \cdot \left(\frac{3}{4}\right)^k + \begin{bmatrix} 1 \\ -1 \end{bmatrix} \cdot \frac{1}{2} \cdot \left(\frac{1}{4}\right)^k \tag{2.94}$$

If written in expanded form, Eq. (2.94) becomes

$$x_1(k) = \tfrac{3}{2}(\tfrac{3}{4})^k + \tfrac{1}{2}(\tfrac{1}{4})^k \tag{2.95}$$

$$x_2(k) = \tfrac{3}{2}(\tfrac{3}{4})^k - \tfrac{1}{2}(\tfrac{1}{4})^k \tag{2.96}$$

The decoupled natural modes are plotted in Figure 2.8 and the system natural responses (Eq. (2.94)) are plotted in Figure 2.9.

So far we have considered state variables representations for systems that are purely continuous time or purely discrete time. This has served to unify the notation developed for state-variable system analysis and highlight the similarities between continuous and discrete systems. Naturally, a physically dynamic system may consist of both continuous and discrete

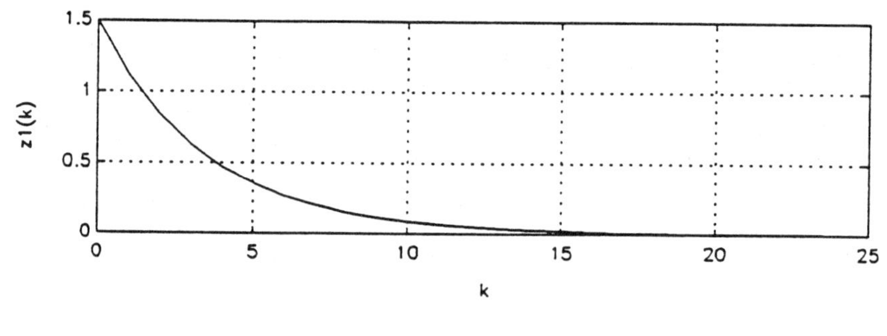

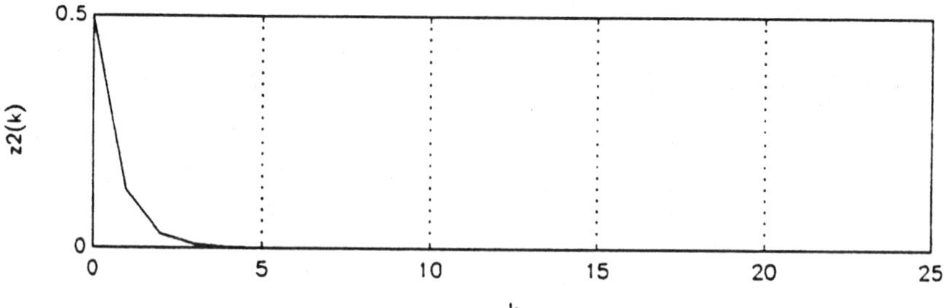

FIG. 2.8. Decoupled natural modes $z_1(k)$ and $z_2(k)$.

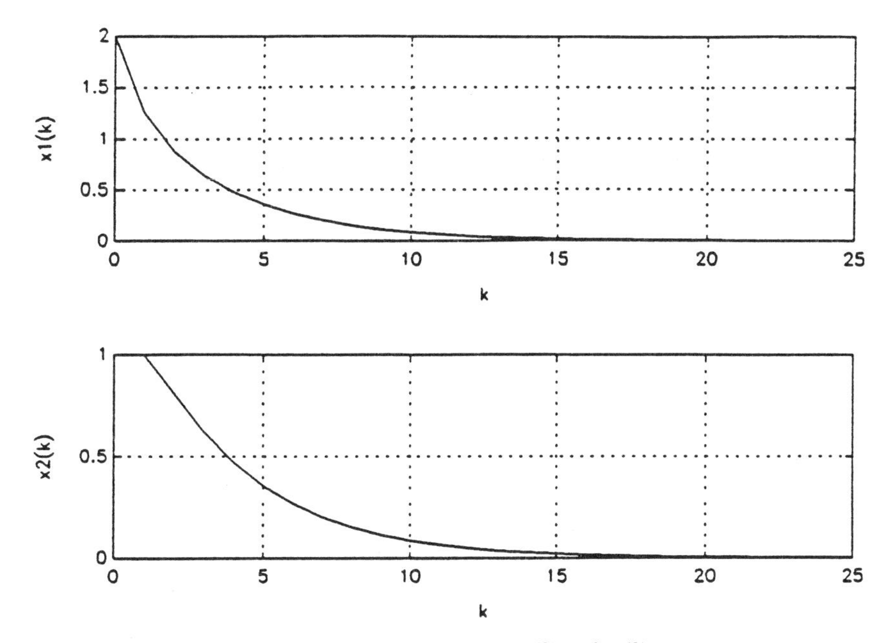

FIG. 2.9. Natural responses $x_1(k)$ and $x_2(k)$.

subsystems. Extension of the state-variable equation formulation to handle hybrid systems is straightforward.

A hybrid system, consisting of a continuous-time linear system represented by a set of state equations such as Eqs. (2.27) and (2.28) with a sampled data or discrete-time input vector is shown in Figure 2.10. Clearly, a closed-loop system may be represented in the same manner. We assume that $u(t)$ follows a zero-order hold (ZOH) digital-to-analog (D/A) converter and therefore may be expressed for $k = 0, 1, \ldots$. The sampling period is denoted by T. Since the linear system in Figure 2.10 may in general contain time-varying components, the solution is given by Eq. (2.35) with $u(\tau)$ preceding the integral sign. Thus,

$$\mathbf{x}(t) = \phi(t, t_0)\mathbf{x}(t_0) + \mathbf{u}(kt)\int_{t_0}^{t} \phi(t, \tau)B(\tau)\,\mathrm{d}\tau \tag{2.98}$$

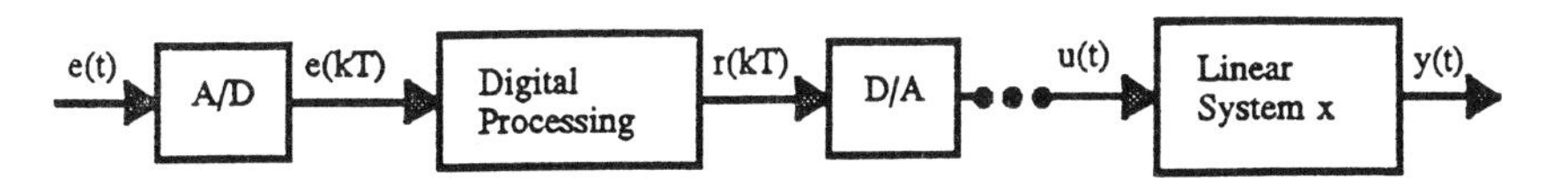

FIG. 2.10. Open-loop hybrid system model.

where $t_0 = kT$, and $kT \le t \le (k+1)T$. The solution for $\mathbf{x}(t)$ given by Eq. (2.98) is valid for all time between sampling instants, but may be simplified somewhat if $\mathbf{x}(t)$ is required at only sampling instants kT. With $t_0 = kT$, $t = (k+1)T$, Eq. (2.98), is modified as

$$\mathbf{x}[(k+1)T] = \phi[(k+1)T, kT]\mathbf{x}(kT) + \mathbf{u}(kt)\int_{kT}^{(K+1)T} \phi[(k+1)T, \tau]B(\tau)\,\mathrm{d}\tau \tag{2.99}$$

The sampling interval is commonly normalized to $T = 1$ sec for convenience; furthermore, we may define (with $T = 1$)

$$\theta(k+1, k) = \int_{k}^{k+1} \phi(k+1, \tau)B(\tau)\,\mathrm{d}\tau \tag{2.100}$$

From Eq. (2.99) with $T = 1$ and Eq. (2.100), a discrete state equation for the hybrid system in Figure 2.10, may be expressed compactly as

$$\mathbf{x}(k+1) = \phi(k+1, k)\mathbf{x}(k) + \theta(k+1, k)\mathbf{u}(k) \tag{2.101}$$

$$\mathbf{y}(k) = C(k)\mathbf{x}(k) + D(k)\mathbf{u}(k) \tag{2.102}$$

It is important to note, however, if the discrete state equation representation defined by Eqs. (2.101) and (2.102) is invoked to describe a hybrid system, that information concerning system dynamics between $t = kT$ and $t = (k+1)T$ has been discarded.

Stability

Most linear systems are designed with the concept of stability implied if not explicitly stated. Thus, it is useful to relate the concept of stability to the parameters of a linear system expressed in state variable form. Since a linear constant coefficient system is completely defined by its state matrix A, we expect that stability may be related to some fundamental properties of A. For our purposes we restrict discussion to three cases: (1) asymptotic stability ($\mathbf{u} = \mathbf{0}$); (2) bounded input–bounded state (BIBS) stability; and (3) bounded input–bounded output (BIBO) stability.

With $\|\cdot\|$ denoting the conventional vector norm, a rather simplified definition of asymptotic stability is

$$\lim_{k \to \infty} \|\phi(k)\| = 0 \tag{2.103}$$

If the eigenvalues of the $n \times n$ matrix A are denoted λ_i, $i = 1, 2, \ldots, n$, the eigenvalues of $\phi(k)$ are λ_i^k, $i = 1, 2, \ldots, n$. Using the property of a matrix norm, which states that

$$|\lambda_i^k|^2 \le \|\phi(k)\|^2 \tag{2.104}$$

we see that the system is asymptotically stable if

$$|\lambda_i| < 1, \qquad i = 1, 2, \ldots, n \tag{2.105}$$

The condition specified by Eq. (2.105) is required for asymptotic stability as defined by Eq. (2.103) regardless whether λ_i, $i = 1, 2, \ldots, n$ represent distinct or repeated roots. If we admit $|\lambda_i| \leq 1$ for distinct roots, and $|\lambda_i| < 1$ for all repeated roots, the system is said to be stable in the sense of Lyapunov (stable i.s.L.). Stable i.s.L. is somewhat less restrictive than asymptotic stability since a bounded but oscillatory state trajectory is allowed.

A linear system is said to be bounded–input bounded output stable if for

$$\|\mathbf{u}(k)\| \leq M, \qquad \text{for all } k \tag{2.106}$$

with M a finite scalar,

$$\|\mathbf{x}(k)\| \leq N, \qquad \text{for all } k \tag{2.107}$$

where N is a finite scalar. It can be shown that the condition $|\lambda_i| < 1$, where λ_i, $i = 1, 2, \ldots, n$ are the eigenvalues of A, assures BIBS stability.

Bounded input–bounded output stability can be tedious to ascertain. The general procedure is to solve the state-variable equations for $x(k)$ and substitute $\mathbf{x}(k)$ with $\mathbf{y}(k) = C\mathbf{x}(k) + D\mathbf{u}(k)$. The system is termed BIBO stable if

$$\|\mathbf{y}(k)\| < N \tag{2.108}$$

where N is a finite scalar and the input vector is bounded as defined by Eq. (2.106).

Stability Example 1

Consider the discrete-time system represented by state equation

$$\mathbf{x}(k+1) = A\mathbf{X}(k) \tag{2.109}$$

with

$$A = \begin{bmatrix} 0 & 1 \\ -0 & 0 \end{bmatrix} \tag{2.110}$$

the eigenvalues of A are $\lambda_1 = j$, $\lambda_2 = -j$, where $j = \sqrt{-1}$. Since $|\lambda_i| = 1$, this system is not asymptotically stable, but is stable i.s.L.

Stability Example 2

Consider the system defined by Eq. (2.77), where we found the eigenvalues of A to be $|\lambda_1| = \frac{3}{4}$ and $|\lambda_2| = \frac{1}{4}$. Since $|\lambda_i| < 1$ for all roots, the system is asymptotically stable and BIBS stable (if $\|\mathbf{u}(k)\|$ is finite). Stability is also verified by Figure 2.9, which shows $\mathbf{x}(k) = [x_1(k) \;\; x_2(k)]'$, $k = 0, 1, \ldots, 25$.

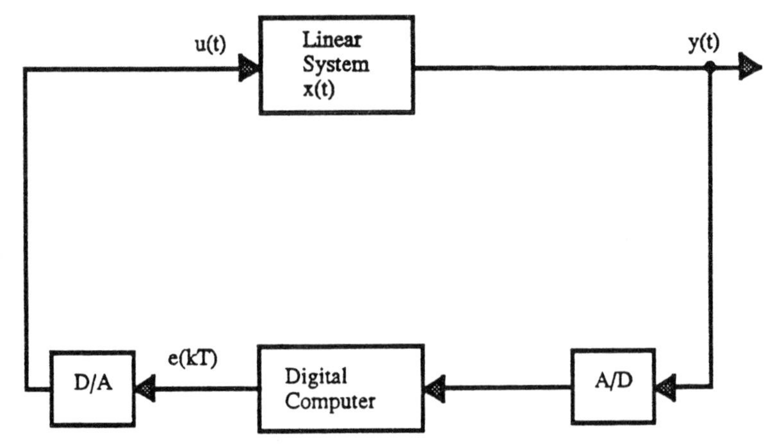

FIG. 2.11. Hybrid control system.

Stability Example 3

This example will clearly demonstrate that when analyzing the stability of a hybrid control system, extra care must be taken with respect to the sample interval T. The system under consideration is shown in Figure 2.11. The linear system in Figure 2.11 is described by the state equations

$$\dot{\mathbf{x}}(t) = \begin{bmatrix} -1 & 0 \\ 1 & 0 \end{bmatrix} \mathbf{x}(t) + \begin{bmatrix} 1 \\ 0 \end{bmatrix} \mathbf{u}(t) \tag{2.111}$$

$$\mathbf{y}(t) = [0 \quad 1]\mathbf{x}(t) + \begin{bmatrix} 0 \\ 0 \end{bmatrix} \mathbf{u}(t) \tag{2.112}$$

From Eq. (2.101), the discrete state equations for this hybrid system are

$$\mathbf{x}[(k+1)T] = \begin{bmatrix} e^{-T} & 0 \\ 1 - e^{-T} & 1 \end{bmatrix} \mathbf{x}(kT) + \begin{bmatrix} 1 - e^{-T} \\ T - 1 + e^{-T} \end{bmatrix} e(kT) \tag{2.113}$$

$$\mathbf{y}(kT) = [0 \quad 1]\mathbf{x}(kT) \tag{2.114}$$

where $e(kT)$ has not been defined. A simple but relatively common choice is $e(kT) = r(kT) - y(kT)$, where $r(kT)$ is some desired output response, $y(kT)$, and thus $e(kT)$ would represent an error signal. For $e(kT) = r(kT) - y(kT)$, which clearly does not require much digital computing power, the discrete state equations are

$$\mathbf{x}[(k+1)T] = \begin{bmatrix} e^{-T} & e^{-T} \\ 1 - e^{-T} & 2 - T - e^{-T} \end{bmatrix} \mathbf{x}(kT) + \begin{bmatrix} 1 - e^{-T} \\ T - 1 + e^{-T} \end{bmatrix} r(kT) \tag{2.115}$$

$$\mathbf{y}(kT) = [0 \quad 1]\mathbf{x}(kT) \tag{2.116}$$

with initial condition $x(0)$ arbitrary, and $r(kT)$ some desired control input. To check system stability we must compute the eigenvalues of

$$A = \begin{bmatrix} e^{-T} & e^{-T} - 1 \\ 1 - e^{-T} & 2 - T - e^{-T} \end{bmatrix} \tag{2.117}$$

clearly, the eigenvalues of A are a function of sampling interval T. From Eq. (2.117) we find

$$\lambda_1 = \frac{2 - T}{2} + \frac{1}{2}\sqrt{T^2 - 4T(1 - e^{-T})} \tag{2.118}$$

$$\lambda_2 = \frac{2 - T}{2} - \frac{1}{2}\sqrt{T^2 - 4T(1 - e^{-T})} \tag{2.119}$$

From Eqs. (2.118) and (2.119), we see that for $T \approx 4$, $\lambda_1 = \lambda_2 = -1$, and the system is unstable. For approximately $T < 4$, $|\lambda_i| < 1$ and the system is stable. Values of $T > 4$ clearly result in an unstable system (see Figure 2.12). To verify this result via simulation, we pick $r(kT) = 1$, $k = 0, 1, \ldots,$ and compute $x(k)$ recursively for $T = 0.1, 1, 4,$ and 5, with $x(0) = [0 \quad 0]'$. The results are given in Figure 2.13.

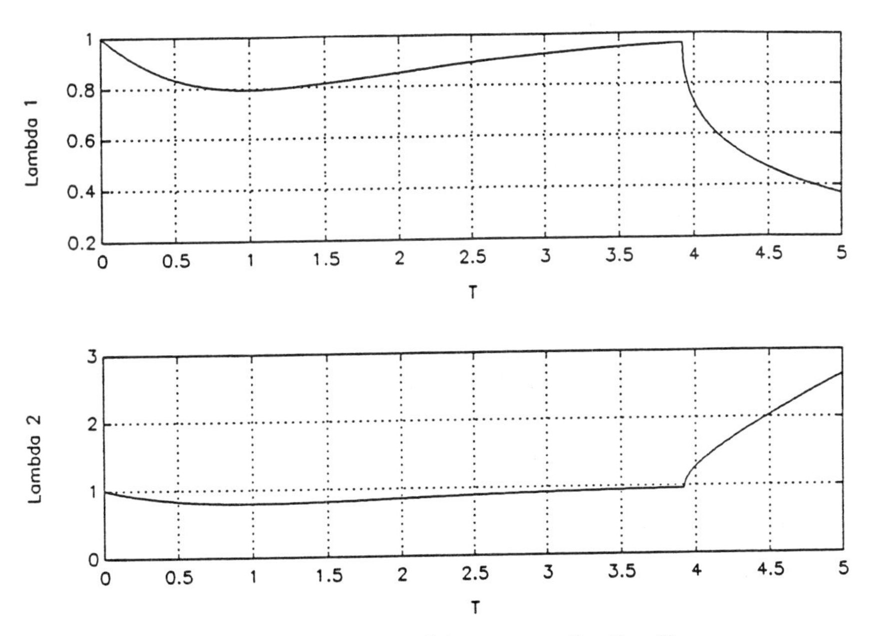

FIG. 2.12. Eigenvalues of A versus sampling time T.

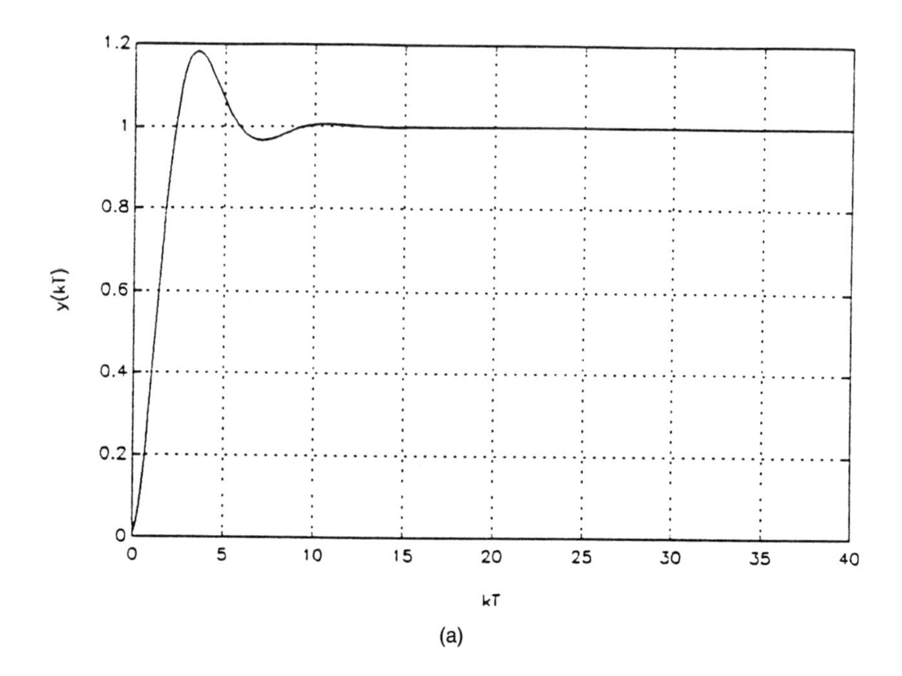
1.2
1
0.8
0.6
0.4
0.2
0
y(kT)
0
5
10
15
20
25
30
35
40
kT

(a)

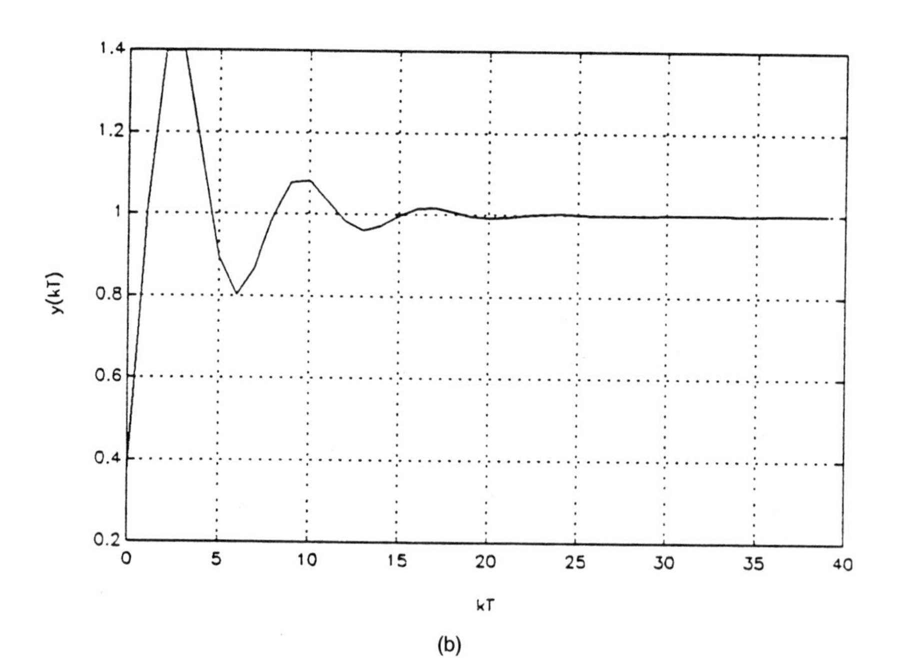
1.4
1.2
1
0.8
0.6
0.4
0.2
y(kT)
0
5
10
15
20
25
30
35
40
kT

(b)

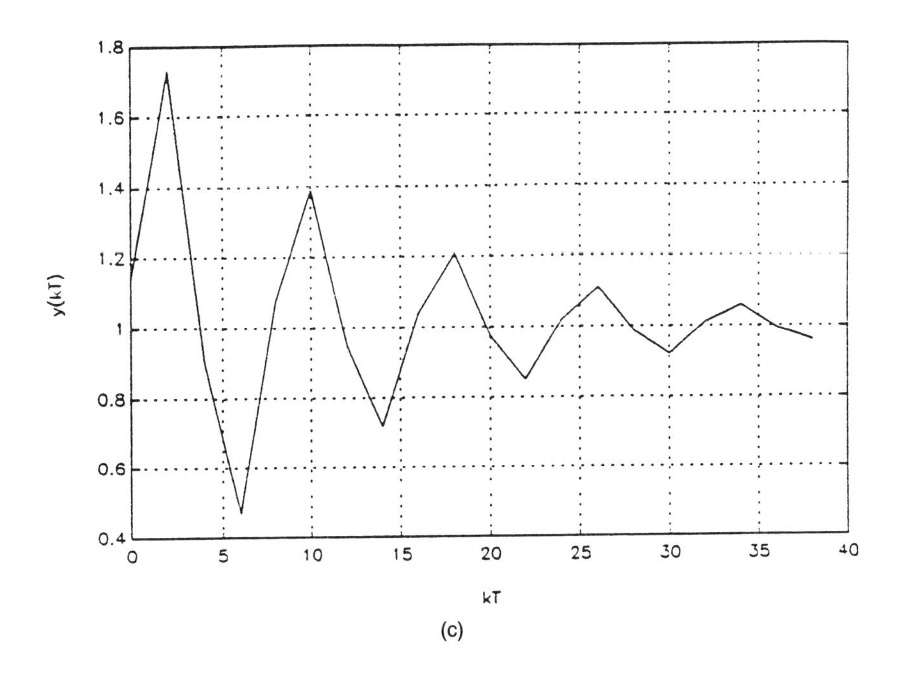

(c)

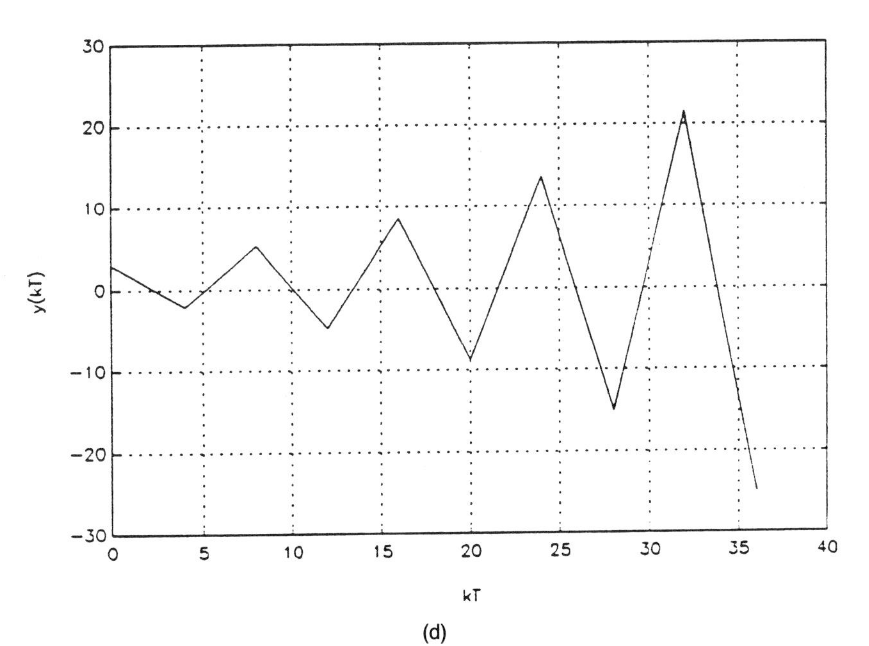

(d)

FIG. 2.13. $y(kT)$: (a) $T = 0.1$, (b) $T = 1$, (c) $T = 2$, (d) $T = 4$.

Controllability and Observability

Although controllability may be defined in various degrees of detail, for our purposes we intend to keep the definition simple and intuitive; the hope is that mathematical rigor is traded for clarity, which we fully recognize is fraught with traps. Controllability is a common requirement for many system design problems, such as minimum settling design, for obvious reasons. For a discrete-time system defined by the state equations

$$\mathbf{x}(k+1) = A(k)\mathbf{x}(k) + B(k)\mathbf{u}(k) \tag{2.120}$$

$$\mathbf{y}(k) = C(k)\mathbf{x}(k) + D(k)\mathbf{u}(k) \tag{2.121}$$

we say that this system is controllable if an input sequence can be found that transfers $\mathbf{x}(k)$ from some arbitrary initial state to any final state in finite time.

First consider the case where A is constant with distinct eigenvalues. Recall that for modal decomposition transformation matrix P, defined by Eq. (2.69), $\Lambda = P^{-1}AP$, and $\Gamma = P^{-1}B$, we formed a decoupled state representation

$$\begin{aligned} \mathbf{z}(k+1) &= \Lambda\mathbf{z}(k) + \Gamma\mathbf{u}(k) \\ \mathbf{y}(k) &= CP\mathbf{z}(k) + D\mathbf{u}(k) \end{aligned} \tag{2.122}$$

If Γ contains an all-zero row then mode z_i cannot possibly be affected by the input; consequently, at least one state variable of $\mathbf{z}(k)$ or equivalently $\mathbf{x}(k)$ is uncontrollable and the system is said to be uncontrollable. Therefore, for a constant coefficient system for which A has distinct eigenvalues, the condition (necessary and sufficient) for controllability is that there are no all-zero rows in the martrix $\Gamma = P^{-1}B$.

Example 1

Consider the discrete time system represented by Eq. (2.77), where

$$P^{-1} = \begin{bmatrix} \frac{1}{2} & \frac{1}{2} \\ \frac{1}{2} & \frac{1}{2} \end{bmatrix} \tag{2.123}$$

$$B = \begin{bmatrix} 1 & 0 \\ 0 & 1 \end{bmatrix} \tag{2.124}$$

$$\Gamma = \begin{bmatrix} \frac{1}{2} & \frac{1}{2} \\ \frac{1}{2} & -\frac{1}{2} \end{bmatrix} \tag{2.125}$$

Since Γ contains no all-zero rows this system is controllable.

For discrete time systems represented by Eqs. (2.120) and (2.121), A may of course contain repeated eigenvalues. It may be shown that such a system is controllable if the $n \times pn$ matrix Q, defined by

$$Q = [B \vdots AB \vdots A^2B \vdots \cdots \vdots A^{(n-1)}B] \tag{2.126}$$

has rank n. The proof is not difficult, but is omitted here to keep the focus on useful system analysis and design tools. Equation (2.126) may also be used if A has distinct eigenvalues.

Example 2

For the discrete-time system described by Eq. (2.77), where

$$A = \begin{bmatrix} \frac{1}{2} & \frac{1}{4} \\ \frac{1}{4} & \frac{1}{2} \end{bmatrix} \tag{2.127}$$

$$B = \begin{bmatrix} 1 & 0 \\ 0 & 1 \end{bmatrix} \tag{2.128}$$

$$Q = \begin{bmatrix} 1 & 0 & \vdots & \frac{1}{2} & \frac{1}{4} \\ 0 & 1 & \vdots & \frac{1}{4} & \frac{1}{2} \end{bmatrix} \tag{2.129}$$

we find rank $(Q) = 2$, and this system is uncontrollable.

If the discrete-time system defined by Eqs. (2.120) and (2.121) contains time-varying coefficients, then the system is controllable if at same time index N, the $n \times n$ matrix

$$\sum_{j=0}^{N} \phi(N, j)B(j)B^t(j)\phi^t(N, j) \tag{2.130}$$

is positive definite. The condition of positive definiteness may be verified by computing the eigenvalues of Eq. (2.130) or by computing the determinant of Eq. (2.130). If no eigenvalues are equal to 0 or the determinant is nonzero, Eq. (2.130) is positive definite and the system is controllable.

The observability property goes hand in hand with the controllability property in system design. A system is termed observable if $\mathbf{x}(k)$ can be found from $\mathbf{y}(k)$ in a finite time. If a system is not controllable, we obviously do not attempt to design a controller such as a minimum energy controller; in a similar manner, if a system is unobservable, we cannot attempt to use some internal state variable in $\mathbf{x}(k)$ since the variable can not be computed from $\mathbf{y}(k)$. Thus, sysytem observability is a very important property.

For a constant coefficient discrete system defined by Eq. (2.122), where A possesses distinct eigenvalues, the system is observable if CP contains no zero columns.

Example 3

Consider the discrete-time system represented by Eq. (2.77), where

$$C = [1 \quad 1] \tag{2.131}$$

$$P = \begin{bmatrix} 1 & 1 \\ 1 & -1 \end{bmatrix} \tag{2.132}$$

$$CP = [2 \quad 0] \tag{2.133}$$

we see that CP contains a zero column. The system is unobservable.

For a discrete time system defined by matrix A with repeated eigenvalues, the system is observable if the $n \times qn$ matrix

$$Q = [C' \vdots A'C' \vdots A^{2\prime}C' \vdots \cdots \vdots A^{n'-1}C']$$

has rank n.

Example 4

For the discrete-time system described by Eq. (2.77), where

$$A = \begin{bmatrix} \frac{1}{2} & \frac{1}{4} \\ \frac{1}{4} & \frac{1}{2} \end{bmatrix} \tag{2.134}$$

$$C = [1 \quad 1]$$

$$Q = \begin{bmatrix} 1 & \vdots & \frac{3}{4} \\ 1 & \vdots & \frac{3}{4} \end{bmatrix} \tag{2.135}$$

we find rank $(Q) = 1$. The system is unobservable.

If the discrete time system defined by Eqs. (2.120) and (2.121) contains the time-varying coefficients, then the system is observable if for a finite time index N, the $n \times n$ matrix

$$\sum_{j=0}^{N} \phi'(k, 0)C'(k)C(k)\phi(k, 0) \tag{2.136}$$

is positive definite. Or equivalently, the $n \times n$ matrix defined by Eq. (2.134) has a nonzero determinant or possesses all nonzero eigenvalues.

Discrete Linear Systems—z-Domain

Z-transform methods are analogous to the role played by Laplace transform techniques invoked to simplify the analysis and design of continuous-time systems. Where the Laplace transform may be used to reexpress differential equations in one domain (e.g., time) as algebraic equations in a transform domain (the s-plane), the z-transform operates on difference equations to produce algebraic equations in the z-plane. As is common in Laplace transform-based linear system analysis, a transfer function may be defined that relates a system output to a system input as a ratio of polynomials in the complex variable z. The concept of transfer function is powerful: issues such as output initial value, output final value, and system stability are easily resolved by inspection or simple algebraic manipulation.

As is necessary for the use of Laplace transform methods, the use of the z-transform is restricted to linear, constant-coefficient, shift-invariant systems. If any of these requirements cannot be guaranteed, the systems analyst must "fall back" on time-domain solution techniques. Many practical systems, although consisting of a great number of complex functional blocks, are accurately characterized by linear or linearized equations with constant coefficients over a sufficiently useful operating range. The useful operating condition of a complex dynamical system may frequently be significantly extended by defining two or more system models. Each model may then, with different transfer functions and different coefficients, cover a unique operational range of the dynamic system. For example, commercial aircraft in a constant velocity cruise altitude flight condition would be specified by a certain linear, shift-invariant, constant-coefficient model, amenable to transfer-domain analysis. Another flight condition, say approach to landing with flaps and gear extended and decreased weight from fuel burn over several hours, would be characterized by a new linear, shift-invariant, constant-coefficient model, which may be analyzed in a transform domain. A caution is in order, however; if the model is being developed for realistic, pilot-in-the-loop, real-time use, a time varying coefficient, most probably nonlinear, and shift-variant time-domain model is required.

Discrete-Time System Transfer Function

The transfer function of a discrete-time system is defined in the usual sense to relate an output variable to an input variable through a ratio of polynomials in the complex variable z. Common properties of Laplace transformation theory, such as linearity and shift relationship, carry directly over to z-transforms; a concise summary of z-transform properties and a table of useful transform pairs may be found in [1–10]. We restrict attention here to causal systems and invoke just the one-sided z-transform.

One nice characteristic of the z-transform not shared by the Laplace transform can be seen from the basic definition. Let a sequence of real or complex numbers be denoted by $x(n)$, $n = 0, 1, 2, \ldots$; the z-transform of $x(n)$, denoted $X(z) = \mathcal{Z}\{x(n)\}$ is defined as

$$X(z) = \sum_{n=0}^{\infty} x(n)z^{-n} \tag{2.137}$$

From the definition given by Eq. (2.137), we see that the z-transform is a special case of a Laurent series; thus, properties of Laurent series (e.g., convergence), a mature field of complex variable theory, may be used as desired or required by the discrete-time systems analyst or designer. One property of particular import, the venerable residue theorem, provides a powerful generalized technique for analytically computing inverse z-transforms.

Consider a linear, constant-coefficient, shift-invariant discrete-time system, whose input–output relationship may be described by the difference equation given by (2.1). Applying the z-transform to the left and right sides of Eq. (2.1), invoking the shift property and linearity property results in

$$\sum_{k=0}^{N} a_k z^{-k} y(z) = \sum_{k=0}^{M} b_k z^{-k} x(z) \tag{2.138}$$

with the transfer function $H(z)$, defined as

$$H(z) = \frac{Y(z)}{X(z)} \tag{2.139}$$

we find that

$$H(z) = \frac{\sum_{k=0}^{M} b_k z^{-k}}{\sum_{k=0}^{N} a_k z^{-k}} \tag{2.140}$$

Note that the coefficients of the difference equation, a_k and b_k, appear unaltered in the z-domain transfer function, $H(z)$. For most textbook problems, the numerator and the denominator polynomials in the complex variable z, which define $H(z)$, seem to possess closed-form summations. This naturally may or may not occur in the real world, but is of little consequence due to the usually finite summation range that admits convenient computer-aided solutions. As is done for Laplace-transform-based transfer functions, we want to factor the denominator of $H(z)$; the resultant system poles (i.e., denominator zeros), as might be expected, are related directly to key linear system characteristics such as stability and response functional form for a variety of common inputs perculiar to control system design (e.g., step, ramp).

Prior to illustrating the concept of a z-transform-based transfer function by way of simple example, we highlight two important z-transform transfer function properties relevant to control system design: the initial value theorem and the final value theorem. These two z-transform theorems are important to discrete-time control system design since system initial response ("time zero") and system steady-state response may be computed prior to finding a general analytic solution. Proposed design changes may then be partially checked prior to more extensive analysis.

Given a linear system function $H(z)$ that relates the system input $X(z)$, to the system output $Y(z)$, the initial value theorem states that

$$y(0) = \lim_{z \to \infty} \{Y(z)\} \tag{2.141}$$

and the final value theorem states that

$$y(\infty) = \lim_{z \to 1} \{z - 1)Y(z)\} \tag{2.142}$$

A necessary condition for the final value theorem is that $Y(z)$ is analytic for $|z| > 1$, which is guaranteed if the poles of $Y(z) = X(z)H(z)$ lie within the unit circle.

Transfer Function Example (Computation, Stability, Initial, and Final Value)

To illustrate the ideas associated with a z-transform-based transfer function, a simple example will suffice. Consider the difference equation defined by (2.3), $y(n) = x(n) + 0.5y(n-1)$, $n = 0, 1, 2, \ldots$, with $y(-1) = 0$, and $x(n)$, a discrete step function. Previously, utilizing time-domain methods, we analytically found that $y(0) = 1$ and $y(\infty) = 2$.

To compute the z-domain transfer function defined for a system defined by (2.3), we either use Eq. (2.137) or apply the z-transform definition and properties directly to Eq. (2.3). Either way, we find that

$$H(z) = \frac{1}{1 - 0.5z^{-1}} \tag{2.143}$$

Earlier we found that the impulse response, $h(n)$, for this system (Eq. (2.8)) was given by $h(n) = (0.5)^n$, $n \geq 0$. We find that $H(z) = \mathcal{Z}\{h(n)\}$ is

$$H(z) = \frac{1}{1 - 0.5z^{-1}} \tag{2.144}$$

with a region of convergence (ROC), $|z| > 0.5$, the exact same functional form as the z-transfer computed for the transfer function given by Eq. (2.140). This is no surprise, of course, convolution in the time domain corresponds to multiplication in the complex z-plane, which is implied by the "simple" algebraic expression for the transfer function $H(z) = Y(z)/X(z)$, or $Y(z) = X(z)H(z)$. For self-consistency, we require $H(z) = \mathcal{Z}\{h(n)\}$, where $h(n)$ is the system impulse response. Directly performing a z-transform of a discrete-time convolution equation (Eq. (2.4) or (2.5)) leads immediately to the same result. Note that after we applied the z-transform operations to the difference equations defined by (2.3), to find transfer function $H(z)$, a convergence region was not readily apparent; however, when the transfer function $H(z)$ was computed by applying the z-transform definition directly to a discrete impulse response function, $h(n)$, the ROC was directly evident from the complex series in powers of z, a consequence of Laurent series theory. For this reason, tables of z-transforms include the ROC, for convenience. From Eq. (2.143), we note that the ROC ($|z| > 0.5$) is coincident with the pole location; this is no coincidence and forms a very convenient shortcut method for computing ROC from expressions such as Eq. (2.143) that were not computed from a closed form series summation (see [14] for more detail on this fascinating topic).

It can be easily demonstrated that, if the *ROC includes the unit circle*, $H(z)$ represents a *stable* system. Note that this is equivalent to saying that the *poles of $H(z)$ lie within the unit circle*, probably a more "natural viewpoint for the engineer accustomed to Laplace transform theory, where stable system poles were restricted to the left half s-plane. For this example a simple pole is located at $z = 0.5$, a point within the unit circle, and therefore $H(z)$ characterizes a stable system. As with the corresponding Laplace transform theory, where $s = j\omega$ forms a stable boundary, $|z| = 1$ forms the stability boundary. Any pole of $H(z)$ with magnitude greater than 1 causes system instability.

To check the initial value for the system output, we first find that $Y(z) = X(z)H(z)$ is given by

$$Y(z) = \frac{1}{1 - z^{-1}} \cdot \frac{1}{1 - 0.5z^{-1}} \tag{1.145}$$

Next, we apply the initial value theorem given by Eq. (2.141) and find $y(0) = 1$. For the final value, $y(\infty)$, we form $(z - 1) \cdot Y(z)$, as prescribed by Eq. (2.142), which results in

$$(z - 1)Y(z) = \frac{z^2}{z - 0.5} \tag{2.146}$$

and therefore taking the limit as $z \to 1$ results in $y(\infty) = 2$. Note that we did not explicitly solve for $y(n)$ to find the initial value, $y(0)$, or the final value, $y(\infty)$.

Finally, from Eq. (2.145), we compute $y(n)$ by partial fraction expansion and table look-up. Equation (2.145) may be expanded as

$$Y(z) = \frac{2}{1 - z^{-1}} - \frac{1}{1 - 0.5z^{-1}} \tag{2.147}$$

and we find that

$$y(n) = 2 - (0.5)^n, \qquad n \geq 0 \tag{2.148}$$

which is identical to Eq. (2.9), which was computed via discrete-time convolution. As with the Laplace-transform-based solution of continuous-time differential equations, the use of z-transforms considerably simplifies solution of discrete-time difference equations.

State-Variable Representations

Previously, we found that a similarity transform (matrix A in Eq. 2.71), which would decouple the state equation in A, if A contained distinct eigenvalues. With z-transform techniques, we now demonstrate that a decoupled set of state equations may be written directly from a discrete system transfer function if there are no repeated roots. When the transfer function contains repeated roots, a minor modification allows a "nearly" decoupled set of state equations to be written, analogous to modal decomposition with repeated eigenvalues.

Let $H(z)$ as shown in Eq. (2.137) be reexpressed in partial fraction form ($M \leq N$) for the simple pole case

$$H(z) = b_0 + \frac{\alpha_1}{z + \lambda_1} + \frac{\alpha_2}{z + \lambda_2} + \cdots + \frac{\alpha_N}{z + \lambda_N} \tag{2.149}$$

where $\lambda_1, \lambda_2, \ldots, \lambda_N$ are the poles of $H(z)$, and $\alpha_1, \alpha_2, \ldots, \alpha_N$ are found from conventional partial fraction expansion techniques. Let $V_i(z)$ denote the transform of the ith state variable corresponding to the partial fraction term

$$V_i(z) = \frac{1}{z + \lambda_i} X(z) \tag{2.150}$$

or

$$v_1(k + 1) = -\lambda_i v_i(k) + x(k) \qquad i = 1, 2, \ldots, N \tag{2.151}$$

Expressing (2.151) in matrix form and using $Y(z) = H(z)X(z)$, with $H(z)$ given by (2.149), we may write

$$\mathbf{v}(k+1) = \begin{bmatrix} -\lambda_1 & 0 & \cdots & 0 \\ 0 & -\lambda_2 & \cdots & 0 \\ \vdots & \vdots & \vdots & \vdots \\ 0 & 0 & \cdots & -\lambda_N \end{bmatrix} \mathbf{v}(k) + \begin{bmatrix} 1 \\ 1 \\ \vdots \\ 1 \end{bmatrix} \mathbf{x}(k) \tag{2.152}$$

$$\mathbf{y}(k) = [\alpha_1, \alpha_2, \ldots, \alpha_N(k)]\mathbf{v}(k) + b_0\mathbf{x}(k)$$

where $\mathbf{v}(k) = [v_1(k), v_2(k), \ldots, v_N(k)]'$.

We see that Eq. (2.152) is identical to Eqs. (2.71) and (2.72) and the system modes are decoupled. The extension for the case of repeated system poles is straightforward, thus it will not be repeated here. As before (i.e., case of repeated eigenvalues) if the transfer function contains repeated poles, the resulting state equations are said to be in Jordan canonical form.

Example

For this example, let a discrete time z-plane transfer function be given by

$$H(z) = \frac{1}{(z+1)(z+2)} \tag{2.153}$$

To find a set of decoupled state equations for this example, we expand $H(z)$ into partial fractions:

$$H(z) = \frac{1}{z+1} - \frac{1}{z+2} \tag{2.154}$$

and by comparison to Eq. (2.152), we write

$$\mathbf{v}(k+1) = \begin{bmatrix} -1 & 0 \\ 0 & -2 \end{bmatrix} \mathbf{v}(k) + \begin{bmatrix} 1 \\ 1 \end{bmatrix} \mathbf{x}(k) \tag{2.155}$$

$$\mathbf{y}(k) = [1 \quad -1]v(k)$$

where $\mathbf{v}(k) = [v_1(k), v_2(k)]'$.

In addition to the method just illustrated in the preceding example, other methods are clearly available to find a set of decoupled state equations. The first canonical form shown in Figure 2.4 with state equations (2.11), (2.12) may be found directly from $H(z)$. Simply multiply the numerator and denominator by z^{-N} and rearrange terms for the desired result (also called the *nested programming method*). Another common method, the so-called direct programming method, produces a set of state equations in the second canonical form. Rather than illustrate these last two methods, we simply note that the coefficients of $H(z)$ *in unfactored form* (a significant advantage at times) are matched to Eq. (2.12) if the first canonical form is desired or matched to Eq. (2.15) if the second canonical form is desired. The trade-off is as follows: decoupled state equations are trivial to solve and reveal potentially hidden system modes, but $H(z)$ must be factored; if $H(z)$ cannot be factored easily or decoupled state equations are not required or desired, the first or second canonical form may be written from an unfactored transfer function by inspection.

Solution of Discrete State Equations via z-Transform

We have previously solved linear discrete state equations (Eqs. (2.63) and (2.64)) with constant coefficients in the time domain. The general time-domain solution is given by Eq. (2.65), however, we must find the state transition matrix to utilize this solution method, a possibly difficult task. Fortunately, z-transforms are very useful for solving discrete state equations. We appeal to the linearity property, take z-transforms of both sides of Eqs. (2.63) and (2.64), and solve for $\mathbf{X}(z)$ as follows:

$$\mathbf{X} = [z\mathbf{I} - \mathbf{A}]^{-1}z\mathbf{x}(0) + [z\mathbf{I} - \mathbf{A}]^{-1}\mathbf{B}\mathbf{U}(z) \tag{2.156}$$

The difficulty intrinsic to Eq. (2.156) is of course the required matrix inverse for solution of $\mathbf{X}(z)$ and subsequently $\mathbf{x}(k)$. The reader may verify that application of Eq. (2.156) to the example by Eq. (2.77) leads to identical results. If the state transition matrix is required, the use of z-transforms greatly simplifies such a computation. It may be shown that the discrete transition matrix may be found from

$$\boldsymbol{\phi}(k) = \mathcal{Z}^{-1}\{z[z\mathbf{I} - \mathbf{A}]^{-1}\} \tag{2.157}$$

Discrete-Time Control System: Regulator Design Example

It is out of the scope of this chapter's purpose to cover the entire spectrum of modern control system design. The interested reader is referred to [15–19] for excellent and thorough treatment of digital control system design. We discuss two basic discrete-time control system design methods: regulator design, with the minimum energy control restraint, and quadratic performance index control. Classical control system design in the s-plane or z-plane is not considered as a basic familiarity with these important techniques has been assumed.

Since we restrict our attention to matrix-based discrete linear systems, a digital computer program or dedicated digital hardware will compute the controller algorithm. The flexibility of digital computer programs in many cases lends great freedom to the design engineer. Additionally, since the discrete-time control system equations, including the embedded computer-based processing subsystem, may be expressed in linear matrix algebraic form, the full power of linear algebraic theory may be directed at the design problem. This is not in general true for continuous-time control system design. Performance criteria, a necessary facet of any design problem, leads to an optimization procedure that follows naturally from solutions to certain basic linear algebraic problems.

The two design problems (regulator design with minimum energy control and quadratic performance index control), though far from complete, serve to illustrate discrete-time linear system design via linear algebraic solution methods and additionally introduce basic concepts of optimal control useful for the understanding of the Kalman filter. The Kalman filter, arguably one of the most fundamental processing algorithms in modern system design and its various applications, particularly system identification, will be discussed in the following section of the chapter. Systems identification is almost always a necessary prerequisite to system feedback design and pole placement.

Regulator Design with Minimum Energy Constraint

For development of the regulator problem, we assume that the linear system is controllable; that is, an input sequence may be found that transfers the state vector $\mathbf{x}(k)$, from some initial state $\mathbf{x}(0)$, to any final state, $\mathbf{x}_f$, in finite time. A simple test for controllability is given by Eq. (2.126), which is valid for a system matrix, A containing distinct or repeated eigenvalues.

For a discrete-time system defined by

$$\mathbf{x}(k+1) = A\mathbf{x}(k) + B\mathbf{u}(k) \tag{2.158}$$

with a single control input, u, the required control vector, $\mathbf{u}$, may be computed by iterating Eq. (2.158) N times and invoking the general condition for controllability defined by Eq. (2.126). This procedure results in the $p \times 1$ control vector, $\mathbf{u}$, assuming the number of iterations, N, is equal to p,

$$\mathbf{u} = Q^{-1}[\mathbf{x}(0) - A^{-N}x_f] \tag{2.159}$$

with Q a $p \times p$ matrix whose columns are given by $-A^{-1}B$, $-A^{-2}B$, $-A^{-3}B, \ldots$. For the case $N = p$, the $p \times 1$ control vector, $\mathbf{u}$, is unique, since Eq. (2.159) consists of a p in p unknowns. For the case $N < p$, it may or may not be possible to find a control vector, $\mathbf{u}$, that solves this regulator problem. If $N > p$, then an infinite number of solutions exists, and the control system designer may add additional constraints to obtain an unique regulator solution. A common auxiliary constraint for the regulator problem is the minimum energy constraint. It may be shown that the minimum energy control vector, $\mathbf{u}$, for $N \geq p$ is given by

$$\mathbf{u} = Q'(QQ')^{-1}\mathbf{x}(0) \tag{2.160}$$

where Q is now a $p \times N$ matrix, and the desired state is $\mathbf{x}_f = \mathbf{x}(0)$, with no loss of generality.

Example

Consider a linear discrete-time system as defined by Eq. (2.158), with

$$A = \begin{bmatrix} 1 & \frac{2}{3} \\ 0 & \frac{1}{3} \end{bmatrix} \tag{2.161}$$

$$B = \begin{bmatrix} \frac{1}{3} \\ \frac{1}{3} \end{bmatrix} \tag{2.162}$$

$$\mathbf{x} = \begin{bmatrix} x_1 \\ x_2 \end{bmatrix} \tag{2.163}$$

Straightforward application of Eq. (2.160), shows that

$$Q'(QQ')^{-1} = \begin{pmatrix} \frac{-3}{2} & \frac{-5}{4} \\ \frac{1}{2} & \frac{1}{4} \end{pmatrix} \tag{2.164}$$

therefore the minimum energy control vector is

$$\mathbf{u} = \begin{pmatrix} \frac{-3}{2} & \frac{-5}{4} \\ \frac{1}{2} & \frac{1}{4} \end{pmatrix} \begin{bmatrix} x_1(0) \\ x_2(0) \end{bmatrix} \tag{2.165}$$

If we let $\mathbf{x}(0) = (1 \quad 1)'$, as a simple example, we find that the minimum energy control vector, $\mathbf{u}$, for $N = 2$, is

$$\begin{aligned} u(0) &= \frac{-11}{4} \\ u(1) &= \frac{3}{4} \end{aligned} \tag{2.166}$$

with a control vector energy of

$$\sum_{i=0}^{1} u_i^2 = \frac{65}{8} \tag{2.167}$$

It is a simple matter to verify that the control vector just calculated drives the system in this example from $\mathbf{x}(0) = (1 \quad 1)'$ to $\mathbf{x}_f = (0 \quad 0)'$ in exactly two iterations; the minimum energy constraint is guaranteed by the minimum norm solution given by Eq. (2.164).

Quadratic Performance Index Control

A very fundamental and very powerful concept in state-variable-based linear system design is based upon quadratic performance criteria. This foundation, which we will introduce in its most basic form, leads in a unified development to the fields of linear quadratic optimal control, least-squares-based system identification, recursive least-squares system identification, least-squares minimization problems, and with appropriate statistical interpretations applied, the discrete Kalman filter. A thorough development of the Kalman filter, with several applications, is given in the following section of this chapter.

Given a system described by the discrete state variable equation

$$\mathbf{x}(k+1) = A\mathbf{x}(k) + B\mathbf{u}(k)$$

when $\mathbf{x}$ is an $n \times 1$ state vector, A is the $n \times n$ state matrix, B is an $n \times p$ control matrix, $\mathbf{u}$ is a $p \times 1$ control vector with initial condition $\mathbf{x}(0)$, the quadratic control problem is to find the control sequence $\mathbf{u}(0)$, $\mathbf{u}(1), \ldots, \mathbf{u}(N-1)$ that minimizes

$$J = \sum_{k=0}^{N-1} [\tfrac{1}{2}\mathbf{x}'(k)Q\mathbf{x}(k) + \tfrac{1}{2}\mathbf{u}'(k)R\mathbf{u}(k)] \tag{2.169}$$

Q is an $n \times n$ positive, semidefinite symmetric weighting matrix, and R is a $p \times p$ positive definite symmetric weighting matrix.

Application of the Lagrange multiplier minimization technique and the Ricatti transformation (nontrivial!) results in

$$\mathbf{x}(k) = -R^{-1}B'(A')^{-1}[P(k) - Q]\mathbf{x}(k) \tag{2.170}$$

with

$$P(k) = Q + A'P(k+1)[I + BR^{-1}B'P(k+1)]^{-1}A \tag{2.171}$$

Note that $P(k)$, as specified by Eq. (2.171), must be solved off-line backward in time with the "initial condition" $P(N) = 0$.

Frequently, it is convenient to define a time-varying feedback gain matrix, $H(k)$, as

$$H(k) = -R^{-1}B'(A')^{-1}[P(k) - Q] \tag{2.172}$$

with the result that the quadratic performance control vector, $\mathbf{u}(k)$, defined by Eq. (2.170), may be compactly expressed

$$\mathbf{u}(k) = H(k)\mathbf{x}(k) \tag{2.173}$$

Equation (2.173) reveals that the solution to the quadratic control problem may be interpreted as a time-varying feedback structure that is an explicit function of the desired weighting matrices Q and R and system matrices A and B. Furthermore, for simplicity, the control system design may be able to allow $H(k)$ to reach a steady-state value as N increases, which permits a closed-loop system description with the $H(k)$ constant.

Quadratic Performance Index Example

For this example, let Q be a 2×2 identity matrix, $R = 1$, $N = 5$, $u(k)$ be a scalar control sequence to be calculated with initial condition $\mathbf{x}(0) = (1 \quad 1)'$. We choose system matrices A and B as

$$A = \begin{pmatrix} 1 & \frac{2}{3} \\ 0 & \frac{1}{3} \end{pmatrix} \tag{2.174}$$

$$B = \begin{pmatrix} \frac{1}{3} \\ \frac{2}{3} \end{pmatrix} \tag{2.175}$$

The quadratic performance index to be minimized is given by

$$J = \sum_{k=0}^{4} \left[\tfrac{1}{2}(x_1^2(k) + x_2^2(k)) + \tfrac{1}{2}u^2(k)\right] \tag{2.176}$$

The calculations required to solve this quadratic control problem have been carried out by computer; the results are shown in Figure 2.14 and Table 2.2.

TABLE 2.2.

QUADRATIC PERFORMANCE EXAMPLE

k	$x_1(k)$	$x_2(k)$	$u(k)$	$h_1(k)$	$h_2(k)$
0	1.0000	1.0000	1.2245	0.6120	0.6125
1	1.2585	−0.4830	0.4541	0.5877	0.5911
2	0.7851	−0.4637	0.1477	0.4868	0.5057
3	0.4627	−0.2530	0.0191	0.2143	0.2857
4	0.2517	−0.0971	0.0000	0.0000	0.0000

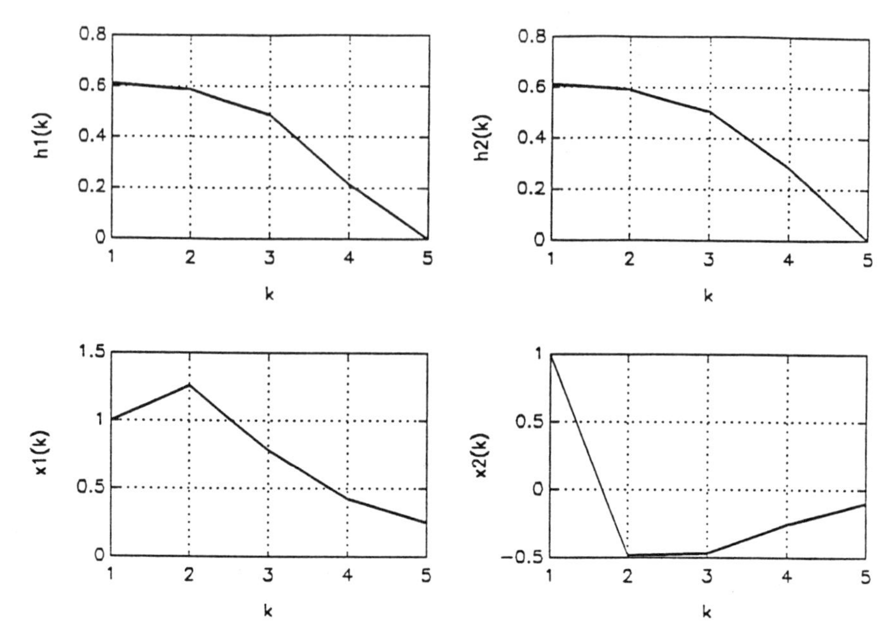

FIG. 2.14. Quadratic performance index controller design example.

Kalman Filtering

In this section, we introduce the idea of a Kalman filter. Many developments in the literature address this topic, and several of those are included for reference at the end of the chapter. Generally speaking, a Kalman filter can be considered an "optimal", minimum mean-squared error (MMSE) estimator of nonstationary Gaussian processes, i.e., a generalization of a Wiener filter [24] to the nonstationary case. The purpose of this section is not to provide yet another derivation of the Kalman tracker. Here, the idea of a Kalman filter itself is somewhat secondary. The real focus in the context of digital system design is to emphasize the *systems* aspect—to demonstrate, by example, how some of the different aspects of systems interrelate as elements in the design of a realistic system. Only by thorough understanding of these interdependencies can the system designer realistically assess the trade-offs they present. Although the purpose of the book is to present the different facets of digital system in one comprehensive volume, the purpose of this chapter is to illustrate the importance of at least some of these various aspects of systems to the system designers.

A thorough study of all of the systems and inter(sub)system communications trade-offs in tracking applications is beyond the scope of this chapter—distributed system optimization is indeed a topic of much further research. However, through the use of examples, we will address at least some of the computational aspects of different tracker types and discuss how practical limitations of the implementation affect optimality criteria and vice versa.

Tracking Defined

A Kalman filter is more often than not referred to as a Kalman *tracker*, probably because of its extensive use in a surveillance context (i.e., to track the positions of objects based on measurements of some aspect of position). The original work by Kalman and Bucy [25] was done in a system control context, however; hence it is also referred to as the *optimal observer* for a linear, quadratic, Gaussian (LQG) problem [26].

In our context, we continue to refer to *tracking* problems, with the understanding that tracking can mean much more (or less) than the tracking of objects in space. In fact, we define the problem loosely as the estimation of a (possibly nonstationary, random) process based on (noisy) measurements of a related process.

In the following subsections, we introduce tracking problems of increasing difficulty, culminating in the Kalman filter, and show why even the general LQG case is too restrictive for the solution of some relatively simple tracking examples. From this, we derive some extensions of the Kalman filter and demonstrate that Kalman tracking in many aspects is only a partial, though sometimes practical, solution.

The "Simplest" Problem: Tracking a Constant

Problem Definition

One of the simplest tracking problems is probably the estimation of a constant in noise. In the traditional tracking context, this constant could be the range of some object, where it is assumed that the object does not move over the observation time of interest. Let the measurements be modeled by

$$z(n) = [x + w(n)]u(n) \tag{2.177}$$

where x is a (random, Gaussian-distributed) constant with mean μ_x and standard deviation σ_x, $u(n)$ is the unit step function, and $w(n)$ is white, stationary, Gaussian noise with average power σ_w^2 and zero mean. The expression in Eq. (2.177) assumes that measurements arrive continuously and indefinitely, starting at time $t = 0$. For negative values of n, the measurements are assumed to be equal to 0—this is often called the *pre-windowed* case. A tracker is simply a filter that estimates the constant based on the measurements. We will discuss several types of trackers, starting with intuitive realizations, leading into the "optimal" one. For each, we will discuss properties of the estimate, as well as implementations and limitations.

Fixed FIR Smoothing

Definition. The most obvious way to estimate the constant x is to simply average all of the measurements:

$$\hat{x}(n) = \frac{1}{N} \sum_{k=0}^{N-1} z(n-k) \tag{2.178}$$

It is clear that the estimate may be obtained as the output from a finite impulse response (FIR) filter with impulse response

$$h(n) = \frac{1}{N} [u(n) - u(n-N)] \tag{2.179}$$

The estimate obtained at time n always consists of a smoothed version of the last N measurements if $n \geq N - 1$, as is demonstrated in Figure 2.15.

Statistical Properties. The mean value of this estimate is clearly equal to

$$\begin{aligned} E\{\hat{x}(n)\} &= \mu_x & n &\geq N - 1 \\ &= \frac{n+1}{N} \mu_x & 0 &\leq n < N - 1 \end{aligned} \tag{2.180}$$

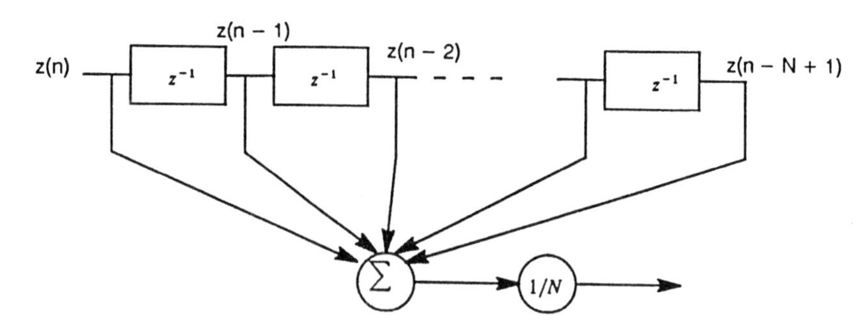

FIG. 2.15. Simple FIR implementation of a smoother.

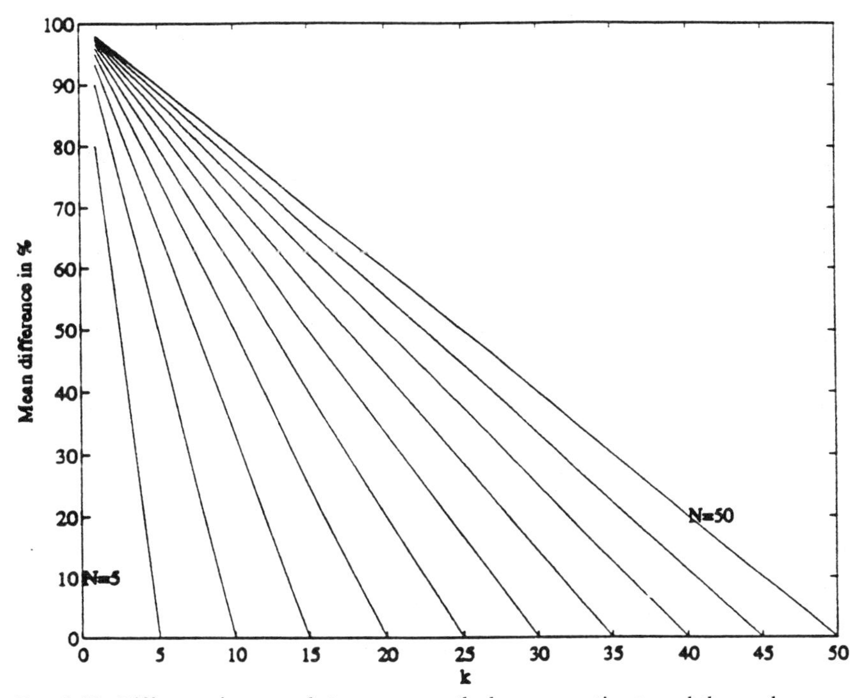

FIG. 2.16. Difference in means between a smoothed average estimate and the random constant to be estimated as a function of time for different window sizes.

For small values of n, the estimate's mean and the constant's mean differ, due to the prewindowing process. This prewindowing process creates a "transient," which results in the different mean values. This difference between the actual constant and the mean of the estimate is shown in Figure 2.16. Note that it is reduced dramatically as the window size, or the length of the FIR, becomes larger, but it also takes longer for it to disappear.

The variance of the estimate is

$$\begin{aligned}\sigma_{\hat{x}}^2(n) &= \frac{n+1}{N^2}[(n+1)\sigma_x^2 + \sigma_w^2] \qquad 0 \le n \le N-1 \\ &= \frac{1}{N}\sigma_w^2 + \sigma_x^2 \qquad n \ge N-1\end{aligned} \tag{2.181}$$

Note that the variance approaches the variance of the constant in question as the window size increases. Also, the variance varies with time during the transient caused by the prewindowing.

In addition to the mean and variance of the estimate, the mean squared error (MSE) is an important measure that describes the statistical quality of the result. It is defined as

$$\text{MSE}(n) = E\{|\hat{x}(n) - x|^2\} \tag{2.182}$$

and is easily calculated for the FIR tracker as:

$$\begin{aligned} MSE(n) &= \frac{\sigma_w^2}{N} \qquad n \geq N - 1 \\ &= \frac{n+1}{N}\sigma_w^2 + \left[\frac{n+1-N}{N}\right]^2 (\mu_x^2 + \sigma_x^2) \qquad 0 \leq n < N - 1 \end{aligned} \tag{2.183}$$

Note that the steady-state mean squared error is inversely proportional with N, and that it takes exactly N time samples for the MSE to reach a constant value.

Implementation. The FIR estimator of a constant is implemented very easily in digital hardware as demonstrated in Figure 2.15. In all, N memory locations are needed to store the measurements, and for every calculated value of the estimate, one needs N additions and one multiplication. Therefore, this implementation lends itself well for realization on digital hardware; high-speed realizations using commercially available signal processors are straightforward. In practice, the filter's arithmetic is implemented in finite precision; this results in additional errors which are not described by the MSE. These errors can be modeled, under certain assumptions, as an additional variance on the filter's output. It is beyond the scope of this chapter to study finite-precision effects carefully; however, because of the simple implementation, finite precision effects can be neglected compared to the measurement noise, unless the number of points in the FIR window becomes very large. For a simple discussion of finite precision effects in FIR filters, see, for example, [4].

Discussion. In high-noise cases, the fixed FIR implementation requires a relatively large window size N. Although the window size is usually not a problem from hardware considerations, due to the availability of inexpensive Digital Signal Processors (DSPs), increased values of N also mean a longer transient, during which the mean of the estimate may significantly differ from the mean of the constant in question. This presents the designer with a classic tradeoff of speed versus performance. The fixed FIR implementation is attractive in the sense that the transient is identically equal to zero after a finite number of time samples. Note that the FIR estimate at time n is a linear combination of measurements from the $N - 1$ previous sample times and the present only. Hence, we often refer to an FIR implementation as having *finite memory*. This is intuitively somewhat contradictory to the knowledge that data comes in continuously for $n > 0$, and that somehow we should take advantage of *all* of this data. In other words, a tracker with *infinite memory* is, at first sight, more appealing.

The "Alpha" Tracker

Definition. An alternative to the fixed FIR implementation from the previous section is now presented. As discussed previously, the smoothing approach only "remembers" measurements over a block of N samples, and completely "forgets" the previous ones. An *infinite memory* estimator can be implemented without physically assigning an infinitely large number of memory locations by using recursion.

A recursive estimation of a constant in the form:

$$\hat{x}(n) = \alpha\hat{x}(n - 1) + (1 - \alpha)z(n^{n \geq 0}) \tag{2.184}$$

is equivalent to passing the measurements through a first order IIR filter, with impulse response:

$$h(n) = (1 - a)a^n u(n) \tag{2.185}$$

It is easy to show that this filter has a single pole at $z = a$; this filter is therefore stable if $a < 1$. The estimate at time n now consists of a combination of *all* previous measurements, where the "oldest" measurements are weighted with a coefficient which decreases exponentially with the measurement's age. This is seen from the convolution of the input with the impulse response:

$$\hat{x}(n) = (1 - a) \sum_{k=0}^{n} a^{n-k} z(k) \qquad n \geq 0 \tag{2.186}$$

For "older" measurements (increasing k) the weight applied to the measurement in the estimate is a^{n-k}, which decreases with $n - k$ since $a < 1$. This simple filter is sometimes referred to as an "alpha" tracker—it is said to have *infinite* memory because it uses measurements from all times, and the coefficient a is often referred to as an *exponential forgetting factor*. a can be interpreted as a parameter which controls the filter's memory size; it does so through *computation* however, as opposed to *direct assignment* as is done in FIR smoothing discussed above.

Statistical properties. The mean of the estimate is easily derived as (for $n \geq 0$):

$$\begin{aligned} E\{\hat{x}(n)\} &= \mu_x(1 - a) \sum_{k=0}^{n} a^{n-k} \\ &= \mu_x(1 - a^{n+1}) \end{aligned} \tag{2.187}$$

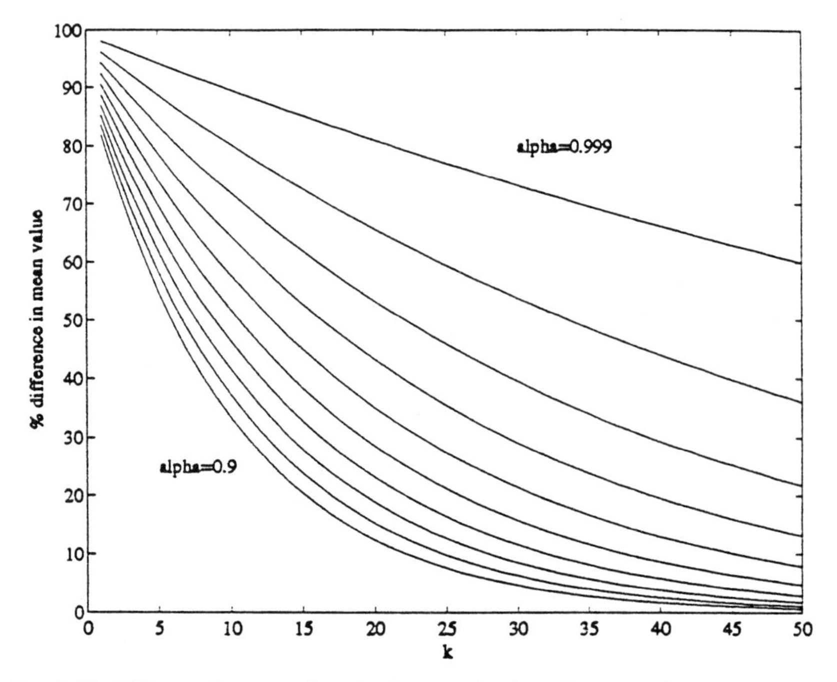

FIG. 2.17. Difference in mean value of estimate and estimated constant for an alpha tracker.

This mean value now only approaches the mean value of the constant in question in the limit, which is illustrated in Figure 2.17 for different values of α as a function of time. Note that the bias never completely disappears; however, it soon becomes negligible, especially for small values of α.

The variance of the estimate is:

$$\sigma_{\hat{x}}^2 = \sigma_{\hat{x}}^2(1 - a^{n+1})^2 + \sigma_w^2 \frac{1 - a^{2(n+1)}}{a + 1}(1 - a) \tag{2.188}$$

Note that again, there is a transient of infinite duration. In steady state, the variance becomes:

$$\sigma_{\hat{x}}^2 = \sigma_x^2 + \sigma_w^2 \frac{1 - \alpha}{1 + \alpha} \tag{2.189}$$

Note that this steady-state variance can be reduced by choosing alpha to be close to 1. The mean squared error of the estimate is obtained as (for $n \geq 0$):

$$\mathrm{MSE}(n) = \alpha^{2(n+1)}(\mu_x^2 + \sigma_x^2) + \sigma_w^2 \frac{1 - \alpha^{2(n+1)}}{\alpha + 1}(1 - \alpha) \tag{2.190}$$

The MSE is shown in Figure 2.18.

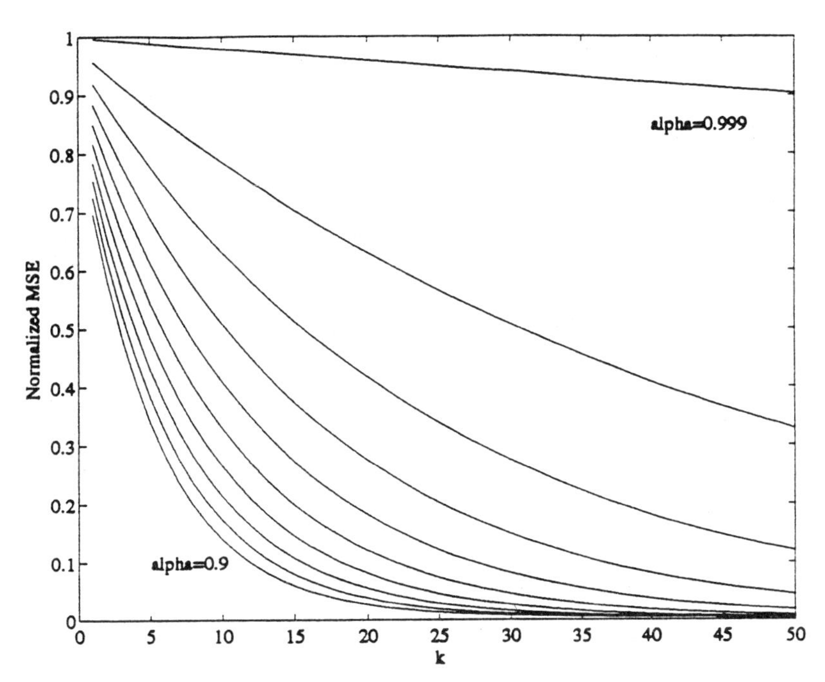

FIG. 2.18. MSE for the alpha tracker as a function of time and for different values of alpha.

Implementation. The alpha tracker can be very easily implemented in fast hardware realizations. Even though it has "infinite memory," it actually uses fewer physical memory locations than the FIR example: only one memory location is needed from one time sample to the next to store the present estimate, one location to store the coefficient alpha, and one to hold the incoming measurement. The implementation is shown in Figure 2.19. From a hardware point of view, even fewer elements are needed to implement the alpha tracker than in the FIR case—a sum and multiplication can,

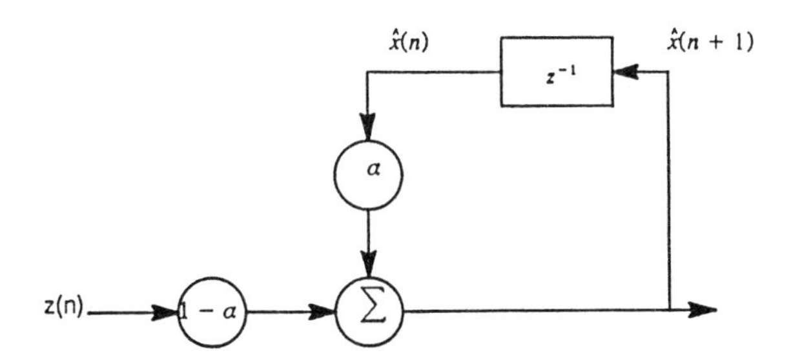

FIG. 2.19. Implementation of the alpha tracker.

in practice, be handled by a single instruction in most commercial digital signal processors. Implementation in finite precision again leads to additional errors, and the constant alpha has to be chosen somewhat more carefully such that instabilities due to finite precision can be avoided. For a more detailed yet simplified discussion of finite precision effects on simple recursive filters, see [27].

Discussion. Although the statistical properties of the recursive implementation are somewhat less desirable than those of the FIR tracker, in the sense that the transients have infinite duration, often this is of no real consequence and the advantage of fewer memory locations outweighs any disadvantage of statistical properties. Hence, the recursive alpha tracker is often the preferred realization when no real optimality criterion has to be optimized. The fact that the recursion can be implemented with minimal hardware makes it ideal where a large number of trackers have to be implemented simultaneously, such as in image processing or spectrum analysis applications.

The Minimum Mean Squared Error Linear Estimator

Definition. From the previous discussions, it is clear that trade-offs exist between the steady-state error, as characterized by the MSE, and the time-length of the transient caused by the "prewindowing" of the data. It may be desired to formulate an "optimal" solution, which minimizes the error to some extent at every point in time. The most pervasive of optimality criteria in signal processing is probably the minimum mean squared error approach (MMSE). For that formulation, let us define the data vector as

$$\mathbf{z}_n = [z(0)z(1)\ldots z(n)]' \tag{2.191}$$

i.e., the accumulated set of measurements up to and including the nth one. Expressing a linear estimate by

$$\hat{x}_n = \mathbf{h}_n'\mathbf{z}_n \tag{2.192}$$

where

$$\mathbf{h}_n = [h_n(0)\ldots h_n(n)] \tag{2.193}$$

is a set of weights that, as we shall see shortly, may be interpreted as the impulse response weights of a time-varying linear filter. Note that we have retained the index n as a subscript to indicate the implicit dependence on n, the number of measurements received.

The MMSE is minimized by setting

$$\nabla_{h_n}\text{MSE}_n = 0 \tag{2.194}$$

where MSE_n is defined as

$$\begin{aligned}\mathrm{MSE}_n &= E\{|x - \hat{x}_n|^2\} \\ &= m_x^2 \mathbf{h}_n' \mathbf{1}\mathbf{1}' \mathbf{h}_n + \sigma_w^2 \mathbf{h}_n' \mathbf{h}_n - 2m_x^2 \mathbf{1}' \mathbf{h}_n + m_x^2 \end{aligned} \tag{2.195}$$

where $\mathbf{1}$ is a vector of length $n + 1$ with all elements equal to 1, and $m_x^2 = E\{x^2\}$. Taking the derivatives with regard to elements of $\mathbf{h}_n$ and setting the result equal to 0 reduces to the following condition on the estimate:

$$\mathbf{h}_n = \frac{1}{n + 1 + (\sigma_w^2 / m_x^2)} \mathbf{1} = h_n \mathbf{1} \tag{2.196}$$

Statistical Properties. The mean of the resulting estimate is found to be

$$E\{\hat{x}_n\} = \frac{n + 1}{n + 1 + (\sigma_w^2 / m_x^2)} \mu_x \tag{2.197}$$

Note that the mean is *not* equal to the mean of the constant unless it is 0; the difference does, however, approach 0 with $n \to \infty$. The resulting MSE is readily obtained from Eq. (2.195).

Implementation. Expression (2.192) indicates that the implementation of this estimator can be readily interpreted as an FIR filter with growing filter size and coefficients that change with n; i.e., a time-varying FIR filter. An increasing number of memory locations is required to store the increasing number of measurements; therefore, the optimal MMSE filter also has infinite memory. No practical hardware implementation has an ever-growing number of memory locations available, and the "optimal" filter has to be approximated.

As an alternative to direct implementation of the estimate, the optimal MMSE estimate can be written recursively as follows:

$$\hat{x}_n = \alpha_n \hat{x}_{n-1} + (1 - \alpha_n) z(n) \tag{2.198}$$

where

$$\alpha_n = \frac{n + (\sigma_w^2 / m_x^2)}{n + 1 + (\sigma_w^2 / m_x^2)} \tag{2.199}$$

as can be seen from combining Eq. (2.196) with (2.192) and (2.193). Note that $\alpha_n < 1$, making the recursion stable. Clearly, this implementation does not require the growing number of memory locations—the memory requirement is handled recursively, similar to the alpha tracker discussed in the preceding subsection. This realization is indeed very similar to the alpha tracker, but the coefficient alpha is now time varying. The implementation

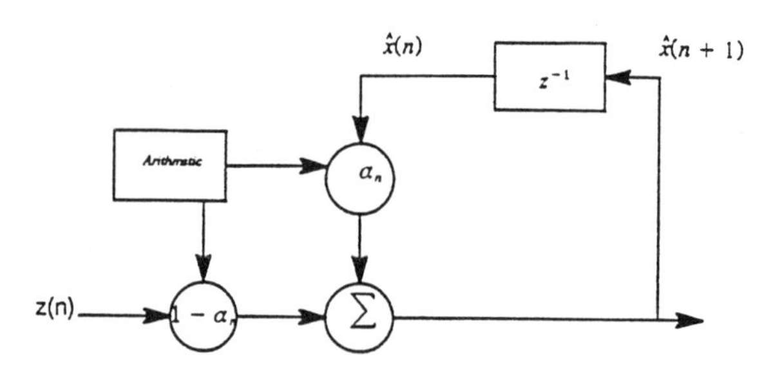

FIG. 2.20. Recursive implementation of the MMSE tracker.

is similar, except that now additional arithmetic is required (addition and division), as is indicated in Figure 2.20. Although the extra additions pose no real problem for typical hardware, division is not always easily implemented. Commercial DSP hardware does not typically provide for a complete division instruction, and hence a division algorithm must be implemented. This may require many additional processor instruction cycles; consequently, a full implementation of the MMSE filter will be limited to lower data rates than the fixed alpha tracker.

With the recursive form in Eq. (2.198), the processor must calculate coefficients from numbers that increase without bound (i.e., n). In practice, exact calculation of the coefficients is therefore limited by the dynamic range of the processor (i.e., the range of numbers the processor can represent). In addition, round-off errors will come into play.

Discussion. The optimal MMSE filter just derived clearly assumes that the statistics of the "signal" to be estimated (the constant x) are known. In practice, this may not be an accurate assumption, and a better model may be to consider x a fixed (as opposed to random), but unknown, constant. Problems 5 through 8 at the end of this chapter demonstrate the difference between that case and the case considered in this example. One may find it remarkable that the MMSE estimator has a different mean from the mean of the constant it estimates. However, it is not uncommon in signal processing to sacrifice some error in mean value for an overall reduced MSE.

To circumvent problems facing a hardware implementation, one needs to make approximations in the arithmetic that computes alpha. Note that, as more measurements are accrued, α_n approaches unity, and hence α_n could be approximated by 1 after a sufficient number of measurements have been collected. This means essentially that the measurement stream is "turned off," and the estimate is no longer updated. In practice, this is undesirable if the constant to be estimated can undergo changes. Note that such a change violates the initial signal model (Eq. (2.177)). Clearly, the "optimal" processor is unable to deal well with inaccuracies in modeling assumptions. If, on the other hand, we limit α_n to a constant <1 after a number of measurements have been collected (i.e., reduce the filter to a fixed "alpha" tracker after a certain period of time), changes in the constant will eventually result in a changed estimate, as is the case for the alpha tracker. Although this estimate is no longer "optimal" according to the MMSE criterion, it is able to deal with incorrect modeling assumptions more effectively. In practice, this sensitivity (actually, the lack thereof) to inaccuracies in assumed models is called *robustness*. As we have seen here, the optimal processor is less robust with regard to changes in the initial model; an implementation that reduces the optimal tracker to an alpha tracker after a certain amount of time sacrifices some optimality in MSE; however, it is more robust.

Estimation with Constraints

Definition. As is evident from the preceding section, the MMSE estimator of a random constant has a different mean from the constant to be estimated. This difference reduces to 0 only after a large number of measurements have been processed (unless the mean is 0). This difference can be avoided by minimizing the MSE in Eq. (2.195) subject to a constraint; i.e., minimize

$$\mathrm{MSE}(n) + \lambda E\{\mu_x - \mu_{\hat{x}(n)}\} \tag{2.200}$$

where λ is a Lagrange multiplier, chosen to satisfy the constraint that

$$E\{\hat{x}(n)\} = \mu_x \tag{2.201}$$

The resulting filter coefficients are now found to be

$$\mathbf{h}_n = \frac{1}{n+1} \tag{2.202}$$

It is no surprise that this is the nth length smoothing filter discussed previously; however, the constrained MMSE estimate changes its "window size" with the number of measurements.

Statistical Properties. The mean of this estimator is, per definition,

$$E\{\hat{x}_n\} = \mu_x \tag{2.203}$$

whereas the MSE is obtained as

$$\mathrm{MSE}(n) = \sigma_x^2 + \frac{\sigma_w^2}{n+1} \tag{2.204}$$

Implementation. The constrained MMSE tracker may be implemented in the same way as the optimal MMSE tracker. The coefficients alpha for the recursive filter implementation in this case are

$$\alpha_n = \frac{n}{n+1} \tag{2.205}$$

The same comments hold regarding precision as followed in Eq. (2.198).

Discussion

The previous is by no means a complete treatment of even the simple problem such as estimation of a constant. In practice, smoothing of this type is typically found in applications where the attribute in question varies sufficiently slowly over a period of time that it can be considered "constant." For example, the range of an aircraft may be measured at a high rate by a radar sensor. Although the phase of the radar return changes sufficiently from pulse to pulse to prohibit coherent analysis over multiple pulses, the measured range is practically constant (within the desired accuracy) so that further temporal smoothing (over a small enough time period) of the range measurements is possible.

Tracking a Constant Rate

Definition

The previous problem, however simple, nevertheless provides good insight in some of the problems and trade-offs encountered in other, more complicated tracking problems. Tracking problems invariably rely on some quantity being known or constant, as expressed in a signal "model." Clearly, different assumptions of the signal model result in drastically different estimation schemes. For instance, the "prewindowing" assumption may not be entirely realistic, yet it resulted in some very specific estimators.

The "constancy," or invariance, expressed by a model is not always as straightforwardly exploited as in the case of a simple constant. To illustrate this, assume that the measured signal in question is represented by

$$\begin{aligned} z(n) &= [x(n) + w(n)]u(n) \\ x(n) &= \dot{x}n\,\Delta T + x_0 \end{aligned} \tag{2.206}$$

where $\dot{x}$ and x_0 are random constants. Note that this model corresponds to a (prewindowed) noisy measurement of a signal that changes at a constant rate. This problem could be related to the estimation of a constant by considering

$$x'(n) = x(n + 1) - x(n) = \dot{x}\,\Delta T \tag{2.207}$$

$$z'(n) = [x'(n) + w(n + 1) - w(n)]u(n) \tag{2.208}$$

Note that we are again estimating a constant, but the measurement noise is no longer "white." We can go through the same derivations as in the previous sections (i.e., the FIR tracker, the alpha tracker, etc.) and derive their statistical properties, but, since the noise is not simply white, the derivation becomes more tedious. Clearly, we want a more formal approach to tracking that applies to a large class of signal models. In the next subsection we formally define such an approach in terms of the Kalman filter. We then return to the problems at hand and demonstrate how the Kalman filter provides a unifying framework to solve them.

Tracking Signals Modeled by a State Equation

Definition

As mentioned in the previous section, tracking or estimation is essentially based upon some "constancy" of parameters that describe the signal(s) in question, through an expressed model.

As already discussed in the chapter on control systems, one of the most general forms of models are the linear models characterized by a finite state equation. It makes sense, therefore, to formulate trackers in the context of this general class and derive properties of the trackers in this framework. The assumption of linear models is more limiting than one may, at first, believe; the linearity assumption does indeed pose a problem for even some of the most simple tracking problems, as will be discussed in later sections. We also limit ourselves to state equations of the discrete-time type; Kalman filters can be derived in similar ways from continuous-time models.

Let a signal be modeled by a state equation in its most general form:

$$\begin{aligned} \mathbf{x}(k + 1) &= \mathbf{A}(k)\mathbf{x}(k) + \mathbf{B}(k)\mathbf{u}(k) + \mathbf{w}_1(k) \\ \mathbf{y}(k) &= \mathbf{C}(k)\mathbf{x}(k) + \mathbf{D}(k)\mathbf{u}(k) + \mathbf{w}_2(k) \end{aligned} \tag{2.209}$$

The signal to be tracked is the state of this model, $\mathbf{x}(k)$, based on measurements of the related process, the model output $\mathbf{y}(k)$. The model allows for some known function, $\mathbf{u}(k)$, a model disturbance $\mathbf{w}_1(k)$, and a measurement error (or noise) $\mathbf{w}_2(k)$.

A General Tracker Form

Definition. A *tracker*, i.e., a linear system that estimates the state, is of the form [26]

$$\hat{\mathbf{x}}(k+1) = \mathbf{A}(k)\hat{\mathbf{x}}(k) + \mathbf{B}(k)\mathbf{u}(k) + \mathbf{K}(k)[\mathbf{y}(k) - \mathbf{C}(k)\hat{\mathbf{x}}(k) - \mathbf{D}(k)\mathbf{u}(k)] \tag{2.210}$$

where the matrix $\mathbf{K}(k)$ is called the *tracker gain*. Typically, the disturbance $\mathbf{w}_1(k)$ and the noise $\mathbf{w}_2(k)$ are assumed to be zero mean, uncorrelated, Gaussian with known covariance matrices. Although the optimal tracker can be derived for the case where the measurement noise and the model disturbance are correlated, we assume in this chapter that they are not—this is consistent with the original work by Kalman and Bucy [25]. It is also assumed that the mean and variance of the initial value of the state are known—this avoids the (unrealistic) prewindowing assumption as in the previous section. Recall that this assumption essentially led to transients during which the estimate's mean and the actual mean were different, even for the optimal MMSE case.

Example: Tracking a Constant. The problem of estimating a constant can be cast in the previous framework easily by letting $\mathbf{A}(k) = 1$, $\mathbf{u}(l) = 0$, $\mathbf{C}(k) = 1$, $\mathbf{D}(k) = 0$, and $\mathbf{w}_1(k) = 0$ for $k \geq 0$. Note that for a constant value of the tracker gain equal to

$$\mathbf{K}(k) = 1 - \alpha \tag{2.211}$$

we obtain the alpha tracker discussed earlier.

Example: Tracking a Constant Rate, or the Alpha–Beta Tracker. The constant-rate problem briefly mentioned in a previous section is also easily expressed in this framework by writing the simple state equation representation of a signal with constant rate, resulting in

$$\mathbf{x}(k) = \begin{bmatrix} \dot{x}(k) \\ x(k) \end{bmatrix} \tag{2.212}$$

$$\mathbf{A}(k) = \begin{bmatrix} 1 & 0 \\ \Delta T & 1 \end{bmatrix} \tag{2.213}$$

$$\mathbf{C}(k) = [0 \quad 1] \tag{2.214}$$

and a tracker of the type

$$\hat{\mathbf{x}}(k+1) = \mathbf{A}(k)\hat{\mathbf{x}}(k) + \mathbf{K}(k)[\mathbf{y}(k) - \mathbf{C}(k)\hat{x}(k)] \tag{2.215}$$

Letting the tracker gain be constant:

$$\mathbf{K}(k) = \begin{bmatrix} \dfrac{\beta}{\Delta T} \\ 1 - \alpha \end{bmatrix} \tag{2.216}$$

we obtain the estimate as

$$\hat{x}(k+1) = \alpha\hat{x}(k) + (1-\alpha)y(k) \tag{2.217}$$

$$\dot{x}(k+1) = \dot{x}(k) + \frac{\beta}{\Delta T}[y(k) - \Delta T\hat{x}(k)] \tag{2.218}$$

This tracker consists of a combination of the previously described alpha tracker, and an estimate of the rate based on a combination of the previous estimate plus a weighted version of the prediction error; i.e., the measurement minus the predicted value of the measurement based on the previous estimate. This tracker is often referred to as an *alpha–beta* tracker, for obvious reasons.

Example: Tracking Straight-Line Motion. The previous case can be directly extended to a situation where an object (an airplane, for instance) moves with constant velocity in a two-dimensional plane. In this case, the state consists of the (x, y) position in the plane, combined with the (x, y) velocity, all relative to some reference point. The state equation ("model") for the motion is determined by

$$\mathbf{x}(k) = \begin{bmatrix} \dot{x}(k) \\ \dot{y}(k) \\ x(k) \\ y(k) \end{bmatrix} \tag{2.219}$$

$$\mathbf{A} = \begin{bmatrix} 1 & 0 & 0 & 0 \\ 0 & 1 & 0 & 0 \\ \Delta T & 0 & 1 & 0 \\ 0 & \Delta T & 0 & 1 \end{bmatrix} \tag{2.220}$$

The model disturbance, $\mathbf{w}_1(k)$, would be equal to 0 for perfect straight-line motion; however, it is often useful to model any inaccuracies in the model by including a model disturbance with nonzero covariance. In this example, the model disturbance may express random motion introduced by wind variations, turbulence, etc.

If a radar system provides noisy measurements of the position in the x, y plane relative to the reference point, the measurement equation is obtained simply with

$$\mathbf{y}(k) = \begin{bmatrix} x \\ y \end{bmatrix} \tag{2.221}$$

$$\mathbf{C} = \begin{bmatrix} 0 & 0 & 1 & 0 \\ 0 & 0 & 0 & 1 \end{bmatrix} \tag{2.222}$$

Random errors in the position measurements (due to radar inaccuracies) are expressed in the measurement noise vector $\mathbf{w}_2(k)$.

If the measurements were taken from a moving platform, as opposed to directly with regard to the reference point, a known function $\mathbf{u}(k)$ can be introduced in the measurement equation to reflect the measurement's offset. If the position and the moving platform relative to the reference point is known to be $\mathbf{x}_r(k) = [x_r(k), y_r(k)]'$, the positional measurements can be represented using

$$\mathbf{u}(k) = \mathbf{x}_r(k) \tag{2.223}$$

$$\mathbf{D} = \begin{bmatrix} 1 & 0 \\ 0 & 1 \end{bmatrix} \tag{2.224}$$

Statistical Properties of Trackers Based on State Equations. To calculate the statistical properties (i.e., the mean and covariance of the estimate) of the tracker in its general form of Eq. (2.210), we need to use the statistics of the state as prescribed by the state equation. These statistics are easily expressed recursively if the initial vcalues of the mean and covariance of the state are known. If it is assumed that the model disturbance is a Gaussian, zero mean, "white" noise sequence, a recursive form for the mean value of the state is given by

$$\boldsymbol{\mu}_x(k+1) = \mathbf{A}(k)\boldsymbol{\mu}_x(k) + \mathbf{B}(k)\mathbf{u}(k) \tag{2.225}$$

and a recursive form of the covariance of the state is

$$\mathbf{R}_x(k+1) = \mathbf{A}(k)\mathbf{R}_x(k)\mathbf{A}(k)' + \mathbf{R}_{w1}(k) \tag{2.226}$$

These recursions can, in turn, be used to express the statistics of the estimate. Assuming that the measurement noise is zero mean, white, Gaussian, and uncorrelated, the mean and covariance of the estimated values can be computed as

$$\begin{aligned}\boldsymbol{\mu}_{\hat{x}}(k+1) = {} & [\mathbf{A}(k) - \mathbf{K}(k)\mathbf{C}(k)]\boldsymbol{\mu}_{\hat{x}}(k) + [\mathbf{B}(k) - \mathbf{K}(k)\mathbf{D}(k)]\mathbf{u}(k) \\ & + \mathbf{K}(k)\boldsymbol{\mu}_y(k)\end{aligned} \tag{2.217}$$

$$\begin{aligned}\mathbf{R}_{\hat{x}}(k+1) = {} & [\mathbf{A}(k) - \mathbf{K}(k)\mathbf{C}(k)]\mathbf{R}_{\hat{x}}(k)[\mathbf{A}(k) - \mathbf{K}(k)\mathbf{C}(k)]' \\ & + \mathbf{K}(k)\mathbf{R}_y(k)\mathbf{K}(k)'\end{aligned} \tag{2.228}$$

where

$$\mathbf{\mu}_y(k) = \mathbf{C}(k)\mathbf{\mu}_x(k) + \mathbf{D}(k)\mathbf{u}(k) \tag{2.229}$$

(the measurement mean) and

$$\mathbf{R}_y(k) = \mathbf{C}(k)\mathbf{R}_x(k)\mathbf{C}(k)' + \mathbf{R}_{w2}(k) \tag{2.230}$$

(the measurement covariance).

In general, the solution of these recursive equations is nontrivial. Closed-form solutions exist if the model matrices in question are time invariant—we refer to the chapter on control system analysis for their solution. It is relatively straightforward, however, to obtain solutions numerically for these recursions; the previous expressions are easily programmed on a digital computer.

Implementations of Trackers Based on State Equations. The tracker defined in (2.210) is itself in the form of a state-variable expression. Therefore, it can be implemented using the same techniques as any linear, discrete-time, state feedback control system. We refer back to the chapter on control systems analysis. The comments made in the introductory sections continue to hold, and, typically, state-space type trackers can be implemented recursively using signal processing hardware (digital signal processors) in a straightforward way. It should be noted, however, that, as the number of state variables grows, the number of memory locations and calculations per time sample grows as well. Hence, we may be able to implement more sophisticated models that approach the true signal more accurately; however, this cannot be done without paying a price.

Optimal MMSE Tracker or Kalman Tracker

Definition and Statistical Properties. The MMSE solution of the tracker problem, based on the state-variable representation is now formulated as the determination of the gain $\mathbf{K}(k)$ such that the MSE,

$$\text{MSE}(k) = E\{[\mathbf{x}(k) - \hat{\mathbf{x}}(k)]'[x(k) - \hat{\mathbf{x}}(k)]\} \tag{2.231}$$

is minimized for all time instances k. A (nontrivial) derivation results in the recursive definition of the optimal MMSE gain sequence $\mathbf{K}_{\text{MMSE}}(k)$ as [26]:

$$\mathbf{K}_{\text{MMSE}}(k) = [\mathbf{A}(k)\mathbf{R}_e(k)\mathbf{C}(k)'][\mathbf{R}_{w_2}(k) + \mathbf{C}(k)\mathbf{R}_e(k)\mathbf{C}(k)']^{-1} \tag{2.232}$$

where $\mathbf{R}_e(k)$, the covariance matrix of the error $e(k) = x(k) - \hat{x}(k)$ is defined recursively as

$$\mathbf{R}_e(k+1) = [\mathbf{A}(k) - \mathbf{K}_{\text{MMSE}}(k)\mathbf{C}(k)]\mathbf{R}_e(k)\mathbf{A}(k)' + \mathbf{R}_{w_1}(k) \tag{2.233}$$

with initialization

$$\mathbf{R}_e(0) = \mathbf{R}_x(0) \tag{2.234}$$

The tracker itself is initialized as

$$\hat{\mathbf{x}}(0) = \boldsymbol{\mu}_x(0) \tag{2.235}$$

In general, solution of this recursion is nontrivial; however, it lends itself relatively well for numerical computation. The following example demonstrates how a simple, nonstationary signal can be tracked using the MMSE tracker of (2.232) and (2.233).

Example: Tracking a Nonstationary Signal. Assume we are to estimate the signal determined by the following model:

$$x(n+1) = a^n x(n) \tag{2.236}$$

based on the measurements

$$y(n) = x(n) + w(n) \tag{2.237}$$

where $w(n)$ is white noise with zero mean and variance σ^2, a is a constant <1. A realization of this signal for $n > 0$ is shown in Figure 2.21.

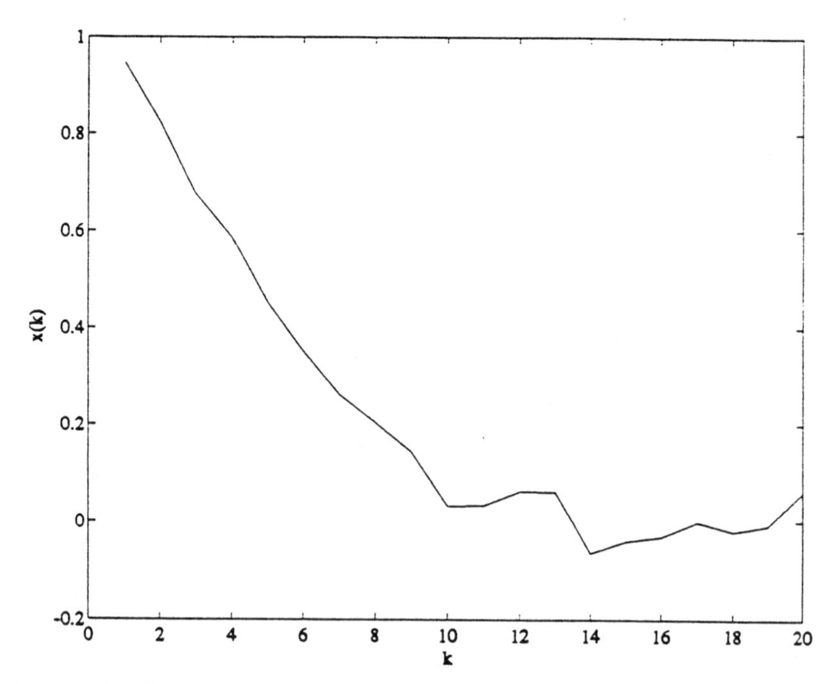

FIG. 2.21. Realization of the nonstationary signal of this example with $\sigma = 0.2$ and $a = 0.95$.

From Eqs. (2.232) and (2.233) we can express the optimal tracker recursively as

$$K_{\mathrm{MMSE}}(k) = \frac{[a^k R_e(k)]}{\sigma^2 + R_e(k)} \tag{2.238}$$

with the variance of the error equal to

$$R_e(k+1) = [a^k - K_{\mathrm{MMSE}}(k)]R_e(k)a^k \tag{2.239}$$

Figure 2.22 shows a realization of this estimate for $a = 0.95$ and $\mu_x(0) = 1$ and $R_x(0) = 0.04$. The Kalman gain is plotted in Figure 2.23. Note that the Kalman gain becomes 0 as $n \to \infty$. In other words, the system "turns off" measurements as it becomes more certain of the estimate—the "optimal" tracker may again not be very robust: if the model is incorrect and the signal changes after a long time, the tracker's output will not reflect this change. Figure 2.24 demonstrates the MSE. Note that, as desired, the MSE rapidly reduces to 0.

Implementation. The optimal MMSE tracker may be implemented in a configuration similar to that of Figure 2.25. Note that *all* operations consist of vector–matrix arithmetic; and the complete model, i.e., the time-varying

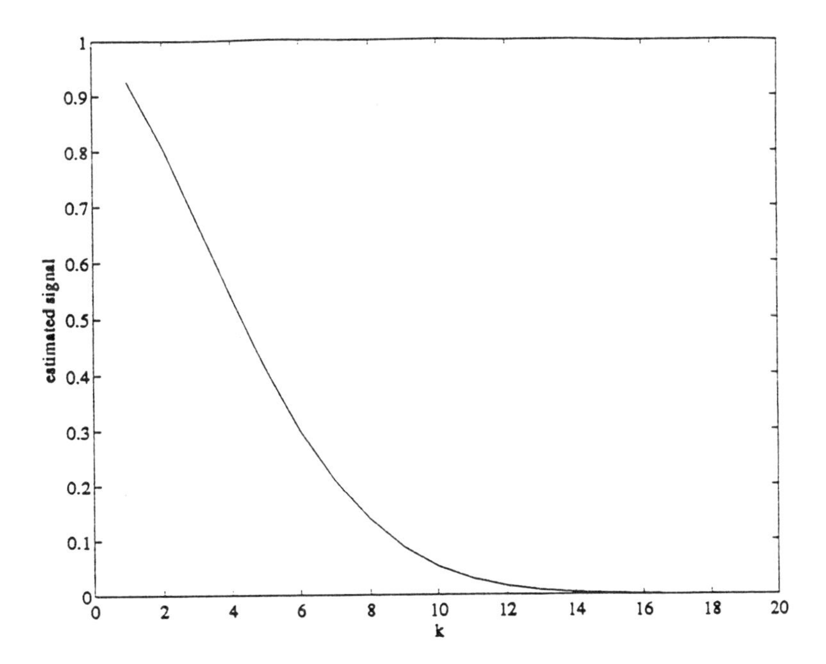

FIG. 2.22. Estimated version of the signal of the same example.

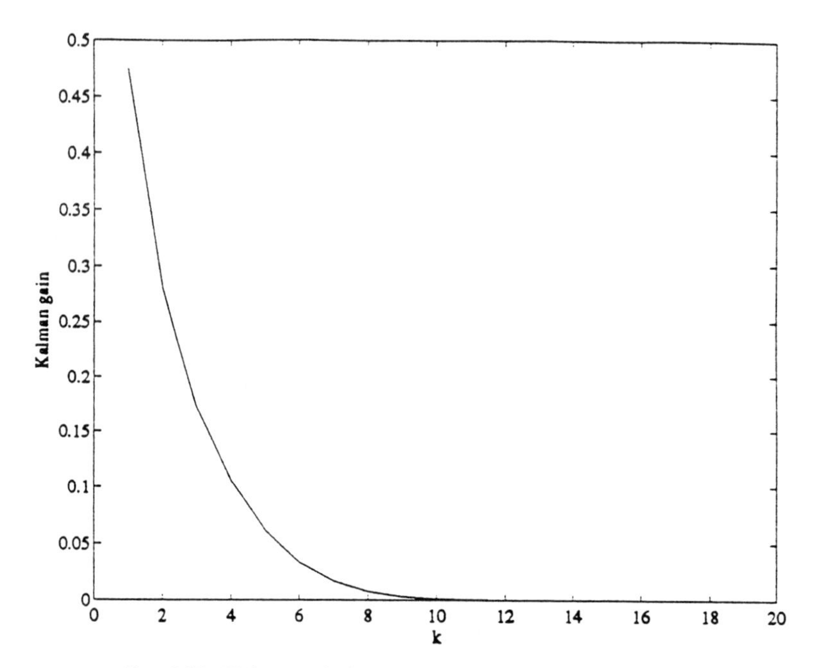

FIG. 2.23. Kalman gain for the MMSE tracker of the same example.

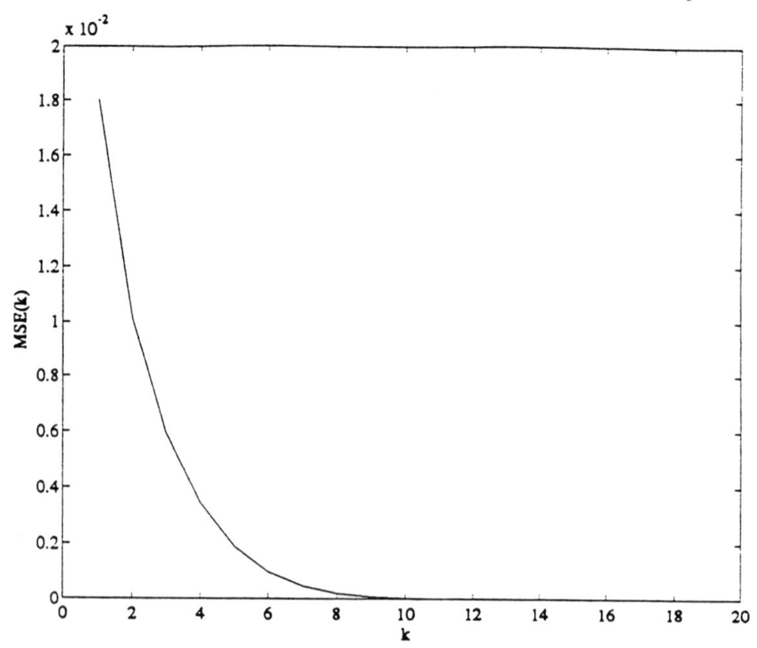

FIG. 2.24. MSE of the estimate of the same example.

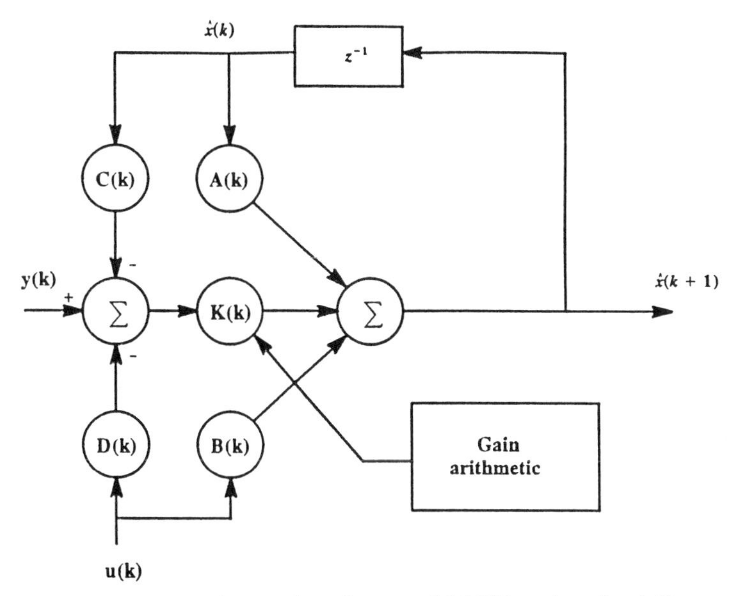

FIG. 2.25. Implementation of a general MMSE tracker: signal filter.

coefficients, need to be stored for every point in time. The arithmetic for the gain computation itself is shown symbolically in Figure 2.26. Note that in addition to vector-matrix arithmetic, the calculation of the gain requires a matrix inverse. Matrix inverses are, in their most general form, extremely computationally intensive, and often sensitive to round-off errors. Although matrix inverses can be implemented in fixed-point arithmetic, one must do so very carefully, and efficient implementation of the optimal tracker is still the subject of a great deal of research (see the discussion on advanced topics later). In general, optimal trackers with a large number of state variables are implemented mainly on floating-point hardware; often the implementation of matrix arithmetic needs to be implemented on parallel processor schemes for faster execution. The gain calculation requires the error variance; hence, the statistical performance (or, actually, an estimate thereof as provided by the model) is a by-product of its implementation.

The Kalman–Bucy Filter for Time-Invariant Models

Definition. In many cases, the model itself does not change appreciably over time, and it becomes possible to model it as a time-invariant system. As seen earlier, this makes the implementation of the Kalman tracker significantly simpler, since the model's state representation matrices need to be stored only once for all time. In addition, the "forcing function"

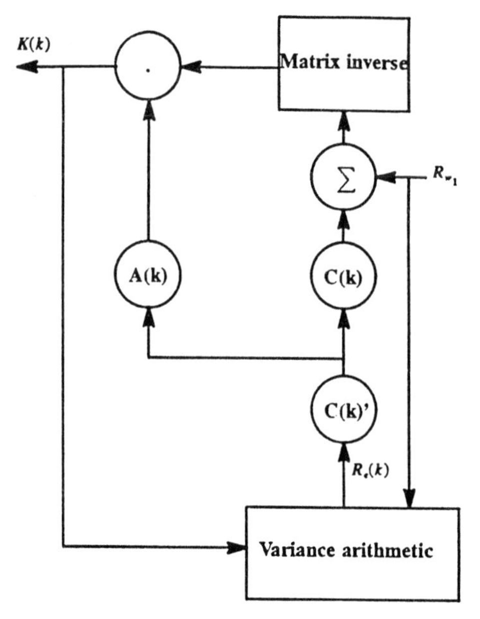

FIG. 2.26. Gain arithmetic for the MMSE tracker (pre- and postmultiplications are not indicated differently).

u( ) in many cases can be taken to equal 0. The Kalman tracker for this case is readily derived from the time-varying expressions (2.232) and (2.233). This results in the following, more standard form of the Kalman tracker:

$$\hat{\mathbf{y}}(k \mid k-1) = \mathbf{CA}\hat{x}(k-1 \mid k-1) \tag{2.240}$$

$$\mathbf{e}(k \mid k-1) = \mathbf{y}(k) - \hat{\mathbf{y}}(k \mid k-1) \tag{2.241}$$

$$\mathbf{R}_{\hat{x}}(k \mid k-1) = \mathbf{AR}_{\hat{x}}(k \mid k-1)\mathbf{A}' + \mathbf{R}_{w_1} \tag{2.242}$$

$$\mathbf{K}(k) = \mathbf{R}_{\hat{x}}(k \mid k-1)\mathbf{C}'[\mathbf{CR}_{\hat{x}}(k \mid k-1)\mathbf{C}' + \mathbf{R}_{w_2}]^{-1} \tag{2.243}$$

$$\hat{\mathbf{x}}(k \mid k) = \hat{\mathbf{x}}(k \mid k-1) + \mathbf{K}(k)\mathbf{e}(k) \tag{2.244}$$

$$\mathbf{R}_{\hat{x}}(k \mid k) = [\mathbf{I} - \mathbf{K}(k)\mathbf{C}]\mathbf{R}_{\hat{x}}(k \mid k-1) \tag{2.245}$$

with

$$\mathbf{R}_{\hat{x}}(0 \mid 0) = \mathbf{R}_x(0, 0) \tag{2.246}$$

$$\boldsymbol{\mu}_{\hat{x}}(0) = \boldsymbol{\mu}_x(0) \tag{2.247}$$

This form of the Kalman tracker partitions the operations into several steps. The first step consists of linear prediction: based on the present estimate $\hat{x}(k-1 \mid k-1)$ and the model, the predicted state covariance $\mathbf{R}_{\hat{x}}(k \mid k-1)$ (Eq. (2.242)) and the predicted measurement at the next time instant $\hat{\mathbf{y}}(k \mid k-1)$ (Eq. (2.240)) are calculated, Based on the model and the predicted state covariance, the Kalman gain is computed (Eq. (2.238)). This is used with the prediction in the state update: error $\mathbf{e}(k \mid k-1)$ (Eq. (2.241)) to obtain the new state estimate $\hat{\mathbf{x}}(k \mid k)$ (Eq. (2.244)). The covariance of the new state estimate, given all of the measurements up to and including time k, is calculated as in Eq. (2.245).

Implementation. It is important to point out that the implementation of the tracker is still a time-varying filter, as in Figure 2.25; even though the model is time invariant. The time invariance helps only in the calculation of the Kalman gain, as in Figure 2.26.

Example. Let us go back to the original simple case of estimating a constant in white noise. The state equation is discussed in Eq. (2.211). If it is assumed that the initial value of the mean of the state and the variance of the state is known, the Kalman tracker can be easily derived. The Kalman prediction is

$$\hat{x}(k \mid k-1) = \hat{x}(k-1 \mid k-1) \tag{2.248}$$

$$R_{\hat{x}}(k \mid k-1) = R_{\hat{x}}(k-1 \mid k-1) \tag{2.249}$$

The Kalman gain is readily computed from Eq. (2.237):

$$K(k) = \frac{R_{\hat{x}}(k \mid k-1)}{R_{\hat{x}}(k \mid k-1) + \sigma_w^2} \tag{2.250}$$

The Kalman update is

$$\hat{x}(k \mid k) = \hat{x}(k \mid k-1) + K(k)[y(k) - \hat{x}(k \mid k-1)] \tag{2.251}$$

and the resulting covariance is

$$R_{\hat{x}}(k \mid k) = [1 - K(k)]R_{\hat{x}}(k \mid k-1) \tag{2.252}$$

This can be combined as

$$\hat{x}(k) = \alpha(k)\hat{x}(k) + [1 - \alpha(k)]y(k) \tag{2.253}$$

$$\alpha(k) = \frac{\sigma_w^2}{R_{\hat{x}}(k-1) + \sigma_w^2} \tag{2.254}$$

$$R_{\hat{x}}(k) = \alpha(k)R_{\hat{x}}(k-1) \tag{2.255}$$

It is not surprising that this results once again in a time-varying version of the alpha tracker discussed earlier.

Advanced Topics

Introduction

The previous discussions are geared towards familiarizing the reader with the system concepts behind the Kalman filter. This topic itself can probably take up several volumes by itself—in this chapter we have hardly scratched the surface. Other issues of implementation, finite-precision effects, parallel computing, dealing with nonlinearities, etc. are all legitimate systems aspects of tracker implementation. In this section, we attempt to summarize some of the more advanced work from the literature and relate it to some of the comments made in this chapter.

Implementation Aspects: Special Architectures

The implementation of the Kalman filter is especially sensitive to numerical errors in the matrix inverse required in the Kalman gain calculation. These errors are particularly noticeable when the covariance matrix is updated in the Kalman update and can lead to covariance matrices that are not positive definite. The so-called square-root Kalman filter addresses this problem by reformulating the Kalman update in terms of matrix square roots [27]. In addition, the number of computations in the Kalman gain calculation, usually dominated by the matrix inverse, often requires special architectures that can handle the computations in real time and provide, to some degree, immunity to computational round-off errors. A wide variety of literature is available on the implementation of the Kalman filter on specialized architectures (see, for instance [28, 29]) and as the field of computation changes, new architectures will become more attractive. In addition to purely computational aspects, other elements of distributed processing for decentralized applications have been studied [30, 31]. In addition to or instead of implementation on (often expensive) specialized architectures, more efficient implementations are obtained through approximation of the Kalman filter by a "suboptimal" filter that approximates the Kalman filter sufficiently closely. An example of this can be found in [32].

Extensions to Nonlinear Models: The EKF and IEKF

In many cases, the simple linear model expressed by the state equation is unrealistic—even for some very simple applications, this turns out to be the case. For instance, let us revisit example tracking straight-line motion, where we assumed an object such as an airplane is traveling on a straight trajectory, and its position is measured in an X–Y plane. In practice, position estimates do not occur in a rectangular coordinate system: radar measurements, for instance, are better modeled by a polar coordinate system. Hence, the real measurements are nonlinear functions of the state of the object in rectangular coordinates, and the measurement equation of the state representation no longer holds. Even though the nonlinear measurement equations can still be used to predict the measurement in the Kalman prediction step, the predicted covariance is not necessarily calculated and may not even be meaningful. In the extended Kalman filter approach, covariances are calculated by locally "linearizing" the nonlinearity through the use of the gradient relative to the state. This simple linearization often leads to biases in the estimate. Some filtering schemes have been proposed with a bias compensation scheme based on retaining higher order terms in the nonlinearity's Taylor series expansion. Alternatively, an iterated scheme is used (IEKF), where the measurement is essentially replaced by a maximum a posteriori (MAP) estimate of the state, which is computed iteratively using a Gauss–Newton type iteration. This results an iterative linearization of the nonlinear measurement equation that, assuming the nonlinearity is sufficiently smooth around the point of linearization, eventually converges to the "best" state estimate. Clearly, because of its iterative character, the IEKF can also be prohibitively computationally expensive.

In the case of nonlinear models, choice of the state becomes extremely important, as the severity of the nonlinearity depends heavily on the state-to-measurement transformation. The bearings-only tracking problem, where an object is tracked using angular measurements only, has given rise to a specialized coordinate system called the *modified polar coordinates* (MPC) [35]. As a general rule of thumb, it is always desirable to choose the state so that the measurement equation of the state representation is (close to) linear, and the state dynamics (or the state equation itself) represent motion in a nonlinear fashion. This is because, usually, the sampling rate is available as a design factor—by making the sampling time arbitrarily small, it is often possible to linearize the state transition from one sampling instant to the next arbitrary well.

Maneuver Models

When tracking physical motion of an object, the forcing function $\mathbf{u}(\,)$ that represents the object's propulsion forces is typically unknown. Thus, when maneuvering targets are being modeled, i.e., when the straight-line model is insufficient, some assumptions need to be made regarding the target's maneuverability. The most simple model for maneuvers is to increase the model's disturbance and simply model the acceleration as "white." Although this may be sufficient in many applications, there is a performance degradation associated with it when the object does indeed follow a straight-line path (i.e., between maneuvers). Consequently, more realistic models may be needed. Some examples of maneuver modeling are found in [36–38].

Problems

1. For the system described by Eqs. (2.161) and (2.162), find the minimum energy control vector, $\mathbf{u}$, for $N = 4$, $\mathbf{x}(0) = (1 \quad 1)^T$, and compare the control vector energy with the control vector energy computed for $N = 2$.
2. Repeat Problem 1 for $N = 8$.
3. For the quadratic performance controller design example, write a computer program to calculate $H(k)$ and $u(k)$ for $N = 20$. Plot $h_1(k)$, $h_2(k)$, $x_1(k)$, $x_2(k)$ as in Figure 2.14; compare these results with $N = 20$ to the results obtained for $N = 5$.
4. For the system in Problem 2, replace the time-varying feedback gain matrix, $H(k)$, with a suitable constant matrix, H, and recompute $u(k)$, $x_1(k)$, and $x_2(k)$. Plot as before and compare to the results for $N = 20$ with the time-varying optimal feedback matrix, $H(k)$.
5. Derive the mean value, the variance, and the MSE of the FIR estimate in the case the constant to be estimated is a deterministic (not a random) parameter. Plot the statistics—do you notice a difference with Fig. 2.16? If, so, how do you explain this difference?
6. Same as Problem 5 for the alpha tracker.
7. Derive the MSE as a function of number of time samples for the MMSE described by (2.196). What is the MSE under steady-state conditions?
8. Derive the MMSE estimator when the constant x is not random, but unknown and fixed. Why is this estimator not realistic?
9. Compare the MMSE of Problem 8 with the one of Problem 7. How do the two compare?
10. A signal is modeled by a constant-rate state-variable model as in the example of the alpha–beta tracker. If the initial statistics on the state are

$$\boldsymbol{\mu}_x(0) = \begin{bmatrix} 1m/s \\ 1m \end{bmatrix} \quad \text{and} \quad \mathbf{R}_x = \mathrm{diag}(1m^2/s^2, 1m^2),$$

and the measurement noise is $0.1m^2$, assuming no model disturbance, calculate and plot the mean and variance of x as a function of time ($\Delta T = 1s$).

11. For the same case as in Problem 10, calculate and plot the mean and variance of $\hat{x}$ as a function of time, assuming that the estimate is obtained with an alpha–beta tracker with $\alpha = \beta = 0.2$.
12. For the optimal MMSE tracker, calculate and plot the MSE if the same signal had been estimated using (a) an alpha tracker (choose appropriate values of alpha) and (b) an alpha–beta tracker (choose appropriate values of alpha and beta). Discuss the difference between your results and the results shown in this section.
13. For the optimal MMSE tracker, calculate and plot the mean value of the estimate, assuming the initial value (for $n = 0$) of the mean equals 1 ($a = 0.95$).
14. Derive the time-invariant tracker expressions of Eqs. (2.240) through (2.245).
15. Derive the Kalman filter for the constant-rate case. Can you write the resulting filter in the form of a time-varying version of the alpha–beta tracker?
16. Compare the results of the preceding text with those of Eq. (2.199). What do you conclude? Can you explain the differences?

References

[1] Oppenheim, A. V., and R. W. Schafer. (1989). *Discrete Time Signal Processing*. Prentice-Hall, Englewood Cliffs, N.J.

[2] Jackson, L. B. (1989). *Digital Filters and Signal Processing*. Kluwer Academic Publishers, New York.

[3] Kamen, E. W. (1990). *Introduction to Signals and Systems*, 2nd ed. Macmillan, New York.

[4] Soliman, S. S., and M. D. Srinath. (1990). *Continuous and Discrete Signals and Systems*. Prentice-Hall, Englewood Cliffs, N.J.

[5] Lathi, B. P. (1987). *Signals and Systems*. Cambridge Press, Berkeley.

[6] McGillen, C. D., and G. R. Cooper. (1984). *Continuous and Discrete Signal and Systems Analysis*. 2nd ed. Holt, Reinhart, and Winston, New York.

[7] Proakis, J. G., and D. G. Manolakis. (1988). *Introduction to Digital Signal Processing*. Macmillan, New York.

[8] Strum, R. D., and D. E. Kirk. (1988). *First Principles of Discrete Systems and Digital Signal Processing*. Addison Wesley, Reading, MA.

[9] Ziemer, R. E., W. H. Tranter, and D. R. Fanin. (1989). *Signals and Systems: Continuous and Discrete*, 2nd ed. Macmillan, New York.

[10] Robert, R. A., and C. T. Mullis. (1987). *Digital Signal Processing*. Addison-Wesley, Reading, MA.

[11] Poularikas, A. D., and S. Seely. (1985). *Signals and Systems*. PWS Publishers, Boston.

[12] Brogan, W. L. (1985). *Modern Control Theory*, 2nd ed. Prentice-Hall, Englewood Cliffs, NJ.

[13] Box, G. E. P., and G. M. Jenkins. (1976). *Time Series Analysis: Forecasting and Control*. Holden-Day, San Francisco.

[14] Chuchill, R. V., J. W. Brown, and R. F. Verhey. (1976). *Complex Variables and Applications*, 3rd ed. McGraw-Hill, New York.
[15] D'Azzo, J. J., and H. H. Constantine. (1988). *Linear Control System Analysis and Design*, 3rd ed. McGraw-Hill, New York.
[16] D'Souza, A. F. (1988). *Design of Control Systems*. Prentice-Hall, Englewood Cliffs, N.J.
[17] Dorf, R. C. (1989). *Modern Control Systems*, 5th ed. Addison-Wesley, Reading, MA.
[18] Kuo, B. C. (1980). *Digital Control Systems*. Holt, Reinhart, and Winston, New York.
[19] Vanlandingham, H. F. (1985). *Introduction to Digital Control Systems*. Macmillan, New York.
[20] Papoulis, A. (1980). *Circuits and Systems*. Holt, Reinhart, and Winston, New York.
[21] Chen, C. T. (1984). *Linear System Theory and Design*. Holt, Reinhart, and Winston, New York.
[22] Stearns, S., and D. R. Hush. (1989). *Digital Signal Analysis*. Prentice-hall, Englewood Cliffs, NJ.
[23] Papoulis, A. (1991). *Probability, Random Variables, and Stochastic Processes*, 3rd ed. McGraw-Hill, New York.
[24] Wiener, N. (1949). *Extrapolation, Interpolation and Smoothing of Stationary Time Series*. J. Wiley and Sons, New York.
[25] Kalman, R. E., and R. S. Bucy. (1969). "New Results in Linear Filtering and Prediction Theory," *J. Basic Eng., Trans. ASME*, ser. D, **83**, 95–108.
[26] Kwakernaak, H., and R. Sivan. (1972). *Linear Optimal Control Systems*. Wiley Interscience, New York.
[27] Kaminski, P. G., P. G. Bryson, and A. E. Schmidt. (1971). "Discrete Square-Root Filtering: A Survey of Current Techniques," *IEEE Trans. Autom. Contr.*, **AC-16**(6), 727–763.
[28] Cheng V. S., et al. (1985). "A High Throughput Matrix Processor for Kalman Filtering," 19th Asilomar Conf. on Circuits, Systems and Computers, Pacific Grove, CA, pp. 716–425.
[29] Baheti, R., et al. (1990). "Mapping Extended Kalman Filters onto Linear Arrays," *IEEE Trans. Automatic Contr.* **AC-35**(12).
]30] Hashemipour, H., et al. (1988). "Decentralized Structures for Parallel Kalman Filtering," *IEEE Trans. Automatic Contr.* **AC-33**(1).
[31] Carlson, N. (1987). "Federated Square Root Filter for Decentralized Parallel Processes," NAECON 1987, Dayton, OH, pp. 1448–1456.
[32] Baheti, R. (1986). "Efficient Approximation of Kalman Filter for Target Tracking," *IEEE Trans. Aerospace and Electron. Sys.* **AES-22**(1), 8–14.
[33] Jazwinski, A. H. (1970). *Stochastic Processes and Filtering Theory*. Academic Press, New York.
[34] Hassab, J. (1989). *Underwater Signal and Data Processing*. CRC Press, Boca Raton, FL.
[35] Aidala, V. J. (1983). "Utilization of Modified Polar Coordinates for Bearings-Only Tracking," *IEEE Trans. Automatic Control* **AC-28**(3).
[36] Fitzgerald, R. J. (1981). "Simple Tracking Filters: Closed-Form Solutions," *IEEE Trans. on Aerospace and Electron. Systems* **AES-17**(6).
[37] Singer, R. A., and K. W. Behnke. (1971). "Real-Time Tracking Filter Evaluation and Selection for Tactical Applications," *IEEE Transactions on Aerospace and Electron. Systems* **AES-7**(1).
[38] Bhagavan, B. K., and R. J. Polge. (1974). "Performance of the *g–h* Filter for Tracking Maneuvering Targets," *IEEE Trans. Aerospace and Electron Systems* **AES-10**(6).

Chapter 3
Coding in Digital Communications

In digital transmission systems, as well as digital storage systems, three fundamental types of coding are introduced with the purpose of improving system performance: source, channel, and line coding. Source coding is used to reduce the redundancy of the information source, and channel coding is used to improve the reliability of the transmission over noisy channels. Line coding has the general purpose of improving the transmission reliability and overcoming the impairments of physical channels. The purpose of this chapter is to present practical channel coding methods with emphasis on block codes. Low-complexity decoding algorithms are particularly emphasized.

Data Transmission and Coding

A communication system connects a data source to a data user (receiver) through a channel such as a microwave link, optical fiber, or a magnetic tape. A communication engineer designs a system to process the information to be sent to match the channel characteristics and processes the output of the channel to determine the transmitted information. Because the channel is subject to various types of noise, distortion, and interference, the channel output might be different than the channel input. One way to combat noise and interference is through the use of error control coding techniques. Data is first processed by the encoder, which transforms a sequence of (information) data symbols into another (typically) longer sequence called the *channel codeword*. The set of all possible codewords form a code. The transformation consists of introducing redundant symbols into the original data sequence. Next a modulator converts each codeword symbol into a corresponding analog waveform, from a set of possible analog waveforms, which is transmitted through the physical channel. The demodulator converts each received channel output signal into another discrete-time analog symbol upon which a decision about the transmitted code symbol can be made. The decoder uses the redundancy in the transmitted codeword to correct as many errors as possible and puts out its best estimate. One very important measure of the reliability of communication is the probability of the decoder not putting out the transmitted codeword, referred to as the *probability of error*. Without coding it is well known that in the presences of Rayleigh fading or worst case finite power interference the bit error probability is an inverse linear function of the received signal energy-to-noise ratio, as opposed to an exponentially decreasing function for broadband additive noise. This can cause an increase of 30–40 dB in required bit energy-to-noise ratio when a probability of bit error of 10^{-5} is desired. Coding techniques for unintentional as well as hostile interference are discussed extensively in the literature.

Coding theory was effectively started in 1948 by Shannon [1]. Shannon showed, by the coding theorem, that associated with a channel there is a nonnegative number C, measured in bits per second, with the following significance. If the transmission rate R in bits per second is less than C, it is possible to design a communication system using error-control codes that results in as small an error probability as desired.

The prime motivation for coding research since 1948 has been Shannon's coding theorem. Although our understanding of the coding theorem has been refined, it still gives no satisfactory answers from a practical viewpoint. This is because the coding theorem is, from a practical viewpoint, an existence theorem. It demonstrates that a certain performance can be obtained by unstructured coding schemes, but fails to specify a particular code that achieves this performance or encoding and decoding methods with reasonable complexity. The two main contributions to complexity are usually taken to be the maximum number of operations required and the number of memory registers needed to perform a certain decoding algorithm. The introduction of linear codes essentially solves the encoding problem for block codes; codes in this class can obtain the performance guaranteed by the coding theorem and can be encoded with algorithms that have low complexity (complexity linear in the length of the code). However, the decoding of linear block codes is, in general, very complex for reasons clarified later. We first, however, describe several classes of channel models that are used throughout the chapter.

Channel Models

To evaluate the performance of an uncoded communications system, the system's designer needs knowledge of the modulation scheme, the demodulation and detection schemes, and the phyiscal characteristics of the channel (that may include multipath fading, thermal noise, hostile interferences, etc.). These partially determine the channel model to be used. The model is complete based on the type of decoding that is used. For instance, whether a whole codeword is decoded at once or each received code symbol is detected separately and then decoding is attempted. Other design options include detecting a symbol at a time and assigning a number to each detected symbol that indicates how reliable is that symbol. Given these techniques, design and evaluation of coded systems is possible.

The channel models we use model the communication system from the input of the modulator to the output of the demodulator. These channels are discrete in time in the sense that the channel input and output are time sequences of letters selected from arbitrary alphabets. Denote the input sequence to the channel as $x_1, x_2, \ldots$ and the corresponding output as $y_1, y_2, \ldots$, where the input and output alphabets are $\mathcal{X}$ and $\mathcal{Y}$, respectively. A channel is memoryless if the output y_i at time i depends only on the input x_i at time i; i.e., the probabilities that $y_1, y_2, \ldots, y_n$ is the output given $x_1, x_2, \ldots, x_n$ is the input is the product $\prod_{i=1}^{n} p(y_i \mid x_i)$, where $p(y \mid x)$ is the conditional probability the output of the channel is y given that the input to the channel is x; also the probabilities are independent of time (i.e., the position in the sequence). In the following models we restrict ourselves to memoryless channels that allow only a finite set of letters in the input alphabet.

The first class of channel models discussed here are the (one-dimensional) binary discrete-time additive channels. Such a channel is depicted in Figure 3.1. The input alphabet $\mathcal{X}$ is equal to $\{0, 1\}$ and the output alphabet $\mathcal{Y}$ is the set of real numbers. Moreover, if $X_1, X_2, \ldots$ are the inputs to the channel at times $1, 2, \ldots$ then the corresponding outputs $Y_1, Y_2, \ldots$ are given by $Y_i = h(X_i) + Z_i$ for all i, where

$$h(X) = \begin{cases} +\sqrt{E_s}, & X = 0 \\ -\sqrt{E_s}, & X = 1 \end{cases}$$

where E_s is called the *code symbol energy*, and $Z_1, Z_2, \ldots$ are independent and identically distributed random variables. Also Z_i is independent of X_j for all i and j. The channel is called an additive white Gaussian noise (AWGN) channel if Z_i is a Gaussian random variable. This channel is used to model antipodal signaling in white Gaussian noise with coherent reception when no quantization is performed at the output of the demodulator. In this case, when coding is used the decoder makes a decision about the input to the channel based on a vector of real-valued outputs from the channel. This is referred to as (pure) soft decision decoding.

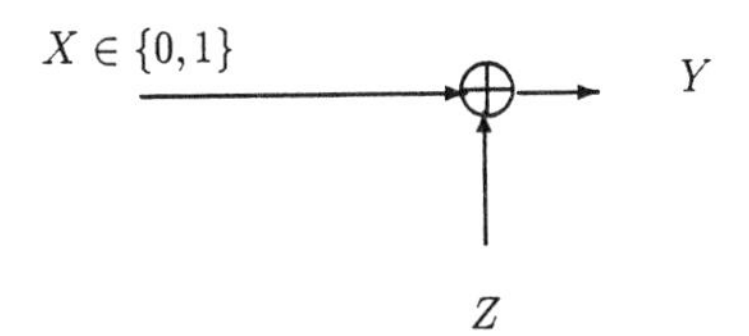

FIG. 3.1. Discrete-time additive channel.

The M-dimensional (vector) additive channel is another additive channel of interest. The input to the channel is one of M symbols,

$$\mathcal{X} = \{0, 1, \ldots, M - 1\}.$$

The vector channel disturbs the transmission and outputs a random vector

$$\mathbf{Y} = (Y_0, \ldots, Y_{M-1}) = F(X) + \mathbf{Z}$$

where $F(X)$ is a vector of length M in which only the Xth component is nonzero and has a value equal to $f_j(X)$; that is, $F(X) = (f_0(X), \ldots, f_{M-1}(X))$ such that $f_j(X) = \sqrt{E_s}$ when $j = X$ and 0 otherwise. Also, $\mathbf{Z} = (Z_0, \ldots, Z_{M-1})$, the error vector, is independent of X, and addition is componentwise. This channel serves as a model for an orthogonal signaling modulator with coherent demodulation. This channel, however, is not applicable to the noncoherent channel (i.e., the case when code symbols are noncoherently demodulated). For a noncoherent receiver the vector channel disturbs the signal in a nonlinear fashion. The preceding class of channel models also characterizes a channel with impulse noise. In this case the channel is characterized by long quiet intervals followed by bursts of high-amplitude noise pulses. This type of noise for instance, can be due to switching transients or lightning discharges. For Gaussian impulse noise, Z_i is conditionally (on burst being active) Gaussian, while the probability of a burst arriving can be modeled as Poisson.

Another important class of channels is that of the multiplicative noise. Such a channel model is important in a fading situation such as encountered in land mobile radio communications systems. In this case the amplitude of the received signal suffers from rapid fluctuations that cause severe signal degradation. In this chapter we do not elaborate on this channel model simply because coding for a multiplicative channel is about the same as that for an additive channel except the optimum coding rate in the sense of minimizing the bit error rate, is different. What we mean by this is an optimum decoder for an additive channel is also an optimum decoder for a multiplicative channel for high signal-to-noise power ratios.

The second class of channel models are the discrete memoryless channels (DMC). Such a channel is characterized by a finite input alphabet $\mathcal{X}$ of, say, M symbols, finite output alphabet $\mathcal{Y}$, and a set of transition probabilities $p(y \mid x)$, defined for each $x \in \mathcal{X}$ and $y \in \mathcal{Y}$ as the probability that the output of the channel is y if the input to the channel is x. When a finite-level quantizer is placed at the output of the demodulator, e.g., the output space of the additive channel model just described is partitioned, the communciation channel between the input to the modulator and the output of the quantizer is discrete, resulting in a DMC. Later we describe two special cases of the DMC.

In many of the applications, the sizes of the input and output alphabets are equal, say to M. Also, in many situations of interest, if a symbol is in error, i.e., the output symbol is not the same as the corresponding input symbol, it is equally likely to be any symbol excluding the transmitted one, and the probability the output of the channel is the same as the input to the channel is the same for all symbols in the alphabet. In such a situation the channel is said to be symmetric. Formally,

$$p(y \mid x) = \begin{cases} \dfrac{p}{M-1}, & y \neq x \\ 1-p, & y = x \end{cases}$$

for all $y \in \mathcal{Y}$ and $x \in \mathcal{X}$. These assumptions give rise to the M-ary symmetric channel shown in Figure 3.2. Decoders for this channel are

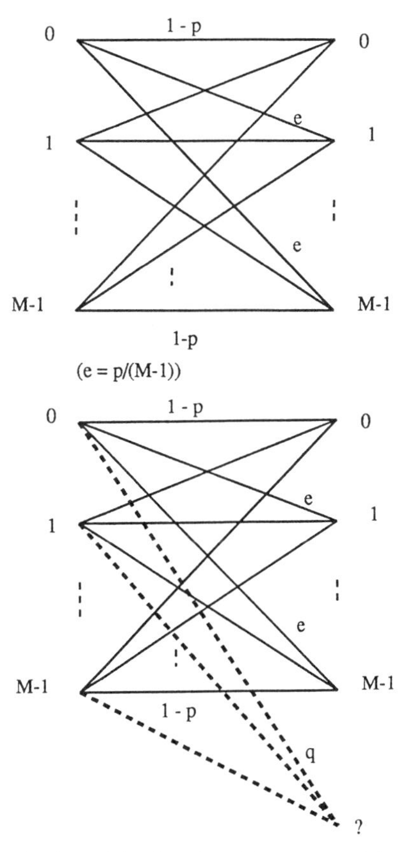

FIG. 3.2. M-ary symmetric channel (top) and an M-ary symmetric-erasure channel (bottom).

called *hard decision decoders*. Also it is convenient to represent both the input and the output alphabets by the integer values $\{0, 1, \ldots, M - 1\}$.

An M-ary symmetric channel can also be represented as an adder channel: if $c \in \{0, 1, \ldots, M - 1\}$ is the transmitted code symbol, then the corrsponding received symbol $y \in \{0, 1, \ldots, M - 1\}$ at the output of the channel is given by $y = c + e$, where $e \in \{0, 1, \ldots, M - 1\}$ is an error symbol added by the channel, and addition is performed modulo M. A code symbol is received in error if and only if $e \neq 0$, which occurs with probability p.

Another DMC with one more output than that of an M-ary symmetric channel is of considerable interest. This DMC is called an *M-ary symmetric errors-and-erasures channel* with M inputs and $M + 1$ outputs. It is shown in Figure 3.2 with q being the probability a received symbol will be erased. The input alphabet of this channel is $\mathcal{X} = \{0, 1, \ldots, M - 1\}$, and the output alphabet is $\mathcal{Y} = \{0, 1, \ldots, M - 1, ?\}$. This channel is characterized by the following transition probabilities:

$$p(w \mid x) = \begin{cases} \dfrac{p}{M - 1}, & w \neq x, w \neq ? \\ 1 - p - q, & w = x \\ q, & w = ?. \end{cases}$$

The additional symbol, called an *erasure* (denoted ?), may reflect symbols which the demodulator determines are very noisy or for which an estimate based on the received symbol is unreliable. This is often done using information, called *side information*, about the channel during the reception of a code symbol. Side information, has been used extensively in the literature when the channel is jammed [2]–[10] or when hits occur in multiple access communication (see [9] and [5]). It can be generated from a number of different sources, some of which are described in [8]; briefly these include predetection and postdetection methods. The predetection methods are based on power measurements applied to the received signal on a symbol-by-symbol basis. This can be accomplished via an automatic gain control (AGC) device. Usually predetection methods are the least reliable due to their high sensitivity to various fluctuations of the signal amplitude. Postdetection methods are based on certain statistics obtained from the output of the demodulator. Examples of this include Viterbi's ratio thereshold technique (see [11] and [3]), which was proven to be very useful in a partial-band interference environment. The errors-and-erasures decoding algorithm takes this additional symbol into account. We shall demonstrate how converting an M-ary symmetric channel to one that includes erasures can improve the performance of a communication system.

The Decoding Problem for Linear Block Codes

In this section we discuss block codes, particularly decoding for linear codes, for the q-ary symmetric channels and the additive channels. In particular we describe standard encoding and decoding algorithms for block codes and discuss the complexity of these algorithms on various channels. We begin with standard definitions.

For a q-ary (discrete-time) input channel, an $[M, n]$ block code $\mathcal{C}$ of length n over GF(q) (a field of q elements) is a collection of M vectors called *codewords*, each of the form $(c_1, c_2, \ldots, c_n)$ with components in GF(q). An (n, k) linear code over GF(q) is a $[q^k, n]$ block code for which the codewords with symbols in GF(q) form a k-dimensional linear subspace of the n-dimensional space. Any such a code is uniquely defined by a set of k linearly independent codewords, which form a generating set. Equivalently any (n, k) code can be defined to be the set of those n-tuples $(c_1, \ldots, c_n)$ satisfying a set of $n - k$ linearly independent linear equations

$$\sum_{i=1}^{n} c_i h_{i,j} = 0, \qquad j = 1, 2, \ldots, n - k \tag{3.1}$$

where $h_{i,j} \in \mathrm{GF}(q)$ are entries in a $(n - k) \times n$ matrix called the *parity check matrix* of the code.

Encoding for a q-ary input, discrete-time channel using a code over GF(q) consists of a one-to-one mapping $\mathcal{F}$ from the k-dimensional message space to the set $\mathcal{C}$ of codewords. That is,

$$\mathcal{F} : \mathcal{X}^k \rightarrow \mathcal{C}$$

where $\mathcal{X} = \{0, 1, \ldots, q - 1\}$ and $\mathcal{C} \subset \mathcal{X}^n$. Decoding for any of the channels described earlier, with output alphabet $\mathcal{Y}$, consists of a composition of two functions $\mathcal{D}_1$ and $\mathcal{D}_2$ such that

$$\mathcal{D}_1 : \mathcal{Y}^{*n} \rightarrow \mathcal{C}$$

$$\mathcal{D}_2 = \mathcal{F}^{-1} : \mathcal{C} \rightarrow \mathcal{X}^k$$

where $\mathcal{Y}^{*n} \subset \mathcal{Y}^n$. The reason for restricting the domain of $\mathcal{D}_1$ to be a subset of the output space will be clear later. When a q-ary code is used on a q-ary symmetric channel $\mathcal{Y} = \mathcal{X}$. When this code is used on a q-ary errors-and-erasures channel $\mathcal{Y} = \mathcal{X} \cup \{?\}$. When this code is used on an additive channel $\mathcal{Y} = \mathcal{R}$ (the real space)..

The Hamming distance $d(\mathbf{x}, \mathbf{y})$ between two q-ary sequences $\mathbf{x}$ and $\mathbf{y}$ of length n is the number of places in which they differ. The minimum distance of a code is defined to be the minimum Hamming distance between any distinct pair of codewords. An (n, k) linear code with minimum

Hamming distance d is sometimes referred to as an (n, k, d) code. When used on a q-ary symmetric channel a code with minimum distance d can correct any pattern of e errors provided $2e + 1 \leq d$ [12] and e is said to be the error correcting capability of the code. When used on an q-ary symmetric errors-and-erasures channel the code can correct all patterns of e errors and τ erasures simultaneously if $2e + \tau \leq d - 1$.

When dealing with additive channels it will sometimes be useful to treat the codewords of a code as real-valued vectors. The real-valued vectors are obtained from vectors with symbols in $\{0, \ldots, M - 1\}$ via the transformations $\mathfrak{F}$ and h discussed in the previous section. It will be clear to the reader which form is being used and should cause no ambiguity. For example, in the simplest case of antipodal signaling (i.e., the additive channel), the one-dimensional transformation consists of the function $h(\cdot)$ defined earlier. Then the Euclidean distance $d_E(\mathbf{x}, \mathbf{y})$ between $\mathbf{x} \in \mathcal{R}^n$ and $\mathbf{y} \in \mathcal{R}^n$ is

$$d_E(\mathbf{x}, \mathbf{y}) = \sqrt{\sum_{i=1}^{n} (x_i - y_i)^2}$$

where $\mathcal{R}$ is the real line. Similar definition holds for the M-ary vector additive channel using the transformation $F(\cdot)$. The minimum Euclidean distance d_E of a code is the minimum Euclidean distance between any distinct pair of codewords with elements in $\mathcal{R}$. A maximum likelihood decoder will map a received vector to the closest codeword; i.e., $\mathcal{Y}^{*n} = \mathcal{Y}^n$. When used on an additive channel a (bounded distance) soft decision decoder will decode correctly only those received vectors with Euclidean distance $d_E/2$ from some codeword.

We assume that after transmission through the q-ary symmetric channel the received n-tuple $(y_1, \ldots, y_n)$ differs from the transmitted codeword by some error sequence $(e_1, e_2, \ldots, e_n)$; that is, $y_j = c_j + e_j$ for $j = 1, \ldots, n$, where addition is performed over GF(q). Also, $e_1, e_2, \ldots, e_n$ are independent and identically distributed random variables with $\Pr(e_i \neq 0) = 1 - p$ and $\Pr(e_i = 0) = p$ for all i. Define s_j, $j = 1, \ldots, n - k$ as

$$s_j \triangleq \sum_{i=1}^{n} y_i h_{i,j} = \sum_{i=1}^{n} e_i h_{i,j} \tag{3.2}$$

The $(n - k)$-tuple $(s_1, \ldots, s_{n-k})$ is known as the syndrome of the received sequence. The (optimal) decoding problem consists of finding the error sequence, producing a given syndrome, that is most probable for a given channel. For a symmetric memoryless channel, the most probable error sequence is that which has the minimum number of nonzero components. In that case the decoding problem reduces to finding the solution to the preceding equation with the minimum weight.

It is generally not feasible to find the most probable solution of (3.2) for an arbitrary syndrome, simply because of the enormous number of possibilities. Furthermore, it has been shown by Berlekamp and McEliece [13] that the algorithm that solves for the most probable solution of (3.2) is in the class of *NP*-complete algorithms. This means that it is (currently) not possible to find an algorithm for (3.2) whose complexity does not grow exponentially but grows polynomially with n. Levitin and Hartman [6], based on a new concept of zero neighbors (a special set of codewords), found an algorithm for which the time complexity is polynomial but the space complexity is exponential in n. Optimal decoding algorithms for other channels are at least as complex as that of the DMC.

For an M-ary symmetric channel, an efficient suboptimal solution to the decoding problem depends on finding a simple method for determining an approximation to the most probable solution of (3.2) for a high-probability subset of the set of all error sequences. This shows why we assumed $\mathcal{Y}^{*n} \subset \mathcal{Y}^n$. For codes with some algebraic structure such as being linear or cyclic, algebraic decoding has led to a practical decoding algorithm for M-ary symmetric errors-and-erasures channels called *bounded distance decoding*. A bounded distance decoder decodes only those received vectors lying in a decoding sphere about a codeword (a decoding sphere is the set of errors and erasures pairs (e, τ) correctable by the decoder such that $2\tau + e \leq t$, where t is called the *radius of the sphere*). Other received vectors that have more than the number of errors and erasures correctable by the code are declared by the decoder as unreconizable, in which case the decoder is said to have *failed*. For instance, the Berlekamp algorithm for linear cyclic codes (codes for which cyclic shifts of a codeword is also a codeword) will correct e errors and τ erasures if $2e + \tau$ is less than the minimum Hamming distance d of the code. The complexity of implementation of this algorithm is proportional to d^2.

Cyclic Codes

An important subclass of linear codes include cyclic codes. These codes are characterized by the following cyclic shift property: if $\mathbf{c} = (c_0 c_1 \ldots c_{n-1})$ is a codeword then $\mathbf{c} = (c_{n-1} c_0 \cdots c_{n-2})$, obtained by a cyclic shift of the elements of $\mathbf{c}$, is also a codeword. As a consequence of the cyclic property, the code possess a considerable amount of structure that can be exploited in the encoding and decoding operations.

When we say two polynomials are equal (or equivalent) mod $f(x)$ we mean that the two polynomials have the same remainder when divided by $f(x)$. With this in mind, it is convenient to represent codewords of a cyclic code by polynomials. The codeword **c** is represented by

$$c(x) = \sum_{i=0}^{n-1} c_i x^i$$

where c_i is an element in GF(q). The polynomial

$$xc(x) = \sum_{i=0}^{n-1} c_i x^{i+1}$$

$$= c_{n-1} + c_0 x + \cdots + c_{n-2} x^{n-1} \bmod(x^n + 1)$$

represents the codeword c shifted cyclically by one position, which is also a codeword. Similarly, if $c(x)$ represents a codeword, then

$$x^i c(x) \bmod(x^n + 1)$$

is also a codeword.

Cyclic codes can be generated using a generator polynomial $g(x)$ of degree $n - k$. The generator polynomial of an (n, k) cyclic code is a factor of $x^n + 1$ and has the general form

$$g(x) = x^{n-k} + g_{n-k-1} x^{n-k-1} + \cdots + g_1 x + 1$$

Also, let the information polynomial $I(x)$ be

$$I(x) = \sum_{i=0}^{k-1} I_i x^i$$

where $(I_0 I_1 \ldots I_{k-1})$ represent k information bits. The codewords are then denoted by

$$c_m(x) = I_m(x) g(x), \qquad m = 1, \ldots, 2^k$$

The codewords possessing the cyclic property can be generated by multiplying the 2^k-message polynomials with a unique polynomial $g(x)$ that divides $x^n + 1$ and has degree $n - k$.

Let $x^n + 1 = g(x)h(x)$, where $g(x)$ denotes the generator polynomial for the (n, k) cyclic code and $h(x)$ denotes the parity check polynomial that has degree k. The term $h(x)$ can be also used to generate another cyclic code with parameters $(n, n - k)$, known as the *dual code*; the code and its dual are orthogonal. The reciprocal polynomial of $h(x)$ is defined as

$$x^k h(x^{-1}) = 1 + h_{x-1} x + h^{k-2} x^2 + \cdots + h_1 x^{k-1} + x^k$$

which is also a factor of $x^n + 1$. Hence $x^k h(x^{-1})$ is the generator polynomial of an $(n, n - k)$ cyclic code.

Examples

It can be verified that

$$x^{15} - 1 = (x^4 + x + 1)Q(x)$$

Thus one can use $g(x) = x^4 + x + 1$ to generate a cyclic code. This happens to be the (15, 11) Hamming code used quite often in practice. This code has a minimum Hamming distance of 3 and, therefore, can correct a single error. In general one can construct a cyclic Hamming code with

$$n = 2^m - 1$$

$$k = 2^m - 1 - m$$

and the Hamming distance of such a code is always 3.

The Golay code is the most familiar binary code that is used in satellite communications and other applications. It is a (23, 12) code with $d_{\min} = 7$. That is, any combination of 3 or less errors can be generated by the code. The Golay code can be generated by one of the two generator polynomials:

$$g(x) = x^{11} + x^{10} + x^6 + x^5 + x^4 + x^2 + 1$$

or

$$g(x) = x^{11} + x^9 + x^7 + x^6 + x^5 + x + 1$$

We point out that cyclic codes can be generated by linear systems with zero inputs. Recall that a linear, time-invariant system is described in discrete-time $k = 1, 2, \ldots$ by the difference equations

$$x(k + 1) = Ax(k) + Bu(k)$$

$$y(k) = Cx(k) + Du(k)$$

where $x(k)$ is an n-dimensional state-vector, $u(k)$ is an m-dimensional input vector, and $y(k)$ is an r-dimensional output vector. The matrices A, B, C, and D define the structure of the system. Let all the elements and operations of these vectors and matrices be in GF(2) (extensions to GF(q) is straightforward).

Let $r = 1$ and assume the preceding system has no input. Denote the sequence $Y[x(0)] = \{y(0), y(1), \ldots, y(iT - 1)\}$ of outputs as the response of the dynamic system to an initial vector $x(0)$. If the system is periodic T; that is, $y(t + T) = y(t)$ for the smallest positive T, then it can be shown that $\{Y[X(0)] : \forall X(0)\}$ forms a cyclic code. This is important since design techniques in system's theory can be applied to coding design and vice versa. Massey and Sain [7] give a brilliant insight into the relations between codes and systems.

BCH Codes

Bose–Chaudhuri–Hocquenghem (BCH) codes are a large class of cyclic codes that include both binary and nonbinary alphabets. These codes are of considerable interest due to the ease of practical implementation of the decoder. Binary BCH codes may be constructed with parameters

$$n = 2^m - 1$$
$$n - k = mt$$
$$d = 2t + 1$$

where $m \geq 3$ and t are positive integers. The generator polynomial for BCH codes can be constructed from factors of $x^{2^m - 1} + 1$. For example, a generator polynomial for a (15, 7) BCH code that can correct two errors is

$$g(x) = x^8 + x^7 + x^6 + x^4 + 1$$

A simple (7, 1) repetition code has the obvious generator polynomial

$$g(x) = x^6 + x^5 + x^4 + x^3 + x^2 + x + 1$$

An important subset of BCH nonbinary codes is the class of Reed–Solomon codes. If q is the alphabet size of the code, then the block length $n = q - 1$. These codes possess an optimal property in the sense that the minimum distance of an (n, k) Reed–Solomon code is $d = n - k + 1$, which is the best distance property for any code with the same parameters. Also, Reed–Solomon codes have a known weight distribution, unlike most other codes. A_i is the number of codewords with Hamming weight i, given by

$$A_i = \binom{n}{i}(q - 1) \sum_{j=0}^{i-d} (-1)^j (i - 1j) q^{i-j-d} \qquad i \geq d$$

One reason for the importance of the Reed–Solomon codes is their good distance properties. Another reason is the existence of efficient hard-decision decoding algorithms that make it possible to implement relatively long codewords. These codes have been used extensively in transmission systems, compact disc players, digital audio, and storage. In 1984 Cyclotomics bit-serial Reed–Solomon encoders were adopted for the NASA standard for deep space communications. Presently, (63, 53) Reed–Solomon decoders can be realized to operate at up to 830 Megabits per second.

Concatenated Codes

The discovery of cyclic BCH codes led to practical (low-complexity) methods of designing the hardware or software for implementing the encoder and decoder. However, as the block length becomes larger the

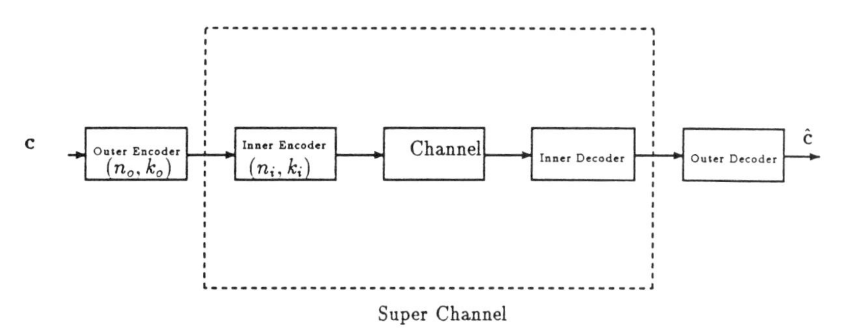

FIG. 3.3. Concatenated coding system.

performance of BCH codes gets worse and the complexity for decoding, although polynomial, becomes substantial. Concatenation of codes, first investigated by Forney [4], is a way of constructing long block codes without requiring a complex decoder. The idea is that the channel is used with an *inner* encoder and decoder, and the combination can be viewed as a "super channel." An outer code is then designed for this discrete super channel as shown in Figure 3.3.

The outer code is typically a Reed–Solomon code. Unfortunately, although Forney's theorem is practical, it is still not constructive in the sense that it does not tell us how to find the appropriate super channel (i.e., the inner code).

Since we are using two codes, we can design the inner decoder to learn about the channel and help the outer code correct as many errors as possible. If the channel statistics are fixed and known, it is appropriate to design the inner code to match the resulting super channel to the outer code, which is a Reed–Solomon code. If, however, the channel parameters vary with time or are unknown but belong to a class of channels, a technique that provides robust performance against a channel with varying statistics involves parallel decoding of the received vector by decoders that have inner decoders matched to different channel parameters followed by a selector to decide which super channel is the most probable for the duration of a codeword. More details about designing the inner decorder will be next.

We start by briefly discussing the basic concepts of concatenated coding. Then we investigate concatenated decoding schemes where we describe a particularly attractive decoding structure called *parallel decoding*, and we discuss some of the earlier work that is relevant to this problem.

An (N, K, D) concatenated code with minimum distance D, block length N, and dimension K consists of two stages: an (n_0, k_0, d_0) outer code $\mathcal{C}_2$ with code symbols belonging to $X = \mathrm{GF}(2^{m_2})$, $m_2 \geq 2$, and an (n_i, k_i, d_i) inner code $\mathcal{C}_1$ with code symbols over $U = \mathrm{GF}(2^{m_1})$, where in general

$m_2 > m_1 \geq 1$. Throughout the chapter, symbols in GF(2^m) are represented as binary m-tuples. With this in mind, codewords are formed as follows. First k_o information symbols from GF(2^{m_2}) are encoded using the outer code into n_o symbols also in GF(2^{m_2}); the resulting $m_2 n_o$ bits are considered to be a sequence of $m_2 n_o / m_1$ (an integer, i.e., parameters are chosen such that m_1 divides $m_2 n_o$) symbols in GF(2^{m_1}). Then each k_i symbols in GF(2^{m_1}) are further encoded using the inner code into n_i symbols in GF(2^{m_1}). If $m_1 = 1$ we have a binary concatenated code. In all cases of interest the outer code used is a Reed–Solomon code that belongs to the class of maximum distance separable codes. These are codes that have the property that $d_o = n_o - k_o + 1$, which is the maximum Hamming distance for any code with the same block length and dimension.

The resultant linear concatenated code has block length $N = n_i n_o$, dimension $K = k_i k_o$, and minimum Hamming distance D that is lower bounded by $D_L = d_o d_i$. Moreover, $D \geq D_L$ with equality if the inner code is a code whose nonzero codewords are of constant weight.

For example the idea is illustrated in the following with an inner codeword that corresponds to one outer code symbol. Let the outer-encoding be characterized by a mapping

$$\mathfrak{F} : \mathfrak{X}^{k_o} \rightarrow \mathfrak{X}_2$$

where $\mathfrak{X}$ is the alphabet of the outer code. Let f be the ith coordinate of $\mathfrak{F}$ and let the inner encoding be

$$g : X \rightarrow U^{n_i}$$

where U is the alphabet of the inner code. Then *concatenation* is defined by

$$F \triangleq g^{n_o}\mathfrak{F} : \mathfrak{X}^{k_o} \rightarrow U^{n_i n_o}$$

where $g^{n_o}f$ is the "composition" of the two functions g^{n_o} and $\mathfrak{F}$ such that $g^{n_o}\mathfrak{F} \triangleq (gf_1, \ldots, gf_{n_o})^T$. The concatenated codeword is the $n_o \times n_i$ matrix, which follows:

$$m \xrightarrow{\mathfrak{F}} \begin{pmatrix} x_1 \\ x_2 \\ \vdots \\ x_{n_0} \end{pmatrix} \begin{matrix} \xrightarrow{g} \\ \xrightarrow{g} \\ \vdots \\ \xrightarrow{g} \end{matrix} \begin{pmatrix} u_{11} & u_{12} & \cdots & u_{1n_i} \\ u_{21} & u_{22} & \cdots & u_{2n_i} \\ \vdots & \vdots & & \vdots \\ u_{n_0 1} & u_{n_0 2} & \cdots & u_{n_0 n_i} \end{pmatrix}$$

where m represents a message ($\in \mathfrak{X}^{k_o}$), x_i is an outer code symbol ($\in \mathfrak{X}$), and u_{ij} is a channel symbol ($\in U$).

Each row in the $n_o \times n_i$ matrix is a codeword of the inner code. For each nonzero codeword of a concatenated code, there exists at least d_0 nonzero rows, each of the nonzero rows contains at least d_i nonzero elements. Therefore, the weight of a nonzero concatenated code is at least $d_i d_o$.

TABLE 3.1.

MINIMUM DISTANCES OF CONCATENATED CODES

N	K	D_L	D_{pr}	n_o	k_o	d_o	n_i	k_i	d_i
70	9	32	30	10	3	8	7	3	4
88	12	36	34	11	3	9	8	4	4
98	12	40	36	12	3	10	8	4	4
98	16	33	32	14	4	11	7	4	3
104	12	44	40	13	3	11	8	4	4
104	24	32	30	13	6	8	8	4	4
105	20	33	32	15	5	11	7	4	3
112	12	48	44	14	3	12	8	4	4
112	24	36	33	14	6	9	8	4	4
120	12	52	51	15	3	13	8	4	4
128	16	52	48	16	4	13	8	4	4
128	32	36	32	16	8	9	8	4	4

Some binary concatenated codes of length 128 or less have been constructed in [14]. Some of these codes, whose parameters are shown in Table 3.1, are superior to the best previously known linear codes with the same block length $n_i n_o$ and dimension $k_i k_o$. Specifically the constructed codes have a larger minimum distance (bound) D_L than the $d_{\min}$ of previously known codes (the actual improvement may be even better, because D_L is a lower bound to D). In the table, D_{pr} is the best known minimum Hamming distance of linear block codes, aside from concatenated codes.

Decoding of Concatenated Codes

Concatenated codes are usually considered to be effective for channels with burst errors as well as random errors. Consider a Reed–Solomon code over GF(2^m) with block length $n = 2^m - 1$. Usually each symbol is represented by m bits. It is evident that such a code is not very effective on a channel with random errors, because one bit error in a symbol means the loss of the whole symbol of m bits. This is because the existing decoding algorithms has no way of taking into account the symbols that are "nearly right," and these decoders are for M-ary symmetric channels (or errors-and-erasures channels). However, the code is effective when errors or erasures come in bursts, since jm consecutive erroneous bits is equivalent to at most $j + 1$ symbols in error. Now if each symbol of the Reed–Solomon code is encoded into, for instance, an (n_i, m) code that corrects random errors, then the resultant concatenated code is effective when used over channels with burst as well as random errors.

In decoding concatenated codes we do decoding in two steps, i.e., we perform the inner decoding and the outer decoding separately. The inner decoder processes the incoming data and uses all the available information (for instance soft decision statistics) to correct random errors and detect burst errors. The output of the inner decoder is predominantly either correct data or stretches of burst errors that may be flagged as unreliable. This output then becomes the input to the Reed–Solomon decoder that corrects errors and erasures. One could think of the inner decoder as one that reduces poor quality data into medium quality data, and the outer decoder reduces medium quality data to very good quality data.

The challenging problem in constructing concatenated codes is to find the appropriate inner code and the inner decoder. The inner decoder is usually designed to "match" the super channel to the outer code. Numerous configurations for the decoder have been considered in particular in spread-spectrum communications systems in the presence of unknown interference. Parallel decoding, described in the following, has proved to be very effective to combat such interference on channels with arbitrarily varying statistics. This is the initial motivation for our work on parallel decoding.

Parallel Decoding

In parallel decoding there is a family of decoders with decoding rules $\mathfrak{D}_1, \ldots, \mathfrak{D}_z$. Each decoding rule is applied to the received vector, say $\mathbf{y}$. Then the output of the parallel decoder is $\mathfrak{D}_i(\mathbf{y})$, where i is chosen such that $d(\mathfrak{D}_i, \mathbf{y})$ is the smallest for all i. The *cost function* d is the appropriate channel distance function (d is the Hamming distance for a q-ary symmetric channel or symmetric errors-and-erasures channel, and d is the Euclidean distance for an additive channel, or the cost function can be the probability of error for an arbitrary channel).

For instance consider a communication system with a noise source that pulses between off and on (or a spread-spectrum communication system with partial-band interference) with fixed total power, where the fraction of the band the noise "on" is constant for a whole codeword but may vary from codeword to codeword. For these types of systems it is desirable to have reliable communication irrespective of the fraction of time (or band) the interference affects the transmitted symbol. Furthermore, assume the decoder knows if a code symbol has been subject to interference. Then one useful decoding algorithm for small pulsing times is to erase symbols that are subject to interference, then use an erasure correcting decoder to correct these erasures. If the erasure correcting capability of the code is larger than the expected number of erasures, this algorithm should perform well. For large duty times, erasing such symbols will cause too many erasures for an erasure correction decoder. In this case it is often better to perform error correction since many of the erased symbols would not have caused an error. A parallel approach using an erasure correcting decorder in parallel with an error correcting decoder will perform well for all values of the duty cycle. Thus parallel decoding with different decoding algorithms "matched" to different channels is a useful way of combating channels with unknown interference. This idea was the original motivation behind the work presented here. Previous studies on parallel decoding in partial band interference begin with Pursley and Stark [10], where perfect side information about the interference was assumed to be available at the receiver. Castor and Stark [2] analyzed parallel decoding for partial band jamming with no side information. Also, Kim and Stark [5] analyzed parallel decoding with no side information for a multiple access environment.

Parallel decoding for concatenated codes has each decoder $\mathfrak{D}_i$, $i = 1, \ldots, z$ consisting of an inner decoder and an outer decoder. The problem then is to design the z inner decoders to optimize for some performance measure (such as $d(\cdot)$ in the preceding). Consider a channel as seen by the inner encoder–decoder pair. Let $\mathbf{x}$ be the transmitted inner codeword and $\mathbf{w}$ be the corresponding output of the channel. If the channel statistics are time invariant and known, then one can design the inner decoder such that the resulting super channel matches the outer code, for instance, to minimize the probability of bit error or to maximize the capacity of the super channel. However, on many occasions, the channel statistics are slowly time varying or unknown; one could think of the channel at a given time interval (such as the duration of a codeword) as belonging to a class of channels. Different channels have different inner decoders that yield the best performance.

In parallel decoding of concatenated codes the channel output $\mathbf{w}$ is processed by several (say z) distinct branches; each branch consists of an inner decoder connected to an outer decoder as shown in Figure 3.4. The ith inner decoder is characterized by a threshold Δ_i for deciding whether to erase or to generate its best estimate to the outer decoder. The output of an inner decoder is either an erasure, a correct estimate, or an erroneus (inner) codeword. Then z identical bounded-distance outer decoders (one for each inner decoder) are used to correct the maximum number of errors and erasures. The decoders produce z candidate estimates of the transmitted concatenated codeword. The final decoding step, performed by the decision device, is to choose the "closest" (i.e., the most likely) concatenated codeword to the received vector for a given channel, as the transmitted one. When designed properly each inner decoder is at least nearly optimal for a subclass of (super) channels. The problem then is that of finding the

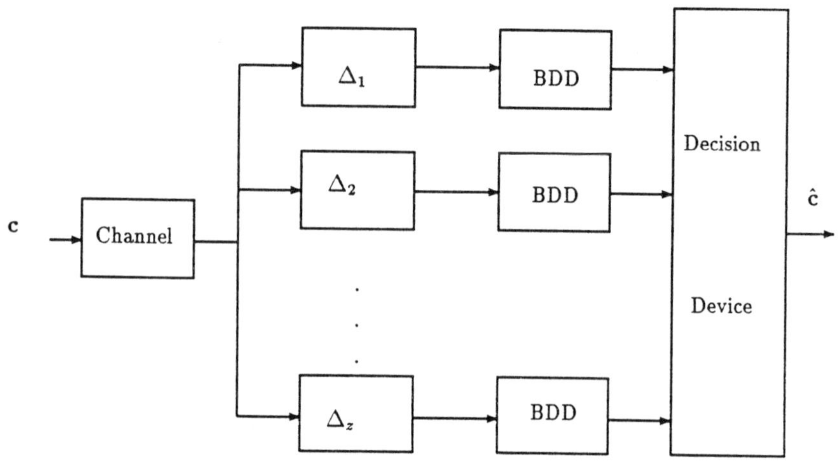

FIG. 3.4. Parallel concatenated decoding.

set of thresholds Δ_i, $i = 1, \ldots, z$ that optimizes some performance criteria. The algorithm for erasing inner codewords (which uses the preceding thresholds for an erasure criteria) depends on the channel model and will be described.

We use parallel decoding for concatenated codes with the preceding description. As noted earlier, the performance measure of the concatenated decoder is the number or size of errors that can be corrected and will be referred to as the *error correcting capability* of the code (using some decoding algorithm and a choice of thresholds). The error correcting capability is defined in different ways depending on the channel model and the applications in mind.

We start by reviewing the work done by Forney. He considered an inner decoder that passes to the outer decoder its best estimate of the inner codeword along with a real number that indicates how reliable it supposes its estimate to be. He showed how such information can be efficiencly used by the outer decoder in a method called *generalized minimum distance* (GMD) decoding; this type of decoding allows the use of likelihood information in algebraic decoding algorithms. If y is the output of the demodulater, $p(y \mid x)$ is the probability density of the output of the demodulator given the input to the modulator is x, and

$$L(y) = \ln \frac{p(y \mid 0)}{p(y \mid 1)}$$

is the bit log likelihood ratio, then the input to the outer decoder is a vector $\alpha = (\alpha_1, \alpha_2, \ldots, \alpha_n)$, ($n$ being the inner code length) such that, for some threshold T, $\alpha_i = q(y_i)$ such that

$$q(y) = \begin{cases} +1 & L(y) \geq T \\ \dfrac{L(y)}{T} & -T \leq L(y) \leq T \\ -1 & L(y) \leq -T \end{cases}$$

Thus the channel considered is that of an additive channel with a soft limiter at the output. The outer decoder processes the received vector $\boldsymbol{\alpha}$ by making hard decisions on each component of the vector $\boldsymbol{\alpha}$ and then attempting to decode with a standard bounded distance error correcting method. If the (bounded distance) error correcting decoding fails, the least reliable symbol is erased and an attempt is made to decode using an errors-and-erasures method. If the decoding fails, the two least reliable symbols are erased and decoding is attempted using an errors-and-erasures decoding. This continues until a codeword is decoded with $(c, r) > n - d_{\min}$, or there are more erasures than can be corrected by the code, where (c, r) is the scalar product of a codeword c and the received vector r and $d_{\min}$ is the minimum Hamming distance of the inner code. Note that there is a vector successfully decoded by the inner decoder with i erasures, where i can take values in $\{0, 1, 2, \ldots, d_{\min} - 1\}$; however, it can be shown that only $\lfloor (d_{\min} + 1)/2 \rfloor$ attempts for decoding are necessary and sufficient for decoding, where $\lfloor x \rfloor$ is the largest integer smaller or equal to x. It is easy to show that errors-only decoding and errors-and-erasures decoding are special cases of this algorithm.

Castor and Stark [2] and Pursley and Stark [10] have considered the use of parallel decoding schemes to mitigate the effects of partial band Gaussian jamming for spread spectrum, M-ary orthogonal, frequency hopped communication systems. Results were presented for the probability of error when the decoders performed hard decision decoding on the received vectors. Their results demonstrate that good performance is achievable in the partial band jamming environment independent of the percentage of bandwidth jammed.

Decoding over *M*-ary Symmetric Channels

For correcting over an M-ary symmetric channel, the logical error-correcting capability is the number of errors correctable by the decoder. It is desirable to have a decoding algorithm that corrects all error patterns with Hamming weight $\lfloor (d_H - 1)/2 \rfloor$ or less, where d_H is the minimum Hamming distance of the concatenated code.

Knowing that the Hamming distance of the code is lower bounded by $d_i d_o$, the maximum error-correcting capability of the code is at least

$\lfloor (d_i d_o - 1)/2 \rfloor$. Designing a decoder that employs the maximum possible capability is not a trivial task. For instance, if the inner code is used to correct $\lfloor (d_o - 1)/2 \rfloor$ errors and the outer code to correct $\lfloor (d_i - 1)/2 \rfloor$ errors, then the decoder $f^{-1}(g^{-1})^{n_2}(u^{n_1 \times n_2})$ can correct only about $d_i d_o/4$ errors. For this case Zyablov [15] found a parallel decoding algorithm that has the maximum possible error-correcting capability, at the expense of increasing the complexity of the decoder. The algorithm was developed for an M-ary input and output channel and depends on errors-and-erasures decoding and the use of several branches with different tentative decisions. Altogether there are $\lfloor (d_i + 1)/2 \rfloor$ branches. The inner code of the ith branch corrects all error patterns with $i - 1$ or fewer errors for $i = 1, 2, \ldots, \lfloor (d_i + 1)/2 \rfloor$, and the outer code corrects all e_i errors and τ_i erasures if $2e_i + \tau_i < d_o$. Of the $\lfloor (d_i + 1)/2 \rfloor$ branches, the one that has the smallest Hamming distance from the received vector is taken as the final result. Then this decoder corrects all error patterns with weight $\lfloor (d_i d_o - 1)/2 \rfloor$ or less. We elaborate on the design of decoders for concatenated codes.

In Figure 3.4 we have a concatenated coded system over an M-ary symmetric channel. The inner code has minimum Hamming distance 9, and the outer code has a minimum Hamming distance 26. For this example we do not care what particular codes are used, but we are told that the inner decoder and the outer decoder are both bounded distance decoders. What are the best possible algorithms for the decoders? At first glance, intuition would suggest that the inner decoder corrects all errors possible, and the outer decoder corrects all errors possible that were not corrected by the inner code. Such a decoder can correct approximately

$$\left\lfloor \frac{9 - 1}{2} \right\rfloor \left\lfloor \frac{26 - 1}{2} \right\rfloor = 48$$

errors (more careful enumeration yield the actual number of errors corrected is 64). The design question is then, can we do any better? Theoretically, the overall concatenated code has a distance of 234 and errors up to 116 can be corrected had we used the code as a one code rather than a concatenated code.

Consider the following algorithm. The inner decoder is allowed to correct all error patterns that have weight of 2 or less. Otherwise the inner decoder will output an erasure. The outer decoder is a bounded distance decoder that corrects all errors e and erasures τ as long as $2e + \tau$ is strictly less than 25. One can show with careful analysis (which will follow later) that the preceding algorithm can correct 77 errors. That can amount to a substantial coding gain.

TABLE 3.2.
ERROR CORRECTING CAPABILITY VERSUS Δ

Δ	Maximum correctable error weight
0	25
1	51
2	77
3	77
4	65

If the inner decoder is allowed to correct Δ errors or less, the overall decoder with have error correcting capability according to Table 3.2. The best threshold is noticed to be $\Delta = 2$ where 77 errors can be corrected by the decoder. The optimal threshold depends only on the Hamming distances of the codes.

In the preceding example, we were able to recover some error correcting capability of the concatenated code. We can actually do better if the system's specifications allow for extra complexity. Consider two branches at the receiver, with the first inner decoder characterized by Δ_1 and the second inner decoder characterized by Δ_2. The optimal choices are

$$\Delta_1 = 1$$
$$\Delta_2 = 3.$$

This decoder can correct 103 errors, which is a substantial increase in the number of errors corrected as compared to the single branch case. Actually for five branches such that inner decoder i is used for $i - 1$ error correction all the errors promised by the overall distance 134 is realized (that is, 116 errors can be corrected).

Let d_i be the minimum Hamming distance of the inner code, and let d_o be the minimum Hamming distance of the outer code. For an arbitrary threshold Δ for the inner decoder, the concatenated decoder can correct all error patterns with weight γ or less, where

$$\gamma = \begin{cases} \min\left\{\dfrac{d_o}{2}(d_i - \Delta), \quad d_o(\Delta + 1)\right\} - 1 & d_o \text{ even} \\[2ex] \min\left\{\dfrac{d_o - 1}{2}(d_i - \Delta) + \Delta, \quad (d_o - 1)(\Delta + 1) + \Delta\right\} & d_o \text{ odd} \end{cases}$$

The optimal threshold Δ that results in most numbers of errors that can be corrected by the concatenated code is given by

$$\Delta = \left\lfloor \frac{d_i - 2}{3} \right\rfloor$$

With this threshold, the number of errors that can be corrected is

$$\gamma = \frac{d_o(d_i + 1)}{3} - 1$$

if the right side is an integer. Otherwise,

$$\gamma = \begin{cases} \dfrac{d_o}{2}\left(d_i + 1 - \left\lfloor \dfrac{d_i + 1}{3} \right\rfloor\right) - 1 & d_o \text{ even} \\ \dfrac{d_o - 1}{2}\left(d_i + 1 - \left\lfloor \dfrac{d_i + 1}{3} \right\rfloor\right) + \left\lfloor \dfrac{d_i + 1}{3} \right\rfloor - 1 & d_o \text{ odd} \end{cases}$$

Decoding over Additive Channels

A decoding algorithm for an M-ary symmetric channel can be used for a discrete-time additive channel by quantizing the output of the additive channel. However, an information loss caused by quantizing will cause degradation in performance. Under most conditions soft decision decoding gives better performance than hard decision decoding or errors-and-erasures decoding mentioned earlier. For instance, for additive white Gaussian noise channel hard decision decoding results in an asymptotic 2 dB loss in signal-to-noise ratio over soft decision decoding in the limit as the code rate goes to 0, both for binary and nonbinary codes. One problem remains: soft decision decoding requires high complexity for codes with large block length. It is desired to recover the loss incurred by quantizing without implementing a highly complex decoding algorithm.

We analyze and optimize the performance of a parallel decoder for concatenated odds on additive channels. Additive channels are motivated by coherent demodulation and the fact that quantization loses performance. Hence, we consider soft decision inner decoders, which process the received (real) vector and generate either an estimate or an erasure. Each of the z inner decoders, say the ith branch, has a different threshold Δ_i for deciding when to erase. If the received vector is within Euclidean distance Δ_i of some inner codeword, the ith inner decoder will generate the information symbols of that codeword; otherwise it will erase the inner codeword and pass the erasure to the outer decoder. Of the z concatenated codewords produced by the parallel branches, the decision device selects the one that is closest in Euclidean distance to the received vector as the transmitted codeword.

This soft decision decoding assumes, implicitly, coherent detection of the received signals. Thus the notion of a correctable Euclidean distance (of the code) is easy to define and is a reasonable performance criteria to consider.

This is particularly true when considering additive white Gaussian noise channel such as in deep space or satellite communications.

The principal result of this section is to present the optimal choice of Δ_i, $i = 1, 2, \ldots, z$, to maximize the guaranteed maximum Euclidean distance correctable by the concatenated code referred to as the *error-correcting capability* of the code. Furthermore, we show that for moderate values of z (3 or 4) this decoding algorithm can correct errors up to something close to half the minimum Euclidean distance of the concatenated code.

Consider the parallel decoding algorithm for a concatenated code and an additive channel, such that the inner decoder of the ith branch decodes all vectors within Euclidean distance Δ_i of some codeword, $i = 1, 2, \ldots, z$ (note that $\Delta_i \in (0, d_{iE}/2)$), where z is the number of decoder branches, and d_{iE} is the Euclidean distance of the inner code. Errors are detected in the ith branch of a received vector (corresponding to an inner codeword) does not fall in any sphere of radius Δ_i, and centered around an inner codeword. In this case the inner decoder outputs an erasure to the outer decoder. The decision device in this case chooses among the z candidate codewords the one that is closest in Euclidean distance to the received vector as the transmitted one.

The Euclidean distance d_{iE} of the inner code depends on the modulation being employed. For example, if we are using a binary inner code and antipodal signaling (with unit energy) then $d_{iE} = 2\sqrt{d_i}$, d_i being the Hamming distance of the inner code, whereas for an M-ary inner code and M-ary orthogonal signal set $d_{iE} = \sqrt{2d_i}$. The exact relation between Euclidean distance and Hamming distance is not important in this chapter since we are dealing with correcting capability with respect to Euclidean distance.

The error-correcting capability of the parallel decoder is evaluated for outer codes defined over GF(q), for all $q = 2^m$, $m \geq 1$, and inner codes over GF(2^l) (usually $l < m$). The outer code is usually a Reed–Solomon code that corrects any set of e errors and τ erasures if $2e + \tau < d_o$. As mentioned earlier, of the at most z possible decoding results, the one that has the smallest Euclidean distance from the received combination is taken as the final result. The optimal decoder maximizes the error correcting capability for a fixed z.

Let $\delta_k = \Delta_k/d_{iE}$ and $f(\delta_k, \delta_{k-1}) = (1 - \delta_k)^2 + \delta_{k-1}^2$. For the case when d_o is an even integer the optimal thresholds for arbitrary number of branches and the largest noise distance (i.e., the Euclidean distance) correctable by the concatenated code are determined by the solution to the following nonlinear equations

$$f(\delta_k, \delta_{k-1}) = \alpha_z$$

where α_z is some unique constant that depends on z and determines the error correcting capability of the code. Given the conditions $\delta_0 = 0$ and $\delta_{z+1} = 1 - \delta_z$; the $z + 1$ equations for $\delta_1, \ldots, \delta_z$, α_z can be solved numerically.

We now can solve for the optimal values of the thresholds Λ_z; that is, we can determine the decoder strategy that maximizes the error correcting capability of concatenated codes when used on q-ary additive channels (recall that $\Delta_i = \delta_i d_{iE}$). These thresholds are strictly a function of the number of decoder branches used in the parallel decoder. One expects that the error-correcting capability of the code to improve with larger z. This behavior is presented in the following.

A similar argument holds for the case when d_o is an odd integer. In this case, the Euclidean distance correctable by the concatenated and the optimum values of the thresholds is the solution to the following set of nonlinear equations:

$$\frac{(d_o - 1)}{2}[(d_{iE} - \Delta_k)^2 + \Delta_{k-1}^2] + \Delta_z^2 = \alpha_z, \qquad k = 1, 2, \ldots, z + 1$$

It can be shown that the optimum values for Δ and the resulting error-correcting capability depends only on z; that is, they are the same regardless whether d_o is an odd integer or an even integer.

The error-correcting capability (squared) of the code when the decoder uses its best strategy is

$$\begin{aligned} \gamma &= \frac{d_o d_{iE}^2}{2}\alpha_z \\ \text{or} \quad \sqrt{\gamma} &= d_{iE}\sqrt{d_o}\sqrt{\frac{\alpha_z}{2}} \\ &= \frac{d_{iE}\sqrt{d_o}}{2}\sqrt{2\alpha_z} \\ &= \frac{d_{iE}\sqrt{d_o}}{2}\beta_z \end{aligned} \tag{3.3}$$

where $\beta_z < 1$; also β_z goes to 1 as z becomes larger.

This implies that the full error-correcting capability of the concatenated code is achieved asymptotically. However, Table 3.3 shows that over 95 per cent of the full error correcting capability is realized for $z = 4$, with values: $\delta_1 = 0.317$, $\delta_2 = 0.395$, $\delta_3 = 0.443$, $\delta_4 = 0.481$. Thus we only need few branches to get a good error-correcting capability. Table 3.4 shows optimal thresholds for few values of z.

TABLE 3.3.

ERROR-CORRECTING CAPABILITY FOR VARIOUS NUMBERS OF BRANCHES z

z	α_z	β_z
1	0.3431	0.828
2	0.4187	0.915
3	0.4500	0.948
4	0.4655	0.965
5	0.4750	0.974
6	0.4800	0.979
7	0.4850	0.984
8	0.4877	0.988
9	0.4900	0.990
10	0.4915	0.991
15	0.4957	0.995
30	0.4982	0.998

TABLE 3.4.

OPTIMAL THRESHOLDS FOR VARIOUS NUMBERS OF BRANCHES z

z	Optimum thresholds
2	$\delta_1 = 0.35288$ $\delta_2 = 0.45757$
3	$\delta_1 = 0.32940$ $\delta_2 = 0.41600$ $\delta_3 = 0.47410$
4	$\delta_1 = 0.317$ $\delta_2 = 0.395$ $\delta_3 = 0.443$ $\delta_4 = 0.481$

The decoding algorithm proposed uses errors-and-erasures decoding and several branches with different tentative decisions, giving rise to parallel decoding. The set of thresholds for each algorithm is chosen to optimize the error-correcting capability of the code. Moreover, the algorithm can be used without modification for a more general case and with no loss of optimality. For instance, it applies when k_o symbols of same coordinates, each symbol from a possibly different codeword of the outer code, are inner encoded.

The error-correcting capability of the code improves with increasing z. We showed that the full error correcting capability is attained asymptotically with z. However, the numerical results shows that $z = 4$ guarantees more than 95 per cent of this capability. In case we need to communicate over a bursty channel with long burst lengths, we can add an outer–outer code to pick the correct outer codeword. Then a decoding algorithm is needed to make best use of the resulting concatenated code.

The inner codes need not be block codes. Convolutional or trellis codes for which the Viterbi algorithm provides a good algorithm for maximum likelihood decoding can be used. We leave such treatment for future work.

Convolutional Codes

Convolutional codes differ from block codes in that the encoder contains memory and the n encoder output at any given time unit depends not only on the k inputs at that time unit but also on ν previous input blocks. An (n, k, ν) convolutional code can be implemented with a k-input, n-output linear sequential circuit with memory ν. Typically n and k are small integers, but ν is made large to achieve low error probabilities. Figure 3.5 shows a block diagram of a convolutional encoder. The message symbols are fed into the shift registers k symbols at a time. The contents of the shift registers are shifted each time a k symbol block is fed in. The linear function generator generates an n symbol block from both the contents of the shift registers and the k input symbols each time an input block is fed in. The number of message symbols from which an output block is generated, $(\nu + 1)k$, is called the *constraint length* of the code. The ratio $R = k/n$ is called the *code rate*.

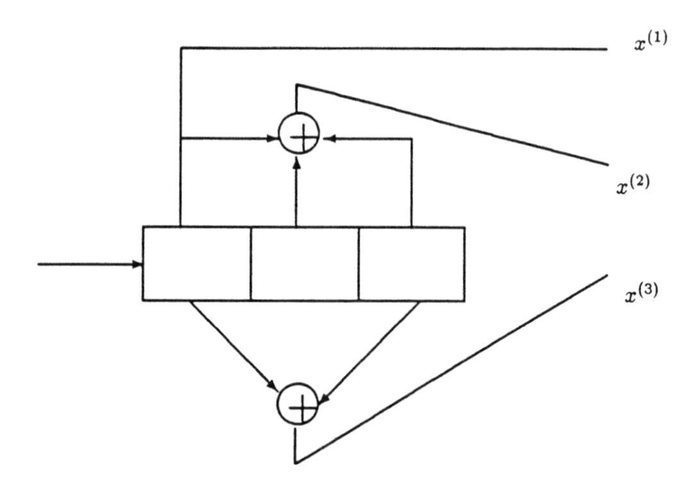

FIG. 3.5. A constraint length 3, $k = 1$, $n = 3$ convolutional encoder.

The input and output sequences for a convolutional encoder is, in general, assumed semi-infinite. The sequences are expressed as power series in D, which represents a unit time delay. Let

$$u_t = (u_t^{(1)} \ldots u_t^{(k)})$$

$$x_t = (x_t^{(1)} \ldots x_t^{(n)})$$

be the input and output blocks at time t, respectively. Then the message sequence and code sequence are expressed as

$$u(D) = u_0 + u_1 D + u_2 D^2 + \cdots$$

$$x(D) = x_0 + x_1 D + x_2 D^2 + \cdots$$

respectively. The operation of a convolutional encoder can be described as

$$x(D) = u(D)G(D)$$

where $G(D)$ is a $k \times n$ matrix of polynomials in D. $G(D)$ is called the *generator matrix* of the convolutional code. The highest degree of the element polynomials of $G(D)$ is equal to the number of stages of the shift registers of the encoder. A convolutional code can also be defined using parity check matrices. A convolutional code is the set of sequences $x(D)$ that satisfy the parity check equation

$$H(D)x(D)^T = 0$$

where $H(D)$ is an $(n - k) \times n$ matrix of polynomials in D, called the *parity check matrix*.

The encoder of a convolution code is a finite state machine, and the contents of the shift registers represent its state. Thus, the encoder of a convolution code over GF(q) with $R = k/n$ and $L = (m + 1)k$ has q^{mk} states. The operation of the encoder is described by a state diagram that has q^{mk} states and q^k branches emanating from each state.

The error-correction capability of a convolution code is measured by the free distance defined to be the minimum Hamming distance between the semi-infinite code sequences generated by the encoder, which is equal to the minimum Hamming weight of the nonzero code sequences generated by the encoder, due to linearity. The free distance is given as the minimum weight path in the state diagram that starts at the all-zero state and ends at the all-zero state.

There are several graph theoretic ways to represent a convolutional encoder: a tree, a trellis, and a state diagram. These are shown in Figure 3.6 for the convolutional code generated as in Figure 3.5.

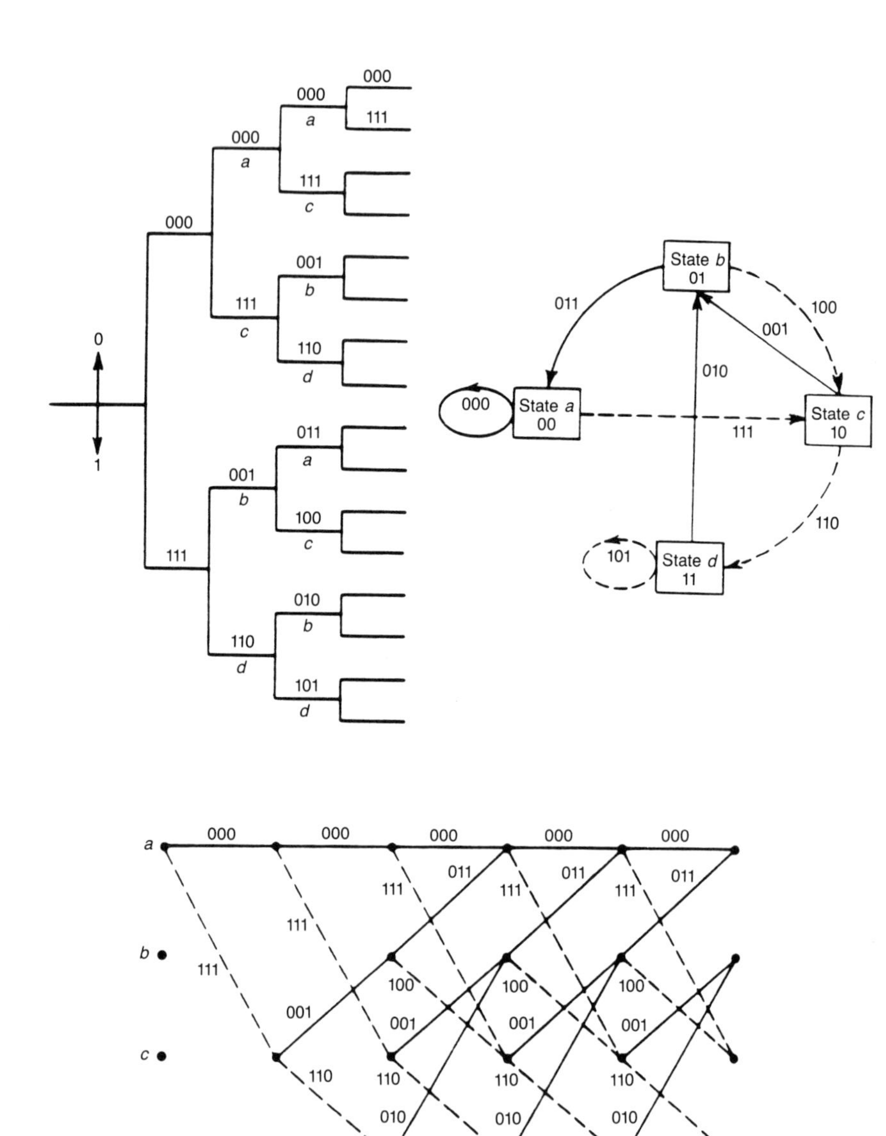

FIG. 3.6. Different representations of convolutional encoders.

The tree for the convolutional code has both input and output sequences to the encoder displayed on the diagram. For this example, an input 0 specifies the upper branch while an input 1 specifies the lower branch. Thus the input sequence 010011110 is indicated by moving up at the first branching level, down at the second, up at the third and so on. From the diagram it becomes clear that after the first three branches the structure becomes repetitive. This leads to the redrawing of the tree diagram to arrive at the more convenient trellis diagram. The repetitive structure of the trellis diagram suggests a state diagram representation shown in Figure 3.6. The states of the diagram are labeled according to the nodes of the trellis diagram. Generalizations of these representations to the nonbinary and arbitrary rate case is straightforward.

Decoding of convolutional codes is simple. The optimum decoding algorithm is the well-known Viterbi algorithm, which follows. Let

$\mathbf{u} = (u_0, u_1, \ldots, u_{L-1})$ of length kL be the information sequence;
$\mathbf{v} = (v_0, v_1, \ldots, v_{L+m-1})$ of length $N = n(L + m)$ be the code sequence generated by the convolutional encoder;
$\mathbf{r} = (r_0, r_1, \ldots, r_{L+m-1})$ be the received vector of the binary transmitted data over an additive channel, M-ary symmetric channel, or M-ary symmetric-erasure channel.

The optimum decoder in the sense of minimizing the sequence error rate is the one that maximizes the likelihood probability $P(\mathbf{r} \mid \mathbf{v})$ or the equivalently its logarithm, which is referred to as the *path metric*. This reasonably assumes that all possible transmitted sequences are equally probable. For a memoryless channel, the path metric is given by

$$\begin{aligned} M(\mathbf{r} \mid \mathbf{v}) &= \log P(\mathbf{r} \mid \mathbf{v}) \\ &= \sum_{i=0}^{N-1} \log P(r_i \mid v_i) \end{aligned}$$

Convolutional decoders are used predominantly on additive channels, because the complexity difference between soft and hard decision decoding is very small, unlike for decoding of block codes. In practice each received symbol is represented by a number of bits depending on the accuracy required. Experience suggests that 4 bits per received symbol yields performance close to the ideal (analog) case.

The Viterbi algorithm searches the trellis for the path with the largest metric in a sequential fashion as suggested by the preceding decomposition of the log likelihood. This is known in optimization as *forward dynamic programming*. At each state, the path metrics ending at that state are calculated. The path with the best metric is kept, called the *survivor*, and the rest of the paths are discarded. This is done at each state at each time until the end of the trellis at which the path with the highest metric is chosen as the transmitted one. To summarize the algorithm,

1. At time $j = m$, store the survivor and its metric for each state.
2. $j = j + 1$; add branch metrics to path metrics; choose survivor.
3. If $j < L + m$, repeat 2; otherwise, stop.

In a previous section we pointed out that time-invariant systems theory can be used to study cyclic codes. Close relationships can also be established between convolutional codes and linear-invariant dynamic systems with a zero initial state as discussed in [7].

Performance Evaluation

The use of coding techniques to correct for errors and erasures, in general, improves on the bit-error-rate (BER) performance. The performance of coded systems is quantified by two measures: the coding gain and the bandwidth expansion factor. The coding gain at a given BER is the amount of E_b/N_o in dB gained by the coded system as compared to the uncoded system. This is sketched in Figure 3.7, where the coding gain at 10^{-4} is shown to be 3 dB. Such a save in energy is very important to increase the capacity of power-limited systems such as satellite communications systems. Coding becomes necessary in fading and jamming channels where reliable communication is not possible without error control techniques. Coding gains of 30–40 dB is not uncommon on such channels.

An important issue in digital communication systems if *how* to use channel coding. However, as important is *when* to use channel coding. There are instances where it is not needed and other instances where coding degrades performance. A typical bit-error-rate performance is more likely to look like that in Figure 3.8, where we show the performance of Reed–Solomon coding on a binary-symmetric channel. Notice that for low channel bit-error rates, corresponding to low E_b/N_o, the curves cross showing worse performance for the coded system than the uncoded system. This means that for signal-to-noise ratios no coding might be employed. This is encountered for example in speech transmission where bit-error-rates on the order of 2 per cent is acceptable.

The bandwidth expansion factor is the excess of bandwidth necessary to transmit the coded signal as compared to the uncoded signal. Usually, for block codes the bandwidth expansion is inversely proportional to the

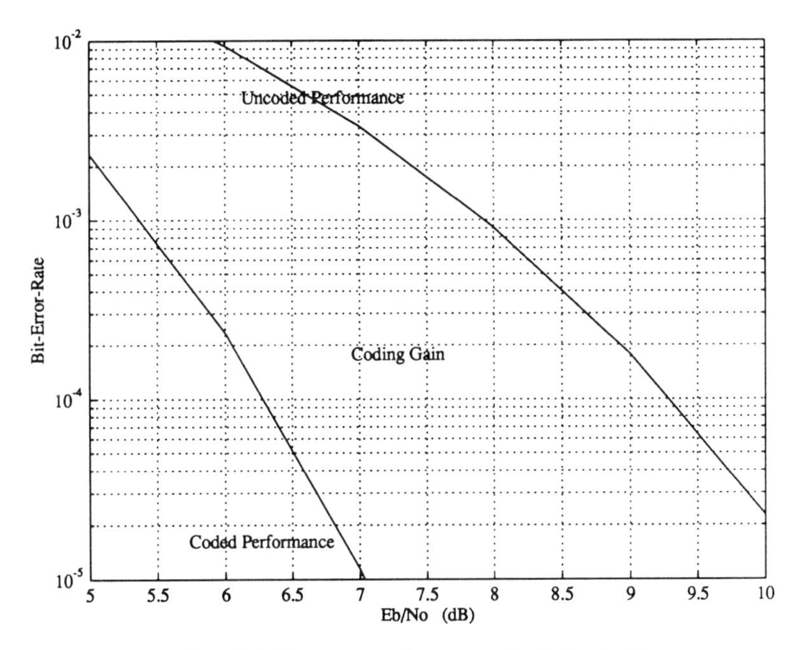

FIG. 3.7. Error rate performance of coded systems.

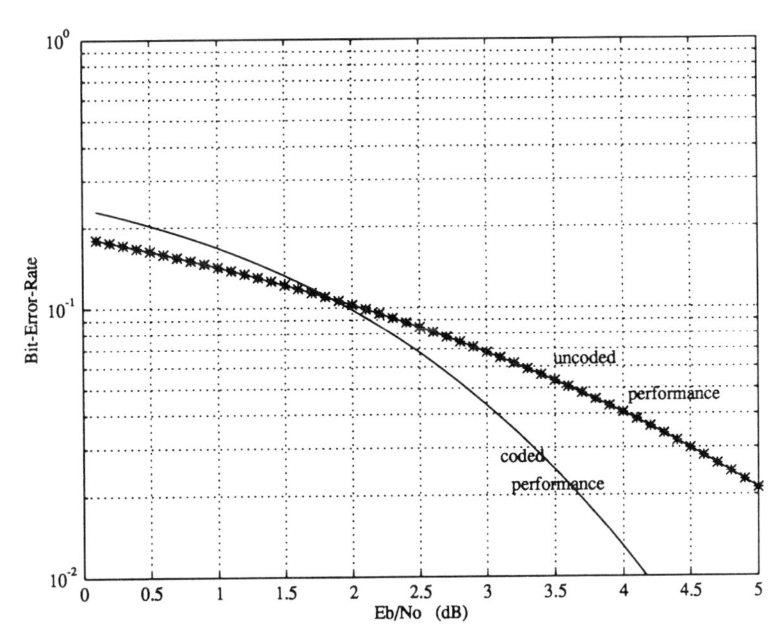

FIG. 3.8. Error rate performance of coded systems.

code rate. That is, when using a code with rate 1/2, twice more bandwidth is required as compared to uncoded systems. An even more important measure (or specification) of bandwidth utilization is the bandwidth efficiency of the combined modulation and coding. This is defined as the data rate divided by the bandwidth occupancy of the transmitted signal and measured in bits-per-second/Hz (bps/Hz). This is particularly important for multiple access systems.

In the heart of coded system design is the calculation of the error rates for the given code parameters and a given mapping of code symbols to waveform signals, known as *modulation*. It is only intuitive to expect the bit-error rate to decrease with an increase in the distance of the code, which is particularly true at high signal-to-noise ratios. This is one reason why the error-correcting capability of codes is emphasized in this chapter.

When the code is used over an additive white Gaussian channel using the common modulation schemes: binary phase shift keying, quaternary phase shift keying, or $\pi/4 - PSK$ (binary and quaternary), the word–error probability P_W is upper bounded by

$$P_W \leq \sum_{d=d_{\min}}^{N} A_d Q\left(\sqrt{\frac{2E_b}{N_o} dr}\right)$$

In this expression, r is the code rate, A_d is the number of codewords with Hamming weight d, N is the number of codewords, and

$$Q(x) = \frac{1}{\sqrt{2\pi}} \int_{x}^{+\infty} e^{-u^2/2}\, du$$

Therefore, to obtain an upper bound on the word–error probability, the weight distribution of the code is required. As pointed out earlier, the weight distribution of most codes is unknown; Reed–Solomon codes have a known weight distribution, which makes it easier to analyze. A less tight upper bound can be used in case the weight distribution is unknown and given by

$$P_W \leq \frac{N-1}{2} A_d Q\left(\sqrt{\frac{2R_b}{N_o} d_{\min} r}\right)$$

For binary frequency shift keying modulation, E_b is substituted by $E_b/2$; that is, a loss of 3 dB is incurred.

These expressions for P_W hold for convolutional codes as well. A_d is then the number of paths with Hamming distance d, and $d_{\min}$ is the minimum free distance of the convolutional code. The upper limit on the summation is theoretically infinite, but usually only up to seven terms are considered at moderate to high signal-to-noise ratios.

The performance of codes when used over an M-ary symmetric channel, or M-ary symmetric-erasure channel is part of the exercises.

Miscellaneous Topics

Coding for computer memories is a little different than coding for transmission. The main differences are in the channel models. In general, "hard" error events in digital systems include the following:

1. Symmetric errors: 1 to 0 and 0 to 1 type errors can occur in a codeword. This chapter has dealt with coding for this channel model in details.
2. Asymmetric errors: Only one of the error type, 1 to 0 or 0 to 1, can occur in a codeword. The error is known a priori.
3. Unidirectional errors: both 0 to 1 and 1 to 0 errors can occur, but they cannot occur in the same codeword.

The following outlines the main results for error correcting capability without any discussion. Let $X, Y \in \{0, 1\}^n$. Denote by $N(X, Y)$ the number of 1 to 0 crossovers from X to Y. Then the Hamming distance of a code is

$$D(X, Y) = N(X, Y) + N(Y, X)$$

and the minimum distance of a code is

$$D_{\min} = \min_{X \neq Y} D(X, Y)$$

Based on this notation and definition, the following theorems are of interest in coding for memory.

Theorem. A code C is capable of correcting t-symmetric errors and simultaneously detecting all unidirectional errors if and only if for all X, $Y \in C$ with $X \neq Y$:

$$N(X, Y) \geq t + 1 \quad \text{and} \quad N(Y, X) \geq t + 1$$

Theorem. A code C is capable of correcting t-symmetric errors and simultaneously detecting $d(d > t)$ unidirectional errors if and only if for all X and Y $(X \neq Y)$ either

$$N(X, Y) \geq t + 1 \quad \text{and} \quad N(Y, X) \geq t + 1$$

or

$$D(X, Y) \geq t + d + 1$$

Problems

1. In certain applications, a symbol is represented as a set of binary digits, or bits. For instance ASCII characters are each represented by seven bits (because eight-bit bytes are common on computers, ASCII is usually embedded in an eight character field with the leftmost either used as a parity or set to 0). Consider transmitting ASCII symbols over a memoryless binary-symmetric channel with bit-error probability p. Find the probability of symbol error. Plot on a semilog scale symbol-error rate versus bit-error rate.
2. To improve on the performance of the preceding transmission, each symbol is repeated three times. The majority symbol is chosen to be the transmitted one.

   (a) Find an upper bound on the decoded symbol–error probability.
   (b) Find an exact expression for the decoded symbol–error probability.

3. The receiver may choose to decode the preceding diversity transmission differently. For instance, each symbol is represented by its seven bits, and each bit of each received symbol is decoded using majority logic.

   (a) Find an exact expression for symbol error rate using the bit combining method.
   (b) Plot on a semilog scale and on the same graph the results of Problems 1, 2b, and 3a.

4. Consider a concatenated coded system as in Figure 3.4. The outer code has minimum Hamming distance 52 and the inner code has minimum Hamming distance 15. If the inner decoder and the outer decoder are designed such that each corrects the maximum number of errors at their respective inputs, what is the maximum number of errors that is always correctable by the concatenated code and why?
5. For the concatenated code in Problem 5 the system's designer allows two times more decoding complexity into your concatenated decoders.

   (a) Find an alternative concatenated decoder that can correct more errors than found in the previous problem.
   (b) How is your design differs if more hardware complexity is not tolerable but twice longer decoding delay is allowed.
   (c) Compare you decoding gains.

6. As a project, consider a coded data transmission system with noncoherent binary frequency shift keying (FSK) using a Golay (23, 12) code [12] for error correction. The transmission uses a frequency-hopped

spread spectrum in which, during each hopping interval (denoted as the dwell time), a fraction of the band is used. In a given hop four known bits are used for synchronization and the rest of the data are code symbols. The codewords are interleaved such that a particular codeword is transmitted in 23 hops.

The channel suffers from multiplicative fading R, which has the following probability density function

$$P_R(r) = \begin{cases} r\,e^{-r^2/2} & r \geq 0 \\ 0 & r < 0 \end{cases}$$

The fading is slow enough to be assumed constant during a dwell interval. Conditioned on the fading random variable $R = r$ the bit-error probability for binary FSK with noncoherent reception is given by

$$p(r) = \tfrac{1}{2}\, e^{-r^2(E_b/N_o)}$$

The communications engineer is asked for more coding gain without changing the system. The engineer can use extra processing only at the receiver.

(a) Calculate the codeword error rate of the original system.
(b) Explain with supporting analysis how can the receiver be modified for better performance if receiver complexity is not an issue.
(c) Explain with supporting analysis how can the receiver be modified for better performance if the receiver-allowable increase in complexity is minimal.
(d) What are the coding gains for these three coded systems.

Hint: Remember that the given system uses the code over an M-ary symmetric channel.

References

[1] Shannon, C. E. (1948). "A Mathematical Theory of Communication," *Bell Systems Tech. Jour.* **38**, 61–656.

[2] Castor, K. G., and W. E. Stark. (1986). "Parallel Decoding of Diversity/Reed–Solomon Coded SSFH Communication with Repetition Thresholding," Proc. 20th. Conf. Information Sciences and Systems, Princeton University.

[3] Chang, L. F., and R. B. McEliece. (1984). "A study of Viterbi's Ratio-Threshold Antijam Technique," Proceedings IEEE Military Communications Conference, pp. 11.2.1–5.

[4] Forney, G. D. (1966). *Concatenated Codes.* MIT Research Monograph No 37, The MIT Press, Cambridge, MA.

[5] Kim, B. G., and W. E. Stark. (1993). "Coding for Spread-Spectrum Communication Networks," *IEEE Trans. Commun.* (To be published.)

[6] Levitin, L. B., and C. R. Hartmann. (1985). "A New Approach to the General Minimum Distance Decoding Problem: The Zero-Neighbors Algorithm," *IEEE Trans. Inform. Theory* **IT-31**, 378–385.

[7] Massey, J. L., and M. K. Sain. (1967). "Codes, Automata, and Continuous Systems: Explicit Interconnection," *IEEE Trans. on Automatic Control.*

[8] Pursley, M. B. (1986). "Packet Error Probabilities in Frequency-Hop Radio Networks—Coping with Statistical Dependence and Noisy Side Information," *IEEE Global Telecommun. Conference Record* **1**, 165–170.

[9] Pursley, M. B. (1987). "Tradeoffs Between Side Information and Code-Rate in Slow-Frequency-Hop Packet Radio Networks," Conference Record, IEEE International Conference on Commun.

[10] Pursley, M. B., and W. E. Stark. (1985). "Performance of Reed–Solomon Coded FH Spread Spectrum Communication in Partial-Band Interference," *IEEE Trans. On Commun.* **Comm-33**(8).

[11] Stark, W. E. (1985). "Coding for Frequency-Hopped Spread-Spectrum Communication with Partial-Band Interference—Part I: Capacity and Cutoff Rate," *IEEE Trans. Commun.* **COM-33**, 1036–1044.

[12] Blahut, R. E. (1983). *Theory and Practice of Error Control Codes.* Addison Wesley, Redwood City, CA.

[13] Berlekamp, E. R., and R. J. McEliece. (1978). "On the Inherent Intractability of Certain Coding Problems," *IEEE Trans. Inform. Theory* **IT-24**, 384–386.

[14] Weng, L. (1977). "Concatenated Codes with Larger Minimum Distance," *IEEE Trans. Inform. Theory* **IT-23**(5), 613–615.

[15] Zyablov, V. V. (1973). "Optimization of Concatenated Decoding Algorithms," *Probl. Peredachi Inf.* **9**(1), 26–32.

[16] Viterbi, A. J. (1982). "A Robust Ratio Threshold Technique to Mitigate Tone and Partial Band Jammer in Coded MFSK Systems," Proceedings of the 1982 IEEE Military Communications Conference.

Chapter 4
Computation

This chapter will deal with computation as a key component of a digital system. It will explore the meaning and place of computation in a digital system and discuss the procedures for performing the computation.

Elementary Functions and Their Fast Approximation

As engineers and applied mathematicians, we often speak of *closed-form solutions*. What we mean by this phrase is that the answer is expressible using only venerable and seemingly universal functions such as the trigonometric functions, logarithmic functions, the error function, Bessel functions, and so on. It is therefore necessary that we spend some time on methods by which some of these important functions can be calculated.[1]

Frequently it is necessary to approximate a continuous function, $y = f(x)$, such as $y = \cos(x)$ or $y = \int_{-\infty}^{x} e^{-z^2} \cos z \, dz$ to within a prescribed accuracy over an interval $[x_a, x_b]$; i.e. $x_a \le x \le x_b$. Of course, a host of possible approximations can be used, and the question of *best* approximation is not well defined without considering what the overall system demands from the approximation. These demands can be for accuracy, or speed, or something else. One trade-off that should certainly be considered as the cost of fast memory continues to decline is the storing of a table of values of y over $[x_a, x_b]$ and simple linear interpolation. Consider that y has been calculated at the set of abscissa values $\{x_j\}$ ordered by increasing value. Then, if we require $y = f(x)$ for $x_i \le x \le x_{i+1}$, where $[x_i, x_{i+1}]$ is the smallest subinterval of $[x_a, x_b]$ containing x, we approximate $y = f(x)$ by

$$y(x) = f(x_i) + \frac{x - x_i}{x_{i+1} - x_i} [f(x_{i+1}) - f(x_i)] \tag{4.1}$$

[1] It is our thesis that most computations of interest to most digital systems admit to approximation. To be sure, many important problems do not so admit, such as the discrete logarithm problem of public key cryptography, Diffie and Hellman [1], "Given α, a primitive root of a prime, p, and given α^x, $x \in$ {positive integers}, reduced modulo p, find x," is an example of a problem that has no approximation, only a strictly correct or incorrect answer.

If the set of abscissa values are sufficiently dense, the magnitude of the maximum error in the linear interpolation specified by (4.1) has an upper-bound at one-eighth of the second difference; i.e.,

$$\tfrac{1}{8}[f(x_{i+2}) - 2f(x_{i+1}) + f(x_i)]$$

[2, p. 66].

Polynomial Approximation

When it is decided that a polynomial approximation shall be used, the question of what is best still obtains. If $p_n(x)$ is to be the degree n polynomial approximation to $f(x)$, we might search for that $p_n(x)$ that minimizes $\int_{x_a}^{x_b} [f(x) - p_n(x)]^2\,dx$. Minimizing a least squares term (such as this) is almost a knee-jerk reaction for many folks, who associate such a criterion with the term *optimal*. Such a choice may, of course, be the best—it depends upon the system requirements and the expected behavior of $f(x)$ in the interval $[x_a, x_b]$. However, a far more useful approximation results from minimizing the *maximum* of $|f(x) - p_n(x)|$ over $[x_a, x_b]$. By selecting this criterion, which is known as the *best uniform* polynomial approximation, we guarantee that no matter what value x assumes in the interval $[x_a, x_b]$, the approximation will be no worse than the preset bound.

The polynomial that realizes this best uniform polynomial approximation is derivable from the Tschebyscheff polynomials. The Tschebyscheff polynomial of degree n is denoted by $T_n(x)$ and defined as $T_n(x) = \cos(n \cos^{-1} x)$. It is easy to show that the following recursion holds:

$$T_{n+1}(x) = 2xT_n(x) - T_{n-1}(x), \qquad n \geq 1 \tag{4.2}$$

The first few values of $\{T_n(x)\}$ for the "standard" interval $[-1, +1]$ are given in Table 4.1. Note that if $-1 \leq x \leq 1$, $|T_n(x)| \leq 1$, *for all n*. (This is a useful property of the Tschebyscheff polynomials.)

With suitable weighting function, the Tschebyscheff polynomials form an orthogonal set and $f(x)$ can be expanded over $[x_a, x_b]$ as

$$f(x) = \sum_{i=0}^{\infty} c_i T_i(x) \tag{4.3}$$

where

$$c_i = \frac{2}{\pi} \int_{x_a}^{x_b} \frac{f(x) T_i(x)\,dx}{\sqrt{(x_b - x)(x - x_a)}} \tag{4.4}$$

where the $\{T_i\}$ have been adjusted for the interval $[x_a, x_b]$ vice $[-1, +1]$. It can be shown that the best uniform degree n polynomial approximation to $f(x)$, which we have denoted as $p_n(x)$, is

$$p_n(x) = \sum_{i=0}^{n} c_i T_i(x) \tag{4.5}$$

TABLE 4.1.

THE FIRST ELEVEN TSCHEBYSCHEFF POLYNOMIALS

$T_0(x) = 1$
$T_1(x) = x$
$T_2(x) = 2x^2 - 1$
$T_3(x) = 4x^3 - 3x$
$T_4(x) = 8x^4 - 8x^2 + 1$
$T_5(x) = 16x^5 - 20x^3 + 5x$
$T_6(x) = 32x^6 - 48x^4 + 18x^2 - 1$
$T_7(x) = 64x^7 - 112x^5 + 56x^3 - 7x$
$T_8(x) = 128x^8 - 256x^6 + 160x^4 - 32x^2 + 1$
$T_9(x) = 256x^9 - 576x^7 + 432x^5 - 120x^3 + 9x$
$T_{10}(x) = 512x^{10} - 1280x^8 + 1120x^6 - 400x^4 + 50x^2 - 1$

Expansion (4.5) can be remarkably computationally beneficial. To quote Kopal [3], "if a power series is arranged in terms of the Tschebyscheff polynomials, it is reduced to its most economic form in so far as *the maximum accuracy can be attained with the minimum number of terms.*"

Tschebyscheff expansion (4.3) develops its terms in order of successively higher orders of Tschebyscheff polynomials. Each of these polynomials is a many-termed function of powers of the polynomial argument. Thus the development of a Tschebyscheff series is a bit different than the more widely experienced Taylor series, in which the exact coefficients of the particular powers of the argument are sequentially developed.

Evaluation of the $\{c_i\}$ by direct application of (4.4) may be quite difficult. They can be well *approximated*, however, by first picking a suitably large N and calculating

$$c_j = \frac{\varepsilon_j}{N} \sum_{\alpha=1}^{N} f(x_\alpha) \cos \frac{j\pi}{2N}(2\alpha - 1) \tag{4.6}$$

where

$$\varepsilon_j = \begin{cases} 1, & N = 0 \\ 2, & N \geq 1 \end{cases} \tag{4.7}$$

$$x_\alpha = \frac{a}{2}\left\{1 - \cos\frac{(2\alpha - 1)\pi}{2N}\right\} + \frac{b}{2}\left\{1 + \cos\frac{(2\alpha - 1)\pi}{2N}\right\} \tag{4.8}$$

As an example, let us consider approximating $f(x) = \cos 2\pi x$ over the interval $[0, 2]$. The first thing to do is to make the change of variable

$$\cos \xi = \frac{2x - x_b - x_a}{x_b - x_a} \tag{4.9}$$

which will keep the argument of $T_n(\,)$ within the interval $[-1, 1]$.

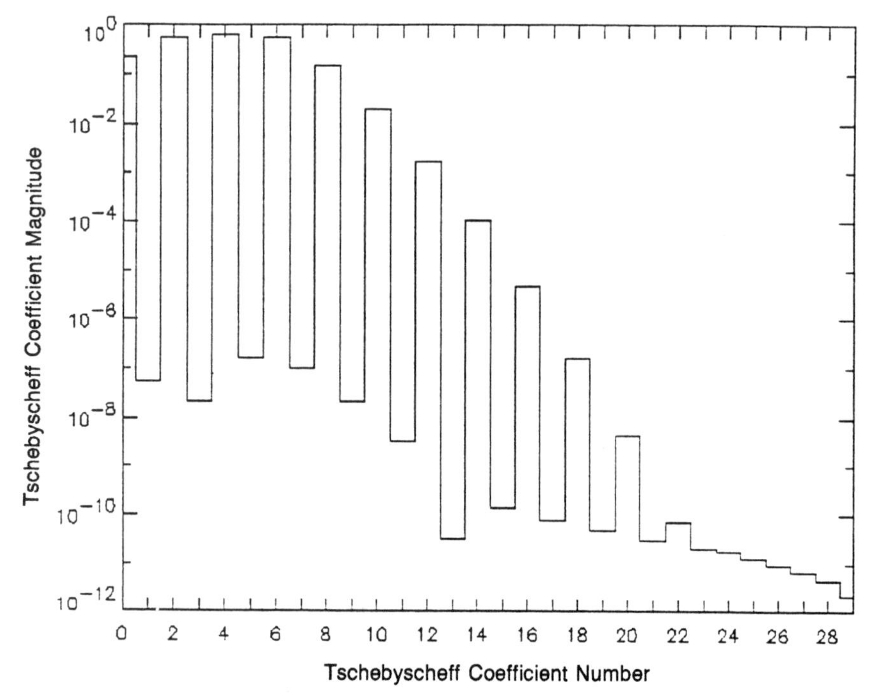

FIG. 4.1. Magnitudes of the first thirty Tschebyscheff coefficients.

For our example we get $\cos \xi = x - 1$ or $\xi = \cos^{-1}(x - 1)$. This allows us to write $T_n(x) = \cos(n\xi)$ or $T_n(x) = \cos[n \cos^{-1}(x - 1)]$. Thus, for our example, we will be using the Tschebyscheff polynomials of Table 4.1 with argument $x - 1$ vice x.

We arbitrarily pick $N = 30$ and use (4.6) to evaluate the first 30 of the $\{c_i\}$. In practice, we usually find that the magnitude of the $\{c_i\}$ drop off rapidly beyond a particular order. That this is so for our example can be seen from the bargraph of Figure 4.1 of the magnitudes of the first 30 of the $\{c_i\}$.

Note that the even-order $\{c_i\}$ are of significantly smaller magnitude than their immediate odd-order $\{c_i\}$ neighbors. This is to be expected as the cosine is an even function.

If we desire our approximation to be within, say, an error of no greater magnitude than 0.1, this can be accomplished by using terms no higher than $T_8(x - 1)$.

Our approximation, $p_8(x)$, is

$$p_8(x) = 0.22027 T_0(x - 1) + 0.575761 T_2(x - 1) + 0.631361 T_4(x - 1) - 0.555377 T_6(x - 1) + 0.146591 T_8(x - 1) \tag{4.10}$$

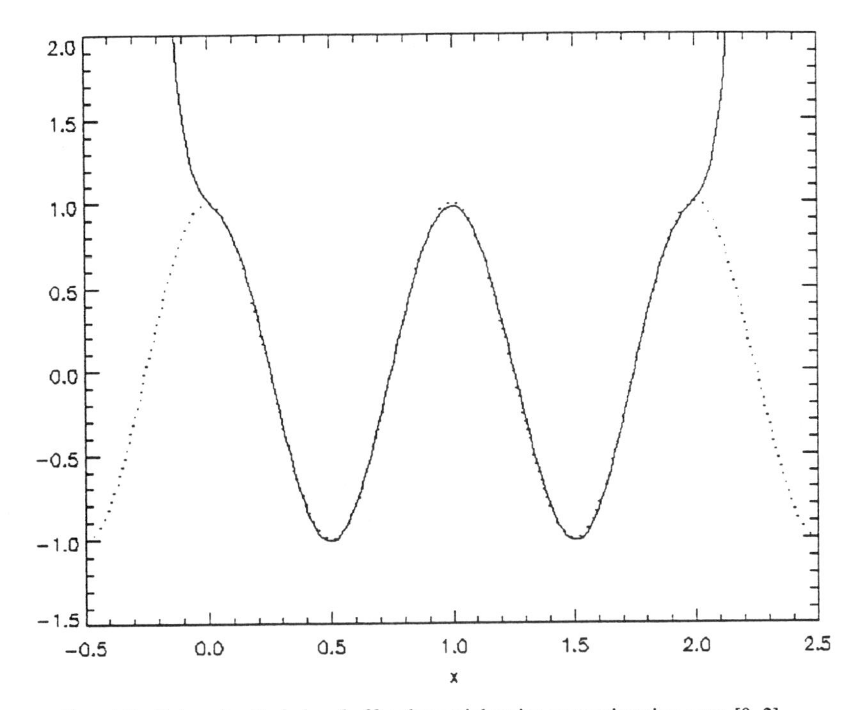

FIG. 4.2. $f(x)$ and a Tschebyscheff polynomial series approximation over [0, 2].

The graph of Figure 4.2 overlays $p_8(x)$ (solid line) on $f(x)$ (dotted line). The magnitude of the largest difference between $p_8(x)$ and $f(x)$ within the interval [0, 2] is 0.022.

Now consider what is perhaps the most "traditional" expansion of a function, the Maclaurin (or Taylor) series. For our example $f(x)$, it is

$$p_n(x) = 1 - \frac{(2\pi x)^2}{2!} + \frac{(2\pi x)^4}{4!} - \frac{(2\pi x)^6}{6!} \cdots \tag{4.11}$$

If we were to require that a truncated version of (4.11) approximate $f(x)$ over [0, 2] with an error not exceeding 0.1, we would require the keeping terms of up to x^{32}! Graphed in Figure 4.3 is $f(x)$ (dotted line) overlaid with

$$p_{32}(x) = 1 - \frac{(2\pi x)^2}{2!} + \frac{(2\pi x)^4}{4!} - \cdots + \frac{(2\pi x)^{32}}{32!} \quad \text{(solid line).}$$

The magnitude of the largest diffference between $p_{32}(x)$ and $f(x)$ within the interval [0, 2] is 0.071.

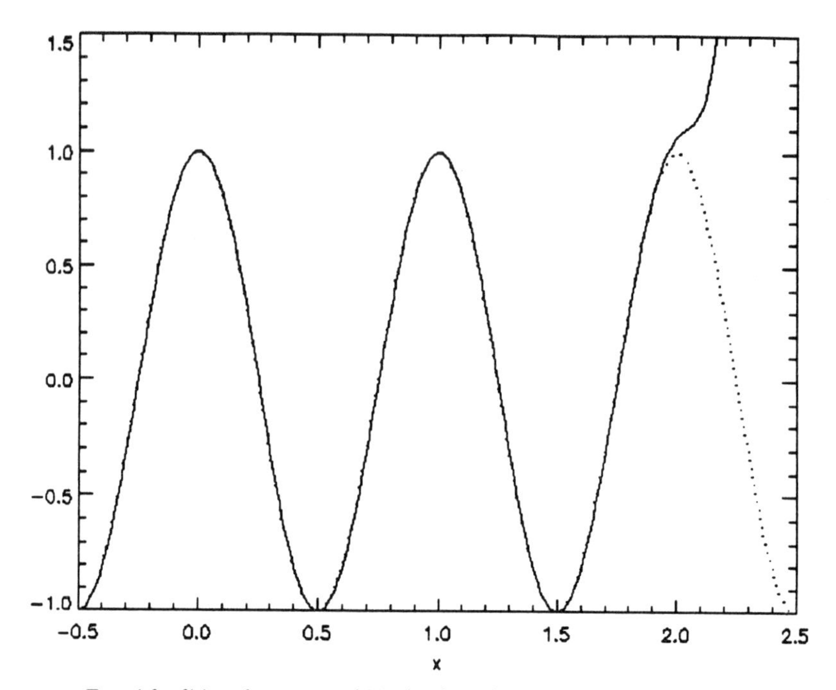

FIG. 4.3. $f(x)$ and a truncated Maclaurin series approximation over [0, 2].

The Cordic Technique

In 1959, Volder [4] reported a remarkable technique he termed *CORDIC*, for coordinate rotation digital computer, for calculating elementary functions such as sin( ) and cos( ). This technique and subsequent refinements forms the basis of the algorithms used in most contemporary pocket calculators to approximate the elementary functions.

At the heart of Volder's technique is a (pseudo) *rotation* technique, the essence of which is as follows. Consider that we have a vector, described by a magnitude R_0 and an angle θ_0, and that we wish to rotate it through an angle θ. The CORDIC technique approximates this rotation by successively rotating the original vector through a series of rotations of angles of decreasing magnitude denoted by $\{\alpha_i\}$ where $|\alpha_0| > |\alpha_1| > |\alpha_2| > \cdots$. The magnitude of the ith rotation is defined to be

$$\alpha_i = \tan^{-1} 2^{-i}, \qquad i \geq 0 \tag{4.12}$$

The diagram in Figure 4.4 will help us to see the wisdom behind this choice of the $\{\alpha_i\}$.

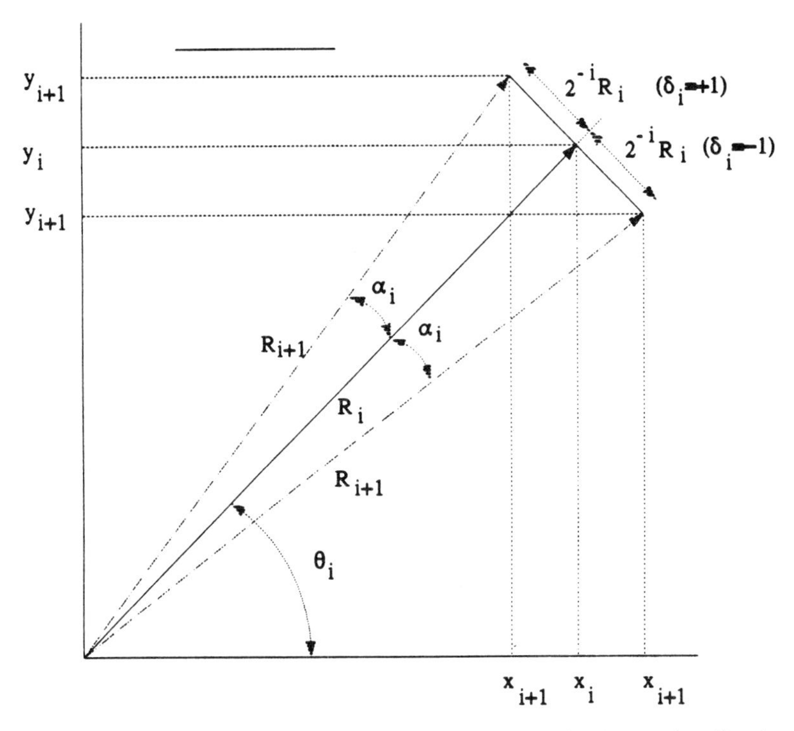

FIG. 4.4. The effect of rotation by α_i; the sign of δ_i specifies the rotation direction.

If we consider the ith rotation, Figure 4.4 allows us to see that

$$
\begin{aligned}
x_{i+1} &= \sqrt{1 + 2^{-2i}}\, R_i \cos(\theta_i + \delta_i \alpha_i) \\
y_{i+1} &= \sqrt{1 + 2^{-2i}}\, R_i \sin(\theta_i + \delta_i \alpha_i)
\end{aligned}
\tag{4.13}
$$

The next rotation results in

$$
\begin{aligned}
x_{i+2} &= \sqrt{1 + 2^{-2i}}\sqrt{1 + 2^{-2(i+1)}}\, R_i \cos(\theta_i + \delta_i \alpha_i + \delta_{i+1}\alpha_{i+1}) \\
y_{i+2} &= \sqrt{1 + 2^{-2i}}\sqrt{1 + 2^{-2(i+1)}}\, R_i \sin(\theta_i + \delta_i \alpha_i + \delta_{i+1}\alpha_{i+1})
\end{aligned}
\tag{4.14}
$$

and we see that we can easily write the expression for x_n and y_n, the results of n rotations starting at θ_0, as

$$
\begin{aligned}
x_n &= \left(\prod_{i=0}^{n-1} \sqrt{1 + 2^{-2i}}\right) R_0 \cos(\theta_0 + \delta_0\alpha_0 + \delta_1\alpha_1 + \cdots + \delta_{n-1}\alpha_{n-1}) \\
y_n &= \left(\prod_{i=0}^{n-1} \sqrt{1 + 2^{-2i}}\right) R_0 \sin(\theta_0 + \delta_0\alpha_0 + \delta_1\alpha_1 + \cdots + \delta_{n-1}\alpha_{n-1})
\end{aligned}
\tag{4.15}
$$

We can make two observations at this point:

1. The rotation operation is not a true rotation, as the magnitude of the vector increases from step to step. From a starting magnitude of R_0, it grows to $\prod_{i=0}^{n-1} \sqrt{1 + 2^{-2i}}$ after completion of the nth step,
2. The change in the magnitude is *not* a function of the $\{\delta_i\}$.

Also, at this point, we must ask two questions:

1. How do we computationally accomplish the "rotation" specified by (4.13)?
2. What is the range of angular rotation that can be provided by $\sum_{i=0}^{n-1} \delta_i \alpha_i$, and if we specify an angle in this range, how accurately can it be approximated and how do we pick the $\{\delta_i\}$?

The answer to the first question encompasses the very heart of the CORDIC technique. We use the identities

$$\begin{aligned} \cos(A + B) &= \cos A \cos B - \sin A \sin B \\ \sin(A + B) &= \sin A \cos B + \sin B \cos A \end{aligned} \tag{4.16}$$

to expand the cosine and sine terms of (4.13) and obtain

$$\begin{aligned} \cos(\theta_i + \delta_i \alpha_i) &= \cos(\theta_i) \cos(\alpha_i) - \delta_i \sin(\theta_i) \sin(\alpha_i) \\ \sin(\theta_i + \delta_i \alpha_i) &= \sin(\theta_i) \cos(\alpha_i) + \delta_i \cos(\theta_i) \sin(\alpha_i). \end{aligned} \tag{4.17}$$

From Figure 4.4 we see that

$$\begin{aligned} x_i &= R_i \cos \theta_i \\ y_i &= R_i \sin \theta_i \end{aligned} \tag{4.18}$$

and so we may write

$$\begin{aligned} x_{i+1} &= x_i - \delta_i 2^{-i} y_i \\ y_{i+1} &= y_i + \delta_i 2^{-i} x_i \end{aligned} \tag{4.19}$$

The recursions expressed in (4.19) involve only additions and subtractions and multiplications by a power of 2, which is easily realized in a binary-based computer by simple shifting.

The answer to the second question deals with the properties of a mixed radix number system; Volder calls it the *arc tangent radix*. (Mixed radix number systems are very useful for many specialized problems. For a discussion and examples of some mixed radix systems see Knuth [5] and Hershey and Yarlagadda [6]. For the CORDIC mixed radix system, selection of $\alpha_i = \tan^{-1} 2^{-i}$ limits the maximum rotation achievable in n steps to $\sum_{i=0}^{n-1} \alpha_i$.

Assume we wish to approximate an angle, r, whose magnitude is less than the maximum possible rotation. Let us define $s_{k+1} = s_k + \delta_k \alpha_k$ for $0 \le k \le n$ with $s_0 = 0$. We pick δ_k such that

$$\delta_k = \begin{cases} 1, & \text{if } r \ge s_k \\ -1, & \text{if } r < s_k \end{cases} \tag{4.20}$$

Then, by induction, it can be shown that

$$|r - s_k| \le \sum_{j=k}^{n} \alpha_j$$

and thus the key result that $|r - s_{n+1}| < \alpha_n$. To set the CORDIC algorithm in a unified framework, it is helpful to augment the equation pair (4.19) with

$$z_{i+1} = z_i - \delta_i \alpha_i \tag{4.21}$$

to represent angular rotation.

Now that the elements of the CORDIC mathematics have been developed, we see that we have a very simple way to compute $\sin\theta$ and $\cos\theta$. By picking $z_0 = \theta$,

$$R_0 = \left(\prod_{i=0}^{n-1} \sqrt{1 + 2^{-2i}} \right)^{-1}$$

and adopting the rule

$$\delta_k = \begin{cases} 1, & \text{if } z_k \ge 0 \\ -1, & \text{if } z_k < 0 \end{cases},$$

x_n will approximate $\cos\theta$ and y_n will approximate $\sin\theta$. R_0, for a particular n, and the $\{\alpha_i\}$ are precomputed and stored in tables.

The CORDIC technique can also be used to approximate many other basic functions, such as the hyperbolic trigonometric functions, $\sqrt{x}$, exp, log, and even multiplication and division itself.

Newton's Method

Newton's method is an iterative procedure for solving the nonlinear equation $g(y) = 0$. Following Strang [7], if $g(y)$ is differentiable, then for a sufficiently small difference between the $k + 1$st approximation and the kth, written respectively as $y^{(k+1)}$ and $y^{(k)}$, we can write

$$g(y^{(k+1)}) \approx g(y^{(k)}) + g'(y^{(k+1)} - y^{(k)}) \tag{4.22}$$

using Taylor's theorem. Our goal is to efficiently drive $g(y^{(k+1)}) \to 0$ as k increases. At the sought value, $y = \xi$, we have $g(y^{(k+1)}) = g(y^{(k)})$.

For this reason, Newton's method is termed a case of *fixed-point iteration.* Proceeding, we set the righthand side of (4.22) to 0 and obtain the general structure of Newton's method; namely,

$$y^{(k+1)} = y^{(k)} - \frac{g(y^{(k)})}{g'(y^{(k)})} \tag{4.23}$$

Perhaps the most widespread use Newton's method is in the calculation of $\sqrt{x}$. To perform this calculation, we set $g(y) = y^2 - x$ and obtain

$$y^{(k+1)} = \frac{1}{2}\left(y^{(k)} + \frac{x}{y^{(k)}}\right) \tag{4.24}$$

as the recursion.

Strang [7] points out that the error after the $k + 1$st iteration is $y^{(k+1)} - \sqrt{x}$, equal to $(1/2y^{(k)})(y^{(k)} - \sqrt{x})^2$ and thus the normalized error is squared at each step. This behavior is termed *quadratic* convergence.

We must, of course, pick a starting approximation; i.e., we must select $y^{(0)}$. So long as $y^{(0)}$ is not 0, this square root procedure will converge but the rate at which it will converge to a desired accuracy of approximation to $\sqrt{x}$ will depend upon the initial approximation. To see the effect that the choice

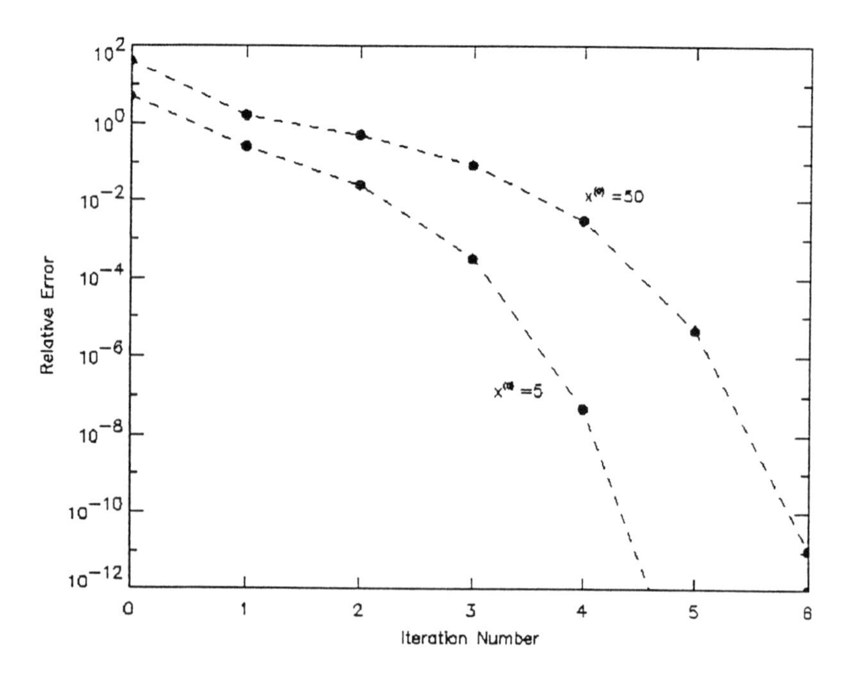

FIG. 4.5. Effect of initial estimates on convergence of Newton's method.

of the initial approximation can have on the rate of convergence, consider the results displayed in Figure 4.5, in which we plot the relative error, $|(\sqrt{x} - x^{(m)})/\sqrt{x}|$, versus the iteration number (m) for $x = 100$ and for two initial approximations, $x^{(0)} = 5$ and $x^{(0)} = 50$.

A lot of work has been done on the question of judiciously picking a good initial approximation, and we are again confronted with a somewhat subjective question: "What does *good* mean?"

A widely used answer was to pick an initial approximation, $I(x)$, to $\sqrt{x}$ that satisfied the condition

$$\max\left|\frac{\sqrt{x} - I(x)}{\sqrt{x}}\right| = \min \qquad x \in [a, b] \tag{4.25}$$

Moursund [8], however, in effect argues that a better approach is to proceed as though we were going to perform m ($m \geq 1$) iterations and ask for $x^{(0)} = I(x)$ to satisfy the condition

$$\max\left|\frac{\sqrt{x} - x^{(m)}}{\sqrt{x}}\right| = \min \qquad x \in [a, b] \tag{4.26}$$

Moursund goes on to derive the (remarkable) result that if $I(x)$ is a fixed-degree polynomial in x, or a rational function of x, then the $I(x)$ found will be the same *for all m* ($m \geq 1$).

Before examining Moursund's results, we should mention a normalization practice pervasive in elementary function computation. When $\sqrt{x}$ (or many other functions for that matter) is sought, the argument, x, is converted to a standard range such as the interval $[\frac{1}{4}, 1]$. This is accomplished by multiplying x by the appropriate integral power, n ($-\infty < n < \infty$) of 4. The square root of the value in the standardized interval is computed and the result multiplied by 2^{-n}.

With this normlizing convention in mind, we first select a standard range for our computations. This selection will most likely be based on our computer hardware. For here, let us arbitrarily pick the interval $[\frac{1}{4}, 1]$. For this range Moursund provides the polynomials for $I(x)$ up to degree 3. They are summarized in Table 4.2 and keyed to $I(x)$ as given in (4.27).

$$I(x) = a_0x^n + a_1x^{n-1} + \cdots + a_n \tag{4.27}$$

The beneficial effects on the rate of convergence achieved by selecting higher values of n for $I(x)$ can be seen in Figure 4.6, where we compute $\sqrt{100}$ by first converting our argument to the interval $[\frac{1}{4}, 1]$; i.e., $100 = 2^8 \cdot 0.390625$. We use the four starting approximations for $n = 0, 1, 2,3$.

TABLE 4.2.
COEFFICIENTS FOR MOURSUND'S INITIAL APPROXIMATION POLYNOMIAL

$n = 0$	$a_0 = 0.707106781186$
$n = 1$	$a_0 = 0.686589047967$
	$a_1 = 0.343294523984$
$n = 2$	$a_0 = -0.316324894525$
	$a_1 = 1.05203265964$
	$a_2 = 0.259280586670$
$n = 3$	$a_0 = 0.287367822508$
	$a_1 = -0.825885236137$
	$a_2 = 1.32256233885$
	$a_3 = 0.217019165859$

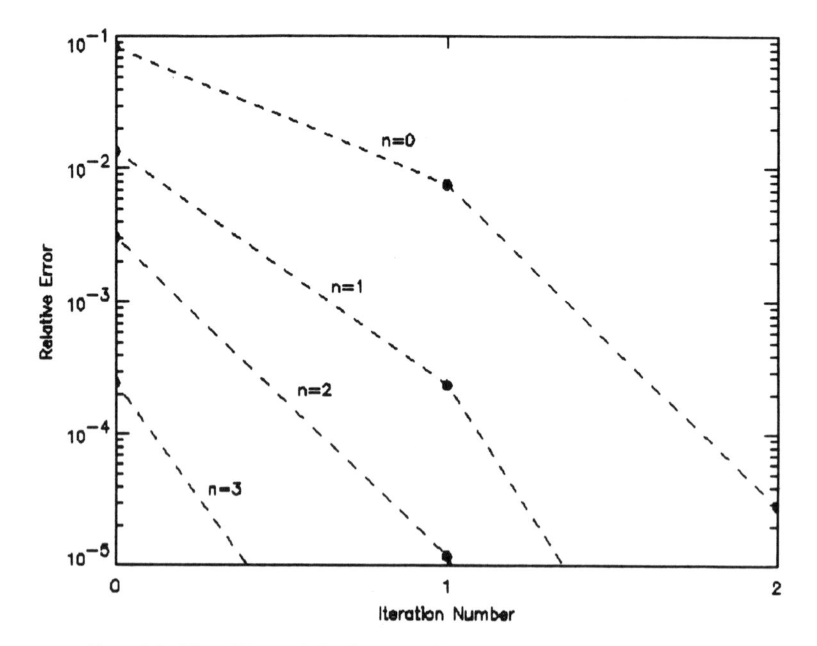

FIG. 4.6. The effects of the four starting approximations on convergence.

Imprecision and Errors

Computation invariably involves imprecision, as quantities are expressed with a finite number of bits. This introduces errors, error propagation, and perhaps error accumulation. It is important to be aware of the error processes and ideally to be able to estimate the effects of errors on key variables and understand the pathways and mechanisms through which the errors may propagate and accumulate.

It is continually surprising (and often alarming) how a small change may have an effect that is seemingly out of all proportion to its magnitude. A classic example from Wilkinson [97] is the solution of the equation

$$\prod_{i=1}^{20} (x - i) = 0$$

The roots are, of course, the integers 1, 2, 3, ..., 20. If, however, we change the coefficient of x^{19} from -210 to $-210 - 2^{-23}$, a change of less than one-ten-millionth of 1%, the roots become as shown in Figure 4.7. Notice that five pairs of the roots are now complex. As Wilkinson notes in his additional comments at the chapter's end, "it is probably true to say that most numerical analysts are shocked when first brought face to face with the result."

Wilkinson's example is an example of what has become termed *ill-conditioned behavior*. Again to quote from Wilkinson, "Clearly ill-conditioned problems are very unsatisfactory because if we wish to be certain of a

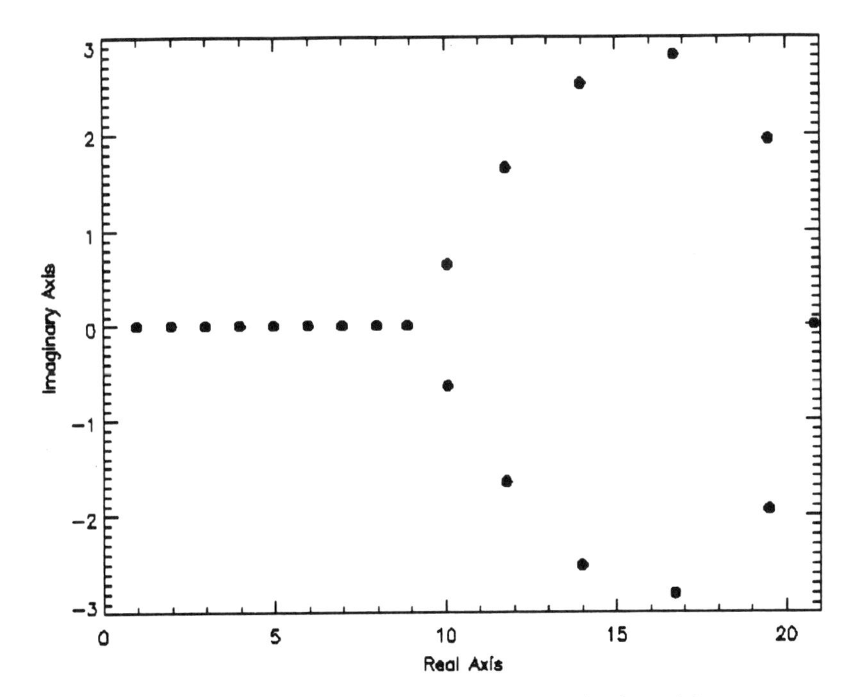

FIG. 4.7. The roots of the slightly perturbed polynomial.

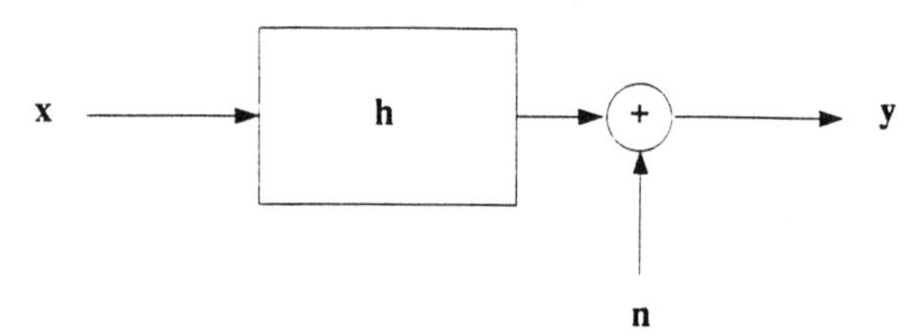

FIG. 4.8. Noise added to the convolution of x with h.

prescribed number of figures in the solutions we must determine accurately many more figures in the parameters. This is particularly undesirable and may indeed by impossible, if the parameters are derived from physical observations."

Another example of ill-conditioned problems comes from contemporary signal processing and concerns the deconvolution problem. The deconvolution problem takes many forms. We will examine the variant shown in Figure 4.8.

The goal of the deconvolution problem is to estimate the input, x, given the observed output, y, perfect knowledge of the filter kernel, h, and knowledge of the *moments* of the observation noise process, n. Philip [10] has studied and characterized those nonnegative kernels that pose the greatest error amplification of observation noise in discrete deconvolution. These kernels are all similar to discretizations of the Gaussian curve; that is, they are approximately binomial in shape. As an example of such, consider the five-point kernel displayed in Figure 4.9. Suppose x is a signal that can be characterized by sampling from a white Gaussian probability distribution function with zero mean, unit variance, and no memory; i.e., the correlation coefficient between samples is 0. For our example, we generate such a 12-point sequence and display it in Figure 4.10.

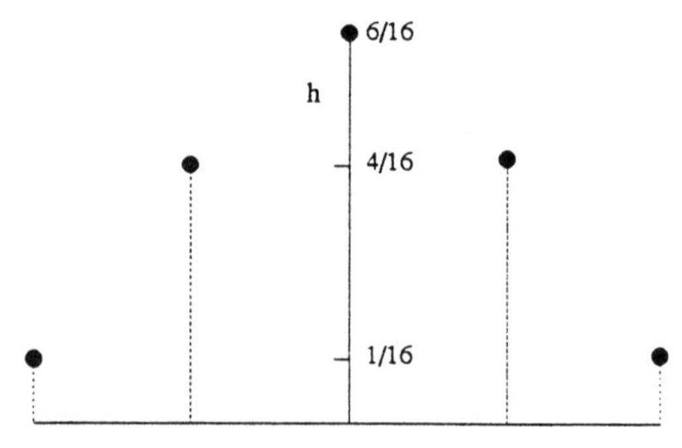

FIG. 4.9. Five-point binomial kernel.

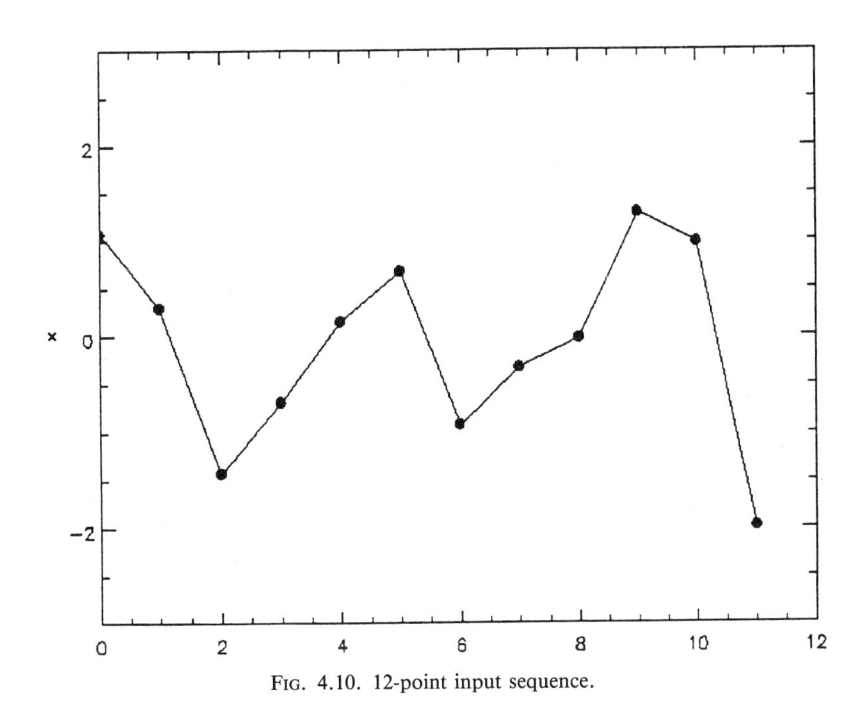

FIG. 4.10. 12-point input sequence.

We now add white Gaussian noise to $h * x$ so that y can be considered as $h * x$ at any desired signal-to-noise ratio. The best *unbiased* (as contrasted to the Wiener minimum variance deconvolution estimate) linear estimator for x, with the least mean square error, is provided by the Moore–Penrose so-called pseudoinverse, $\hat{x} = (H^t H)^{-1} H^t y$, where H is the matrix naturally created from h in order that we may represent the convolution operation in terms of matrix operations. In Figure 4.11 we show the effect on the deconvolution estimate for various signal-to-noise ratios. As you can see, for this particular kernel, unbiased deconvolution is an extremely ill-conditioned problem as just a small amount of noise vastly perturbs the best estimate of the sought input.

Depending on our particular system, then, it is clearly crucial that we have a way of estimating the havoc that errors can work. Computational errors arise from two sources:

1. Inability to represent the measured parameter exactly in the terms of the computer's word structure; e.g., 1/3 is not usually representable in base 2 with a finite number of bits.
2. Inability of the computer to perform computations without incurring round-off errors. (It might help to think of the digital computer as

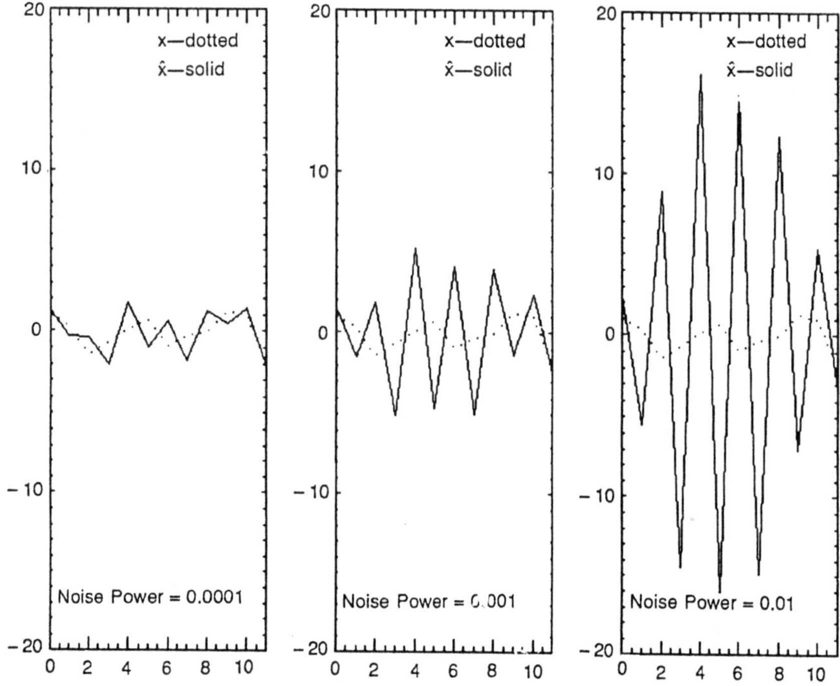

FIG. 4.11. The results of different signal-to-noise levels on example deconvolution.

a large finite lattice of discrete points. The points represent the individual computer words. Visualize, then, a bug jumping from one lattice point to the other. This is the program flow and the only spots the bug can rest on are the finite number of possible computer words.)

The first of these error sources is often subsumed under the analog-to-digital converter, which measures a continuously variable parameter and represents it by a binary word, thus introducing the error. The second error source is a function of the ways the computer does arithmetic. We will look at this briefly and discover that in general, addition, in particular, is *not* independent of the order of summation insofar as the relative error of the computed sum to the true sum is concerned.

Most computers of interest to system designers use floating-point arithmetic. In this type of number representation, t-bits are reserved for the mantissa,[2] also called the *fractional part*, which is used to represent a number between two bounds, such as $\frac{1}{2} \leq mantissa < 1$, and other,

[2] The term *significand*, introduced in 1967, is often used in place of the term *mantissa*.

additional, bits for the exponent, which is the power of 2 that multiplies the mantissa to represent any particular number. The sum of the number of bits used for the mantissa and the exponent is the word size. Addition takes place by first aligning the mantissas so that the words have the same exponents and then adding the mantissas. If one number is much larger than another, it is clear that a loss of precision will result as some of the mantissa precision will be lost in the alignment process. From this reasoning it follows that it is probably best to add a sequence of numbers in order of increasing magnitude, and this has become a rule of thumb in computer practice.

The great numerical analyst J. H. Wilkinson wrote a signal treatise on errors in computer arithmetic [9] in which he developed a calculus for computer precision. He introduced the function fl( ), which denotes a floating point computation of what is specified within the parentheses. The operation is obviously dependent upon the computer's structure. He developed the important representation

$$\mathrm{fl}(x_1 + x_2) = x_1(1 + \varepsilon_1) + x_2(1 + \varepsilon_2) \tag{4.28}$$

where the $\{\varepsilon_i\}$ are on the order of 2^{-t}. Expression (4.28) is true if the addition is performed using t-bit arithmetic. If, however, the addition uses a double precision intermediate step, i.e., $2t$-bits for the addition followed by rounding to a t-bit result, then, as Wilkinson showed,

$$\mathrm{fl}(x_1 + x_2) = (x_1 + x_2)(1 + \varepsilon) \tag{4.29}$$

where $|\varepsilon| \leq 2^{-t}$.

Using (4.29), Wilkinson showed that the finite precision sum, S^*, of $x_1, x_2, \ldots, x_n$ is expressible as

$$S^* = x_1(1 + \eta_1) + x_2(1 + \eta_2) + \cdots + x_n(1 + \eta_n) \tag{4.30}$$

where

$$(1 \quad 2^{-t})^{n+1-r} \leq 1 + \eta_r \leq (1 + 2^{-t})^{n+1-r}, \qquad r = 1, 2, \ldots, n \tag{4.31}$$

Note that the error,

$$S^* - \sum_{i=1}^{n} x_i = \sum_{i=1}^{n} \eta_i x_i,$$

and thus the error bounds depend upon the summation order. From (4.30) we can see that the rule of thumb regarding adding numbers in order of increasing magnitude to reduce precision loss is justified as it tends to reduce the error bounds. Further reading on increasing the accuracy of floating-point summation can be found in Linz [11] and Malcolm [12].

Multiplication and division are far "tamer" than addition. Using $2t$-bits for intermediate computation and rounding off as in addition, Wilkinson obtains

$$\mathrm{fl}(x_1 x_2) = x_1 x_2 (1 + \varepsilon) \tag{4.32}$$

$$\mathrm{fl}\left(\frac{x_1}{x_2}\right) = \frac{x_1}{x_2}(1 + \varepsilon) \tag{4.33}$$

where $|\varepsilon| \leq 2^{-t}$.

Parallel computation

As the need for computational throughout continues to increase, it becomes increasingly clear that no single processor will be able to bear the entire load. It thus becomes evident that parallel or concurrent computation will probably be required in most large, advanced systems. Parallel processing seeks to partition a problem over a set of processors and thereby reduce the overall time required to perform a particular computation. A couple of terms are prevalent regarding parallel processing: *speed-up* and *efficiency*. Speed-up, S_P, is defined as the ratio of the time it takes a single processor to do a particular computation to the time it takes P processors, working together, to perform the same computation. Thus, if T_1 is the time required by one processor and T_P is the time required by P processors,

$$S_P = \frac{T_1}{T_P} \tag{4.34}$$

Efficiency is defined as the ratio S_P/P. It measures, in a sense, the effective utilization of the P processors. Unlike the speed-up, efficiency may not be a very useful parameter for the system's designer.

Let us take a look at a number of elementary problems to see if we can get a feel for parallel or concurrent computation. First, consider the coprocessor question. It is often the case that single processor (serial) computers will have their problems sized in time as the ratio of millions of floating-point operations required to solve the problem divided by the megaflops (millions of floating-point operators per second, or Mflops) capability of the machine. It is not unusual for the actual time for solution to exceed three times this estimate. Surprising and disheartening, this outcome is easily understood by the following example, adapted from Parkinson and Liddell [13].

Let t_c be the cycle time required to fetch an operand from memory (or to write an operand into memory), t_i be the time required to perform integer arithmetic, t_L be the time required to perform a logical test, and t_{FM} be the time required to perform a floating-point multiply.

Let us examine what is involved in the following program:

```
  DO 1 I = 1,N
1 Z(I) = X(I) * Y(I)
```

Each pass through the loop requires that we

1. Fetch two operands from memory: $X(I)$ and $Y(I)$,
2. Floating-point multiply the operands,
3. Store the result, $Z(I)$, in memory,
4. Increment an integer counter $I \leftarrow I + 1$,
5. Logically test the counter to see if it exceeds N.

The time, T, required to perform a single replication of the loop, i.e., steps 1–5 is

$$T = 3t_c + t_i + t_L + t_{\mathrm{FM}} \tag{4.35}$$

If the majority of the computation of T is taken up by the floating-point multiply operation, then we might opt to invest in a high-speed floating-point coprocessor, that is, we might be attracted to a device that had a high $1/t_{\mathrm{FM}}$, a large number of megaflops. But what really happens? Let us assume that the t_{FM} before coprocessor speed-up is t_{FM_1} and t_{FM_2} after speed-up. We would be tempted to anticipate that we had reduced our program's execution time $t_{\mathrm{FM}_2}/t_{\mathrm{FM}_1}$. Unfortunately this is not so. Let us designate T_1 as the value of T in (4.35) before floating-point speed-up and T_2 as the value of T after floating-point speed-up. The true ratio of times, the speedup S, is then

$$S = \frac{3t_c + t_i + t_L + t_{\mathrm{FM}_2}}{3t_c + t_i + t_L + t_{\mathrm{FM}_1}} \tag{4.36}$$

If, for example, $t_c = 200$ nsec, $t_i = 100$ nsec, $t_L = 100$ nsec, $t_{\mathrm{FM}_1} = 1200$ nsec, and $t_{\mathrm{FM}_2} = 200$ nsec, we find that the time is reduced by only 50% and not by one-sixth, which is the ratio between t_{FM_2} and t_{FM_1}. The overhead that accompanies floating-point operations diminishes the ratio. This concept of overhead is crucial.

Note that even if t_{FM_2} were to vanish entirely (become 0) in (4.36), the result would scarcely improve. This analysis led Parkinson and Liddell to opine that "Mflops seems to be more popularly used as a measure for systems whose floating point hardware is so powerful that the run time is dominated by all the other terms!"

Second, consider the question of calculating the inner product

$$\mathbf{x} \cdot \mathbf{y} = (x_1 x_2 \ldots x_{2^n})(y_1 y_2 \ldots y_{2^n})^T \tag{4.37}$$

Calculation of (4.37) can be done using 2^n multiplies and $2^n - 1$ additions. How can we speed up this calculation by parallel processing? Well, we could certainly do all 2^n multiplies concurrently by using 2^n multipliers, but what about the additions following the multiplications? We cannot form the sum of 2^n numbers in one step even with an unlimited number of adders. The best we can do is to use 2^{n-1} adders to add 2^{n-1} pairs of numbers at the first step, and then add the resulting 2^{n-2} pairs of numbers using 2^{n-2} adders, and so on. In this case the addition associated with computing (4.37) requires $\lceil \log_2 2^n \rceil = n$ steps and makes very inefficient use of the adders. The key thing to notice is that the speed-up of the addition, S, is $S = (2^n - 1)/n$, which may be significantly smaller than $2^n - 1$. Concurrent addition of M numbers is one of the problems in the class for which maximum speed-up is on the order of $M/\log_2 M$.

Models

It is often very useful to have a model for a processs, and if one is using the model for insight, it is best to keep the model as simple as reasonable. Ware (see [14]) proposed a very simple single-parameter model for parallel processing speed-up, S.[3] It is written succinctly as

$$S = \frac{1}{(1 - \alpha) + \alpha/P}, \qquad 0 \le \alpha \le 1 \tag{4.38}$$

where α is the fraction of the problem that can be "parallelized," i.e., done concurrently, and P is the number of processors used in parallel. If $\alpha = 0$, there is no sense in trying to achieve a speed-up through distributing the computations over different processors; if $\alpha = 1$, the problem can be perfectly partitioned. Note that if $\alpha < 1$, then

$$\lim_{P \to \infty} S = \frac{1}{1 - \alpha}$$

This clearly demonstrates that the best we can do in speed-up is critically governed by α, α needs to be nearly unity to make effective use of a large number of processors.[4]

[3] Also called *Amdahl's law*, see [15].

[4] There are some who believe that multiprocessing has gotten a "bad rap" by this seemingly pessimistic limit. Some folks have made an excellent argument for what they term *scaling*. Their thesis is that, as more processors become available, it is unrealistic to believe that they would be applied to the same problem. They believe that the problem size should also be scaled. Their arguments are worth reviewing and are, we believe, probably valid under many circumstances. For a defined system problem and specific requirement, however, we believe that the problem does not, in general, scale and that this "pessimistic" limit is realistic. The interested reader is referred to Gustafson [16] and Zorbas, Reble and Van Kooten [17].

Buzbee [14] introduced an additional term into Ware's model. This new term, $\sigma(P)$, attempts to account for the increased overhead of managing parallel algorithms. This overhead includes such things as synchronization and interprocessor communications. With this new term we have the following expression for S:

$$S = \frac{1}{(1-\alpha) + \alpha/P + \sigma(P)} \tag{4.39}$$

Notice that now, for efficiently partitioned problems, the speed-up has an upperbounded of

$$\lim_{\alpha \to 1} S = \frac{1}{1/P + \sigma(P)}.$$

Parallel Computational Architectures

In this section we will introduce some of the more common parallel computational structures. Our introduction will be by way of considering the parallel implementation of the fast Fourier transform. But first, a little philosophy.

The discrete Fourier transform of a real $N = 2^n$-point data record $x(0)$, $x(1), \ldots, x(N-1)$ is defined as

$$X(k) = \frac{1}{N} \sum_{m=0}^{N-1} x(m) W^{km}, \qquad k = 0, 1, \ldots, N-1 \tag{4.40}$$

where $W = e^{-j(2\pi/N)}$. It is clear that all $N = 2^n$ values of $\{X(k)\}$ could be computed in parallel by assigning 2^n processors to the problem. Looked at this way, α in (4.38) or (4.39) is unity, and the efficiency of the computational speed-up is unity. The Fourier transform is rarely computed directly as expressed in (4.40) because there is an algorithm for computing it that requires far fewer computations. This is, of course, the FFT. Therefore, even though we can achieve an efficiency of unity in parallelizing the computation of the Fourier transform by assigning $N = 2^n$ processors, we would probably be grossly inefficient in doing so as we would have chosen the wrong algorithm to parallelize. There is another consideration, however. It is not clear in general that a *faster* algorithm can be efficiently parallelized.

A simple parallel architecture for doing the FFT is to put P processors and a centralized memory on a controlled access as depicted in Figure 4.12. Bhuyan and Agrawal [18] analyzed the performance of the radix-2 fast Fourier transform on the distributed architecture of Figure 4.12. Assume we want to perform an N-point transform, where N is a power of 2, i.e., $N = 2^n$, and that the "butterfly," the basic unit of the FFT, requires B

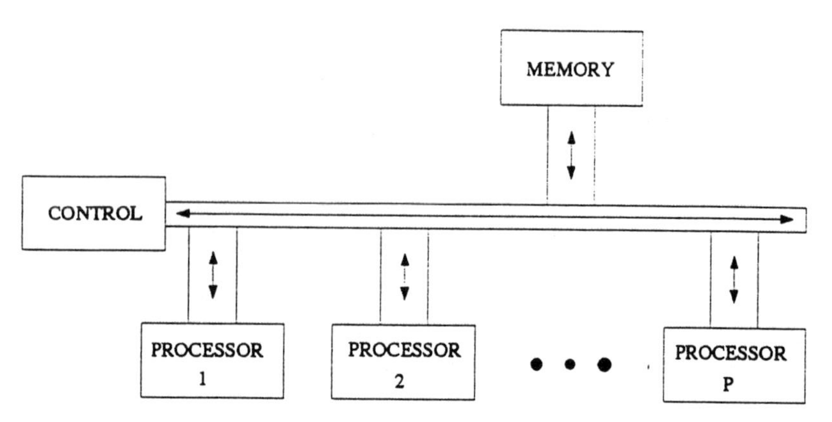

FIG. 4.12. Multiprocessors and a centralized memory sharing a bus.

time units. We know that the total time required on a single processor, T_1, would be $T_1 = nNB/2$. Let us allow $P = 2^m$ processors to work on the FFT in parallel and perform communications as shown in Figure 4.12; i.e., we transfer data from processor to processor through the memory. If a processor to–from memory transfer takes τ time units, then a processor-to-processor transfer will consume 2τ time units. Bhuyan and Agrawal showed that the time required to perform the N-point FFT using this architecture, T_P, is $T_P = (nNB/2P) + mN\tau$. It is gratifying and not difficult to discover [19] that the speed-up, $S = T_P/T_1$, can be written as

$$S = \frac{1}{(1/P + 2m\tau/nB)}$$

and thus can be "mapped" onto the Ware–Buzbee model (4.39), resulting in

$$\alpha = 1 \tag{4.41a}$$

$$\sigma(P) = \left(\frac{2\tau}{nB}\right) \log_2 P \tag{4.41b}$$

It is clear that the dimensionless τ/B is critical to the parallelism achieved, and we conclude that interprocessor communication is an extremely important issue.

A contemporary important multiprocessor architecture is known as the *hypercube*. The hypercube is a very popular multiprocessor architecture. It consists of a power of 2, say, 2^d processors that run independently, have their own local memory, and are interconnected in the following fashion. Each processor is situated at a unique lattice coordinate in d-dimensional space. The 2^d lattice points have locations $(x_1, x_2, \ldots, x_d)$, where $x_i \in \{0, 1\}$.

The processor located at coordinate $(X_1, X_2, \ldots, X_d)$ is "connected to," i.e., may send and receive messages or data packets from its d-nearest neighbors (in the Hamming sense), the d-processors located at coordinates $(X_1 + 1, X_2, \ldots, X_d)$, $(X_1, X_2 + 1, \ldots, X_d)$, ... and $(X_1, X_2, \ldots, X_d + 1)$, where the plus here is the exclusive-or. The processors and their communication links thus outline a d-dimensional cube, hence the name *hypercube*.

The hypercube topology is remarkable as it can be configured into many different geometries that may be of use to different problems. It was an answer[5] to an important statement that Unger [20] had issued: "A general purpose digital computer can, in principle, solve any well defined problem. ... However, they are relatively inept at solving many problems where the data is arranged naturally in a spatial form. ... It appears that efficient handling of problems of the type mentioned above cannot be accomplished without some form of parallel action." It is also a highly versatile and in some sense a "natural" computational vehicle onto which many problems can be mapped. This is singularly true for those problems that are spatially decomposable, such as those found in finite-element modeling. The hypercube can be configured to represent a nearest neighbor interconnected mesh, a torus, a ring, and other useful topologies. So versatile is the hypercube that some have proclaimed that all militarily significant computational problems can be profitably executed on a hypercube architecture.

As an example of how a hypercube can be used, we will look at Fox, Otto, and Hey's [22] algorithm for doing matrix multiplication on a hypercube. Assume we have P processors configured as a two-dimensional square mesh with $\sqrt{P}$ lattice points in each row and column. For this example, let us further assume that $\sqrt{P} = 2^m$ and that $m = 1$. Consider that we want to form the product, C, of two square matrices, A and B. All matrices are square and, for this example, of dimension $2^n \times 2^n$. The algorithm is based on the fact that we can represent A, B, and C as partitioned into equal size subblocks:

$$A = \begin{pmatrix} A_{11} & A_{12} \\ A_{21} & A_{22} \end{pmatrix} \tag{4.42}$$

$$B = \begin{pmatrix} B_{11} & B_{12} \\ B_{21} & B_{22} \end{pmatrix} \tag{4.43}$$

$$C = \begin{pmatrix} C_{11} & C_{12} \\ C_{21} & C_{22} \end{pmatrix} \tag{4.44}$$

[5] For another, earlier, answer, the reader may wish to look at some very important work reported by Slotnick, Borck, and McReynolds [21].

Where each subblock is of dimension 2^{n-m} (which is 2^{n-1} for this example), and the product, C, can be written as

$$C_{rt} = \sum_{s} A_{rs} B_{st} \tag{4.45}$$

The algorithm involves two communication processes that at first blush appear similar but are really quite different. The first is copying or broadcasting. The second is rolling. Our specific example proceeds as follows:

- The data is assumed prestored with subblocks A_{11} and B_{11} at the processor at location (0, 0), subblocks A_{12} and B_{12} at the processor at location (0, 1), A_{21} and B_{21} at the processor at location (1, 0) and A_{22} and B_{22} at the processor at location (1, 1) as shown in Figure 4.13.

A_{11}, B_{11}	A_{12}, B_{12}
A_{21}, B_{21}	A_{22}, B_{22}

FIG. 4.13. Quantities stored in the four processors' local memories.

- The diagonal subblocks of A are broadcast or copied to all processors in the row in which they occur. The results of this operation are depicted in Figure 4.14.

A_{11}, B_{11}	A_{12}, B_{12}, A_{11}
A_{21}, B_{21}, A_{22}	A_{22}, B_{22}

FIG. 4.14. Quantities stored in the four processors' local memories.

- The processors now form the appropriate products and begin to accumulate the values of the product matrix C. The matrices copied and broadcast can be erased (written over). This is depicted in Figure 4.15.

$A_{11}, B_{11}, A_{11}B_{11}$	$A_{12}, B_{12}, A_{11}B_{12}$
$A_{21}, B_{21}, A_{22}B_{21}$	$A_{22}, B_{22}, A_{22}B_{22}$

FIG. 4.15. Quantities stored in the four processors' local memories.

- The B subblocks are now rolled vertically. The situation is now as depicted in Figure 4.16.

$A_{11}, B_{21}, A_{11}B_{11}$	$A_{12}, B_{22}, A_{11}B_{12}$
$A_{21}, B_{11}, A_{22}B_{21}$	$A_{22}, B_{12}, A_{22}B_{22}$

FIG. 4.16. Quantities stored in the four processors' local memories.

- The "diagonal plus one" subblock elements of A are now broadcast to all processors in the row in which they occur, resulting in the situation depicted in Figure 4.17.

$A_{11}, B_{21}, A_{12}, A_{11}B_{11}$	$A_{12}, B_{22}, A_{11}B_{12}$
$A_{21}, B_{11}, A_{22}B_{21}$	$A_{22}, B_{12}, A_{21}, A_{22}B_{22}$

FIG. 4.17. Quantities stored in the four processors' local memories.

- The processors now form the appropriate products and complete the accumulation of the values of the product matrix C. The matrices copied and broadcast can again be erased (written over). This is depicted in Figure 4.18.

$A_{11}, B_{21}, A_{11}B_{11} + A_{12}B_{21}$	$A_{12}, B_{22}, A_{11}B_{12} + A_{12}B_{22}$
$A_{21}, B_{11}, A_{21}B_{11} + A_{22}B_{21}$	$A_{22}, B_{12}, A_{21}, A_{22}B_{22}$

FIG. 4.18. Quantities stored in the four processors' local memories.

Thus, the algorithm forms

$$C = \begin{pmatrix} A_{11}B_{11} + A_{12}B_{21} & A_{11}B_{12} + A_{12}B_{22} \\ A_{21}B_{11} + A_{22}B_{21} & A_{21}B_{12} + A_{22}B_{22} \end{pmatrix} \tag{4.46}$$

with the matrix partitioned in the same fashion as matrices A and B. The algorithm is naturally extended in the "broadcast-multiply-roll" loop. Fox *et al.* [22] analyze the algorithm for its speed-up value over the purely sequential (single-processor) case. They define three timing quantities:

1. t_{comm} as the time required to pass a floating point quantity from one processor to another,
2. t_{start} as the time required to start up a pipeline to broadcast a subblock,
3. t_{flop} as the time required to perform a floating-point multiply or floating-point addition.

The total time, T, for execution turns out to be

$$T = \frac{2 \cdot 2^{3n}}{P} t_{\text{flop}} + \frac{2 \cdot 2^{2n}}{\sqrt{P}} t_{\text{comm}} + \sqrt{P}\,(\sqrt{P} - 1)t_{\text{start}} \tag{4.47}$$

If just the first term of (4.47) were present, this would represent a totally efficient parallelization. In the Ware–Buzbee model, we would find that $\alpha = 1$ and $\sigma = 0$. The latter two terms call attention to the various communication overheads.

The operation of rolling is quite natural to a hypercube. Information is passed from nearest neighbor to nearest neighbor in a simple ring. Broadcasting or copying is very different. Here the same data is sent to an entire subset of hypercube nodes. This involves developing an efficient communication strategy. Developing such a strategy requires the system designer to understand and model the exact architecture of the candidate hypercube design. For example, Lubeck and Faber [23] found that an acceptable model for the time required for a node to send an L-byte message to a nearest neighbor was $t_0 + ([L/B] - 1)t_b + Lt_e$ where B is the buffer size, t_0 is a general startup time, t_b is a buffer start-up–overhead time, and t_e is a function of the signaling rate available on the iner-node channel. All of these parameters are machine dependent. It is also necessary to know whether the particular hypercube will support pipelining, simultaneous sending and receiving, multiport simultaneous operations, and so on. For further study, the reader is referred to Berntsen [24] and Bertsekas *et al.* [25].

The hypercube belongs to the MIMD class within a taxonomy proposed by Flynn [26]. This taxonomy attempts to dichotomize parallel processing into

- SIMD (single instruction stream–multiple data stream)—a computer architecture having a single originator of instructions that operates on various data streams simultaneously. A computer that uses pipelining would fall within this class, as would a multiprocessor configuration all of whose processors are slaved to the same instructions.
- MIMD (multiple instruction stream–multiple data stream)—an array of processors each producing different instruction streams to operate on different data streams. The processors are coupled in the sense that they can pass information to each other.

Flynn's taxonomy has proved very useful as a shorthand for the art. But taxonomies and models must be used with proper perspective. One should not cabin one's thinking into immediately forcing a new computational architectural concept under the taxonomic rubrics.

Returning to the hypercube, perhaps the greatest challenge to the algorithm designer and programmer is the question of effective load balancing. If a problem is partitioned over a hypercube, it should be done in such a way that each node finishes at approximately the same time, as the time to solution is clearly bounded by the node that finishes last. For some problems this is a straightforward task; for others, especially those algorithms that involve branching decisions into code streams of unequal time-execution segments, the problem is far from trivial. Because a hypercube is a general programmable computer, it is not optimized for any particular feature. One potential bottleneck is input–output. It may be difficult to both preload data and read data out at necessary system rates.

In an attempt to alleviate the scheduling problems just addressed and take advantage of "natural data flow," many designers prefer what has become known as the *systolic approach*. This approach attempts to devise efficient parallel algorithms that

1. can be realized by an array of processing elements favoring only local interconnections that are also "regular" or similar in pattern,
2. can be decomposed into very nearly equal time-computational time pieces.

Such algorithms are easily realized with VLSI techniques and the computational architecture is termed *systolic*. Kung [27] labels systolic arrays as a new pipelined-array architecture. Systolic arrays tend to do best when used for executing algorithms whose data flow is local and whose basic operations are of approximately the same complexity. Algorithms that require branching may thus be difficult to implement on a systolic array. The FFT is also difficult to implement on a systolic array as execution of the FFT requires interprocessor communication that is not local.

Perhaps the best way to get a quick feel for a systolic array is to look at one of the matrix manipulation tasks for which systolic arrays are so eminently suited—that of matrix multiplication. Our goal is to compute the elements of

$$C = \begin{pmatrix} c_{11} & c_{12} \\ c_{21} & c_{22} \end{pmatrix},$$

where $C = AB$, a product of 2×2 matrices; i.e.,

$$C = \begin{pmatrix} a_{11} & a_{12} \\ a_{21} & a_{22} \end{pmatrix} \begin{pmatrix} b_{11} & b_{12} \\ b_{21} & b_{22} \end{pmatrix} \tag{4.48}$$

Consider the systolic array in Figure 4.19, where we show four computing elements, represented by square boxes, each fed by two data "pipes."

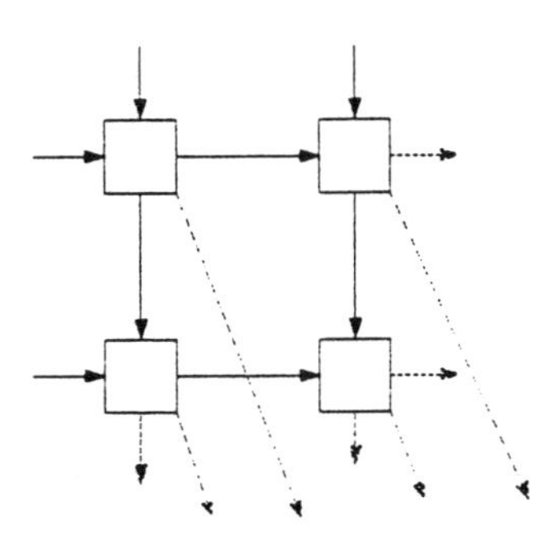

FIG. 4.19. Systolic array.

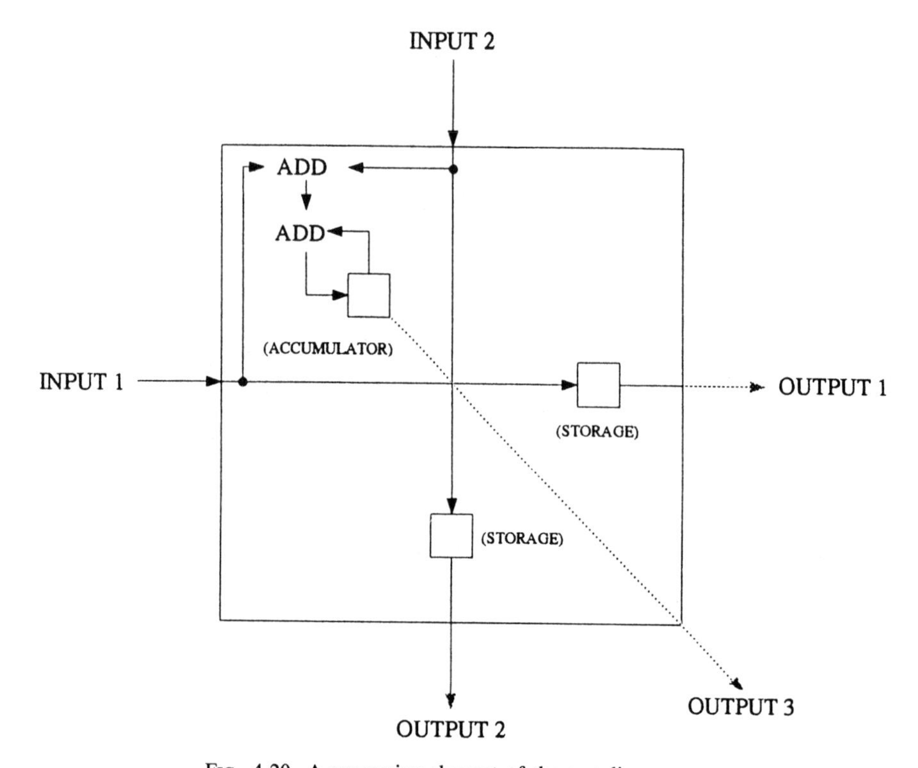

FIG. 4.20. A processing element of the systolic array.

At each clock instant, each processing element accepts the two values waiting at the input pipes, multiplies them together, adds the result to an accumulator, and simultaneously sends the previously input values on their way on the output pipes unaltered. The processing element also simultaneously sends the previous content of its accumulator on a third (diagonal) pipe. A conceptualization of the processing element's function is depicted in Figure 4.20.

In Figure 4.21 we set up the data pipes to "flow" matrices A and B through the systolic array. Notice that the input pipes are appropriately padded with leading and trailing zeros. The accumulators of the individual processing elements each contain the correct value for c_{ij} after four time steps. These values can then be clocked out or extracted from the accumulators along the diagonal data pipes for presentation to an output bus or perhaps another systolic array for further processing.

Systolic structures can take many forms. It is possible to think of systolic units that make decisions on routing data even though this is usually

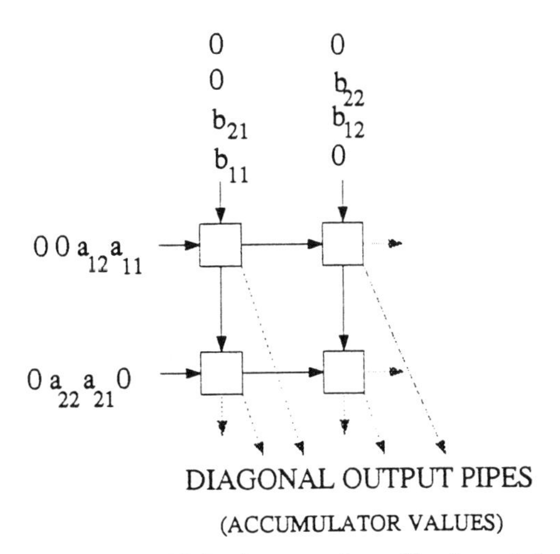

FIG. 4.21. Matrix multiplication as performed by the systolic array.

considered within the purview of data flow machines. An ingenious example of this type of structure, although not presented in this light by its author, was the convolutional tree computer introduced by Jenq [28]. As we know, convolution is a basic and important signal processing function. Signal processing engineers usually perform convolution via the FFT. The sequences to be convolved are both Fourier transformed, the transforms multiplied together, term by term, and the inverse Fourier transform taken of this product sequence. Jenq cites potential drawbacks to this:

1. The FFT will require complex multiplications even though the sequences may be entirely real.
2. To perform the FFT, one must calculate (or retrieve from a pre-calculated table) the appropriate values of trigonometric functions.
3. One must also zero-pad the sequences effectively doubling their lengths so that the cyclic convolution does not alias.

Jenq proposed doing the convolution directly, and his construction of a suitable computational flow is remarkable for its regularity, its simplicity, and its potential cost-effective buildability. His device is a tree with a root at which the sequences to be convolved are entered. The data flow will be down the tree to the leaves and then back up the tree, where the convolution coefficients will become present at the root. The tree's general form is sketched in Figure 4.22.

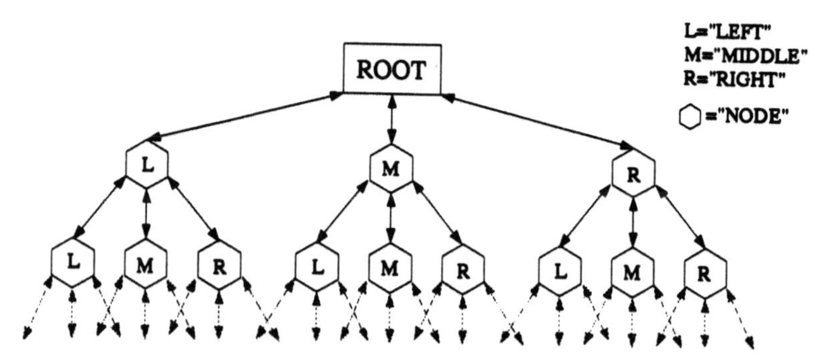

FIG. 4.22. The general form of Jenq's convolver.

To convolve two N-point sequences[6]

$$\{A(1), \ldots, A(N)\} \qquad \text{and} \qquad \{B(1), \ldots, B(N)\}$$

entered at the root, we must use a tree with depth equal to n. Jenq's algorithm uses two modules:

1. Divide: operates on data moving down the tree.
   - SET $n = N$
   - AS LONG AS $n > 1$, THEN EXECUTE:
     - send $\left\{A(1), \ldots, A\left(\frac{n}{2}\right), B(1), \ldots, B\left(\frac{n}{2}\right)\right\}$ to the left descendant node (L);
     - send $\left\{A(1) + A\left(\frac{n}{2} + 1\right), \ldots, A\left(\frac{n}{2}\right) + A(n),\ B(1) + B\left(\frac{n}{2} + 1\right), \ldots, B\left(\frac{n}{2}\right) + B(n)\right\}$ to the middle descendant node (M);
     - send $\left\{A\left(\frac{n}{2} + 1\right), \ldots, A(n),\ B\left(\frac{n}{2} + 1\right), \ldots, B(n)\right\}$ to the right descendant node (R);
     - divide n by 2.
   - WHEN $n = 1$, (the "bottom" of the tree has been reached) execute:
     - $C(1) = A(1) * B(1)$;
     - send $C(1)$ to the parent node.

[6] For convenience we will assume that $N = 2^n$.

2. Combine: operates on data moving up the tree. Each node receives a sequence of length m from each of the nodes below it. Let these sequences be denoted by $\{C_L(1), \ldots, C_L(m)\}$, $\{C_M(1), \ldots, C_M(m)\}$, and $\{C_R(1), \ldots, C_R(m)\}$ for left, middle, and right node, respectively.
   - FOR $i = 1, \ldots, m$ COMPUTE $C_\Lambda(i) = C_M(i) - C_L(i) + C_R(i)$;
   - FOR $i = 1, \ldots, \frac{m+1}{2}$ SET $C(i) = C_L(i)$;
   - FOR $i = \frac{m+3}{2}, \ldots, m$ COMPUTE $C(i) = C_L(i) + C_\Lambda\left(i - \frac{m+1}{2}\right)$;
   - FOR $i = m + 1$ SET $C(i) = C_\Lambda\left(\frac{m+1}{2}\right)$;
   - FOR $i = m + 2, \ldots, \frac{3m+1}{2}$ COMPUTE $C(i) = C_R(i - m - 1) + C_\Lambda\left(i - \frac{m+1}{2}\right)$;
   - FOR $i = \frac{3m+3}{2}, \ldots, 2m + 1$ SET $C(i) = C_R(i - m - 1)$.

As an example, let us look at the convolution of the two four-point sequences $\{A(1), A(2), A(3), A(4)\}$ and $\{B(1), B(2), B(3), B(4)\}$. Direct evaluation gives

$$\begin{aligned}
C(1) &= A(1)B(1) \\
C(2) &= A(1)B(2) + A(2)B(1) \\
C(3) &= A(1)B(3) + A(2)B(2) + A(3)B(1) \\
C(4) &= A(1)B(4) + A(2)B(3) + A(3)B(2) + A(4)B(1) \qquad (4.49) \\
C(5) &= A(2)B(4) + A(3)B(3) + A(4)B(2) \\
C(6) &= A(3)B(4) + A(4)B(3) \\
C(7) &= A(4)B(4)
\end{aligned}$$

Let us now use Jenq's convolver to convolve the two four-point sequences. Figure 4.23 displays the first part of the Divide module.

Proceeding up the tree, the nodes that are directly below the root receive data as outlined in Figure 4.22 by application of the Combine module. (Note that for this node, $m = 1$.) The data displayed in Figure 4.24 now flows up to the root where the Combine module forms the autocorrelations (4.49). (The verification of this example is left as Problem 8.)

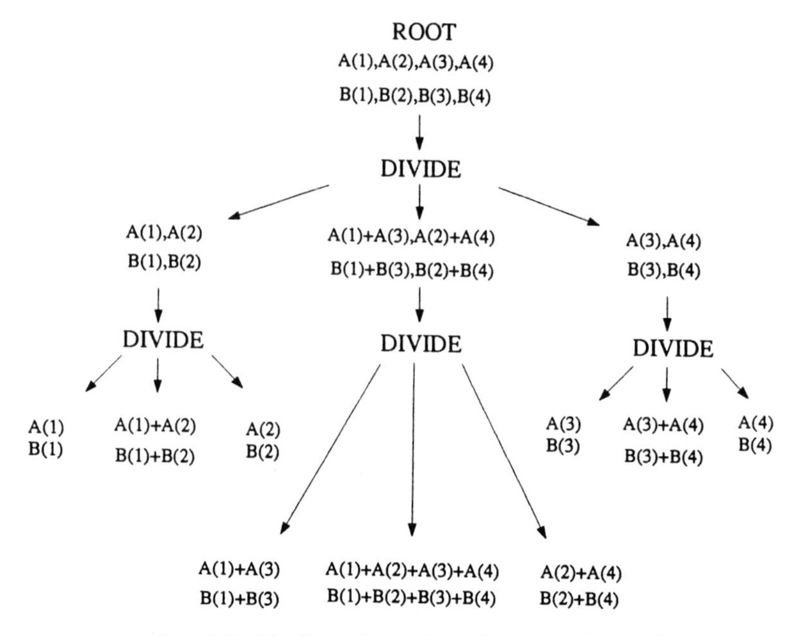

FIG. 4.23. The flow of data down the tree during Divide.

DATA RECEIVED AT LEFT NODE	DATA RECEIVED AT MIDDLE NODE	DATA RECEIVED AT RIGHT NODE
$C_L = A(1)B(1)$	$C_L = A(1)B(1) + A(1)B(3) + A(3)B(1) + A(3)B(3)$	$C_L = A(3)B(3)$
$C_M = A(1)B(1) + A(1)B(2) + A(2)B(1) + A(2)B(2)$	$C_M = A(1)B(1) + A(1)B(2) + A(1)B(3) + A(1)B(4) + A(2)B(1) + A(2)B(2) + A(2)B(3) + A(2)B(4) + A(3)B(1) + A(3)B(2) + A(3)B(3) + A(3)B(4) + A(4)B(1) + A(4)B(2) + A(4)B(3) + A(4)B(4)$	$C_M = A(3)B(3) + A(3)B(4) + A(4)B(3) + A(4)B(4)$
$C_R = A(4)B(4)$	$C_R = A(2)B(2) + A(2)B(4) + A(4)B(2) + A(4)B(4)$	$C_R = A(4)B(4)$

FIG. 4.24. The data received at the nodes directly below the root as Combine proceeds.

In Search of Parallel Algorithms

Devising new parallel architectures has been a highly successful undertaking. Devising algorithms for efficient parallel solution of a problem, however, can be very difficult if even possible. It is usually not possible to straightforwardly parallelize serial algorithms. Some folks even claim that, if your goal is to devise a parallel algorithm, you should scrap all the known serial algorithms before starting.

Consider the following (corrected) note from Fateman [29]. Suppose we wish to compute $\Sigma = A * B * C + A * B * D + A * E + F$. Assuming the asterisk and plus operators are two-input operators that each take one time unit, we could determine Σ in five time units as shown in Figure 4.25. If we wish to compute Σ in as short a time as possible we could proceed as shown in Figure 4.26. This new approach, using up to two operators per unit time, calculates Σ in four time units. The structure of Figure 4.26 is very different from the structure of Figure 4.25. Unfortunately there is no simple "bridge" from one structure to the other.

The field of parallel algorithm development is not without its triumphs, however. In a signal success, Miranker and Liniger [30] gave an excellent and early discussion concerning the parallelization of predictor–corrector methods for the numerical integration of ordinary differential equations (ODEs). As the need for numerical solution of ODEs is encountered in many large-scale systems problems it seems appropriate to touch on Miranker and Liniger's work if not for the method itself, then for the success they had in parallelizing the method.

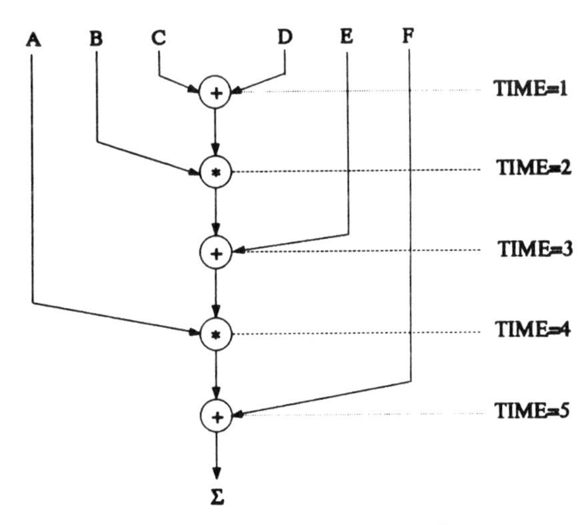

FIG. 4.25. Serial computation of Σ.

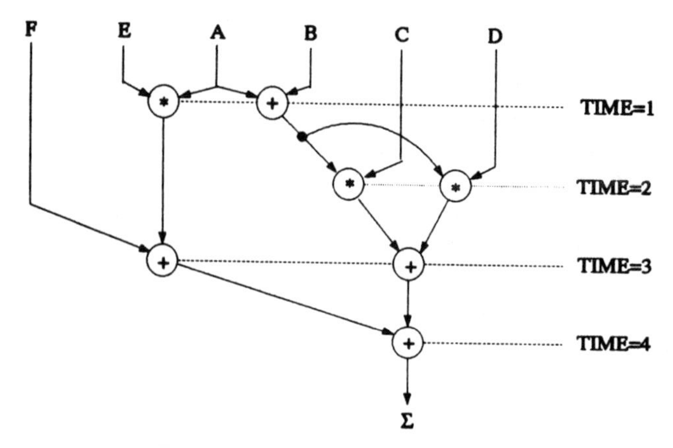

FIG. 4.26. Parallel computation of Σ.

A first-order ODE is an equation of the form $y' = f(x, y)$. Typically, we are given a boundary condition, such as $y(0) = y_0$ and asked to compute $y(x)$ for $x > 0$. There are, as you might expect, many different ways of doing this. These methods exhibit different stability behaviors and different computational complexities. One method that has been used is the Runge–Kutta (RK) iteration technique. The simplest form of the Runge–Kutta methods is an iteration of the following form:

$$y(nh + 1) = y(nh) + ak_1 + bk_2 \tag{4.50}$$

where h is the extrapolation mesh or step size, n is an integer, and where $k_1 = hf(x = nh, y(nh))$, $k_2 = hf(x = nh + \alpha h, y(nh) + \beta k_1)$; a, b, α, and β are constants to be determined to reduce the extrapolation error [31]. As you can see from (4.50), the Runge–Kutta method essentially "throws away" past information as it moves forward. This cannot help the stability of the method and that is why many numerical analysts advise against using the Runge–Kutta method for numerical integration of ODEs. A method that uses past information, exhibits better stability, and even has a way to assess solution accuracy as the iteration progresses is known as the predictor–corrector (PC) method. This method computes a predicted value, calculates the derivative at the predicted value, and then uses this derivative along with previously computed derivatives to further refine the "predicted" value into a "corrected" value. There are many excellent sources for reading about PC methods. One we particularly suggest is [32].

As a very elementary example, we will contrast the RK and PC methods of "order" 2. The RK equations corresponding to (4.50) are (adapted from [31]):

$$y(nh + 1) = y(nh) + \tfrac{1}{2}(k_1 + k_2) \tag{4.51}$$

where

$$k_1 = hf(x = nh, y(nh))$$
$$k_2 = hf(x = nh, y(nh) + k_1) \quad (4.52)$$

The PC equations[7] for order 2 are (from [30]):

$$y_{n+1}^p = y_n^c + \frac{h}{2}(3f_n^c - f_{n-1}^c)$$
$$y_{n+1}^c = y_n^c + \frac{h}{2}(f_{n+1}^p + f_n^c) \quad (4.53)$$

where y_n^p is the predicted value of y at $x = nh$, y_n^c is the corrected value of y at $x = nh$, f_n^p is f evaluated at $x = nh$ using y_n^p, and f_n^c is f evaluated at $x = nh$ using y_n^c.

As an example contrasting the RK and PC methods of order 2, let us look at the differential equation describing simple atmospheric drag effects on a sphere. Newton's Third Law states that force is equal to mass times acceleration. If we have a sphere moving through an atmosphere we can approximate the force on the sphere by atmospheric drag as equal to $(-k/m)v$, where k is the drag coefficient in kilograms/second, m is the mass in kilograms, and v is the velocity in meters/second. Thus, the differential equation describing the velocity of the sphere with time is

$$v' = -\frac{k}{m}v \quad (4.54)$$

Equation (4.54) can be integrated in closed form to yield

$$v(t) = v_0 e^{-kt/m} \quad (4.55)$$

where v_0 is the initial velocity in meters/second. For $k = 0.1$ kilograms/second, a 10 gram sphere initially traveling at 2500 meters/second will have its velocity reduced as shown in Figure 4.7 over 1 second. We used the RK equations (4.51) and (4.52) and the PC equations (4.53) to numerically integrate (4.54) with a mesh size of $h = 1$ millisecond. The errors, the absolute differences between the true answer (55) and the RK and PC approximations, are displayed in Figure 4.28.[8]

[7] There are many formulations for the predictor. The one used by Miranker and Liniger is an Adams–Bashford type.

[8] One further point worth making concerns the question of starting the PC iterations, as they require more history than is provided by v_0 alone. A common way to obtain these extra data is to use the first terms of a Runge–Kutta iteration, and this is what we have done.

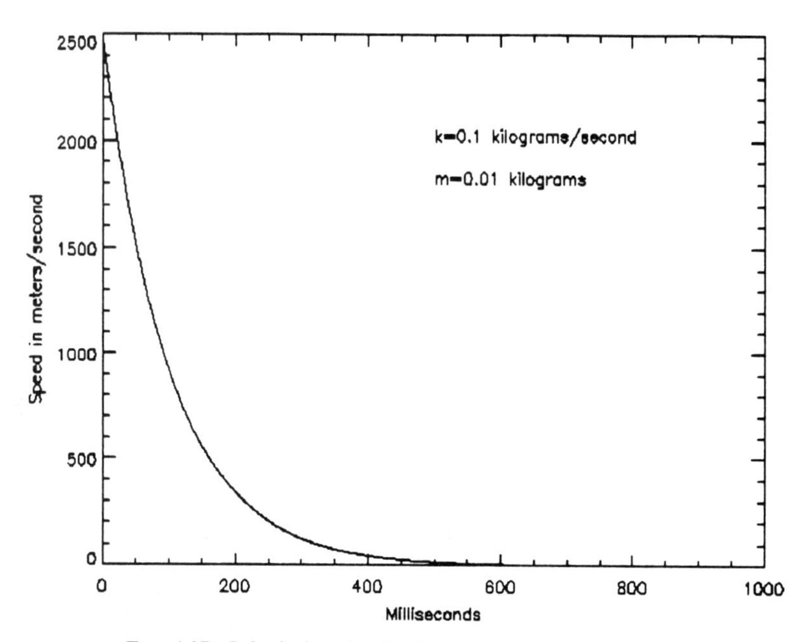

FIG. 4.27. Spherical projectile slowdown—exact solution to (4.56).

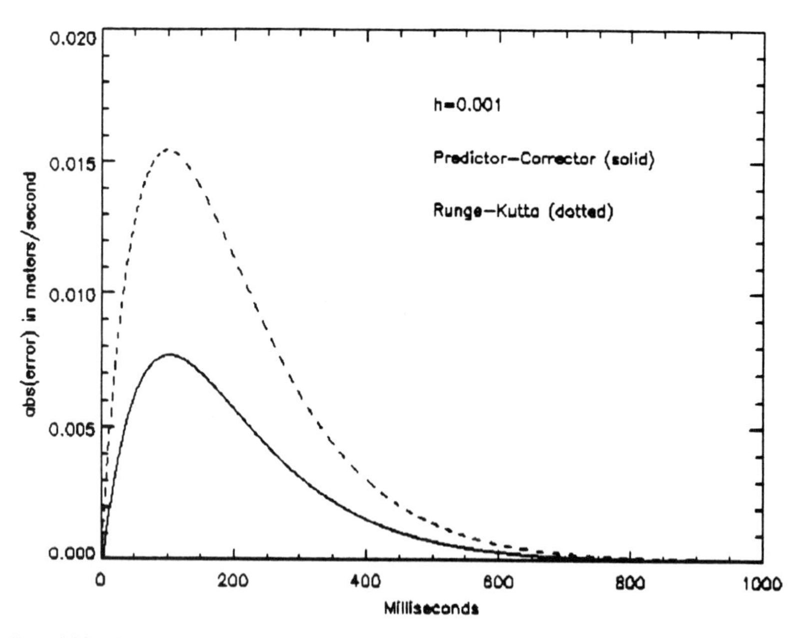

FIG. 4.28. Errors exhibited in integration of (4.56) using second-order RK and PC algorithms.

This example seems to indicate that the PC may outperform the RK for accuracy. This seems consistent with the following from Acton [32]: "we usually summarize by saying that the Runge–Kutta requires *twice* as much work as predictor–corrector for the same accuracy." The choice of the best numerical procedure for integrating ODEs requires much study, and it is not our intention here to recommend one method over another. We do recommend, however, that much study go into selecting the best method for a particular system.

Let us now address the key question of parallelization. Miranker and Liniger made a key observation concerning the flow of computation implied by (4.53). They observed that the order of computation is

$$\rightarrow y^p_{n+1} \rightarrow f^p_{n+1} \rightarrow y^c_{n+1} \rightarrow f^c_{n+1} \rightarrow$$

and that this order is representable by a *front* of computation, where calculations at $x = nh + 1$ involve information from both sides of the front, as depicted in Figure 4.29.

Miranker and Liniger transformed the predictor–corrector equations (4.53) so that the coupling depicted in Figure 4.29, which required information from both sides of the computation front, was eliminated. For the parallel PC method of order 2, these equations are

$$\begin{aligned} y^p_{n+1} &= y^c_{n-1} + 2hf^p_n \\ y^c_n &= y^c_{n-1}\frac{h}{2}(f^p_n + f^c_{n-1}) \end{aligned} \tag{4.56}$$

Note that now the order of computation is separable; i.e.,

$$\rightarrow y^p_{n+1} \rightarrow f^p_{n+1} \rightarrow \quad \text{and} \quad \rightarrow y^c_n \rightarrow f^c_n \rightarrow.$$

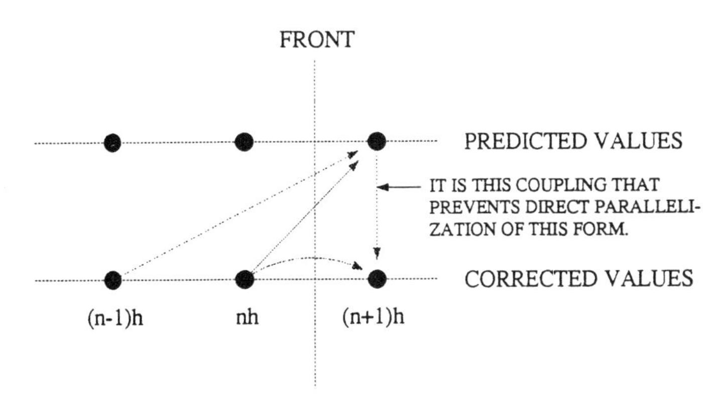

FIG. 4.29. The computational front for the serial order-2 PC equations.

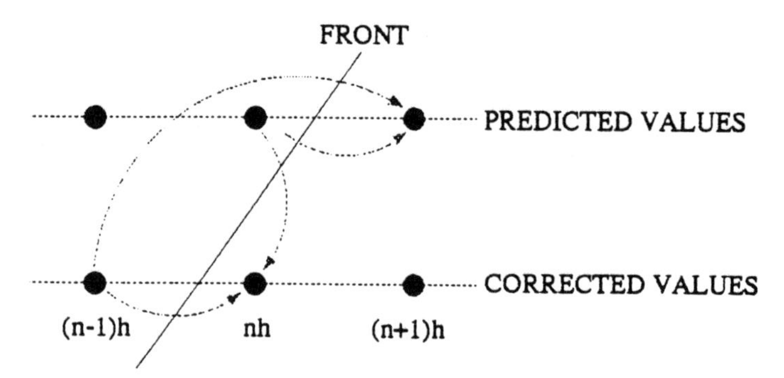

FIG. 4.30. The computational front for the parallel order-2 PC equations.

The computation front respecting (4.56) depicts computation that depends only upon information behind the front as depicted in Figure 4.30.

The calculations of the two equations (4.56) can now proceed in parallel. Miranker and Liniger also develop similar parallel formulations for higher order PC methods.

What can we do with these results? Well, we can use the extra accuracy that the PC method provides over the RK to integrate with a larger step or mesh size, h, and thus derive results equal in accuracy to the RK results in shorter time. Or, we can increase the mesh size *and* do the PC computations in parallel to gain an even greater speed advantage over the RK with the same accuracy. The practice of systems analysis is, once again, the development and study of trade-offs.

For comparison, the graph in Figure 4.31 displays the errors incurred in integration of (4.54) with two different step sizes, using the PC method. One step size is the same h as used in Figure 4.28. The second step size is $\sqrt{2}\,h$. Note that this increase in h doubles the error to the error rendered by the 1000-step RK method but requires about 29% fewer iterations than the 1000-step RK.

Again, the art of integrating ODEs is ever changing and improving. For example, methods for dealing with dynamic mesh spacings (variable h) are often recommended. Also the choice of order must be made along with its implications of increased computational complexities. Some additional useful references are [33–37]. It seems almost certain that parallel computational algorithms will play a key role in integrating ODEs in systems of the future. As a point of interest and an additional reference, the reader is referred to Khaddaj [38], who discusses an integration architecture utilizing transputers.

Another extremly important problem usually encountered in the design of a large system is that of solving a large set of linear equations representable

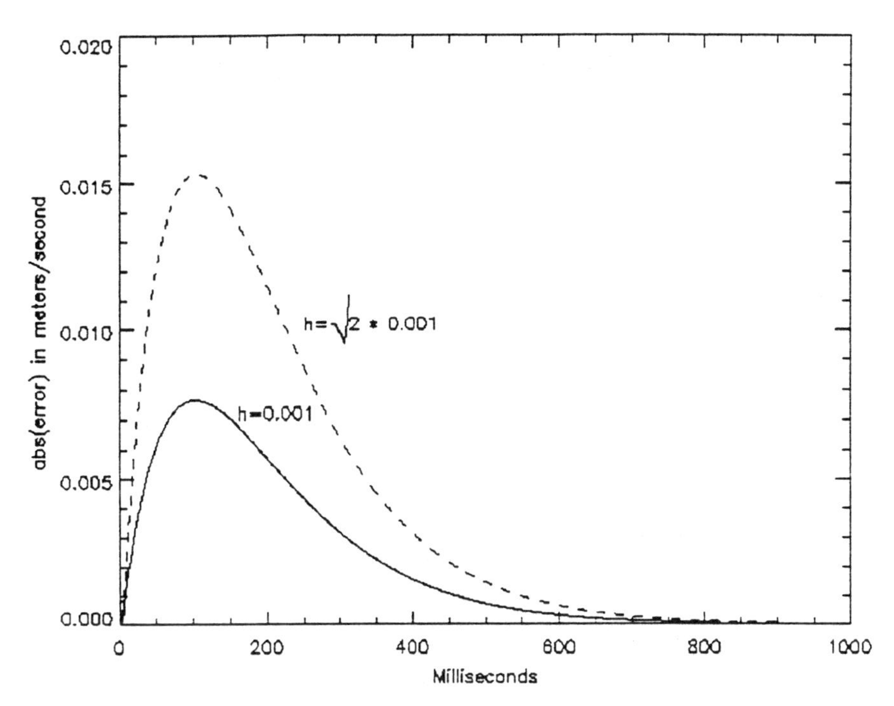

FIG. 4.31. Errors exhibited in integration of (4.54), using a second-order PC algorithm with different mesh sizes.

by the general equation $Ax = b$, where $A = (a_{ij})$ is a general $n \times n$ dense matrix; i.e., most of the $\{a_{ij}\}$ are nonzero and there are no special properties of A such as equal element bands or other symmetries. Much attention has been paid to this problem over the years by mathematicians interested in the problem qua a mathematical problem and by applied mathematicians and engineers seeking to parallelize a solution. Sameh and Kuck [39] produced an algorithm that requires $O(n)$ steps using $O(n^2)$ processors. Their algorithm is based on the elementary but extremely powerful matrix operation known as the *Givens rotation*. The algorithm is worth examining in and of itself for possible implementation or just as an example of a good parallel algorithm development effort. It is primarily for the latter reason that we look more closely.

As we have hinted, an efficient parallel algorithm is not easy to develop in general. One approach is to break an algorithm into a set of simple steps that can be executed in parallel. In doing this, the algorithm designer must be continuously sensitive to the stability of the resulting algorithm and its error performance.

The Givens rotation allows the zeroing or annihilation of a specific element of a matrix. The rotation can be expressed as the matrix

$$G(i, j, \theta) = \begin{pmatrix} 1 & \cdots & 0 & \cdots & 0 & \cdots & 0 \\ \vdots & \ddots & \vdots & \ddots & \vdots & \ddots & \vdots \\ 0 & \cdots & c & \cdots & -s & \cdots & 0 \\ \vdots & \ddots & \vdots & \ddots & \vdots & \ddots & \vdots \\ 0 & \cdots & s & \cdots & c & \cdots & 0 \\ \vdots & \ddots & \vdots & \ddots & \vdots & \ddots & \vdots \\ 0 & \cdots & 0 & \cdots & 0 & \cdots & 1 \end{pmatrix} \begin{matrix} \\ \\ \text{—row } i \\ \\ \text{—row } j \\ \\ \\ \end{matrix} \quad (4.57)$$

if we form $Y = G(i, j, \theta)A$, then the elements of $Y = (y_{i,j})$ can be explicitly written as

$$y_{uv} = \begin{cases} ca_{iv} - sa_{jv} & \text{if } u = i \\ sa_{iv} + ca_{jv} & \text{if } u = j \\ a_{uv} & \text{otherwise} \end{cases} \quad (4.58)$$

It is clear that we can zero y_{jv}, for example, by selecting s and c so that $sa_{iv} + ca_{jv} = 0$.[9] We must, of course, apply the same multiplication of $G(i, j, \theta)$ to the column vector b so that the solution vector, x, $G(i, j, \theta)Ax = G(i, j, \theta)b$ will be unchanged.

By sequentially zeroing selective elements of A using successive Givens rotations, we see how the matrix premultiplying x can be transformed or factored into a matrix, R, that is upper triangular; i.e., it has zeros below the main diagonal.[10] The system $Rx = b'$, where b' is the vector created by the product of Givens rotations operating on b, has the same solution vector, x, as the original system and is easily and quickly solved by back substitution.

Sameh and Kuck suggested parallel or simultaneous application of different Givens rotations to reduce the time to transform A into R. The trick is to apply the Givens rotations in an order so that they do not interfere with each other. Thus the two rows affected by any particular Givens rotation cannot be used in any other Givens rotation applied at the same time. This is a rather mild restriction. A good way to see how the algorithm would proceed is to consider a 10×10 matrix A. Figure 4.32

[9] The following constraint is observed by c and s: $s^2 + c^2 = 1$. The application of the Givens rotation thus apparently involves a square root operation.

[10] This is called *QR factorization*: R is upper triangular and Q is an orthogonal matrix. The Givens rotation is orthogonal, and thus the product of successive Givens rotations is also equivalent to premultiplying x by an orthogonal matrix.

*	*	*	*	*	*	*	*	*	*
9	*	*	*	*	*	*	*	*	*
8	10	*	*	*	*	*	*	*	*
7	9	11	*	*	*	*	*	*	*
6	8	10	12	*	*	*	*	*	*
5	7	9	11	13	*	*	*	*	*
4	6	8	10	12	14	*	*	*	*
3	5	7	9	11	13	15	*	*	*
2	4	6	8	10	12	14	16	*	*
1	3	5	7	9	11	13	15	17	*

FIG. 4.32. The order of application of the Givens rotations.

shows a logical order in which the lower 45 elements of A are annihilated in parallel in 17 time steps. Written in the annihilated element's position (i, j) is the time step at which it is annihilated. The annihilation of the element at (i, j) is performed in each case by using rows i and $i - 1$; i.e., $G(i - 1, i, \theta)$. For a general $n \times n$ matrix A, it is clear that there will be $n(n - 1)/2$ elements to be annihilated. If a Givens rotation takes one time step to execute, then Sameh and Kuck's parallel Givens rotation procedure will peform the annihilations in parallel in $2n - 3$ time steps. It is easily concluded that we can solve a dense $n \times n$ system of linear equations in $O(n)$ time steps using $O(n^2)$ processors.

For more recent results on using parallel Givens rotations, see Golub and Van Loan [40] for a discussion of "Fast Givens Transformation" in which the number of required multiplications is reduced and explicit square rooting eliminated. Also see Duato [41] for executing square-root-free Givens rotations on a transputer network. Finally, because of its many desirable properties, it should be noted that the Givens rotation is an element of choice in many optical processing architectures.[11]

Suboptimal Parallel Algorithms

It is almost an inbred dictum that demands a system's designer to fervently seek the optimal algorithm to be applied to the particular system problem. Most often the optimal algorithm will remain unknown for a variety of reasons.

[11] Another nice aspect to the algorithm is that it can use an error analysis done by Wilkinson [42] on the product of Givens rotations. Wilkinson also addressed the error analysis of the back substitution. Both the product of Givens rotations and the back substitution appear to be quite stable in general.

One of these reasons is the sheer complexity of the problem. It is simply intractable to optimal solution. The celebrated Traveling Salesman problem was such for many mathematicians.

Another of the reasons that the optimal algorithm will remain elusive is that the problem will not be completely specifiable and rather approximated *ab initio*—the noise may be assumed to be additive, white, and Gaussian. Various linearizations may have to be made.

The problem must still be addressed despite these woes, and what is done by default, out of necessity, is to pick what amounts to a suboptimal algorithm. Such a choice is not necessarily bad. The Traveling Salesman problem, for example, has a suboptimal algorithm that guarantees finding, in polynomial time, a tour whose length will not exceed the minimum possible length by more than 50% [43].

Quite often a suboptimal algorithm is significantly simpler than the optimal, and for a parallel processing implementation, much easier to parallelize, verify, program, *and* debug. Additionally, something very surprising may happen on the parallelization of a suboptimal algorithm, which will recoup some of the penalty initially incurred through its adoption. Let us explore this question with the following problem, adapted from Hershey and Yassa [44].

Suppose we have a system that has N image forming sensors. Each sensor has P pixels. Each of the N different sensors stares at a different scene. An example of this might be a space-based sensor system viewing non-overlapping sectors of space. The mission of each sensor is to warn of the presence of targets. All sensors sample their respective scenes, and the sample values are relayed to a central computation facility, where they are processed and tested for target presence.

The intelligence available to the system designer suggests expectation of an initial attack in one monitored scene only, and all scenes should be considered as equally likely candidates to view the initial attack. The background of each pixel is expected to be cluttered, and the clutter process is adequately describable as a pixel-to-pixel and pixel-sample-to-pixel-sample independent Gaussian process $G(\mu_c, \sigma_c^2)$. Intelligence advisors allow that each target can be considered to reside in one and only one pixel and that a target occupied pixel will exhibit a pixel value that is also describable by a Gaussian process $G(\mu_t, \sigma_t^2)$. We define π as the probability that a particular pixel exhibits clutter only and $1 - \pi$ as the probability that the pixel contains a target. Unfortunately, no reliable estimate is available for the pentad $(\mu_c, \sigma_c^2; \mu_t, \sigma_t^2; \pi)$, and to complicate matters even further, we also do not know what fraction of the pixels in the scene viewing the attack will contain targets; i.e., we do not know the expected strike size. It may also be the case that μ_c and σ_c^2 are *different* for each of the N

sensor images. The system designer's job is to (1) pick an algorithm for processing the scenes and (2) devise a computational architecture to implement the processing.

This particular problem involves components of two very difficult and well-known larger problems. The first of these larger problems is the question of identification of a finite mixture of probability distributions. A very good reference to this problem is Titterington, Smith, and Makov [45]. The second of the larger problems concerns a particular genre of dynamic optimal allocation of resources, and it is often referred to as the *p-arm bandit problem*. A very good reference to this problem is Gittins [46]. In this case study we will not attempt to produce the best answer, once we define *best* itself, but we will do fairly well. Above all, what we hope to do is to motivate some interesting trade-off discussions.

As we do not know what $(\mu_c, \sigma_c^2; \mu_t, \sigma_t^2; \pi)$ is, we might as well consider our testing problem as developing a razor between the hypotheses:

H_0: the null hypothesis that the pixel values of each scene are produced by a single Gaussian process; i.e., that we are sampling only $G(\mu_c, \sigma_c^2)$.

H_1: the hypothesis that our samples come from sampling a mixture of the two different Gaussian processes $G(\mu_c, \sigma_c^2)$ and $G(\mu_t, \sigma_t^2)$.

There are many statistical testing candidates to choose from, and we arbitrarily decide that the candidate discrimination method we pick need not be optimal but it should be nominally sensitive and respect computational costs.

Because we know so little about the values of the five defining parameters of our problem, let us seek a statistic that is robust yet sensitive. A good candidate may be found in the higher order central moments, viz. $\{\nu_i\}$, where

$$\nu_i = E[(x - \bar{x})^i] \tag{4.59}$$

and $\bar{x}$ denotes the mean. The kurtosis, denoted historically as β_2, of a probability density function, $f(x)$, is defined as

$$\beta_2 = \frac{\nu_4}{\nu_2^2} \tag{4.60}$$

A remarkable property of a Gaussian random variable is that its kurtosis is identically 3. It is independent of the two Gaussian defining parameters μ and σ^2. Thus it seems reasonable that a reasonable test between H_0 and H_1 for our problem might be provided by the kurtosis particularly in light of our lack of knowledge about the specific parameters of our problem.

The calculated kurtosis of a set of samples from a single Gaussian distribution is itself a random variable and has been studied by many of the great statisticians in their anticipation that β_2 might be used just as we are suggesting. Such a study, which also contains useful bounds on measured kurtosis, is to be found in Pearson {47].

For our problem, pixel values produced under H_1 will be describable by the mixture probability density function

$$f(x) = \pi G(\mu_c, \sigma_c^2) + (1 - \varepsilon)G(\mu_t, \sigma_t^2), \tag{4.61}$$

The expected value of the kurtosis under H_1 is found by evaluating (4.60) where

$$\begin{aligned} \nu_4 = {} & \pi\{(\mu_c^4 + 6\mu_c^2\sigma_c^2 + 3\sigma_c^4) - 4\mu(\mu_c^3 + 3\mu_c\sigma_c^2) \\ & + 6\mu^2(\mu_c^2 + \sigma_c^2) - 4\mu^3\mu_c + \mu^4\} \\ & + (1 - \pi)\{(\mu_t^4 + 6\mu_t^2\sigma_t^2 + 3\sigma_t^4) - 4\mu(\mu_t^3 + 3\mu_t\sigma_t^2) \\ & + 6\mu^2(\mu_t^2 + \sigma_t^2) - 4\mu^3\mu_t + \mu^4\} \end{aligned} \tag{4.62}$$

$$\begin{aligned} \nu_2 = {} & \pi\{(\mu_c^2 + \sigma_c^2) - 2\mu\mu_c + \mu^2\} \\ & + (1 - \pi)\{(\mu_t^2 + \sigma_t^2) - 2\mu\mu_t + \mu^2\} \end{aligned} \tag{4.63}$$

where μ, the weighted mean, is

$$\mu = \pi\mu_c + (1 - \pi)\mu_t \tag{4.64}$$

As an example, let us pick $\sigma_c^2 = 1.0$ and $\sigma_t^2 = 1.3$. Isograms of the kurtosis are displayed in Figure 4.33. The independent variables chosen for the two axes are the mixing parameter π and the magnitude of the difference between the clutter and target means. These particular parameters were chosen to display the relative sensitivity of the kurtosis to them in the regions considered.

Continuing with the selection of our example, let us pick $\mu_c = 2.0$, $\mu_t = 4.0$, and $\pi = 0.98$. Under these conditions, the expected kurtosis under H_1 will be 3.355, the second central moment, ν_2 will be 1.0833, and the mean of the mixture will be 2.04.

To appreciate the sensitivity of the kurtosis as a test between the hypotheses, consider Figures 4.34 and 4.35. In Figure 4.34, the probability density functions (pdfs) for clutter and target, $G(\mu_c, \sigma_c^2)$ and $G(\mu_t, \sigma_t^2)$, respectively, are displayed.

In Figure 4.35, the probability density function of the mixture is displayed overlaid by a Gaussian pdf possessing the same mean and variance as the mixture pdf. Note in Figure 4.35 how close the two pdfs are.

For our simulation, we assume each sensor has $P = 4096$ pixels. In Figure 4.36 we display the kurtosis as it is progressively calculated for the

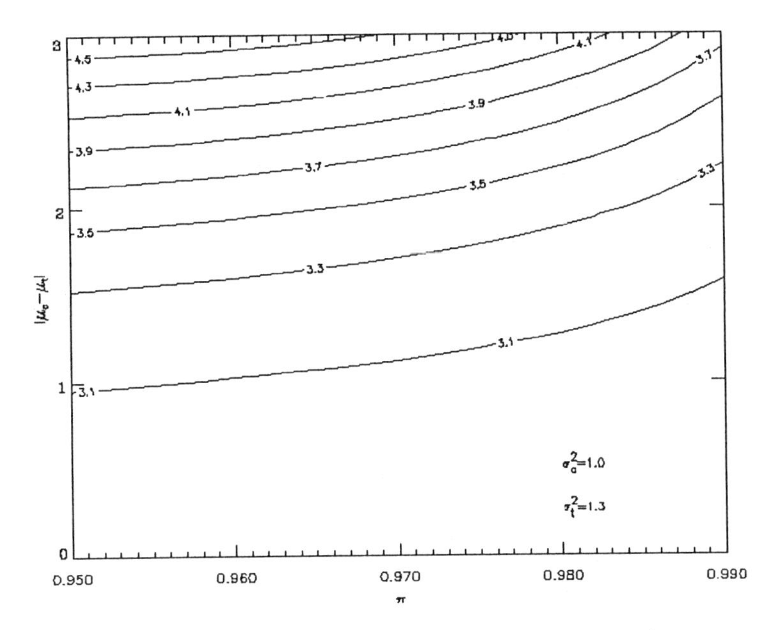

FIG. 4.33. Isograms of the kurtosis for the present example.

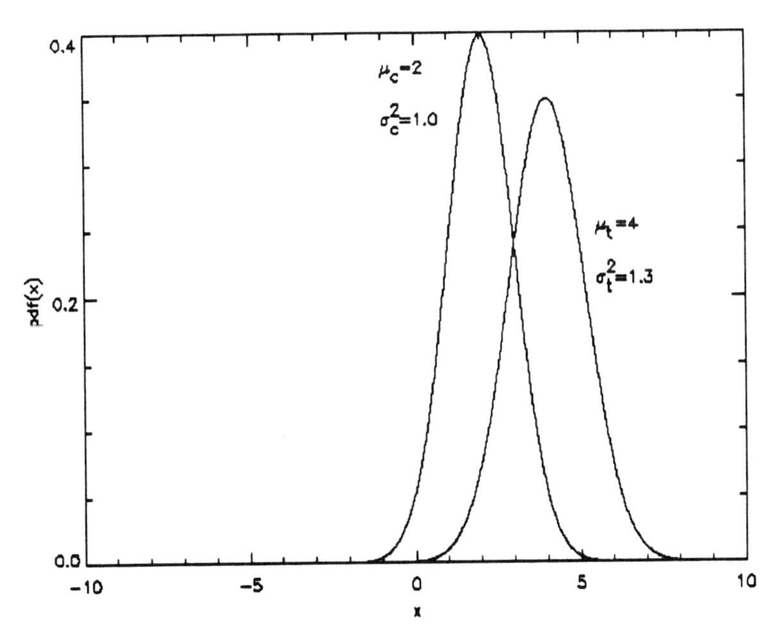

FIG. 4.34. The pdfs for clutter and target.

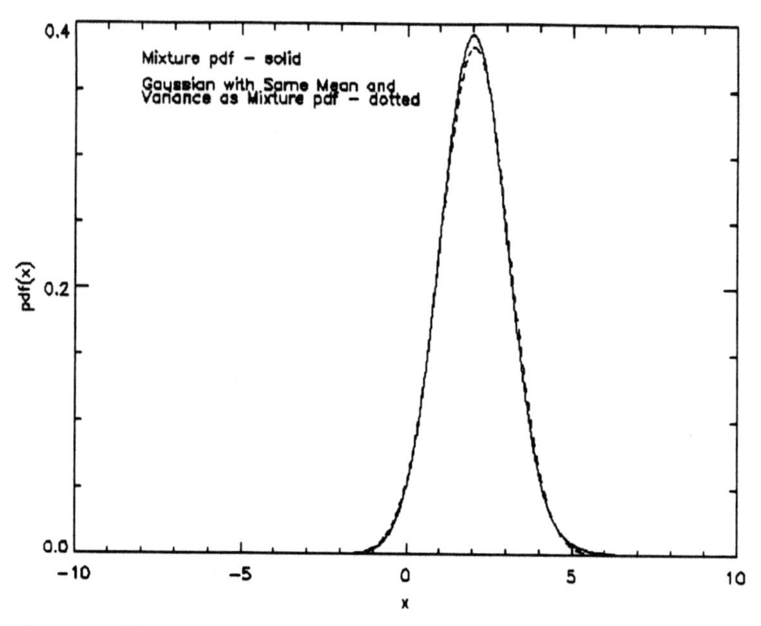

FIG. 4.35. The mixture pdf and a Gaussian pdf with the same mean and variance.

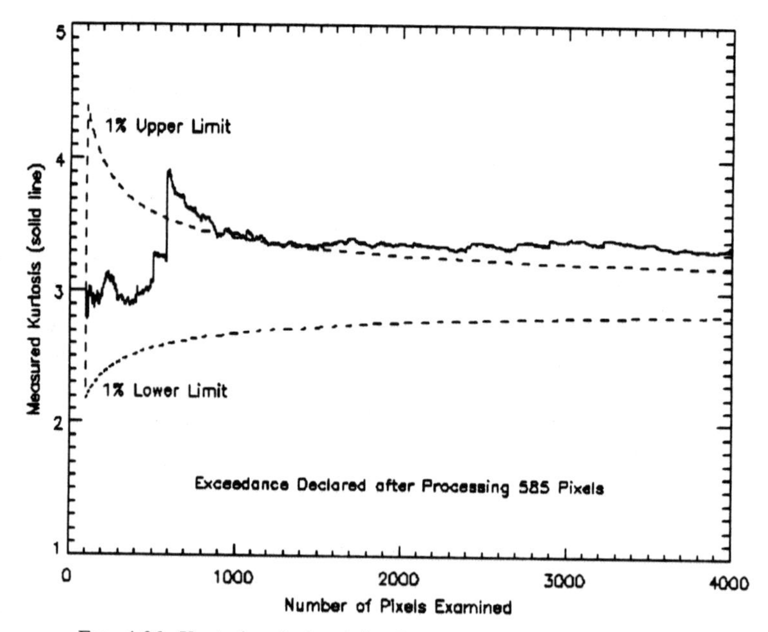

FIG. 4.36. Kurtosis calculated for the example under condition H_1.

sensor viewing the attack. The bounds on the kurtosis are from Pearson [47] and essentially specify the "false alarm" probability of 1%; i.e., that the kurtosis computed under H_0 will exceed the bound values.

Now let us look at parallelizing our surveillance task. This is a natural question as many significant computational problems, especially those respecting a real-time constraint, will be implementable only if the computation can be divided over a number of processors that will work in simultaneity.

As we recall, the benefit from parallel processing is frequently expressed in the term *speed-up*, which is defined as the ratio required by a single processor to do a problem to the time required by N processors working together on the same problem.

It seems intuitively obvious that the speed-up must have an upper bound of N. In 1977, Wilkes [48] posited a fascinating possibility. In effect, Wilkes said to consider a case where a unique something was present in exactly one of N different settings. Assume that it takes τ time units, on the average, to test and reject a setting as not host to the something and τ_0 ($\tau_0 \leq \tau$) time units, on the average, to declare the something found once the appropriate setting is examined. If N processors are put on the problem, one processor per setting, the expected speed-up, S, in determining the setting with the something will be

$$S = \left(\frac{N-1}{2}\right)\frac{\tau}{\tau_0} + 1 \tag{4.65}$$

If the average time to accept is less than half the average time to reject, it appears that the speed-up will be greater than unity. This is termed a *superunitary speed-up*—a term derivative from Miya [49]—as a counter to the prevalently used misnomer *superlinear speed-up*.

The case study problem we have just reviewed seems to be a realization of Wilkes's concept. The kurtosis can be estimated for a given image only after a portion of the particular image is analyzed. If we declare success in finding the target when the dynamically developed kurtosis exceeds preset limits, as in Figure 4.36, then we can think of this average time to exceed the limits as τ_0 and τ as the time to reject an image. For our example, $\tau_0 \approx 1500$, and if we reject an image only after processing it completely, then $\tau = 4096$ and we see that $\tau/\tau_0 > 2$ and, therefore, if we were to use N processors, one per image, we would experience a superunitary speed-up.

We found that the kurtosis appears to be a robust test for mono-Gaussianity. It is particularly appealing because it does not require parameters to be known or assumed as it is an invariant statistic over samples from a single Gaussian process.

Regarding superunitary speed-up, as intriguing as it appears, it indicates only that a suboptimal algorithm has been parallelized Faber, Lubeck, and White [50]. There are more efficient ways of sequentially testing our set of images, and this is the domain of Gittins [46], as we indicated previously. However, we should not eschew a suboptimal algorithm a priori.

Fault Tolerance and Graceful Degradation

Today, many systems are designed for deployment where they will not be accessible or accessible in a timely fashion, and they must continue to be able to operate at some level to fulfil the overall mission into which they are integrated. It is essential therefore that the system designer understand, specify, and ensure that the system is imbued with sufficient fault tolerance. To do this, the system designer must undestand the potential failure mechanisms, the appropriately pessimistic failure rates, and the allowable mission trade-offs. Fault tolerance and graceful degradation or, in contemporary parlance *operate through*, are attributes that should not be left to the end of the design cycle. They can become extremely costly if not well integrated into it.

In this section, we will examine some basics of fault tolerance that is algorithmic based and fault tolerance that is hardware-based. We will also examine the increasingly important concept of graceful degradation. We must note that the field of fault tolerance is expanding at a tremendous rate in techniques and approach. Two references which especially reflect this, and are worthy of study in their own right are Bastani and Ramamoorthy [51] and Chatterjee and d'Abreu [52]. The first presents an intriguing illustration of a fault tolerant distributed process-control system for vehicle control. The second presents a novel technique of diagnosing and locating a type of fault known as a *functional delay*. This type of fault occurs when a computational module produces the correct output but at an unacceptably slow rate. The fault may be very difficult to directly localize due to an insufficient number of access points into a densely integrated module. Chatterjee and d'Abreu propose modeling the module by state equations and data flow graphs and then using syndrome analysis to candidate the most likely point of failure. In our opinion, both of these papers illustrate the sophistication and ingenuity of modern fault tolerance research.

Algorithmic-Based Fault Tolerance

Many computation-intensive system functions comprise massive linear operations. This is especially true of matrix operations. Huang and Abraham [53] introduced the concept of algorithm-based fault-tolerant linear encoding of data that undergoes operation over an array of processors. Their method applied to checking and single-error correcting matrix multiplication is elegant and incurs only a nominal operational overhead. It is an excellent example of naturally incorporating fault tolerance into an extant algorithm.

Consider that we have an $r \times s$ matrix A and an $s \times t$ matrix B. We want to form the product $C = AB$. We define an m-component unit vector; i.e., $u_m = (11 \cdots 1)$. We denote a column check-sum matrix with the subscript c, a row-checking matrix with the subscript r, and a full check-sum matrix with the subscript f. We define these matrices by forming them out of A, B, and C as follows:

$$A_c = \begin{pmatrix} A \\ u_r A \end{pmatrix} \tag{4.66}$$

$$B_r = (B \quad Bu_t^T) \tag{4.67}$$

$$C_f = A_c B_r = \begin{pmatrix} AB & ABu_t^T \\ u_r AB & u_r ABu_t^T \end{pmatrix} \tag{4.68}$$

As an example, let

$$A = \begin{pmatrix} 1 & 2 & 3 \\ 4 & 5 & 6 \end{pmatrix} \tag{4.69}$$

$$B = \begin{pmatrix} 1 & 4 \\ 2 & 5 \\ 3 & 6 \end{pmatrix} \tag{4.70}$$

then

$$A_c = \begin{pmatrix} 1 & 2 & 3 \\ 4 & 5 & 6 \\ 5 & 7 & 9 \end{pmatrix} \tag{4.71}$$

$$B_r = \begin{pmatrix} 1 & 4 & 5 \\ 2 & 5 & 7 \\ 3 & 6 & 9 \end{pmatrix} \tag{4.72}$$

$$C_f = \begin{pmatrix} 14 & 32 & 46 \\ 32 & 77 & 109 \\ 46 & 109 & 155 \end{pmatrix} \tag{4.73}$$

A single error can be detected by simply checking C_f to see if the elements in each row sum to the checks and similarily for the columns. In implementing this procedure, we must, of course, allow a reasonable tolerance for

$$C_f = \begin{pmatrix} 14 & 10 & 46 \\ 32 & 77 & 109 \\ 46 & 109 & 155 \end{pmatrix}$$

FIG. 4.37. The faulty row and faulty column overlap at the faulty element.

floating-point arithmetic imprecision. Draw a line through the row and column that do not check The element at the intersection of these two lines is the element in error. There are two possible cases: either (a) a check sum is in error, or (b) an element of the basic matrix, C, is in error. In either case, the error can be corrected by using either row or column checks summing.

As an example, let us imagine that element (1, 2) of C_f is in error and we have computed the check sums and indicated the row and column where the check sums do not check. We display the situation in Figure 4.37. The faulty value is 10. Let x be the true value. Then, if we work the row we have $14 + x = 46$; if we work the column we have $x + 77 = 109$. From either approach we find that the true value is $x = 32$.

Hardware-Based Fault Tolerance

In his celebrated paper, Avizienis [54] states "The presence of fault-tolerant features does not add any performance advantages during normal (fault-free) operation. On the contrary, fault-tolerance requires additional hardware and/or software that is *redundant* during normal operation and could be entirely superfluous in a completely fault-free machine." It is then a challenge to the system designer to ensure that adequate fault tolerance is insinuated into the system in a cost-effective manner.

One of the oldest techniques for adding fault tolerance was to simply triplicate critical functions and operate according to the majority decision.[12] Triplication is extremely costly. The fault tolerance planner may be able to find properties within the system algorithm that can be cleverly exploited to reduce the overhead incurred by the fault tolerance requirements.

[12] The purist may object that the voter module may not be capable of being triplicated as the "final decision" has to be a single action. For some hydromechanical systems, it is possible to actually fuse the commands from three independent control modules. For example, in control surface activation, it may be possible to triplicate the control loops and actually attach three separate actuators to a single control surface. If one actuator fails, the other two may be sufficient to mechanically force the surface to the correct attitude.

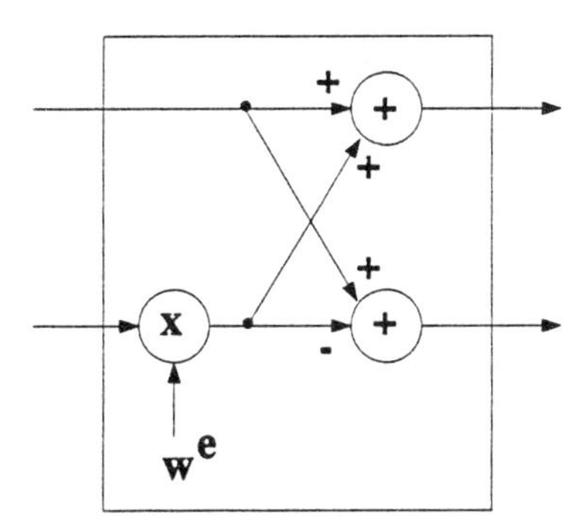

FIG. 4.38. The basic FFT butterfly.

A very nice example of such is given by Choi and Malek [55]. They propose adding an extra stage to an FFT processor. The extra stage will allow faults to be detected, permanent fault to be localized, fault-free operation following the excision of a *single* fault providing no other fault occurs. In achieving this fault tolerance, it should be noted that some of the ancillary fault tolerant hardware is assumed to operate fault free.

The fault-tolerant algorithm is intimately tied to the structure of the FFT. It has its basis in the fact that many possible paths or butterfly routings will produce the same computation.

The basic FFT module is the butterfly depicted in Figure 4.38. Here e is the appropriate power of $w = e^{-j(2\pi/N)}$. It is assumed that the appropriate twiddle factors, the set $\{w^e\}$, are prestored in the butterflies.

We will not replicate Choi and Malek's algorithm as our purpose is to only illustrate a concept. We will, however, demonstrate its application to a four point transform; i.e., $N = 4$. (Their algorithm and hardware structure is good for arbitrary N, where $N = 2^n$.)

The hardware heart of the fault-tolerant FFT is the augmented butterfly module shown in Figure 4.39. The $N = 4$-point FFT fault-tolerant processor is constructed out of the augmented FFT butterflies and contains an extra stage as shown in Figure 4.40.

The algorithm basically depends upon the linearity of the Fourier transform. If an error enters a butterfly that is operating correctly, then *both* of this butterfly's outputs will be in error. Thus, if the computation is repeated in a manner so that each butterfly module processes different inputs than it did the first time, the two output FFTs will differ detecting the fault. Localization of the fault can then be pursued.

The computations are channeled through alternate paths for fault detection as follows. First the data are entered in order $i_0, \dots i_{N-1}$ (here i_0, i_1, i_2, i_3). All switches are *unset*. Next the checking computation

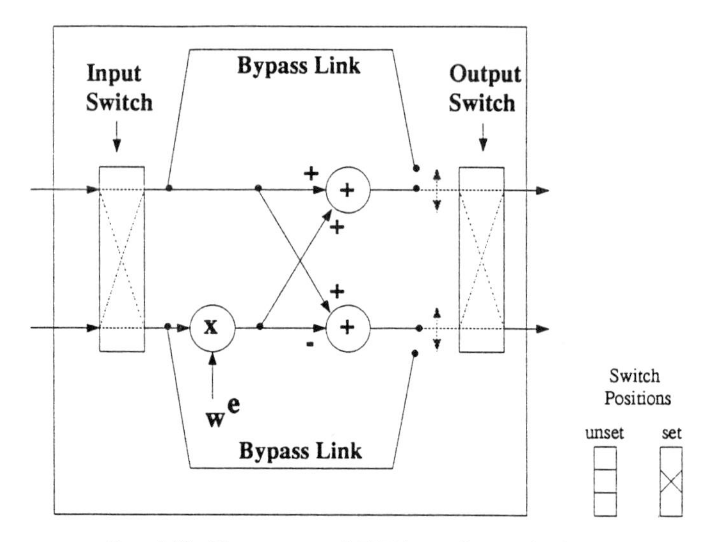

FIG. 4.39. The augmented FFT butterfly standard module.

(one cycle after the first) is performed by entering the data in order $i_{N/2} \ldots i_{N-1}, i_0 \ldots i_{N/2-1}$ (here i_2, i_3, i_0, i_1). During this cycle the input switch to stage n (here $n = 2$) is *set*. This is required so that the coefficients $o_0 \ldots o_{N-1}$ are produced in the same order as in the previous cycle. The situation is diagrammed in Figures 4.41 and 4.42.

The coefficients produced in the two cycles are compared. If there is a difference, a fault is declared detected. Fault isolation may now commence. We can understand fault isolation by the following argument. There are three computational elements in each butterfly: a multiplier and two adders. If an adder fails, only one of the outputs of a butterfly will be in error; if the multiplier fails, both outputs will be faulty. The location of the stage of the *single* fault is thus determined to within one stage by simply counting the number of coefficients that disagree. From all the previous discussion it

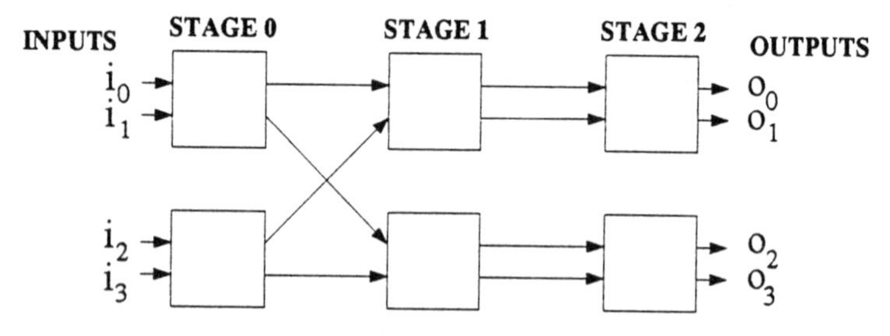

FIG. 4.40. The fault tolerant four-point FFT processor.

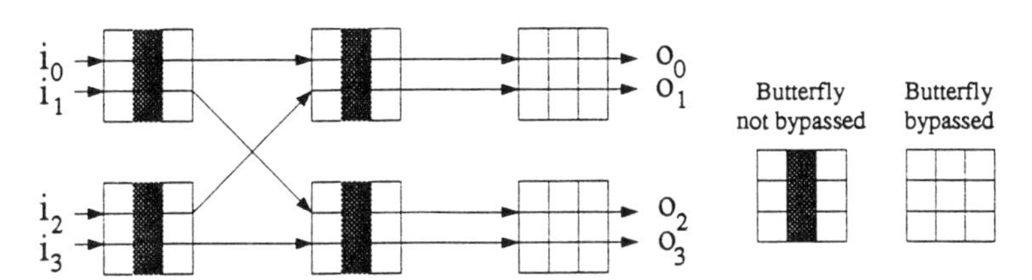

FIG. 4.41. The first of the two cycles of computation for performing and checking the $N = 4$-point FFT.

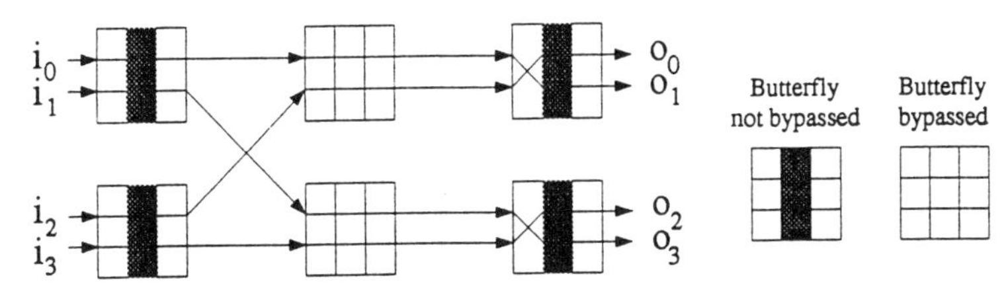

FIG. 4.42. The second of the two cycles of computation for performing and checking the $N = 4$-point FFT.

can be concluded that the number of coefficients in error, E, must be a power of 2; i.e., $E = 1, 2, 4, \ldots, 2^N$. The stage that contains the faulty butterfly is stage $n - \log_2 E$ if an adder has failed or stage $n - \log_2 E - 1$ if a multiplier has failed.

Discrimination tests are then performed. At this juncture we are searching for the stage with the faulty butterfly and not seeking to perform an FFT. We do not therefore need to reorder the input data; i.e., we enter $i_0 \ldots i_{N-1}$. By setting the appropriate bypass and output switches, we can selectively bypass either stages $n - \log_2 E$ or $n - \log_2 E - 1$ and perform comparison tests as before.

Once we have determinbed the faulty stage, we can reconfigure the FFT network to continue to perform FFTs. By resetting the twiddle factors, the set $\{W^e\}$, and the appropriate bypass links, we can "write out" the stage containing the faulty butterfly and continue to perform FFTs, without the checking feature of course.

Graceful Degradation

Graceful degradation is a concept receiving increasing attention. What it implies is best discussed in reference to an admittedly difficult-to-define quantity or attribute that we term *Utility*. *Utility* is the essence of the information's importance to the recipient. For graceful degradation we are interested in means by which Utility will decay in a "smooth" fashion as the data production or transport medium decays. Such behavior may often be purchased at the price of information quality. The information that is the object of our Utility–quality trade-off may be a computed quantity or data received over a communications channel. The concept is an extremely general one, and we believe it best to introduce it via an example. The reader is advised to be sensitive to a system's potential need for graceful degradation attributes and encouraged to be creative as there is no set "nostrum" for insinuating it.

Imagine that a remote electro-optical sensor on a remotely piloted vehicle is performing reconnaissance over a hostile area. The images are radioed back to us through a channel that experiences heavy jamming. The effect of the jamming is to cause errors in the received bits of the transmitted image. We believe we know approximately the capability of the opposition's jamming equipment but we do not want to bet everything on it.

The image *quality* at the sensor is that detail provided by 8-bits per pixel sampling. At the receiver, the digital image is displayed so that the 256 values of gray level are used. This is done by simply noting the minimum and maximum values of the pixel values received and using these limits to linearly scale the pixels over the range 0–255.

The information Utility is defined by a photointerpreter's conclusions as to the presence or absence or various strategic or tactical targets at various locations. The utility is thus a very complicated function and not reducible to familiar engineering units for patent information content metrology. The question to the systems designer is how to protect the data so that their utility degrades gracefully in the presence of greater than expected jamming.

It is almost a knee-jerk reaction to reach for error correcting codes. They have, after all, proven their worth countless times. In using them, however, you must generally have the channel noise well specified. If not, if the noise is higher than expected or of a different nature than modeled, a code may do more harm than good.

We will represent the 8-bits of every pixel by the sequence MSB, 2, 3, 4, 5, 6, 7, 8 where MSB denotes the value (0 or 1) of the most significant bit and 2, 3, 4, 5, 6, 7, 8 represent the binary values of the subsequent bits. We will code each pixel in two different ways and study how the Utility is served by each. The methods are summarized in Figure 4.43. The first scheme is to use a systematic (7, 4) SEC (single error correction) Hamming code to protect the two 4-bit words MSB, 2, 3, 4 and 5, 6, 7, 8. The specific code used is detailed in Table 4.3. A pixel whose value is 143, for example, would thus be converted first to its binary representation 10001111. Each of the 4-bit halves would then be encoded and in this case would yield 1000011 and 1111111, respectively. Each Pixel value thus requires 14 bits,

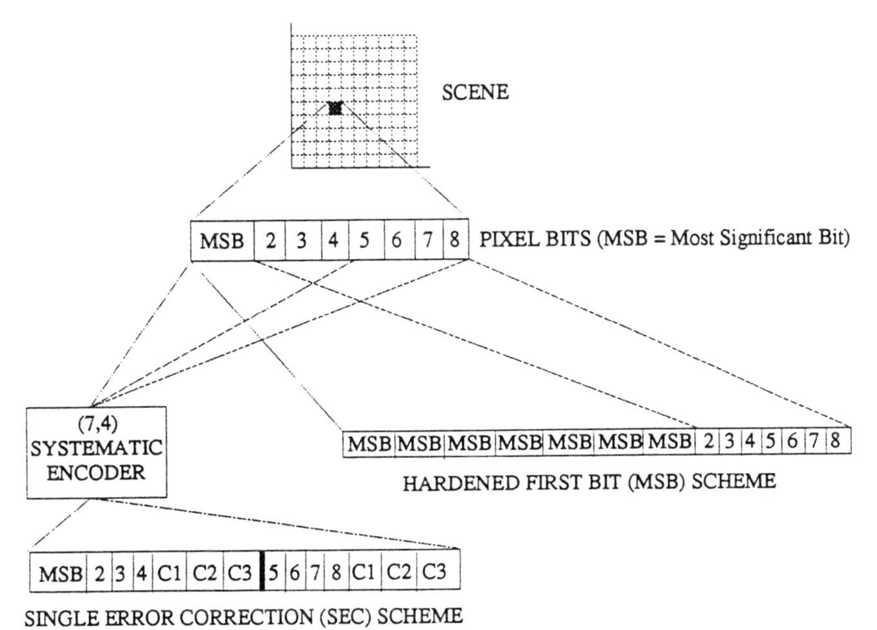

FIG. 4.43. The SEC and the MSB pixel encoding schemes.

TABLE 4.3.
THE SPECIFIC (7, 4) SYSTEMATIC CODE USED IN THE EXPERIMENT

	Information bits			Parity bits		
x_1	x_2	x_3	x_4	c_1	c_2	c_3
0	0	0	0	0	0	0
0	0	0	1	1	1	1
0	0	1	0	1	1	0
0	0	1	1	0	0	1
0	1	0	0	1	0	1
0	1	0	1	0	1	0
0	1	1	0	0	1	1
0	1	1	1	1	0	0
1	0	0	0	0	1	1
1	0	0	1	1	0	0
1	0	1	0	1	0	1
1	0	1	1	0	1	0
1	1	0	0	1	1	0
1	1	0	1	0	0	1
1	1	1	0	0	0	0
1	1	1	1	1	1	1

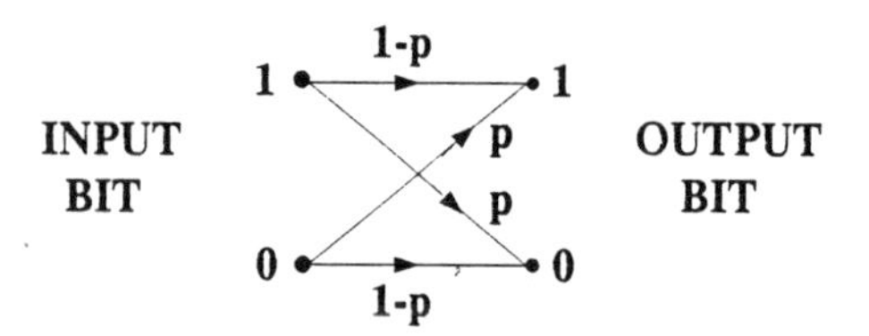

FIG. 4.44. The binary symmetric channel (BSC) model.

and the encoding is such that the pixel value can be recovered without error providing that there is no more than a single error in either of the 7-bit code words received.[13]

The second scheme is to simply repeat the MSB six times and send bits 2–8 as is, i.e., unprotected. We say that this scheme "hardens" the first bit and is an example of what is known in coding theory as *unequal symbol protection* coding. Decoding the MSB is a simple majority decision on the received seven versions of the MSB. Bits 2–8 are accepted as received.

We model the channel as a binary symmetric channel (BSC). This, the simplest of channel models, is a memoryless channel that inverts any particular bit with probability p as depicted in Figure 4.44.[14] Figure 4.45 displays the results of using the two schemes (SEC and BSC). The image consists of approximately 10,000 pixels. The scene is a low-resolution overhead picture of a portion of the Schenectady County Airport. The first row of pictures is for $p = 0.02$. This is an extremely high error rate for many "normal" communication scenarios but not at all abnormal for communications subject to jamming. Note that the MSB scheme appears to have lost some sharpness of detail whereas the SEC scheme preserves the sharpness. This is due to there being absolutely no protection for bits 2–8 in the MSB scheme. If we were sure that the opposition could not insinuate a higher error rate than $p = 0.02$, we would be tempted to select the SEC scheme. But now see what happens as p is forced higher and higher. The SEC scheme degrades severely and quickly. If the Utility of the information is to allow a photointerpreter to discern gross detail and understand the image, then the SEC scheme produces a "cliff" effect in Utility versus p. The MSB scheme, however, allows this particular Utility function to degrade gracefully with increasing p.

[13] Decoding of the Hamming (7, 4) code is done by finding the codeword of minimum Hamming distance to the received codeword and extracting the first four (information) bits.

[14] As an aside, we must add that in a jamming environment we would probably encrypt the bits and then transmit them in a random order so that the opposition could not jam intelligently. This would accomplish random interleaving. A BSC channel model is probably not a bad choice in this case. See Hershey and Yarlagadda [6].

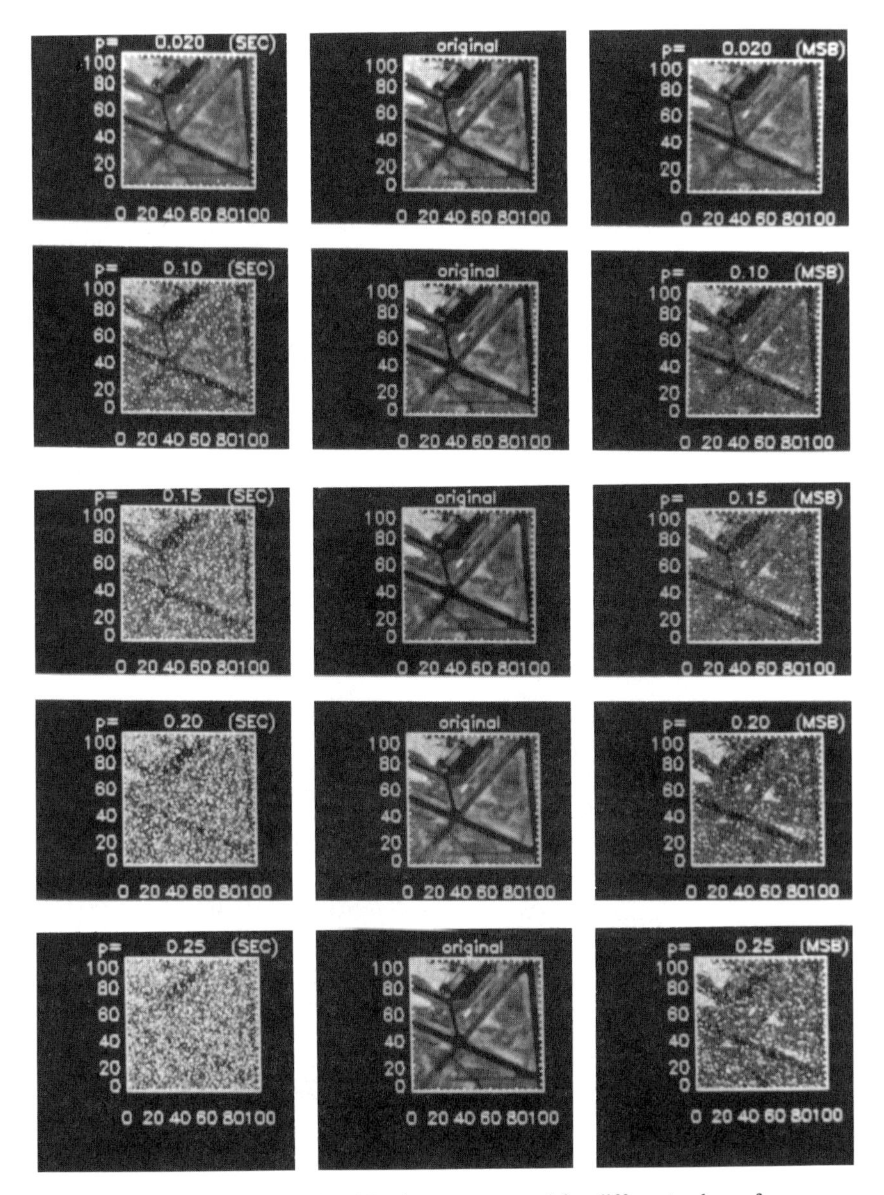

FIG. 4.45. The SEC and MSB schemes compared for different values of p.

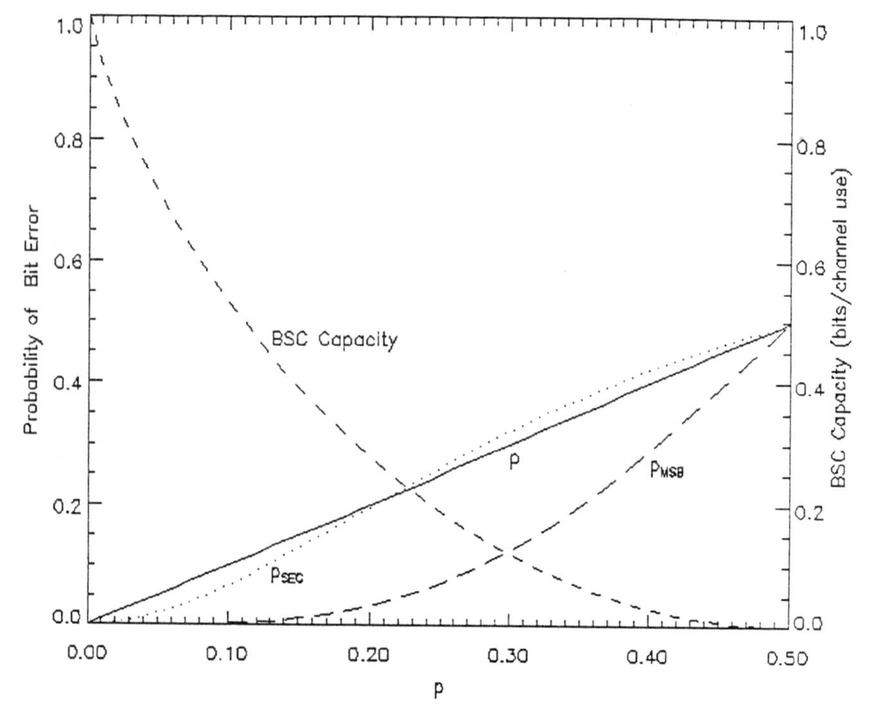

FIG. 4.46. Parameters of interest to the unequal symbol protection example.

A more analytical look is provided by Figure 4.46. In this figure four different quantities are graphed:

1. p itself.
2. P_{MSB} that is the probability that the MSB will be in error when the MSB scheme is used.
3. The probability of error in a decoded information bit using the SEC scheme.
4. The BSC channel capacity[15] in bits per channel use. The capacity of a BSC is $1 + \log_2 p + (1 - p)\log_2(1 - p)$, see Shannon [56].[16]

When p exceeds approximately 0.22, it is clear that the (7, 4) code actually yields a worse performance than would be obtained by sending the bits unencoded through a BSC with the same p. This is a consequence of the

[15] *Capacity* refers to the maximum information rate that is transportable through a channel error free.

[16] The channel use here is a bit, so we are really talking about capacity in information in bits transportable per transmitted bit.

(7, 4) code's being a *perfect code* and thus admitting no erasure space. For example, the codeword representing the information bits 0000 is 0000000. If just the first two bits are received incorrectly, i.e., if 1100000 were received, the closest codeword would be 1110000 and the information bits delivered by the decoder would be 1110 resulting in an error multiplication of 150%.

It is thus very important to know what is expected of the system to be designed; i.e., the system designer must clearly understand the system's Utility function and how it can be best served through judicious selection of the communications, control, computation, and signal processing modules.

Conclusion

Computation is a critical element of almost every contemporary large-scale system. As the designer proceeds, it is best to remember that system design is a both a series of trade-off steps and innovative synergy. There are three axes to the computational problem—hardware, algorithms, and architectures—as depicted in Figure 4.47. The solution to any particular problem can be accelerated by pushing along any one of the three axes. For example, we could select improvement of the hardware and seek to develop or procure faster circuits. But the synergy may be absolutely dramatic when we attempt to simultaneously push on two or more axes. A simple qualitative example is depicted in Figure 4.48. The gradual convex

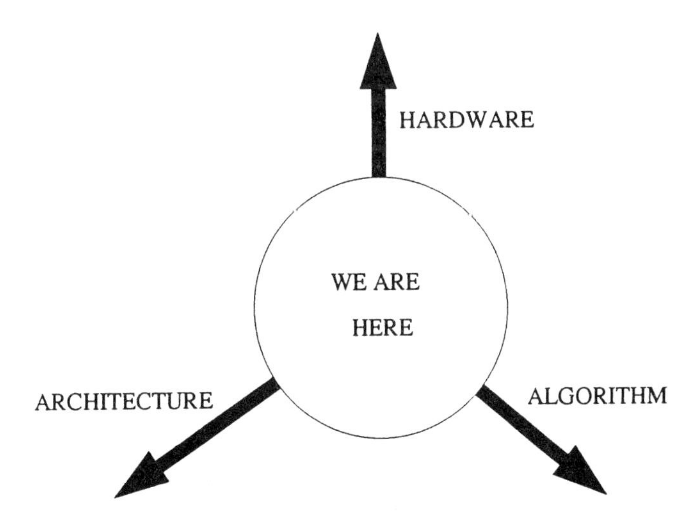

FIG. 4.47. The three axes of computation.

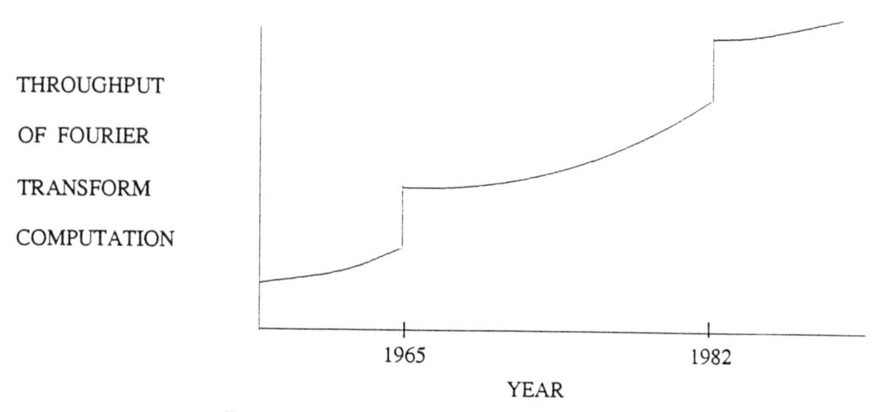

FIG. 4.48. Fourier transform throughput rate.

slopes reflect speed increases provided by hardware advancement. The discontinuity or "jump" in 1965 reflects the discovery of the fast Fourier transform, the FFT. This was an algorithmic advance. The jump, pegged somewhat arbitrarily, at 1982 reflects the viability of a multiprocessor architecture for performing the FFT. The question for thought is simply, "Where would be *now* if we had pursued the hardware axis only?"

Problems

1. Discuss the commonly used term *real time*. Does it have any widely agreed upon meaning? Attempt to quantify it within a system or class of systems.
2. Not all approximations are practical or useful. For example, $1 - \frac{1}{3} + \frac{1}{5} - \frac{1}{7} + \cdots$ converges to $\pi/4$ but the convergence is very slow. Not all approximations to a function, $f(x)$, are friendly either. Knopfmacher and Knopfmacher [57] have shown that a power series of the form $S(x) = 1 + a_1x + a_2x^2 + \cdots$ can be uniquely written as $S(x) = \prod_{i=1}^{\infty} (1 + b_ix^i)$.

   The product expansion for $\cos 2\pi x$ is easily seen to be

$$\cos 2\pi x = 1 - \frac{(2\pi x)^2}{2!} + \frac{2\pi x)^4}{4!} - \cdots$$

$$= (1 - 2\pi^2x^2)\left(1 + \frac{2\pi^4}{3}x^4\right)\cdots$$

   In general, if we try to use this product expansion as a route to approximation, we may wind up with more trouble than help. Consider that we approximate $\cos 2\pi x$ by the product of the first two terms (the solid line), we get Figure 4.49.

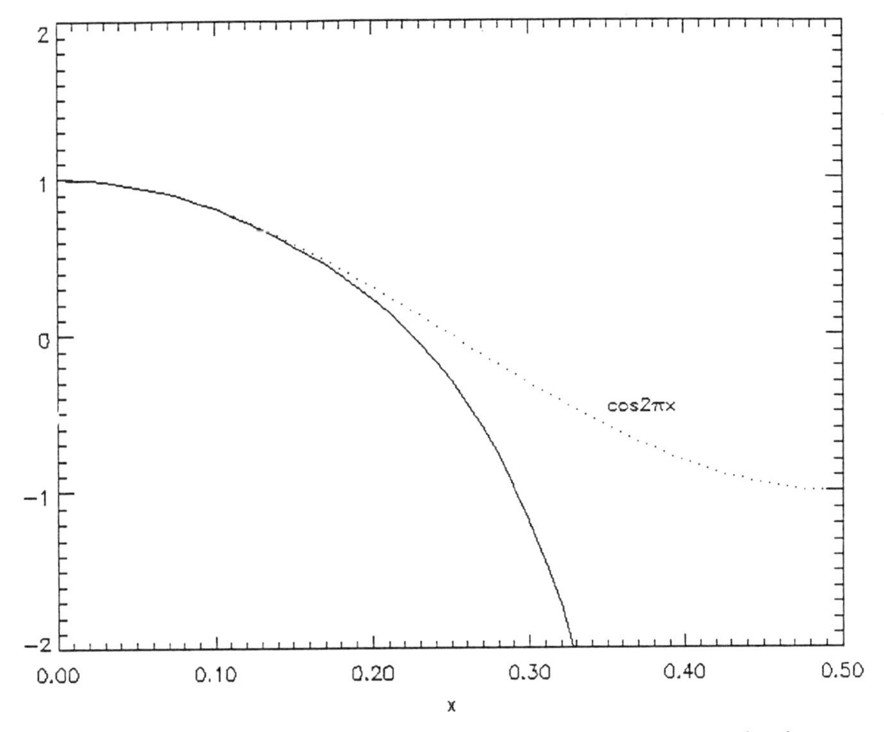

FIG. 4.49. Comparison of the cosine function and a two-term product approximation.

Note that we have a 0 at $x = 1/\sqrt{2}\,\pi$. This 0 does not, of course, exist and is termed a *pseudo zero*. As long as a finite number of terms are included in the product approximation, this zero (and other pseudo zeros) will remain.

Expand e^z, z may be complex, in a product expansion and comment on some of the pseudo zeros.

3. There is another mode to the CORDIC technique. It is called *vectoring* (in contrast to rotation). In this mode, y_n is forced to 0 rather than θ. Show that if we set $z_0 = 0$ and iterate n times using (4.19)–(4.21), but use the rule

$$\delta_k = \begin{cases} 1, & \text{if } y_k < 0 \\ -1, & \text{if } y_k \geq 0 \end{cases},$$

z_n will approximate $\tan^{-1}(y_0/x_0)$ and x_n will approximate

$$\left(\prod_{i=0}^{n-1} \sqrt{1 + 2^{-2i}}\right)\sqrt{x_0^2 + y_0^2}.$$

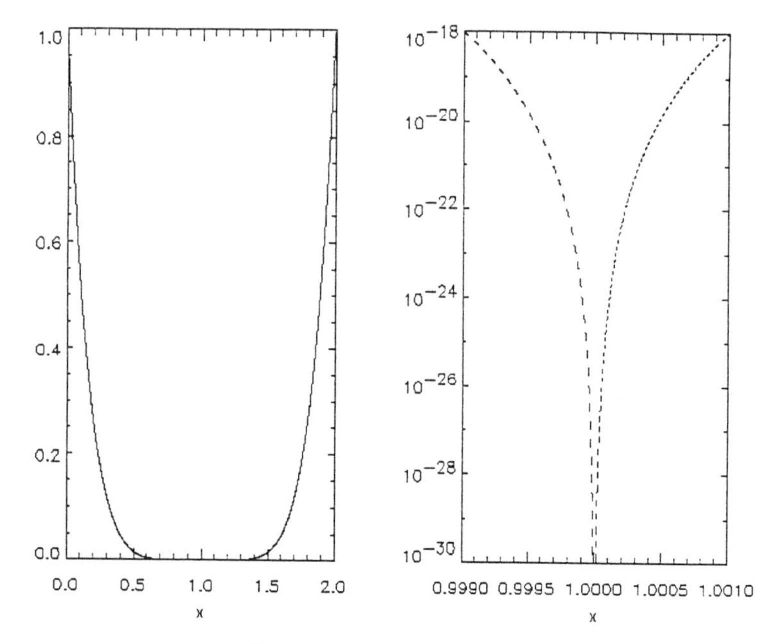

FIG. 4.50. $y_1(x) = (1 - x)^6$ for the two ranges $0 \le x \le 2$ and $0.999 \le x \le 1.001$.

4. The two expressions
   (a) $y_1(x) = (1 - x)^6$
   (b) $y_2(x) = 1 - 6x + 15x^2 - 20x^3 + 15x^4 - 6x^5 + x^6$

   are, of course, equivalent. They do not produce equivalent results when computed in finite precision near the minimum at $x = 1$, however. Rice [58] uses essentially this expression to demonstrate "how round-off can make a theoretically smooth curve into a jumbled mess." In Figure 4.50 we graph $y_1(x)$ in the two ranges $0 \le x \le 2$ and $0.99 \le x \le 1.01$.

   In Figure 4.51 we plot $y_2(x)$ for the range $0.999 \le x \le 1.001$ using both single and double precision arithmetic. We should think about the conditions that underlie such radically different results in plotting what are equivalent mathematical expressions.

   Hyslop [59] refers to essentially $(1 - x)^6$ as "pathologically flat" because the first nonvanishing derivative at $x = 1$ is of such a high order. The consequence of this is that it may be very difficult to locate the maximum or minimum of such a function. Hyslop argues that for a function, $y(x)$, where the first nonvanishing derivative at $x = x_0$ is of high even order, the accuracy in computing the point of local maximum or minimum is greatly reduced and may seriously affect the outcome of applying typically used hill climbing schemes.

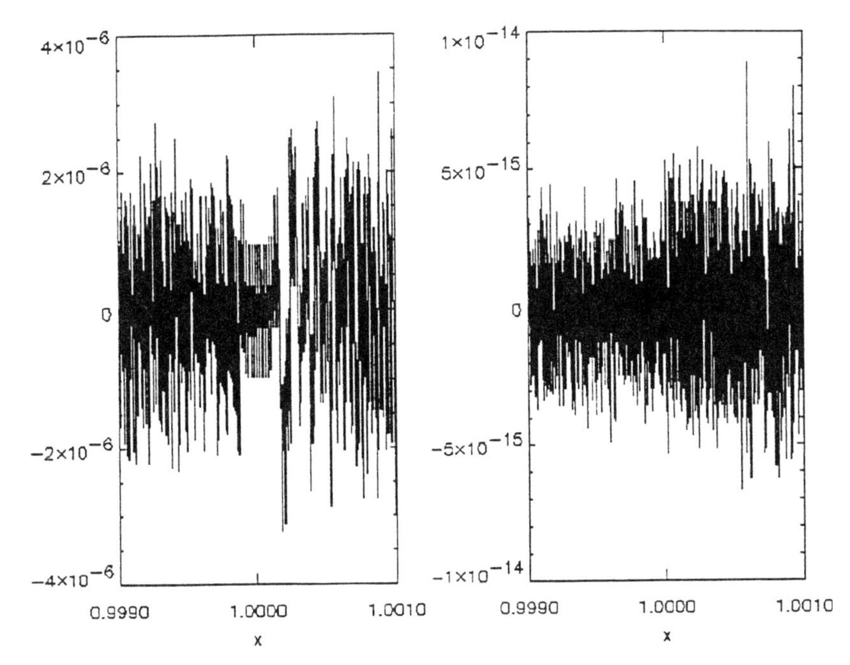

FIG. 4.51. $y_2(x)$ computed for the range $0.999 \leq x \leq 1.001$ in single precision (left) and in double precision (right).

Similarly investigate the function $y(x) = \cos(x) + \cosh(x)$ near $x = 0$. Attempt to derive an iterative method which will find the minimum which occurs there.

5. It will be important to be able to test or benchmark the computational modules in the designed system. Most contemporary large systems will be required to perform operations on large matrices. Over the years, various researchers have developed what are known as *test matrices*. Test matrices allow linear algebra program packages or system modules to be tested for accuracy and stability. One such test matrix is the following tridiagonal form

$$\begin{pmatrix} 3 & -1 & 0 & \dots & 0 & 0 \\ -1 & 2 & -1 & \dots & 0 & 0 \\ 0 & -1 & 2 & \dots & 0 & 0 \\ \vdots & \vdots & \vdots & \ddots & \vdots & \vdots \\ 0 & 0 & 0 & \dots & 2 & -1 \\ 0 & 0 & 0 & \dots & -1 & 1 \end{pmatrix}$$

This particular matrix is relatively "tame." Its inverse, for example, is

$$\frac{1}{2}\begin{pmatrix} 1 & 1 & 1 & 1 & 1 & \cdots \\ 1 & 3 & 3 & 3 & 3 & \cdots \\ 1 & 3 & 5 & 5 & 5 & \cdots \\ 1 & 3 & 5 & 7 & 7 & \cdots \\ 1 & 3 & 5 & 7 & 9 & \cdots \\ \vdots & \vdots & \vdots & \vdots & \vdots & \ddots \end{pmatrix}$$

This particular form is a special case of a set of test matrices presented by Gear [60]. It is included in a Report on Test Matrices by Fosdick and Kim [61]. Fosdick and Kim note that LU decomposition or Gaussian elimination require no row exchanges as the pivots will always be maximum. It should be relatively easy to invert this matrix accurately. We presented this matrix to a commercially available program and the results (in Figure 4.52) seem to bear out the intuition.

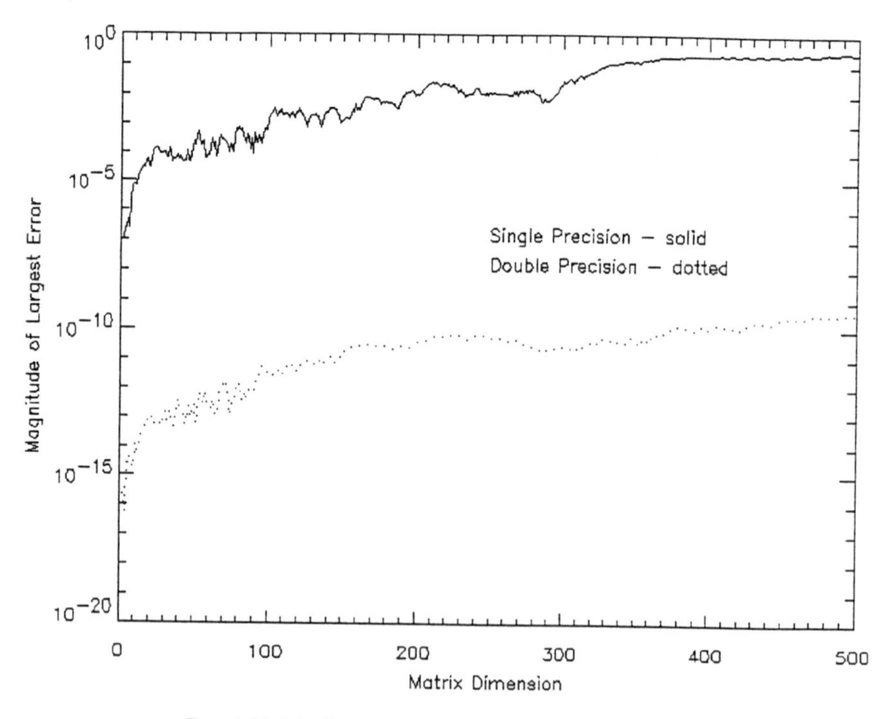

FIG. 4.52. Maximum error in inverting a specific test matrix.

Try the preceding experiment with various sizes of the matrix generated by the pattern

$$\begin{pmatrix} 1 & \frac{1}{2} & \frac{1}{3} & \frac{1}{4} & \frac{1}{5} & \cdots \\ \frac{1}{2} & \frac{1}{3} & \frac{1}{4} & \frac{1}{5} & \frac{1}{6} & \cdots \\ \frac{1}{3} & \frac{1}{4} & \frac{1}{5} & \frac{1}{6} & \frac{1}{7} & \cdots \\ \frac{1}{4} & \frac{1}{5} & \frac{1}{6} & \frac{1}{7} & \frac{1}{8} & \cdots \\ \frac{1}{5} & \frac{1}{6} & \frac{1}{7} & \frac{1}{8} & \frac{1}{9} & \cdots \\ \vdots & \vdots & \vdots & \vdots & \vdots & \ddots \end{pmatrix}$$

This matrix is called the *Hilbert matrix*. Moderately sized truncations of this matrix are extremely ill-conditioned. For your experiment, pick various dimensions for truncation of the Hilbert matrix, present them to a math package or module for inversion, and multiply the returned answer times the truncated Hilbert matrix. See how close you come to an identity matrix. For further discussion, see Fosdick and Kim [61].

6. Evaluation of $p(x) = c_n x^n + \cdots + c_0$, such as would be required to evaluate a series approximation, can be peformed on a single computer using n multiplications and n additions by using Horner's rule, which is the recursion

$$p(x) \leftarrow c_n \qquad \text{(initialization)}$$

$$p(x) \leftarrow xp(x) + c_{n-i} \qquad \text{(do for } i = 1 \text{ to } n)$$

Notice that Horner's rule can be viewed as the nested expression

$$p(x) = \{\ldots [(c_n x + c_{n-1})x + c_{n-2}]x \ldots\} + c_0$$

Using two processors that can pass information to each other, find a parallel algorithm that surpasses a single processor's performance in evaluating

$$p(x) = c_4 x^4 + c_3 x^3 + c_2 x^2 + c_1 x + c_0$$

Assume that the requisite coefficients are prestored at the processors and that the independent value, x, is also present at both processors. For further investigation, see references [62–65].

7. Multiplication of matrices is an extremely important and pervasive computation. Straightforwardly, it can be accomplished for two matrices of dimension $N \times N$ using N^3 multiplications and $N^3 - N^2$ additions. Strassen [66] found a method that required only $O(N^{2.81})$ arithmetic operations as opposed to the $O(N^3)$ arithmetic operations required by the "straightforward" or what we shall refer to as the *conventional* method.

Strassen's remarkable concept rests on the following method of forming the product, C, of two 2×2 matrices, A and B:

$$\begin{pmatrix} c_{11} & c_{12} \\ c_{21} & c_{22} \end{pmatrix} = \begin{pmatrix} a_{11} & a_{12} \\ a_{21} & a_{22} \end{pmatrix} \begin{pmatrix} b_{11} & b_{12} \\ b_{21} & b_{22} \end{pmatrix}$$

The "conventional" method would compute

$$c_{11} = a_{11} \times b_{11} + a_{12} \times b_{21}$$

$$c_{12} = a_{11} \times b_{12} + a_{12} \times b_{22}$$

$$c_{21} = a_{21} \times b_{11} + a_{22} \times b_{21}$$

$$c_{22} = a_{21} \times b_{12} + a_{22} \times b_{22}$$

which requires 8 multiplications and 4 additions, a total of 12 arithmetic operations. Strassen discovered that the product can be formed by first forming the 7 intermediate terms $T_1, T_2, \ldots, T_7$, where

$$T_1 = (a_{12} - a_{22}) \times (b_{21} + b_{22})$$

$$T_2 = (a_{11} + a_{22}) \times (b_{11} + b_{22})$$

$$T_3 = (a_{11} - a_{21}) \times (b_{11} + b_{12})$$

$$T_4 = (a_{11} + a_{12}) \times b_{22}$$

$$T_5 = a_{11} \times (b_{12} - b_{22})$$

$$T_6 = a_{22} \times (b_{21} - b_{11})$$

$$T_7 = (a_{21} + a_{22}) \times b_{11}$$

and then forming

$$c_{11} = T_1 + T_2 - T_4 + T_6$$

$$c_{12} = T_4 + T_5$$

$$c_{21} = T_6 + T_7$$

$$c_{22} = T_2 - T_3 + T_5 - T_7$$

This requires 7 multiplications and 18 additions for a total of 25 arithmetic operations. This hardly seems a gain but yet the implications are profound. Now consider that the matrices A and B are of dimension 4×4. We can express them as

$$A = \begin{pmatrix} A_{11} & A_{12} \\ A_{21} & A_{22} \end{pmatrix} \qquad B = \begin{pmatrix} B_{11} & B_{12} \\ B_{21} & B_{22} \end{pmatrix}$$

where A_{ij} and B_{ij} are 2×2 matrices. We form T_1–T_7 using A_{11} for a_{11}, A_{12} for a_{12}, etc. We perform additions of the matrices when addition is called for, but when we run into multiplication, we recursively call the procedure. There is one multiplication indicated in each of the $\{T_i\}$, so there are $7 \times 18 = 126$ additions and $7 \times 7 = 49$ multiplications created by the recursive call. The eight additions involved at the "top" level involve elements that are 2×2 matrices and therefore, at the top level, we must perform $4 \times 18 = 72$ additions. Thus, using Strassen's method, we find that the total additions required is $126 + 72 = 198$, and the total number of multiplications is 49. For matrices of dimension $2^n \times 2^n$, Strassen's method requires 7^n multiplications. The number of additions required is precisely calculable from the recursion $A(2^n) = 7A(2^{n-1}) + 18 \cdot 4^{n-1}$, where $A(\ )$ is the total number of additions required. (For an *excellent* motivation, analysis, and discussion of Strassen's method, see Section 2.4 in Wilf [67].)

Let the total number of operations (additions plus multiplications) required by the "conventional" method for multiplying two square matrices of dimension $2^n \times 2^n$ be given by $\Omega_c(2^n)$ and let $\Omega_s(2^n)$ be the total number of operations required by Strassen's method. From Figure 4.53, we see that Strassen's method requires fewer operations for $n \geq 10$. It can be shown that $\Omega_c(2^n) = O(2^{3n})$ and $\Omega_s(2^n) = O(2^{2.81n})$. For further discussion of Strassen's method and methods that outperform Strassen's method, see [68].

(a) Substitute the $\{T_i\}$ into the $\{c_{ij}\}$ and verify that Strassen's method correctly results in the 2×2 matrix product.
(b) Consider implementing Strassen's method at the nodes of a hypercube implementing Fox and Otto's algorithm of matrix multiplication. Compare the overheads required by Strassen's algorithm and the conventional approach.
(c) In the section "Suboptimal Parallel Algorithms" we stated that "Quite often a suboptimal algorithm is . . . much easier to parallelize." Investigate and discuss the possible parallelization of Strassen's method.

8. Complete the example used to illustrate Jenq's convolver by demonstrating that the *root* computations under Combine do indeed produce the equations (4.49).

9. A closed-form expression involving matrices may be aesthetically pleasing but it does not necessarily indicate how to perform the computations efficiently. The purpose of this problem is to highlight this observation and stimulate further thinking and awareness about the problem.

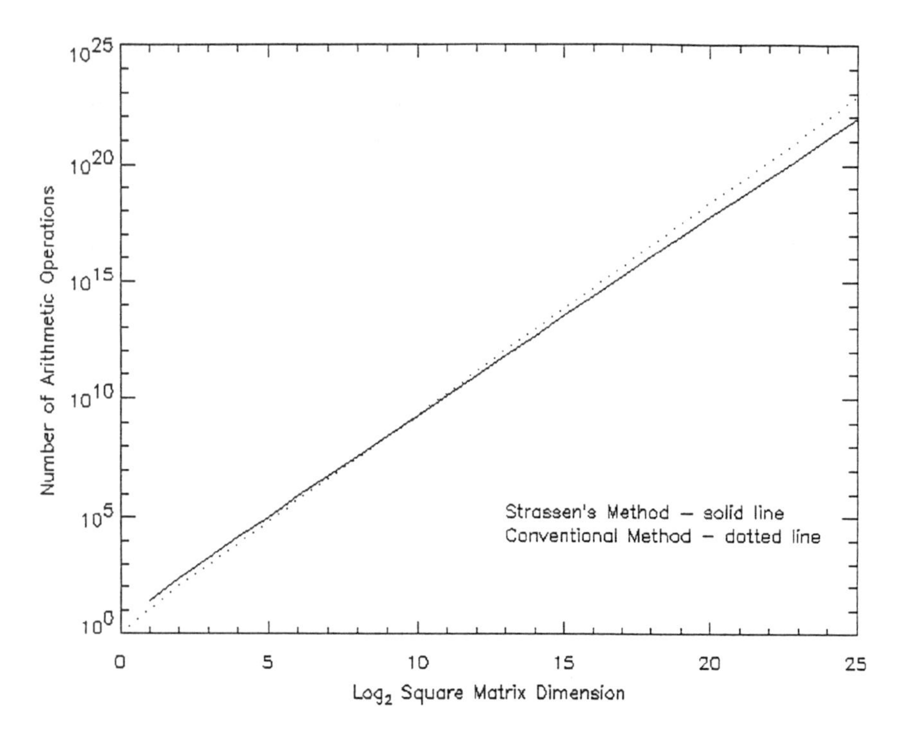

FIG. 4.53. The comparative complexities of conventional matrix multiplication and Strassen's method.

Let M_1 be a matrix of dimensions $n_0 \times n_1$ and M_2 be a matrix of dimensions $n_1 \times n_2$. The number of operations required to compute the product $\prod_2 = (\pi_{ij}) = M_1 M_2$, by the standard method whereby π_{ij} is calculated by $\pi_{ij} = \sum_{k=0}^{n_1-1} M_{1_{ik}} M_{2_{kj}}$, is

- $n_0 n_1 n_2$ multiplications,
- $n_0(n_1 - 1)n_2$ additions.

Imagine we have n matrices that are conformable in that the dimensions of the kth matrix are $n_{k-1} \times n_k$ so that the product $\prod_n = M_1 M_2 \ldots M_n$ is defined. We know from Niven [69] that there are $(2n - 2)!/n!(n - 1)!$ different ways in which the product $\prod_n$ may be evaluated. For example, if $n = 3$, there are two possible ways. We may form $\prod_3 = (M_1 M_2)M_3$ or $\prod_3 = M_1(M_2 M_3)$.

Study the $n = 3$ case. What conditions, expressed in terms of n_0, n_1, n_2, and n_3, would you suggest for determining the order of multiplication? For further study, see Muraoka and Kuck [70].

10. (a) In some cases we may model the speed-up in parallelizing a suboptimal algorithm in the following way. We augment the Ware–Buzbee model so that it becomes

$$S_P = \frac{1}{(1 - \alpha) + \alpha/P + \sigma(P) - \pi(P)}$$

where $\pi(P)$ is the contribution to the speed-up that comes from parallelizing a suboptimal algorithm [6]. Note that the sign preceding the term is *negative* implying a gain in speed-up. For the case discussed under Suboptimal Parallel Algorithms, show that if P processors are assigned to find the single something in N different settings, the model yields $\alpha = 1$, $\sigma(P) = 0$, and $\pi(P) = 1 - 2(\tau_0/\tau)$.

(b) Devise and investigate other sequential algorithms that outperform the suboptimal algorithm used in Suboptimal Parallel Algorithms. Study and discuss the computational aspects regarding these more nearly optimal algorithms.

11. Determine the correct switch setting and twiddle factors needed to reconfigure an eight-point fault tolerant Choi and Malek FFT processor given that a single fault has been localized to stage i, $i = 0, 1, 2$.

References

[1] Diffie, W, and M. E. Hellman. (1976). "New Directions in Cryptography," *IEE Transactions on Information Theory* **IT-22**(16), pp. 644–654.

[2] Davis, P. J. (1975). *Interpolation and Approximation*. Dover, Mineola, NY.

[3] Kopal, Z. (1955). *Numerical Analysis*. John Wiley & Sons Inc. New York, N.Y.

[4] Volder, J. E. (1959). "The CORDIC Trigonometric Computing Technique," *IRE Transactions on Electronic Computers*, pp. 330–334.

[5] Knuth, D. E. (1981). *The Art of Computer Programming*, Vol. 2 *Seminumerical Algorithms*, 2nd ed. Addison-Wesley, Reading, MA.

[6] Hershey, J. E., and R. Yarlagadda. (1985). "Probabilistic Signal Processing," 1986 IEEE Military Communications Conference (MILCOM), 19.2.1–19.2.3.

[7] Strang, G. (1986). *Introduction to Applied Mathematics*. Wellesley–Cambridge Press, Wellesley, MA.

[8] Moursund, D. G. (1967). "Optimal Starting Values for Newton–Raphson Calculation of $\sqrt{x}$," *Communications of the ACM* **10**(7), 430–432.

[9] Wilkinson, J. H. (1963). *Rounding Errors in Algebraic Processes*. Prentice-Hall, Englewood Cliffs, NJ.

[10] Philip, J. (1987). "The Most Ill-Posed Non-Negative Kernels in Discrete Deconvolution," *Inverse Problems*, Vol. 3, pp. 309–328.

[11] Linz, P. (1970). "Accurate Floating-Point Summation," *Communications of the ACM* **13**(6), 361–362.

[12] Malcolm, M. A. (1971). "On Accurate Floating-Point Summation," *Communications of the ACM* **14**(11), 731–736.

[13] Parkinson, D., and H. Liddell. (1983). "The Measurement of Performance on a Highly Parallel System," *IEEE Transactions on Computers* **C-32**(1), 32–37.

[14] Buzbee, B. L. (1983). "The Efficiency of Parallel Processing," *Los Alamos Science* (Fall), p. 71.

[15] Amdahl, G. M. (1967). "Validity of the Single Processor Approach to Achieving Large Scale Computing Capabilities," AFIPS Conference Proceeding, pp. 483–485.

[16] Gustafson, J. L. (1988). "Reevaluating Amdahl's Law," *Communications of the ACM* **31**(5), 532–533.

[17] Zorbas, J. R., D. J. Reble, and R. E. VanKooten. (1989). "Measuring the Scalability of Parallel Computer Systems," Proceedings Supercomputing '89, pp. 832–841.

[18] Bhuyan, L., and D. Agrawal. (1982). "Applications of SIMD Computers in Signal Processing," National Computer Conference, AFIPS Conference Proceedings, Houston, pp. 135–142.

[19] Yarlagadda, R., and J. E. Hershey. (1989). Signal Processing, *General, Encyclopedia of Telecommunications* (Robert A. Meyers, Ed.), pp. 391–411. Academic Press, Boston.

[20] Unger, S. H. (1958). "A Computer Oriented Toward Spatial Problems," *Proceedings Institute Radio Engineering* (USA) **46**, 1744–1750.

[21] Slotnick, D. L., W. C. Borck, and R. McReynolds. (1962). "The SOLOMON Computer," *AFIPS Conference Proceedings* **22**, 97–107.

[22] Fox, G. C., S. W. Otto, and A. J. G. Hey. (1987). "Matrix Algorithms on a Hypercube I: Matrix Multiplication," *Parallel Computing* **12**(4), 17–31.

[23] Lubeck, O. M., and V. Faber. (1988). "Modeling the Performance of Hypercubes: A Case Study Using the Particle-in-Cell Application," *Parallel Computing* **00**(9), 37–52.

[24] Berntsen, J. (1989). "Communication Efficient Matrix Multiplication on Hypercubes," *Parallel Computing* **00**(12), 335–342.

[25] Bertsekas, D. P., C. Ozveren, G. D. Stamoulis, P. Tseng, and J. N. Tsitsiklis. (1991). "Optimal Communication Algorithms for Hypercubes," *Journal of Parallel and Distributed Computing* **11**, 263–275.

[26] Flynn, M. J. (1972). "Some Computer Organizations and Their Effectiveness," *IEEE Transactions on Computers* **C-21**(9), pp. 948–960.

[27] Kung, S.-Y. (1984). "On Supercomputing with Systolic/Wavefront Array Processors," *Proceedings of the IEEE* **72**(7), 867–884.

[28] Jenq, Y.-C. (1981). "Digital Convolution Algorithm for Pipelining Multiprocessor Systems," *IEEE Transactions on Computers*, 966–973.

[29] Fateman, R. J. (1969). "Optimal Code for Serial and Parallel Computation," *Communications of the ACM* **12**(12), 694–695.

[30] Miranker. W. L., and W. Liniger. (1967). "Parallel Methods for the Numerical Integration of Ordinary Differential Equations," *Mathematics of Computation*, 303–320.

[31] Conte, S. D., and C. de Boor. (1980). *Elementary Numerical Analysis: An Algorithmic Approach*, 3rd ed. McGraw-Hill, New York.

[32] Acton, F. S. (1970). *Numerical Methods That Work*. Harper & Row, New York.

[33] Shampine, L. F., and H. A. Watts. (1964). "Block Implicit One-Step Methods," *Math. of Computation* **23**, 731–740.

[34] Rosser, J. B. (1967). "A Runge-Kutta for all Seasons," *SIAM Review* **9**(3), 417–452.

[35] Worland, P. B. (1976). "Parallel Methods for the Numerical Solution of Ordinary Differential Equations," *IEEE Transaction on Computers*, 1045–1048.

[36] Franklin, M. A. (1978). "Parallel Solution of Ordinary Diferential Equations," *IEEE Transactions on Computers* **C-27**(5), 413–420.

[37] Birta, L. G., and O. Abou-Rabia. (1987). "Parallel Block Predictor-Corrector Methods of ODE's," *IEEE Transactions on Computers* **C-36**(3), 299–331.

[38] Khaddaj, S. A. (1989). "The Numerical Solution of ODEs on an Array of Transputers." In *CONPAR 88* (C. R. Jesshope and K. D. Reinartz, eds.), pp 492–499. Cambridge University Press, Cambridge.

[39] Sameh, A. H., and D. J. Kuck. (1978). "On Stable Parallel Linear System Solvers," *Journal of the Association for Computing Machinery* **25**(1), 81–91.

[40] Golub, G. H., and C. F. Van Loan. (1989). *Matrix Computations*, 2nd ed. Johns Hopkins University Press, Baltimore.

[41] Duato, J. (1988). "Parallel Processing of the Square Root Free Givens Rotations by Means of a Transputer Network." In *Parallel Processing and Applications* (E. Chiricozzi and A. D'Amico, eds.), pp. 257–264. Elsevier Science Publishers B.V., Amsterdam, The Netherlands.

[42] Wilkinson, J. H. (1965). *The Algebraic Eigenvalue Problem.* Clarendon Press, Oxford.

[43] Christofides, N. (1976). "Worst Case Analysis of a New Heuristic for the Travelling Salesman Problem." Technical Report, Graduate School of Industrial Administration, Carnegie-Mellon University, Pittsburgh.

[44] Hershey, J. E., and F. F. Yassa. (1991). "The Kurtosis and Superunitary Speedup: A Case Study," International Signal Processing Workshop on Higher Order Statistics, pp. 199–202.

[45] Titterington, D. M., A. F. M. Smith, and U. E. Makov. (1985). *Statistical Analysis of Finite Mixture Distributions.* John Wiley and Sons, New York.

[46] Gittins, J. C. (1989). *Multi-Armed Bandit Allocation Indices.* John Wiley and Sons, New York.

[47] Pearson, E. S. (1930). "A Further Development of Tests for Normality," *Biometrika* (July) **22**, 239–249.

[48] Wilkes, M. V. (1977). "Beyond Today's Computers," *Information Processing* **77**, 1–5.

[49] Miya, E. (1988). "Beyond Today's Computers," *Network News Posting* (December).

[50] Faber, V., O. M. Lubeck, and A. B. White, Jr. (1986). "Superlinear Speedup of an Efficient Sequential Algorithm Is Not Possible," *Parallel Computing* **3**, 259–260.

[51] Bastani, F. B., and C. V. Ramamoorthy. (1987). "Fault-Tolerant Distributed Process-Control Systems," Proceedings 1987 Fall Joint Computer Conference, pp. 522–527.

[52] Chatterjee, A., and M. A. d'Abreu. (1991). "Syndrome-Based Functional Delay Fault Location in Linear Digital Data-Flow Graphs," Proceedings IEEE International Conference on Computer Design (ICCD), pp. 212–215.

[53] Huang, K.-H., and J. A. Abraham. (1984). "Algorithm-Based Fault Tolerance for Matrix Operations," *IEEE Transactions on Computers* **C-33**(6), 518–528.

[54] Avizienis, A. (1978). "Fault-Tolerance: The Survival Attribute of Digital Systems," *Proceedings of the IEEE* **66**(10), 1109–1125.

[55] Choi, Y.-H., and M. Malek. (1988). "A Fault-Tolerant FFT Processor," *IEEE Transactions on Computers* **37**(5), 617–621.

[56] Shannon, C. E. (1948). "A Mathematical Theory of Communications," *Bell Systems Technical Journal* **27**, 379–423.

[57] Knopfmacher, A., and J. Knopfmacher. (1989). "Infinite Products for Power Series," *Journal of Approximation Theory*, Vol. 59, pp. 276–281.

[58] Rice, J. R. (1983). *Numerical Methods, Software, and Analysis: IMSL Reference Edition.* McGraw-Hill, New York.

[59] Hyslop, J. (1972). "A Note on the Accuracy of Optimisation Techniques," *Computer Journal* **15**, 140.

[60] Gear, C. W. (1969). "A Simple Set of Test Matrices for Eigenvalue Programs," *Mathematics of Computation* **23**, 119–125.
[61] Fosdick, L. D., and Y. J. Kim. (1970). "Test Matrices I," Report No. 403, (COO-1469-0166), Department of Computer Science, University of Illinois at Urbana-Champaign.
[62] Leach, R. J., O. M. Atogi, and R. R. Stephen. "The Actual Complexity of Parallel Evaluation of Low Degree Polynomials," *Parallel Computing* **13**, 73–83.
[63] Dowling, M. L. (1990). "A Fast Parallel Horner Algorithm," *SIAM Journal of Computing* **19**(1), 133–142.
[64] Munro, I. (1973). "Optimal Algorithms for Parallel Polynomial Evaluation," *Journal of Computer and System Sciences* **7**, 189–198.
[65] Kosaraju, S. (1986). "Parallel Evaluation of Division-Free Arithmetic Expressions," Proceedings of the 18th Annual ACM Symposium on Theory of Computing, pp. 231–239.
[66] Strassen, V. (1969). "Gaussian Elimination Is Not Optimal," *Numerische Math.* **13**, 354–356.
[67] Wilf, H. S. (1986). *Algorithms and Complexity*. Prentice-Hall, Englewood Cliffs, NJ.
[68] Pan, V. (1984). "How Can We Speed up Matrix Multiplication?" *SIAM Review* **26**(3), 393–415.
[69] Niven, I. (1965). *Mathematics of Choice*. Random House, New York, NY.
[70] Muraoka, Y., and D. J. Kuck. (1973). "On the Time Required for a Sequence of Matrix Products," *Communications of the ACM* **16**(1), 22–26.
[71] Lanczos, C. (1938). "Trigonometric Interpolation of Empirical and Analytical Functions," *Journal of Mathematics and Physics* **17**, 123–199.

Index

E

F

G

H

I